MISS CUTLER
& the Case of the Resurrected Horse

HISTORICAL STUDIES OF URBAN AMERICA

Edited by Timothy J. Gilfoyle, James R. Grossman, and Becky M. Nicolaides

ALSO IN THE SERIES

*The Transatlantic Collapse of Urban Renewal:
Postwar Urbanism from New York to Berlin*
by Christopher Klemek

*I've Got to Make My Livin': Black Women's
Sex Work in Turn-of-the-Century Chicago*
by Cynthia Blair

*Puerto Rican Citizen: History and Political
Identity in Twentieth-Century New York City*
by Lorrin Thomas

*Staying Italian: Urban Change and Ethnic
Life in Postwar Toronto and Philadelphia*
by Jordan Stanger-Ross

*New York Undercover: Private Surveillance
in the Progressive Era*
by Jennifer Fronc

*African American Urban History since
World War II*
edited by Kenneth L. Kusmer and
Joe W. Trotter

*Blueprint for Disaster: The Unraveling of
Public Housing in Chicago*
by D. Bradford Hunt

*Alien Neighbors, Foreign Friends:
Asian Americans, Housing, and the Transformation of Urban California*
by Charlotte Brooks

*The Problem of Jobs: Liberalism, Race, and
Deindustrialization in Philadelphia*
by Guian A. McKee

*Chicago Made: Factory Networks in the
Industrial Metropolis*
by Robert Lewis

*The Flash Press: Sporting Male Weeklies in
1840s New York*
by Patricia Cline Cohen, Timothy J.
Gilfoyle, and Helen Lefkowitz Horowitz
in association with the American Anti-
quarian Society

*Slumming: Sexual and Racial Encounters
in American Nightlife, 1885–1940*
by Chad Heap

MISS CUTLER

& the Case of the

Resurrected Horse

SOCIAL WORK AND THE STORY OF POVERTY
IN AMERICA, AUSTRALIA, AND BRITAIN

MARK PEEL

The University of Chicago Press   Chicago and London

MARK PEEL is professor of modern cultural and social history and head of the School of History at the University of Liverpool. A former professor of history at Monash University, he is the author of three books, most recently *The Lowest Rung: Voices of Australian Poverty*.

The University of Chicago Press, Chicago 60637
The University of Chicago Press, Ltd., London
© 2012 by The University of Chicago
All rights reserved. Published 2012.
Printed in the United States of America

21 20 19 18 17 16 15 14 13 12   1 2 3 4 5

ISBN-13: 978-0-226-65363-1 (cloth)
ISBN-10: 0-226-65363-3 (cloth)

Library of Congress Cataloging-in-Publication Data

Peel, Mark, 1959–
    Miss Cutler and the case of the resurrected horse : social work and the story of poverty in America, Australia, and Britain / Mark Peel.
        p. cm. — (Historical studies of urban America)
    Includes bibliographical references and index.
    ISBN-13: 978-0-226-65363-1 (cloth : alk. paper)
    ISBN-10: 0-226-65363-3 (cloth : alk. paper)   1. Poor—
Services for—United States.   2. Poor—Services for—
England.   3. Poor—Services for—Australia.   4. Social case
work—United States.   5. Social case work—England.
6. Social case work—Australia.   I. Title.   II. Series:
Historical studies of urban America.
    HV43.P44 2012
    362.5'53—dc22
                                                    2011016218

To SCOTT, *for everything,*
and for my friend LOUISE PERSSE,
who always rather liked Miss Cutler

Contents

Acknowledgments ix
Introduction 1

Part One MELBOURNE

Case 1: Miss Cutler and the Case of the Resurrected Horse 23

1 Service, Sympathy, and Efficiency 33
2 Mr. Smith and the Importance of Modern Casework 38
3 Wise Discrimination 46
4 Lady Detectives 51
5 There Are Those Who Feel Their Position 61
6 But Most Will Never Better Themselves 67
7 A Growing Sense of Justice 71
8 The Citizens' Welfare 80

Part Two LONDON

Case 2: Miss Hedges and the Stupid Client 87

9 The Man with the Repulsive Face 95
10 We Are at a Crossroads 99
11 They Are Somewhere Down the Stairs 107
12 Little People 111
13 Dense and Low Grade, but Still He Builds Great Castles in the Air 118
14 Nightmare Days 125

Part Three BOSTON

Case 3: Miss Wells and the Boy Who Wanted to Be an American 133

15 Changing Jerzy 139
16 Closed Mouths and Wise Guys 143
17 She Has Found Herself, and He Will Make a Good American 153
18 The Primitive Becoming More and More Dominant 162
19 More Sinned Against Than Sinning 165

Part Four MINNEAPOLIS

Case 4: Miss Lindstrom and the Fried Potatoes 177

20 The Discovery and the Remedy 185
21 He Is Too Willing for Us to Assume Responsibility 190
22 His Attitude of Helplessness Is Exasperating 197
23 An Insecurity of Terrifying Proportions 206

Part Five OREGON

Case 5: Miss Perry and the Boy Who Knew Numbers 213

24 Policing Relief 221
25 Evasive Types and Plausible Women 228
26 Into the Backwoods 234

Part Six MEN IN SOCIAL WORK

Case 6: Mr. O'Neill and the Seductive Client 247

27 In a Woman's World 257
28 He Must Be Bent to Our Will and Made into a Man 261
29 Confronting the Nagger 266
30 Mr. O'Neill and Mr. Mattner 271

Conclusion 277
Appendix 1: Sources 283
Appendix 2: Cast of Characters 287
Appendix 3: Case Notes 289
Notes 297
Index 319

Acknowledgments

A book that takes years to write, and a research project that began a long time ago, will always generate debts that might now be forgotten. So I shall try and start at the beginning. I first looked at the case files of the Citizen's Welfare Service in 1994 at the suggestion of Tony Birch, then in History at Melbourne University. I will be forever grateful to him for trusting me with the idea and the inspiration. The first people who heard about the idea were my colleagues at the Urban Research Program at the Australian National University; it might have seemed a diversion, but Patrick Troy, Tim Bonyhady, Alastair Greig, Steven Bourassa, Nicholas Brown, and Max Neutze always encouraged me to pursue it.

To the organizations whose case files are featured in this study, I am exceedingly grateful: Melbourne's Citizen Welfare Service, London's Family Welfare Association (especially Helen Dent, chief executive, and Loraine Toone); the Massachusetts Society for the Prevention of Cruelty to Children (especially former president David Robinson; Nancy Scannell, director of planning; and Michael Ames, director of research); the Home for Little Wanderers (especially then president Robert Raye); and the Minneapolis Family and Children's Service (especially the director, Terrence J. Steeno). There would be no archives without archivists, who were to a person generous, knowledgeable, and patient; those overseas were also remarkably welcoming to a long-distance traveler. I especially want to thank the staff at the University of Melbourne's Special Collections; Elizabeth Mock and Dale Freeman from the University of Massachusetts, Boston, Archives and Special Collections; David Klaassen from the Social Welfare History Archives, University of Minnesota Libraries; Bridget Howlett and the excellent staff at the London Metropolitan Archives; and Tim Bakke, who did an immense amount to help me at the Oregon State Archives. During my trips to London, Boston, and Minneapolis, I benefited from some very generous people: to Clay and Carolyn McShane in Boston, my undying thanks for a place to stay, great conversations, and Carolyn's baked beans. Thanks also to David Klaassen for a couple of car trips on some very cold Minneapolis days and for organizing a seminar attended by the great Clarke Chambers; to Pat Thane in London for the seminar, the dinner, and so much good advice; and to Selina Todd, then at Manchester, for the opportunity to visit and speak.

Most of the research and writing for this book took place while I was a member of the Department of History and then the School of Historical Studies at Monash University, Melbourne. I benefited from the interest and advice of a wonderful community of scholars, not least in a school seminar in 2005 that emboldened me to continue writing the dramatizations that are featured in this book. Barbara Caine read much of this manuscript in draft and improved it as only someone of her commanding intellect could. Leah Garrett read my introduction and helped me revise many of the themes of the entire project. I was asked telling questions and given great advice all the way through this project by Monash colleagues—I think especially of Bain Attwood, Graeme Davison, Jane Drakard, David Garrioch, Michael Hau, Peter Howard, Carolyn James, Pauline Nestor, Seamus O'Hanlon, Marian Quartly, and Christina Twomey—and by a host of historians and friends in other places: John Murphy, who generously read drafts and shared his own work in progress; Mike Savage, who also shared some of his own writing prior to publication; and Janet McCalman, who always knows how to make me think more and write better. For her general enthusiasm and good sense, my thanks to Rosemary Johnston, and for always being interested in everything, my thanks to my mother, Jean Peel. I am also grateful for the thoughts and reactions of my many postgraduate students, but especially to Megan Blair and Barbara Russell, who acted a part and taught me a few things; Stephen Powell and Piers Lumley, both of whom did sterling service as research assistants; and Paul Sendziuk, who arranged an invitation to speak in Adelaide. I am also grateful to the Australian Research Council for Large Grant A00103361, which funded the research time and travel necessary to make this a comparative account.

The very last stages of this book were completed in a new location, the School of History at the University of Liverpool. My thanks to Andy Davies, Brigitte Resl, and Dmitri Van Den Bersselaar for helping to refresh a project so long in the making, and to Pat Starkey, Stephen Kenny, and the other participants in a Northwest Historians Network seminar in May 2010 who made me think again about possibilities and connections. I am also very grateful to the three scholars who read this manuscript for the University of Chicago Press for their accurate critiques and suggestions for improvement.

I was able to present papers and seminars on various aspects of this project in all kinds of places, and I am grateful to all of those who asked questions, challenged my approach, and—usually—confirmed that it was worth doing. Particularly important opportunities to share the work were provided by the South Australian and New South Wales Councils of Social Service, the Tasmanian Historical Society, the South Australian State History Conference, the University of Manchester's Centre for Research in Socio-Cultural Change, the Lancaster University Dynamics of Memories Group, the Sociology Department at Macquarie University, the University of London's Institute for Historical Research, the History Council of Victoria, the University of Adelaide Labour Studies Department and the same university's History Seminar Series, the Menzies Centre for Australian Studies, the Museum of Brisbane, and the Simmonds Graduate School of Social Work in Boston.

Parts of the book have appeared before, and I am grateful to the following journals for permission to use the material, more or less revised, as well as for the opportunity to publish the work in the first place: the *Journal of Men's Studies* ("Male Social Workers and the Anxieties of Women's Authority: Boston and Minneapolis, 1920–1940," *Journal of Men's Studies* 15 [2007]: 282–95); the Australian Historical Association ("'Feeling Your Position': Charity, Social Work and the Drama of Class in Melbourne, 1920–1940," *History Australia* 2 [2005]: 83.1–83.15); and the *Griffith Review* ("The Imperfect Bodies of the Poor," *Griffith Review* 4 [2004]: 83–93).

As it nears its appearance, this book is drawing on the talents, experiences, and wisdom of the people at the University of Chicago Press, and my thanks go especially to Robert Devens for his expert advice and good offices and to Anne Goldberg for answering every question I could think of. I am also grateful to Kathy Swain for improving my words as only great editors can.

All along the journey, books draw on the sustaining power of friendships, and as the dedication shows, this one carries a particular link to a lasting one. I hope that Louise Persse likes the Miss Cutler who has emerged here. It is also important to recognize Orlando and Doris, two cats wise and serene, who listened to the odd difficult passage, clumsy transition, and half-baked idea in the way only cats can listen. Perhaps Oliver and Ruby will develop the same skill. And this book, like anything I do, rests on the solid foundations of a partnership for life. In our more than eleven years, Scott and I have moved in and out of several houses and to a new continent, and we have carried Miss Cutler with us. It is time, I think, that she moved on.

The task of casework is to make the discovery and apply the remedy.

Minneapolis Associated Charities, 1922

They appear to us only at intervals, so that we catch glimpses of their lives as one might see a film through an opening in a curtain.

Charity Organisation Society Council, London, 1924

Our workers seek to know.

Massachusetts Society for the Prevention of Cruelty to Children, 1927

Most welfare organizations have a story that is worth the telling, a story terse with human interest, and stratified with pathos, dramatic situations and often a vein of humour.

Charity Organisation Society, Melbourne, 1928

Introduction

An apparently resurrected horse and a man accused of lying. A pregnant Londoner who wouldn't go to the hospital. A boy called Jerzy and a man called George. Children with fried potatoes for lunch. A boy who could do multinumber divisions in his head. A mother accused of a clumsy seduction. All were characters in stories that were, and are, worth the telling. In the thousands of case files produced by inquiry officers, investigators, charity agents, visitors, and social workers, we read about people, lost now to the apparent anonymity of the past, who are trying to say something. What we read is fleeting, uncertain, and sometimes incidental. But it is what we have. If their words and ideas are scattered and torn, perhaps history can mend them and do them justice. After all, if we don't put words in their mouths, they remain silent. So this is a book about stories, the ones we know and the ones we can—and must—imagine.

This is primarily a history of what the people who encountered the poor during the 1920s and 1930s heard them saying and of how they formed what they heard into dramatized explanations of poverty's origins and remedies. It is a comparative study of Australians, Americans, and Britons, of people who shared a commitment to tackling poverty, as well as a set of investigative methods they thought would reveal the best solutions. They shared some presumptions and prescriptions, though in some ways their responses to the problem of poverty were intriguingly different. This is an account of what we see through their eyes: the assumptions they made about their own places and times, the evils they wanted to tackle, and the good they thought they could do. It is a history of their convictions and of the ideas that inspired and sometimes failed them.

These visitors and investigators usually assumed that the poor lied and dissembled or did not comprehend the real causes and consequences of their situations. The poor were often thought to be cunning and deceitful. They "feigned simplicity" or pretended to look for work when all they wanted was to get something for nothing. They went from one agency to another, drawing too deep from the shallow well of charity. They invented stories and pretended that they weren't responsible. They said that they'd been unlucky or that there was no hope and no help for the "common people" or the likes of them. Because they were presumed to tell lies and because they were supposed to be hiding things and avoiding responsibility for their own failings, the poor had to be questioned, examined, and visited. Only thorough and rigorous investigation could establish the facts and distinguish true need from deceptive fraud.

For the new kind of professional and mostly female caseworkers who took over much of the conversation with the poor in American, British, and Australian charity and welfare after 1920, it was especially important that clients understood the truth about their poverty and that they "felt their position." The poor could not be helped until they had accepted a true diagnosis of their condition and the cure that might end their problems. This usually meant a careful exchange of questions and answers in which workers struggled to unearth secrets and lies. Often with little material and financial aid to give, workers tackled the difficult problem of proving beyond a doubt that an applicant actually deserved help. They probed for details, looked for possible aliases, contacted other agencies for case histories, asked local shopkeepers, and interviewed neighbors. They probed the silences and the omissions and tried to find truth in the applicants' language. Yet they knew words could be deceptive, especially when they were spun into stories. The choreography was physical as much as verbal: caseworkers evaluated gestures, expressions, dress, and physical surroundings. People could learn how to simulate genuine feeling and could mimic the truly needy. It was delicate and demanding work.

From the testimonies of the poor, and from whatever other evidence they could gather of circumstance and character, these women—and a few men—wrote dramas of negotiation, dispute, and detection, which emerge in the thousands of case files they drafted and amended. Theirs was a form of "charitable writing" that took very seriously the need to create knowledge for broader publicity and education as well as about the individual case itself.[1] This book is based on those files, produced by eight different agencies in Melbourne, London, Boston, Minneapolis, and Oregon.[2] The record of encounters with the poor is patchy and depends on where such case files have survived. In a sense, these places appear in this book because someone—a librarian or archivist, an earlier historian, or a prescient social worker who stood against the discarding zeal of the 1950s and 1960s—thought to preserve a large collection of files and make them accessible to the scholars of the present and future. In Melbourne, London, Boston, and Minneapolis, I could also read these files alongside more or less complete records of the administration and policies of the agency, including annual reports, discussions of casework, and, sometimes, publicity material.

These agencies appear in this story not only because of the fortuitous survival of their records, however, but also because of their significance and because they offered some intriguing comparative possibilities. During the 1920s and 1930s, the Charity Organisation Societies of London and Melbourne, the Massachusetts Society for the Prevention of Cruelty to Children, the Boston Children's Aid Society, and the Minneapolis Family Welfare Association were leaders in the transition from an earlier model of charity visiting to professional casework; the files of Oregon's Child Welfare Commission, Public Welfare Bureau, and Associated Charities provide a glimpse into the sometimes turbulent mix of public and private charity. These were major local and sometimes national institutions during a period of significant transformation. All played an important part in training the first two generations of paid, professional "inquiry officers," "agents," and "investigators" who would in time begin to call themselves "caseworkers" and "social workers." All were part of local welfare landscapes in which they were particularly influential as interpreters, dramatizers, and publicists of new forms of charity investigation, casework, and social work, in part because the more humdrum tasks of dealing with the poor were managed by public authorities or by agencies representing other faiths, including the Salvation Army and Catholic and Jewish charities. The agencies in this study were always able to rely on others to help the absolutely destitute and could therefore focus more confidently on judging, policing, and defining the poor. All did a great amount of general welfare work, including the two Boston organizations that were primarily focused on child protection. And because these agencies amassed evidence and made inquiries in all possible directions, their case files and records bristle with letters to and from other organizations, government bodies, reform groups, and professional associations in their own territories and beyond. They wrote to each other, participating in a national and international exchange of ideas. In examining them, we can hear a much broader conversation about poverty.

★   ★   ★

Miss Cutler and the Case of the Resurrected Horse has three goals. First, it continues a strong scholarly tradition of using social work's case files to explore how the origins and solutions of social problems such as poverty were understood, dramatized, and enacted, largely between women, during a period when many of those who would shape the social welfare systems of the mid-twentieth century were being trained in, and shaped by, particular forms of investigation and inquiry. Second, it is a comparison of different places at a roughly similar time. It explores how interpretations of poverty—and casework itself—were shaped by local histories and contexts and by the gender of the interpreter. Yet it also emphasizes strong similarities between these dramatizations of poverty, especially an assumption that because poverty's roots lay first and foremost in the deficiencies of the poor, its solutions would involve transforming or at least controlling the poor. Finally, the book explores the possibility of using case files (and a little imagination) to dramatize and rewrite encounters between the poor and their investigators in ways that restore to history the voices, perspective, and knowledge of poor people themselves.

For interwar investigative social work, and the stories about poverty for which it was the foundation, the case file took on profound importance. It was the hallmark of professional investigation and the guarantee of a just outcome. Each file began with a profile of the applicant, to which the worker added details of home visits and other investigations. The home visit was especially crucial, for it was here, as social casework pioneer Mary Richmond argued, that the client's "whole atmosphere" could be revealed.[3] Mary Birtwell, a charity visitor in Boston, described the home visit as "a study of the entire history, character, and resources of the whole family, a gathering of all the information from every available source, with a view to searching out the real causes of need."[4] With such aims persisting into the 1920s and 1930s, it is little wonder that some files contained dozens and even hundreds of pages.

Often brimming with impressions, descriptions, documents, and detailed narratives, busy files were a testament to the caseworkers' professional rigor. They were also produced for audiences. Overseeing officials defaced neat pages with penned exclamations and penciled underlining. Workers produced shortened versions of the most "telling" cases for executive committees and the increasingly common case conferences. As they wrote up and revised, they added flourishes and dramatic momentum, turning their clients into characters and highlighting the truths about poverty they seemed to convey. In the training, publicizing, and political activity of these agencies, or what one called its "propaganda," those stories introduced appeals for donations, made up the evidence in submissions to public inquiries, and appeared in newspapers next to staged photographs of the "grateful recipients," the "sympathetic women" who helped them, and the older men who presided over agency committees and boards.[5]

Before decisions could be made about poverty's remedies, either in the intimate encounters between caseworkers and their clients or on the larger canvas of political and social debate, poverty's true causes and characteristics first had to be dramatized and explained. Poverty must always have a story that explains the present and looks into the future. The story can focus on what is wrong with the poor and how they must be saved or transformed. Or it can speak of the larger wrongs that poverty reveals and how those might be put right. Of course, the poor themselves also have a story. For them, it was important to offer explanations that would secure them what they needed, ideally without too much time-consuming and intrusive interrogation and in a way that said something about the burdens they carried and preserved something of their dignity. In this way, case files form an archive of interactions, debates, and competing versions of the truth.[6] This was sometimes a prolonged war of words and sometimes a brief skirmish, but it was always, as Eileen Yeo recognizes, "a fascinating theatre of encounter."[7]

Case files provide us with a stock of stories drawn from life and shaped by their writers toward conclusions and lessons, as they turned what they saw and heard into dramas and melodramas, comedies, and satires. The best stories presented tableaux in a theater of class, with more or less stock characters performing scripts of detection, redemption, and salvation. They captured the dilemmas of proving entitlement, praising the grateful and deserving poor, and condemning the ungrateful graspers who imperiled the whole business of charity. They proved that investigative methods and professional expertise could help the needy, unmask the deceiver, and identify the person who could be transformed as well as the pauper who should only be deterred. Above all, caseworkers claimed to tell the truth about poverty. As Linda Gordon reminds us, case records were not always "scrupulously honest," and sometimes a worker needed "to note what she ought to have done, not what she did do."[8] But if we are interested in case files as dramatizations of what was meant to be, as stories written by narrators, that makes the choices they reflect even more significant, especially when some of these stories were used to justify some forms of charity and turn others into "pauperization" or "useless benevolence."[9]

The most telling stories cast an especially interesting light on what their narrators thought others would find convincing and moving. They help us grasp the good that they thought they were doing and for whom it was being done. Such narrative, as Thomas Laqueur points out, aims to "make 'is' seem, at least for a moment, to imply 'ought.'"[10] And it is important to remember that these stories had a real impact on the poor themselves, both in the determination of individual outcomes and in the shaping of a broader understanding of poverty and inequality.[11] These stories had real power. They shaped poor people's experience, and they shaped other people's assumptions and convictions. They described, and they prescribed. Above all, they provide a crucial window into what people who were not poor thought was true about those who were.[12]

As a history of how poverty and inequality were explained by stories, this is also a history of how social and economic hierarchies were described and defended. This was not so much a war as a series of inconclusive skirmishes, but it was a struggle all the same. Daniel Walkowitz argues that the professional welfare workers of the first three decades of the twentieth century played a crucial role in the real and symbolic construction of class identity and authority. As they "patroled" the "borders of class," they also dramatized and enacted them.[13] In Britain, too, "class superiority" was the crucial factor linking earlier forms of charity and benevolence with the more modern "social work."[14] Autobiographies and testimonies make clear that many twentieth-century people learned about the consequences of their class position from their contacts with social workers, child protectors, and charity investigators, as well as police officers, teachers, priests, ministers, missionaries, and welfare nurses.[15] This was especially true for women and children and for men rendered dependent by unemployment, illness, or incapacity. And as they examined and investigated others, social workers also, of course, made and remade themselves. The writer wrote her own life story, as well as her client's. The dramatizing of these encounters was not just a matter of attracting funding or shaping public perception. It was also a means of satisfying the worker's own sense of accomplishment and, I argue, creating her own sense of certainty about how the story of poverty should end.

Class distinctions are forged in public arenas, such as in factories and mines or on the political stage. But they are also made in private realms, such as on doorsteps and porches, in kitchens and living rooms, and in the intimate skirmishes between investigators and investigated.[16] Then and now, those conversations focus less on labor, exploitation, and economic justice and more on virtue, vice, character, and morality.[17] They also take place largely between women. Men served as leaders and officials in most of these agencies, and a few young men specialized in fields such as juvenile delinquency or "industrial work," in which their gender was considered an advantage in dealing with boys. The dramas they imagined, wrote, and enacted differed in significant ways from those written by their female colleagues. But the daily work of welfare—and the most frequent forms of encounter between classes—was more and more the terrain of professional women. On the other side, too, women made up most of the clients in social work's dramas; in the United States, no less than in Britain and Australia, working-class wives and mothers tried as far as possible to keep exchanges with outsiders in their own hands. Certainly, in the times and places described in this book, women entered ever more centrally into the encounters between those who were and were not poor.

The dominance of women in everyday investigation does not make them in some way more responsible than men for creating the hierarchies and justifications of inequality. Nor did they necessarily benefit in the same way as men. Certainly, as an emphasis on social reform, amelioration, and welfare increased the range and number of class interactions during the late nineteenth and twentieth centuries, such interactions often became the responsibility of female professionals. Women did—and still do—much of the hardest and most exacting work in the management of class inequalities. Yet this was always an ambivalent and limited authority. As Angela Woollacott argues, women endured a long struggle to establish their authority on "competence and rights" rather than innate morality; "even now at the end of the twentieth century," she says, "the ghosts of female moral authority and a belief in women being inherently maternal have not been laid to rest."[18] As Lori Ginzberg notes of America, a "conflation of femaleness and morality" has always had both "conservative and radical implications" for professional women.[19] The benefits women derive from professional status are always somewhat fragile; even if middle class and white, as women these professionals never gain the "full dividend" of their class, racial, and ethnic privileges.

In the agencies represented in this study, female workers still tended to report to—and be supervised by—male secretaries and committees on which men outnumbered women. Even as this became less true by the 1930s, the rise of women into supervisory positions often created new dilemmas. In distinguishing themselves from the friendly visitors and benevolent ladies of an unprofessional past, for instance, these women, Regina Kunzel argues, sometimes tried to "de-gender the act of helping" and "equated professionalism with masculinity."[20] Walkowitz describes women adopting "the 'male' work ethos of the dispassionate expert, even while continuing, with evident discomfort, to defer to her male colleagues and bosses."[21] In a comparative view, the shift from "female" benevolence to "male" expertise seems more complicated, especially because women caseworkers in Melbourne and London seem to have developed another response to the problem of female authority: they created new forms of gender-specific capacity, based on women's specific contributions to tasks such as detective investigation and case writing. Among American social workers, too, as Karen Tice argues, women often claimed a clear link between a specifically "feminized, personal knowledge of clients" and social work's most important means of professional expression: the well-written case file.[22] They assumed that they heard more, and listened more effectively, than men.

At the same time, it is important to consider how the relative dominance of women might have mattered to social work and especially its emerging conceptualizations of poverty and inequality. If we can ask how social work helped create certain kinds of professional femininity or female leadership, we can also ask, following historians such as John Cumbler or Steven King, how women's involvement in charity, welfare, and casework made a real difference to how those movements grew and what they achieved.[23] In each of the cities explored in this book, it is possible to say that women tempered social work and shaped the experience of poor people in a number of ways. For instance, they tended to be more impatient with men, especially those they termed the "able-bodied," and to be less forgiving of men's failings. Women also believed themselves to be better and more patient questioners of children and were more likely to be impressed by poor women's struggle to keep their houses and children clean. As working women, too, they exhibited a better understanding than men of the importance—and also the very great fragility—of women's independence, even if they always tended to impress the importance of good housekeeping on their married women clients. If they were advising other and especially younger women, they often emphasized the importance of a skill or a trade and the capacity to care for yourself if need be. It may have been patronizing, and sometimes they assumed too easily that their own lives as working women should be a model for women who had little chance of economic self-sufficiency. But it made rather better sense than insisting, as some of the male visitors did, that for young women, a life of domestic toil and obedience to a husband was a matter of like it or lump it.

Most important, gender mattered in the relationships women workers developed with their clients. It is true, as Elizabeth Lunbeck argues, that women social workers "dealt in morals, bandying about terms such as feebleminded, immoral and slovenly on the one hand and intelligent, upright and refined on the other."[24] But they did so—at least in part—having at least seen and confronted those they were labeling. Proximity to the poor—and the focus on everyday welfare work rather than policy, politics, and planning—was itself gendered: by and large, women talked to the poor, whereas men talked to each other about poverty. Accordingly, women were much more likely to be in a position to listen to the poor and to recognize and repeat alternative stories about poverty. I argue that some of what the poor said about unfairness, injustice, and unearned disadvantage could make sense to some women in a way it did not to most men. Woollacott argues that her social and welfare workers and policewomen "claimed the right to make judgements" but also "came to view their clientele as having legitimate interests."[25] Ellen Ross claims that her London charity women seemed to have chronicled poverty in rather dif-

ferent ways from men, helping to "write new and different 'legends' ...
that would now include factory girls and worn mothers, domestic interi-
ors rather than street scenes, schoolchildren rather than child beggars." As
she argues, women also focused much more attention on aural information
and interviews, whereas men often emphasized poverty's visual surfaces.[26]
In these works, and in Beverly Stadum's meticulous study of welfare relationships in Minneapolis, it is also clear that female interpreters of poverty
took greater note of family conflicts and the burdens as well as the importance of mothering.

In this book, I show how poverty's stories were normally constructed in
ways that demeaned the poor, casting them as characters in dramas about
inadequacy, deceit, and inferiority in which their willingness to accept
transforming guidance distinguished the worthy from the unworthy. But
I also want to suggest that some of the female caseworkers who listened
to poorer women helped reconstruct the story of poverty, inequality, and
welfare in the first half of the twentieth century. It wasn't all or nothing,
and much of the work in case files and archives that might challenge or
bear out this claim remains to be done. But it reminds us that as women
caseworkers grappled with the problems of translating expected practice
into practical social work, they could—and sometimes did—begin exploring an alternative story. As Linda Gordon puts it, "Individual caseworkers were usually better (though sometimes worse) than the official agency
policies they were supposed to follow."[27] Our testimonies of poverty were
and are largely produced by women who listened to other women. Perhaps
poorer women could say things to other women they could not have said
to men, even across a boundary of class. This is why case files are so important. In them we see that caseworkers could bear witness to the truths
that poor people, and especially poor women, had been speaking all along.
Some caseworkers never wavered from their belief in the inferiority, ignorance, and even stupidity of the poor. But in some places and times, in
conversations among women, others began to wonder whether what the
poor were saying about their poverty might be true after all.

★ ★ ★

In its focus on case files (and especially the theater of encounter), the nar-
ration and enactment of inequality, and the importance of women, this
study draws on the insights of a particularly rich scholarly literature. In
the United States, Roy Lubove first emphasized the importance of casework and the "accumulation and interpretation of social evidence." The
history of social work and poverty was then transformed by Michael Katz,

who was one of the first to draw attention to the fascinating "drama of sacrifice and gratitude" that case files contained, and by Linda Gordon, whose study of domestic violence in Boston established the importance of case records as a window into the construction of social problems and their remedies.[28] Social work continues to attract some of the best North American historians, with case files used to reconstruct the experience of people living in poverty and to examine the nature of welfare work, especially the professionalizing dilemmas of its female workers. The rich vein of writing includes Franca Iacovetta and Wendy Mitchinson's pathbreaking edited collection *On the Case* and Karen Tice's superb *Tales of Wayward Girls and Immoral Women*, both published in 1998. Tice showed how case records "transformed clients' biographies into professional representations," and hers was one of the first studies to deal seriously with the narrative choices and genres of social work writing.[29] Daniel Walkowitz amplified the crucial links between case writing and class identity, and Elizabeth Lunbeck showed, in her study of American psychiatry, that casework was one among a variety of methods that allowed social workers "to imagine that in implementing a police-like investigatory strategy they were acting in the name of science, not morality."[30] Records of negotiation have also proved important in reinforcing the claim, made by Lynn Hollen Lees and Bruce Bellingham, among others, that "applying for relief was an active, negotiated process" in which historians must seek the "reconstruction of struggle and accommodation" rather than simple imposition.[31] The imaginative use of case files and other agency records as a window into the negotiations between social workers and clients is also a feature of recent work by Emily Abel and Joan Waugh on New York City and especially by Beverly Stadum on Minneapolis.[32]

In British history, Ellen Ross's *Love and Toil* and Seth Koven's *Slumming* underscored the importance of charity records in the imaginative reconstruction of what Ross called "special, carefully orchestrated relationships."[33] In her most recent work, Ross has also reminded us of the importance of narratives of encounter, which take ideas about charity relationships "beyond sentimentalized images of female selflessness, satirical 'lady bountiful' stereotypes, or social-control simplifications."[34] Although Stephen Page's call for a more detailed use of case files in "reconstructing the lives of the poor" has been only partly heeded, Pat Starkey has shown how the detailed notes of her amateur social workers in Liverpool and other cities change our sense of how Britons became aware of the "problem family."[35] This focus on the "vocabulary" and "sites and occasions of class encounter" also follows the imaginative lead of Peter Bailey, who was among the first to raise the issues during the 1970s.[36]

Relatively few Australian welfare historians have used case records; in some agencies, only registers or index cards were used, and others did not preserve or amalgamate the accumulating evidence that created a story. Because the bulk of its case files were preserved, Melbourne's Charity Organisation Society/Citizen's Welfare Service has attracted the most attention, including the pioneering work of Shurlee Swain, Tony Birch's caustic interrogation of social workers' interventions in working-class family life, and Nell Musgrove's illuminating analysis of welfare surveillance in the 1940s and 1950s.[37] Here, too, case files tend to tell a more complicated story than accounts relying largely on publications, pamphlets, and propaganda, most especially by uncovering the war of words and putting clients back into encounters in which neither they nor the social worker held all the cards.

The agencies that appear in this study all practiced and fostered investigative casework, and all played a crucial role in the development of welfare ideas and practices in their respective societies. Accordingly, and as the chapters that follow show, accounts of their relationships with the poor can draw on numerous broader histories of charity, welfare, and social work. On the broadest canvas are studies that trace the emergence of casework on a national scale, including Stanley Wenocur and Michael Reisch's *From Charity to Enterprise*.[38] Another group—such as Eric Schneider's *In the Web of Class* and Susan Traverso's *Welfare Politics in Boston*—deals with particular cities, and others, including Robert Humphreys' *Poor Relief and Charity*, Jane Lewis's *The Voluntary Sector, the State and Social Work in Britain*, and the work of Richard Kennedy, R. A. Cage, and Geoff Spenceley, provide detailed histories of specific agencies.[39] Any historian of women's lives in Boston must also begin with a close reading of Sarah Deutsch's superb *Women and the City*.[40] In what follows, my debt to these scholars who have shown the way should be clear.

* * *

My work differs from most earlier accounts in one crucial respect: it is a comparative history that examines similar organizations in different contexts. Some of these variations stem from their different missions: in London and Melbourne the case files were produced by charity organization societies, in Minneapolis by a general family welfare association, in Oregon by the public family and children's welfare commission, and in Boston by child rescue and protection agencies. There are differences, also, in their relationships with other organizations and public authorities, in the kinds of information I have been able to gather on their administration, and in the weight that must be given in the chapters that follow to their ideological battles and internal arguments. In both Melbourne and London, for instance, it is especially important to examine how charity organization societies enmeshed themselves in larger debates about public and private welfare, using the accumulated stock of case files to defend their positions, before undergoing their own transformations during the late 1930s and 1940s.

But similarities and differences in their dramatizations of poverty were not simply an outcome of contrasting objectives. Accordingly, they can help illuminate what the people of these different places wanted to say and do. And by focusing on those files that contain the richest and most detailed conversations about poverty's origins and solutions, the comparisons stand clear of simple differences in the mission or clientele of the various agencies. The worth of the approach is shown as well by existing comparative insights. Jane Lewis, for instance, emphasizes how far the British charity organization movement lagged behind American agencies in the development of professionalized casework practice before 1930, and Kathleen Woodroofe's pioneering work on Britain and the United States highlights common dilemmas and different characterizations of how the problem of poverty might best be ameliorated.[41]

Following the strategy so well deployed by David Goodman in his account of "gold seeking" in mid-nineteenth-century California and Victoria, I base my historical comparison on a series of questions: How did the people of different places interpret a similar set of problems, responsibilities, and opportunities? If poverty must always be explained by means of a story about its origins and overcoming, to what extent did those stories differ or not differ in place, and change or not change across time? With what interpretations of poverty did the people of different places begin their accounts? How did they dramatize and explain poverty and inequality? What were their scripts and characters, and what were the conclusions they wanted to reach? If social workers chose different colors from the palette of possibilities, what might that tell us about what really mattered to them, and what was most influential about the context in which they were making their decisions? What were the social problems that preoccupied them? What did they focus on, and what did they ignore?

This is a comparative study, though it might also be, in the way suggested by Ian Tyrrell, a "transnational" one because it tracks ideas and practices that themselves moved across national boundaries to influence the work of charity and welfare in other places.[42] In my view, the two approaches work together. Certainly, I am interested in the light that comparison sheds on what people in different nations made of themselves;

social workers' idea of America, or Britain, or Australia was expressed in the way they dramatized their cases and in the cultural references they used to explain their situations. As such, these people, who were often very "transnational" in their careers, their thinking, and their travels, were also very "national" in the way they understood social and economic problems. And they were also local; they did their social work in specific times and places, and as Susan Kleinberg's illuminating comparative study shows, local control and patterning was a crucial factor in the uneven development of American welfare into the Depression and beyond.[43] Again following Goodman, I am interested in the light that comparison casts on these more specific, local differences: "We may," he argues, "only understand what is truly local by invoking comparison."[44]

Accordingly, the comparisons in my study are contextual; they ask if and how stories differed, and if and when they changed, across a roughly similar period of time. They are local as well as national, emphasizing the links between British and Australian ideas as well as the striking variations within the American stories of poverty. For "scientific charity" in interwar Melbourne and London, class was everything, and it was the policing and detective elements of investigation that counted for most. In the United States, stories of superiority and inferiority were just as powerfully shaped by race, while an American faith in redemptive transformation, at least for some of the poor, stood in strong contrast to a British and Australian conviction that poverty stemmed mostly from almost ineradicable flaws of character. The case files written in Minneapolis and especially Boston, for instance, emphasized the dramas of changing some immigrants into Americans who could plot out the social mobility and self-improvement that were assumed to characterize "superior" lives. In Boston, social workers wrote of themselves as magicians who helped the ethnic poor—though not African Americans—unpick the threads of their heritage and reassemble themselves as Americans. In Minneapolis, much faith rested on every white American's capacity for wise planning, self-management, and social uplift. Oregon's welfare workers, however, dramatized a different kind of frontier. As they looked out into what they described as a disordered backwoods of fanatics, hunchbacks, and half-breeds, their dramas traced degeneration at a scale that justified segregation, institutionalization, and even sterilization.

In Melbourne and London, workers witnessed and described their tasks as defining and policing but hardly ever, in the way their American counterparts did, as transforming. What is striking about the story of poverty in interwar London is its sense of unshakable class difference. This was charitable writing as travel writing, casework as fieldwork, or sometimes almost humorous social commentary. In Melbourne, too, a sense of difference was important. But there, exemplary stories had a different slant, I think because what seemed solid at the center of the British world always needed reinforcement at its edges. Melbourne's characteristic tales were of forensic investigation, of lady detectives engaged in a search for truth and lies. But in both Melbourne and London, the certainties of class would in time be shaken by events, or at least by how those events starkly revealed the deficiencies and contradictions of what had once been taken for granted. Here, in charity organization, hardly a place where anyone might have expected reforming revelation, minds could change. Melbourne's Depression, and London's sufferings in war, would see some of those who listened to the poor and the unlucky begin to explore new and sometimes very challenging ideas about the links between social position, character, and fortune.

Yet even if they differed in their assumptions about what do with the deficient poor, how much change could be expected, and how that change might be brought about, American, Australian, and British interpreters of poverty shared and carried into their social work a common idea that poverty's origins lay in the problems of the poor, and its solutions in managing and perhaps even overcoming those deficiencies. In this period of transition, when methods of social work were carried out into encounters between new kinds of social workers and their clients, people were asked to produce accounts of themselves, to narrate their struggles and their suffering in a kind of "compulsory autobiographical activity."[45] As is so often the case, poor people's autobiographies emphasized vulnerability and the weight of accumulated disadvantage. They talked about the importance of work for fathers, schooling and opportunities for children, and investments in the health and capacities of mothers. They made clear poverty's tangled roots. Of course, poor people didn't share everything with the visitors, investigators, and interpreters, who couldn't always be trusted with the truth and who so often seemed to want a performance of bravery, pluck, and gratitude rather than a serious conversation about the "whole atmosphere" and the "real causes of need." But even if the words of the poor were coherent and consistent, and even if social work's storytellers could learn to listen, most did not. In these places and times, there was change, and there were differences. But there was also a fundamental and almost unshakable unwillingness to do what actually makes most sense if you want to tackle poverty: see the world through the eyes of the poor.

* * *

Any historian working with case files or similar records is enthused by their possibilities and challenged by their limitations. Even if, as Iacovetta and

Mitchinson argue, they "do not provide the client's unmediated voice," the descriptions and understandings of poverty we find in case files tell us much about those who met, questioned, and listened to the poor.[46] Of course, as these caseworkers recapitulated and wrote, they also preserved something of the words they heard. Each "I said" responded to a "he said" or a "she said," and part of my reading of those files is to try to recapture something of the other side of the welfare encounter. What the poor said was reshaped, summarized, and amended into phrases they wouldn't have used. But their words remain visible because the visitors, investigators, and inquiry officers used them as evidence. They quoted their clients at length or garnished their summaries with telling snippets and idiosyncratic expressions. Sometimes they tried to capture accents and unusual pronunciations in deliberately misspelled words. They took care to note, remember, and write down angry, dismissive, or challenging words into their files, as well as words that struck them as particularly revealing of the truth.

Clients knew how important words were. They often asked what was being written or showed concern about the permanence of what might be woven from their words. They tried to control the content of their case by insisting that certain facts be recorded or by helping their neighbors and local shopkeepers learn their "lines." They sent in their own letters or had letters written on their behalf by someone they assumed the charity investigators would respect, such as a priest or a local dignitary. They tried to inject their own prerogatives into their conversations with workers and insist that those asking questions of them also answer questions in return. They wanted to know, as one East Boston woman asked, "what is being written about me in your books." It would be many years before the poor won the right to see at least part of what was being written about them. But their demand for that right was long-standing.

Words are an important weapon for the strong, but they are just as important for the weak. The poor have always shared stories that shame those who happen to be rich, reestablish a sense of worth battered by the humiliations of distrustful welfare, or challenge the cruel common sense of inequality. Words express entitlements and obligations and describe ideal worlds. More or less openly, words help the powerless hold the powerful to account. Used imaginatively and carefully, the record of their words is our best resource for understanding what the poor were trying to say and what they were struggling to establish as true. As a number of historians have noted, the words of the poor also help us understand how they insisted on turning individualized charity based on character into a collective entitlement based on need, emphasizing their moral independence and their own prerogatives in ideas about justice.[47]

Such evidence can be aural, as in slave songs, and it can be heard in the "hidden transcripts" of oral tradition so brilliantly deployed by James Scott in *Weapons of the Weak*.[48] As some of the most imaginative and illuminating historians of welfare have realized, it can also be found in the documentation of claim, entitlement, and responsibility that form the archive of charity and social work. In an edited collection titled *Chronicling Poverty*, Tim Hitchcock, Peter King, and Pamela Sharpe point to the value of "forms of written evidence created when the poor confronted, and were confronted by, the hierarchies and institutions of authority"; from "the places where rich and poor interacted," they argue, stem the materials for careful investigation of "particular documents, negotiations and strategic ploys."[49] Peter Mandler makes a similar call, insisting that the history of charity and philanthropy is never just "a chapter in the cultural history of the upper classes" but also one in the social history of class interaction, and Michael Katz shows how case files allow us to "negotiate the terrain" with charity's clients.[50] Linda Gordon describes clients using words to encourage or to deflect competing judgments of their situations. Their interventions and interruptions help us grasp their agency: "not merely manipulated, but also manipulators," they were "active in attempting to get help according to their own values and goals."[51]

Case files are a source for the voices of the poor, though perhaps a less secure one than pauper letters and petitions. These are not written demands, and although a study of the letters that applicants sent to these agencies would be very interesting in its own right, relatively few clients wrote them. Like court transcripts or records of interrogation, these are not documents over which their subjects could easily gain or retain control. In addition, case files were written after the fact and were never intended to be verbatim accounts of everything that was said. Although perhaps not as potentially dangerous as a legal proceeding, the encounter with social workers was nonetheless difficult and risky. The truth was not always a client's best friend, especially when the truth might in some way confirm workers' assumptions about dependence and depravity. And sometimes, of course, confronted by someone who couldn't understand the truth or whose empathy couldn't stretch too far beneath herself, clients had to tell half-truths and even lies.

As I examined these case files, I could see that many clients wanted to say something. I wanted to know what it was, what they were saying under their breath. As a client is questioned and examined, I found myself wondering what she was thinking, what she would like to say, what were the words that might have been pressing against those pursed lips. Workers could see things in clients' eyes, but they weren't always sure what those things were. Clients might "seem indignant," "grimace slightly," or even start to speak before checking themselves. There is something there, but it is fleeting and half-seen. This isn't the comfortable introspection of the diary or the private letter. It is public, it is potentially dangerous, and it can mean the difference between getting and not getting something you need.

The desire to give voice to the weak presses me on, as it has pressed others on before. Can we hear and even speak for any of the people who were under investigation? Some would say no, and emphatically, perhaps wondering whether the case files reveal anything of "experience" at all.[52] I am not so much interested in questions of agency; in many respects those questions have already been raised, addressed, and closed. Instead, I want to explore another challenge: whether it is possible to use these files for a kind of historical writing that tries—imaginatively and truthfully—to write clients back into the story, to draw back into the spotlight what James Scott so luminously calls "the offstage conversations of the repressed."[53]

Employing the imaginative skills they must always use, historians can turn relatively one-sided stories into dramas that give all their characters more of a voice. That ambition means trying to imagine both what clients might have wanted to say, or what they knew, and exploring a greater range of the emotions and characters of the investigators, inquiry officers, or welfare workers themselves. Such an approach means understanding these files as records of encounter and exchange in which some parts of the conversation are missing and must be imagined or, if possible, drawn in from other, similar conversations. Sometimes there are hints that reveal something. There are facts that weren't understood or were forgotten. There are twists and turns in the story that make things clearer in hindsight. And sometimes the client has left us something: a word or a phrase, a drawing, a clue, or a fragment that suggests another way the story happened and might be told.

Such writing has to be done carefully. History isn't fiction, and we can't just invent the outlines of the story or change the ending. History is an imaginative and inventive discipline, but it is also a truthful one, and it must always make clear the difference between evidence and artifice. Yet we can draw on the tools of fiction—especially its focus on dramatization, dialogue, and drama—to create an account that is real and realistic. It is possible to be truthful—to convey the true meaning of the past—by incorporating material that is dramatized and even fictional, so long as the reader is informed of the difference and always knows where the boundaries lie.

In refashioning these stories, I draw largely on the work of Dominick La Capra, especially the arguments about writing ethical, engaging history laid out in his book *Writing History, Writing Trauma*. In my view, it is possible to use some of these case files to achieve two of the goals La Capra describes (and leaves tantalizingly open when it comes to practical application). First, by providing readers with the substance of the file and the story that I create out of it, I can display something of the writing of history, engaging the reader in the challenges and opportunities posed by the discipline of history (as opposed to fiction) and revealing the judgments I have made about how—and how much—to invent and assume in order to create a truthful story.

The second goal identified by La Capra is capturing something of what he calls the "true impact" of the past by "attending to, even trying, in limited ways, to recapture the … affective dimension of the experience of others."[54] It is to enact the past, and give voice to its various actors, because not to do so is to compound the problem of relative invisibility. In other words, if all we have are the voices of the powerful talking about the powerless, this does not mean we are somehow released from the responsibility of finding a way to include the powerless in our stories about the past. This approach focuses attention on how history's sources are read: against the grain, for their silences and their strategies, and for what lies half-spoken on their edges. But it also focuses attention on how history might be written. It suggests that we try to realize the narrative possibilities of those sources in order to perform the past more truthfully and with a more complete range of actors.

In a broad sense, the task of social and cultural history must always be to account for what people made of themselves, not just what others made of them. And the point is to stress their imprint as well as their agency. Of course, they appear mostly in what French historian Antoine De Baecque describes as the past's "intermittent lightning."[55] These are testimonies and transcripts they don't control. They are in places they sometimes don't want to be. They are in court or incarcerated. They are in case files and hospital records and prison musters. They are sometimes just recorded and sometimes asked for more. And sometimes they must tell stories they don't want to share. They must think about tactics, about what they dare and dare not say. We see them almost always through the eyes of others.

But they are at least there. Like Linda Gordon's ill-used wives, Michael Katz's impudent woman, Carolyn Steedman's servants, Karen Tice's American girls, Tim Hitchcock's unmarried mothers, or Jeremy Boulton's pensioner petitioners, the clients in these case files speak, often at length, about the world they knew. They are trying to tell us something. History is always made from what the people of the past left behind, from what they imagined would tell their story. It is made from what the people of the past projected into their future. For a tiny few, we have a lot, but for most we have only fragments. But if the words and ideas of the weak are shadowy and disjointed, then perhaps it is up to historians to make them whole in ways that do justice to the people who spoke them, as well as those who listened to them. Having read more than a thousand case files, I think I can imagine what might and sometimes must have been. This is, in part, an attempt to fulfill James Scott's request that we respect the words and tactics of history's bit players, perhaps especially their "tenacity of self-preservation."[56] But it rests as well on a simple observation: if we deny ourselves the capacity to tell stories about most of the people who lived in the past because they have not left us enough with which to write a more narrowly understood "history," then we compound the neglect that silenced them in the first place.

The bulk of this book is made up of more usual forms of historical writing. But to illustrate the possibilities of these sources, and a kind of writing that tries better to convey the to-and-fro of investigation, assumption, success, and failure, I have written short dramatizations of six encounters: "Miss Cutler and the Case of the Resurrected Horse"; "Miss Hedges and the Stupid Client"; "Miss Wells and the Boy Who Wanted to Be an American"; "Miss Lindstrom and the Fried Potatoes"; "Miss Perry and the Boy Who Knew Numbers"; and "Mr. O'Neill and the Seductive Client." The longest is some five or six pages, the shortest around two. Each example turns the true details of a case history into a dramatized script. What workers and clients said and thought is assumed from this file, brought in from another file, or imagined as a realistic version of what might or must have been said. In appendix 3, readers will have the notes on which the story is based so that they can see what was there.

Each drama is followed by a resolution, which points out what is and is not known and what a historian may and may not do and explains why the encounter was dramatized in a particular way. In each, there is something of a secret or a mystery, something that can't now be known for sure, something that helps show how difficult were the tasks assigned to charity and social work's foot soldiers. "Miss Cutler" focuses on the dilemmas of judgment, especially when it comes to the assumptions that are made about the needy, and "Miss Hedges" reveals the ways in which good intentions could override a poor woman's own prerogatives. "Miss Wells" shows how the changes desired of clients by social workers might not always have been what they seemed. "Miss Lindstrom" tries to understand the reasons for a conflict between a social worker and her clients. The "Miss Perry" story uses fragments left by a "stubborn" and perhaps "feeble-minded" boy to ponder how hard it was then—and remains now—to make difficult decisions. And "Mr. O'Neill" is a tale of seduction from South Boston, which ends up asking who was playing with whom.

In the end, the point of writing these six scripts is to insist that the people who are featured here, the poor but also the mostly female investigators who heard them, not be ciphers, marionettes in a drama that gives them no life, no passion, no feelings, and no voice. It is to make them actors in a more fully realized story than the actual record makes possible. It is to do them as much justice as I can. But it is also to stress what I take to be the particular task of any history of poverty: to write dramatically and truthfully about the past in order to move hearts and, perhaps, change minds about the present and the future.

Part One

MELBOURNE

Miss Cutler and the Case of the Resurrected Horse

Dramatis Personæ

AGNES CUTLER, a charity investigator
HAROLD ALDERMAN, an unemployed man
VIOLET ALDERMAN, his oldest daughter
DAPHNE ALDERMAN, a younger daughter

· · · · · · · · · · · · · DRAMA · · · · · · · · · · · ·

But for the foolishness of men, Agnes Cutler thinks, she would be making good time. She'd left ten minutes ago but was still waiting in a queue of cars to pass an accident. The queue was slow moving, in part because the two drivers were now engaged in an animated public dispute about the right of way. This wasn't helping her dislike of driving, nor of careless men. She drove well, of course, but she did not enjoy it. Cars were unhelpful machines, and the attention they demanded seemed to her rather a waste of time. Still, the Aldermans lived nearly twenty miles from the Charity Organisation Society's office, so she would have to drive.

Clear of the confusion, she gathers a little speed, though the gears are as uncooperative as ever. Agnes Cutler prefers to walk. She is more used to Melbourne's closer streets and lanes, in Fitzroy and Collingwood, or in Richmond. Walking makes for a less obvious arrival, though in those dreary little streets she knows that the news of an impending visit by "the Charity lady" ripples just ahead of her. Early mornings are the best time for visits. In the morning, Cutler finds, you can see into a household with a particular clarity. You can see the family as it is when you are unexpected and they are unsuspecting. You can find the men still in bed, the children unwashed or unfed, the women with their hair unclipped, and their stories not yet straight. It was the women you have to talk to, of course. The men are usually rather dull and sullen. Or they talked too much and tried to charm you. "All teeth and trousers," Cutler remembers someone saying once. It mightn't be a polite way of making the point, but you can't doubt its accuracy.

For an experienced charity investigator, mornings also produce the clues that distinguish the merely slovenly from the scroungers, cheats, and liars. There will be the same crumbs on the table and the sour milk you can smell before you see it, but the evidence that an applicant is undeserving takes more time to discern. The cigarette butts won't yet have been thrown away, and the fingerprinted glasses of last night's liquor remain on the draining board. Sometimes there are too many people for the beds. Or there are the signs of a man whose presence might be denied but whose shade lingers: a pair of boots too carelessly pushed under a bed, a razor strop not hung back behind a door, or the smell of shaving soap and workman's sweat. People cannot hide the truth that character etches upon them. Their eyes will flicker, and their faces will reveal their deceit.

Well, this won't be an early morning call. Whitehorse Road is quiet and grows more so as she leaves Box Hill, and the houses become more scattered. Nor will she have a chance to ride on the train and do a little reading. In her satchel, inherited from her schoolmaster father, are two keenly awaited pleasures, Miss Agatha Christie's short story collection *The Thirteen Problems* and Miss Dorothy L. Sayers's new Lord Peter Wimsey novel, *Murder Must Advertise*. She'd read *Five Red Herrings* and *Have His Carcase* last year, and although Lord Peter could be irritating, Cutler wants to see if Harriet Vance appears again. Miss Christie's Poirot is a good detective, more interesting than Father Brown, but her new collection includes a woman, Miss Marple. Agnes Cutler always contends that women make the skilled detectives. Women are better at spotting lies and deceptions. She would not say that she drew inspiration from these characters, for life was neither so simple nor so straightforward as in a two-hundred-page novel, but Cutler enjoys the occasional similarities between their fiction and her fact. Like her, they had a nose for secrets. She does like some of the men. Miss Margery Allingham's Albert Campion is growing on her. But her brief forays into American writers have not been successful. There is that awful Philo Vance, a "Manhattan aristocrat," no less. And of Mr. Dashiell Hamnett, she thinks, the less said the better.

Leaving the main road and traveling down an unmade street, she looks for the turning that leads down to the Aldermans' block. She'd had only a few minutes to look at the file before leaving; the case stretched back three years, to January 1931, when Harold Alderman first sought free treatment from the Dental Hospital. He and wife, Ada, had come from London in 1921, but like a good many of the British migrants of those years, they hadn't enjoyed much success. With five children under ten, Harold was out of work, relying on sustenance and owed nearly four pounds in payments on a house they were buying.

Agnes Cutler had done that first home visit, too, which is helping her to remember the way. "Impressed favourably," she'd written of them then. The situation had been worse than first presented, as there was nearly two pounds owed to a grocer and twenty-six shillings to the baker. Ada Alderman was attending the Women's Hospital for internal trouble, while Harold still suffered a great deal with his chest and with stomach trouble, both from war service with the British forces in France.

They are, Cutler now thinks, rather a hapless couple. Harold had visited the central office in July 1931 to say he couldn't work due to an accident; he had "evidently been drinking," she had written in the file, for although "he was not drunk," his breath "smelt of whiskey." He'd come in again in October and "smelt strongly of whiskey." In the winter of 1932, he was in again; diagnosed with tuberculosis, he needed clothing, pajamas, and shaving equipment so he could attend the Amherst Sanatorium. A few months later, Ada Alderman reported that their house payments were in arrears, and they owed £4 in rates, but there was little the COS could do for such large amounts. Harold did receive the invalid pension from that September, but it was only seventeen shillings a week; with the Child Welfare Department allowance of twenty-four shillings a week, they had just over two pounds left once they'd paid for the house. Then, in November 1932, Ada and her eldest daughter were knocked down by a motor truck in Mitcham and injured; Cutler, ever aware of the need for accurate records, clipped the story from the *Herald* and glued it to a page in the file.

Though she is visiting today in order to gather more information for Ada's most recent inquiry, made last week, there is another thing Agnes Cutler wants to ascertain. There is something she has not been told, something that will need to be uncovered and examined. Back in 1931, the society loaned the Aldermans four pounds. Harold's horse had died. He wanted another, and a cart, so he could make money by delivering wood to neighboring houses and farms. Always keen to steer applicants away from dependence, Cutler had discussed the case with the society's secretary, Stanley Greig Smith. He had, in turn, taken it to the Executive Committee. Cutler had never seen the new horse, though Harold reported it to be good-natured and a hard worker.

The horse turned out to be as hapless as its owners, Ada later reporting that it had been destroyed in September 1931 following an accident. Three years on, Cutler is still puzzled by that, and she wants some answers. She had impressed upon them the very great investment that the society had made and asked that they keep her informed. To lose one horse might be an accident, but to lose two beggared belief, and she had wondered if Harold had been drinking. Back then, Ada had seemed very forlorn—and she said the children were very sad—so Cutler had let the matter rest. Harold was a returned serviceman, so a little generosity of spirit didn't go astray. But she wants to hear his version of events, and this visit will be a good opportunity to shine the light of investigation into some of his story's darker corners.

The gate is closed, but a girl of around ten or eleven runs up and opens it. As Cutler drives onto and along the path, the gate opener skips ahead, joining three younger girls, all rather watchful. The group is completed by a little boy, maybe two years old, who runs across the porch before descending the ill-made steps with the quiet intensity of a still unsteady walker.

Cutler steps down from the car, smiling at the girls and then at the boy.

"Are your parents here, dear?"

"Yes," says the tallest.

Cutler can't quite remember the girls' names. Rose, perhaps. Or Daphne. The child ventures nothing further, so Cutler smiles at her again. She steps off the rough drive and looks around the side of the small weatherboard house, the children following her from a distance. The place is sturdy enough, though they must bake in the heat under that iron roof. The general impression is of a kind of half-realized ingenuity. A somewhat askew pipe runs from the roof to a water tank, but it is dripping slowly from an ungainly bend in its middle. Some kind of homemade pump is rattling away, though its purpose isn't obvious. An old washtub, almost orange with water stains, holds two potted geraniums and what looks like a mint bush. There is an apple tree; one of its limbs has been cut off, and it looks about to topple over.

Cutler steps back onto the drive and walks to the other side of the house. The children again move behind her, as if she is their scout and they are tied to her by some long yet invisible thread.

"Is your father here, dear? Daphne, isn't it?"

"I'm not Daphne."

Cutler's smile becomes a little more forced. "I don't quite remember your names," she says.

"That's Daphne." The girl pointed out by her sister nods.

"Oh, yes, that's nice."

Stepping farther out so she could see around the house, Cutler trips and then catches herself; it is, oddly, the rollers of an old mangle, which have been screwed to what looks like a baking tray. She shakes her head, but looks more carefully at the ground as she takes a few more steps, the children still shadowing her every move.

"I'm Violet."

"Yes, dear, lovely. Now, is your father here?"

"No."

"But," says Cutler, turning, "you said your parents were here."

"He's not there. He's here."

This is an exasperating child.

"What do you mean," Cutler begins, just as Harold Alderman appears from the side of the house.

"See. He's here," offers Violet helpfully.

The children all look at their father. "It's a lady, Dad. She's got a car."

So Daphne can speak, thinks Cutler.

"Yes, love, I can see that. Now make yourselves scarce, you lot."

Violet picks up the toddler, Daphne grabs the two smaller girls by the hand, and all retreat around the side of the house from which Alderman emerged.

The first impression is not altogether favorable, Cutler thinks. A slight man, he seems deflated and worn. He is around forty, she knows, but looks more like fifty. His trousers are old, and his boots are even older.

"Good morning, Mr. Alderman. Are you well?"

"Good morning. Yes, well. Quite well."

He clearly isn't sure who she is. Perhaps he has forgotten the visits from two and three years ago, or perhaps he just can't place her.

"Miss Cutler, Mr. Alderman. Your wife came in last week."

He looks more blank, if anything.

"Miss Cutler, from the Charity Organisation Society."

"Oh, yes, Miss Cutler. Yes. Forgive me, I hadn't realized you would be visiting us."

"We always visit, Mr. Alderman. We need to check details, of course, but many people prefer to discuss their plans at home rather than in the office."

"Yes, of course. I remember that you visited us last time, when my wife was so ill."

Cutler is pleased. She likes to be remembered.

"Yes, I did. That was three years ago now."

"Really," says Alderman, his face still rather blank.

"Yes, it was at that time that we procured you a horse, Mr. Alderman."

He is still blank.

"So you could cart wood. Deliver wood to other houses."

"Yes, Miss Cutler."

"The horse for which the society paid four pounds."

"Well, that was very generous. We've had a good deal of help from generous people."

"Well, let's get on." Agnes Cutler walks around to and down the other side of the house. Harold Alderman, expecting that she would want to go inside and speak to Ada, is unsure about her interest in the yard and is taken aback by the quickness of her step.

"You maintain the house yourself, Mr. Alderman?"

"Yes, yes, I do."

"And the vegetable garden, where is that?"

"Begging your pardon, Miss Cutler?"

"The vegetable garden, Mr. Alderman? You surely grow vegetables?"

He looks puzzled. "There's not really enough water, Miss Cutler. Not in the summer. We try and... "

"Well, I should think growing vegetables would help a little, Mr. Alderman. Help you help your family, you see."

"Yes, I see, but ... "

"Perhaps around the back. Around here."

She strides toward the back of the house.

"Perhaps rabbits, Mr. Alderman. Or chickens."

"There aren't any rabbits or chickens here, Miss Cutler."

She stops. "That, Mr. Alderman, is my point. Where are the rabbits and the chickens, Mr. Alderman? Where are the measures of self-reliance? Where is the evidence of standing on your own two feet? This is why I'm here, Mr. Alderman, to gauge your needs and find the most effective remedy. Best to help yourself rather than being helped by others, don't you agree?"

"I'm not sure how we'd manage all of those animals."

"Come now, Mr. Alderman. I'm hardly suggesting that you re-create Noah's ark. But a bit of self-reliance never goes astray, does it? You seem to be able to turn your hand to some home improvements."

It is important to be encouraging, she thinks, though Cutler would not trust Harold's ungainly handiwork in any but the least important of jobs.

"Pressing on, Mr. Alderman, pressing on."

"But don't you want to see Ada, Miss Cutler? She's in the house."

He hurries to catch up with her and then steps in front of her.

"You'll need to walk back this way, Miss Cutler. The ground's a bit bad, a bit stumbly here. I think Ada's probably put the kettle on. The children would have told her you're here."

She steps sideways. "Surely we can go in through the back door. I'm not unaccustomed to back doors, even the tradesman's entrance, Mr. Alderman. Have no fear. No pomp and ceremony is necessary."

Then she sees it. She stops and turns toward him. He is affecting a rather uncertain smile. No wonder he wants to deflect her, interrupt her progress, and bar her way. He clearly hasn't remembered that she leaves no stone unturned, no angle unexamined. She thinks quickly about how best to force an admission.

"And what, Mr. Alderman, is that?"

"What's what, Miss Cutler?"

He is either very stupid or very cunning. His eyes are flickering, but he's still trying to smile. Of course, he is looking into the sun, but there's more to the flickering than the sun's glare.

"That, Mr. Alderman, that." She points and then points again.

"Do you wish to make a clean breast of it now, or shall I continue?"

"Miss Cutler, I'm not sure what you mean."

"My meaning is very clear, Mr. Alderman."

He is looking nervous and feigning simplicity.

"Miss Cutler, I don't know what you mean. What are you referring to?"

She stays controlled. "That to which I refer, Mr. Alderman, is directly in front of you."

His eyes are flickering again.

"The paddock, Miss Cutler?"

She hopes her gaze is withering.

"Was your wife lying, Mr. Alderman? Was she lying? We give you help and assistance, to the measure of four pounds, Mr. Alderman, four pounds, and this is how you repay our charity? Think carefully about what you say, Mr. Alderman, think very carefully!"

He is taking refuge in silence and trying to appear puzzled.

"It was dead, Mr. Alderman, and now it walks. It was dead, and now it breathes. Has there been a miracle, Mr. Alderman? A heavenly event? It was dead, Mr. Alderman, dead and, I presume, buried, and yet it has returned!"

Harold blinks and looks around. He hopes Ada might come out of the house. He hopes that whatever this strange woman is doing will begin to make sense. He hopes that maybe she'll go away.

"That, Mr. Alderman, over there, larger than life and enjoying what I assume to be its oats?

"It's all very well looking vague, Mr. Alderman. It's all very well looking vague. But that," Agnes Cutler says with the flourish of a hand, "is a piece of evidence that is impossible even for you to hide!"

· · · · · · · · · · · RESOLUTION · · · · · · · · · · ·

Harold Alderman must have wondered what had happened and what he had done wrong. Despite the exacting details provided in this case file, I can't be sure when, where, and how he was confronted, but confronted he certainly was. Agnes Cutler had spotted a horse, a horse where there should be no horse, a horse that was supposedly destroyed and long gone, a horse that had apparently come back from the dead. Even if it was not a case worthy of Lord Peter Wimsey, or even of Miss Marple, it was an occasion for the display of Cutler's detective skills. I don't know if she read detective novels, but her case files read as if she did, and her impatience with foolish, extravagant, or evasive men is very evident in the hundreds of investigations she conducted in the years between her first appointment in 1922 and her retirement in 1943. I have characterized Agnes Cutler as a kind of detective because that—in a very important way—is how I think she saw herself.

Two years on, she remembered that there was a horse and the £4 it had cost the society. She remembered what Ada Alderman had said and what had been written in the file. She remembered the horse, and she remembered that there was also a cart, which he admitted, after the initial confrontation, "could be used all right." Her notes on the incident are short and to the point: "I told him [what] his wife said on 27 September 1932," and he "looked vague." Looking vague offered scant protection from Miss Cutler's ire. Yet it seems she did not press her advantage. Ada Alderman received the order for her free glasses, and Cutler reserved the moral of her tale for the case record: "He still impresses me as a decent man, but he and his wife appear to expect a great deal from the Government."

The Aldermans did not approach the society again. They seem to have managed better by themselves. Or perhaps they simply wanted nothing more to do with Agnes Cutler. By 1937 the older girls worked to help support the family; for impoverished parents before the war, the wage of a teenager often meant the difference between needing charity and getting along. Although his tuberculosis could not be cured, Harold remained well enough to be at home. Cutler did see the Aldermans one more time, in 1939, when she was visiting a nearby family. It was a habit of hers, this dropping in unexpectedly on current and former clients, and it rested on a prodigious memory. The house was "much improved," she wrote. Harold had occasional work at a golf links, and the eldest daughters were working in a laundry and bringing home their earnings. They were, she recorded, "bright & happy & very pleased about being visited." They were perhaps even more pleased to make their last farewells.

We can't be quite sure what the Aldermans made of their confrontation with the Charity Organisation Society's most adept investigator in the summer of 1934. Like the other case files that form the basis for this book, the drama—and the moral—of the story was written by the inquiry officer and not by the claimant or client. We see the world through her eyes, and we read what she wanted to say about the poor and their poverty and progress. We can only imagine what Harold Alderman was thinking. Was he stumbling for an answer to a question he hadn't expected to face? Was he caught out, unsure what Ada had said to this woman? Was he worried about what he might be risking?

One thing is certain. It never crossed Agnes Cutler's mind that she might be wrong. There are questions she might have asked but did not. In a semirural locality still caught between the city and the farm, with market gardens and scattered bungalows and no high school within miles, is it possible that the Aldermans found a way to buy, beg, or borrow another horse in the three years since the other one had died? Was this actually the same horse? Did Cutler know what kind of horse and cart was purchased in 1931, a task that appears was left to Harold Alderman once the sum of £4 had been agreed on? Perhaps this was a different horse. Did Harold think better of contradicting her, fearing that to do so might endanger the expensive special glasses that Ada needed?

I feel for Agnes Cutler and what she was asked to do. She was the instrument of a flawed practice. The Miss Cutlers of the 1920s and 1930s—like the welfare "compliance officers" of our own time—are as kind or as unkind as they are allowed to be. As they enact what is always a demanding theater of obligation and entitlement, they are always torn between a desire to give assistance and a fear that some of that assistance might end up in the wrong hands. It is up to them to achieve the impossible, to size up the poor, make the right judgment, and provide the right kind of help, doing it quickly enough to ensure that it is effective and all the while ensuring that each and every drop of kindness is deserved. On them are heaped all the dilemmas that stem from the struggle to care. Cutler was a variation on a theme, not its inventor. In the end, perhaps, we should be as impressed by the tenderness of her mercies as by her occasional ferocity. Detective she was, but she was not always judge and jury.

But it remains possible to hold her to account for the questions she did not think to ask. Perhaps she was right about the horse, but perhaps she was wrong, deeply wrong. The Aldermans were an unlucky and seemingly hapless couple, but there is little that suggests they were cheats and liars. Indeed, their resilience might have earned them what the case file makes clear they didn't get: an assumption of innocence.

I wonder, too, if people now reading the story of the supposedly resurrected horse assumed—along with Agnes Cutler—that the Aldermans were hiding something. I chose to dramatize this encounter in part because it speaks so directly to the enduring suspicion that poor people are deceivers, liars, and frauds and that those who interpret their claims are best advised to model themselves as detectives. Did the reader expect that Harold and Ada Alderman must have been telling lies? Did the reader see heroes and villains or something in between? Did you anticipate a revelation and a triumph of detection rather than the much more typical messiness of real people's poverty? It's easy to believe that the poor lie or cheat or don't know any better. It's certainly then easier to cope with what is done to them or is allowed to happen to them. It's a bad conclusion, even if it's often made by good people. Miss Cutler wanted to help, and there is ample evidence in this file and her dealings with others that she could be an effective advocate, a helpful ally, and even a friend. But she always thought that she knew best, that the poor didn't understand their poverty and would need to be told what to do and that it was always best to approach them with a degree of skepticism and even suspicion. However many horses were or weren't resurrected, this was the story she always tended to tell. Even if it was the most reassuring, it was also the most misleading.

CHAPTER I

Service, Sympathy, and Efficiency

The Charity Organisation Society (COS) always took a particular interest in sorting the deserving from the undeserving, and it shaped both the story and the experience of poverty in Melbourne between the wars. A city of around a million people, Melbourne, like Australia as a whole, rose and fell according to the rhythms of global fortunes; the 1920s and 1930s were hard times. In 1922 the six women who worked under Secretary Stanley Greig Smith, including Assistant Secretary Doris Cumberland, handled around seven hundred new cases per year. There were nine women on the staff by 1930, but the number of applicants soared to more than a thousand per year by the middle of the 1920s. In earlier years, the society's annual reports divided cases into those deriving from "misfortune," "misconduct," and "imposture." Male and female applicants were tabulated, and careful note was taken of referrals. In 1922, for example, 37 came from clergymen and doctors, 50 from the society's subscribers, and 112 from the State War Council. In 1931 the annual report simply states a number: 2,669 new cases. Volume had defeated the capacity and perhaps even the desire for categorization. It was, the society's Executive Committee recorded, "an abnormally arduous year."[1] It would worsen: the scale and duration of Melbourne's Depression meant that there were two thousand or so new cases every year for the rest of the decade. Even if the other inquiry officers were impressed—or daunted—by Agnes Cutler's forensic skills, they had little time in which to emulate them.

Melbourne's interwar poverty had familiar wellsprings: large families, unemployment, low wages, illness, old age, and disability. In what they said to Agnes Cutler and the other inquiry officers, people normally began with the frailties of their bodies and the telltale ailments of insecurity. Their teeth were so bad that they could no longer chew solids. They had diabetes and couldn't afford to replace the bread and cakes that filled them up with the nourishing food they needed. They had chronic bronchitis from damp houses. They were going deaf, but hearing aids cost too much. Their newborns struggled to thrive; their children slept three and four to a bed, didn't get enough to eat, and fell asleep in school. The rent of an unheated room in inner suburban Carlton took up half of the pension, so old people and invalids lived on thinning diets and in chronic pain. Some drank that pain away; others, unable to cope with bad teeth or bad eyes, asked for help. If they could be proved deserving, they waited a year—perhaps two years when demand was high—for free treatment at the Dental Hospital on Spring Street or joined the long queue for cheap spectacles from the Eye and Ear Hospital at Eastern Hill.

There were lonely old men, broken by hard work at age forty or fifty, in constant pain from bad backs and bad knees. There were jobless drifters aged nineteen and twenty, hard eyed and bitter before their time, along with drinkers who were too sober or too troublesome for the inebriates' homes. There were people who needed somewhere to live, and people who needed somewhere to die but couldn't secure a bed in one of the few hospices. There were people who needed to bury a husband, killed on the railways or on the wharves, when a decent funeral might cost a month's wages. Some applicants had "weak minds," like the self-styled "Russian secret service count" who survived a torpedoed troopship but then turned to alcohol. Children died in agony from tubercular spines and hips; men aged twenty-five were too weak from rheumatism, asthma, and untreated infections to earn a living; women, worn out by hard work, poor diet, and self-sacrifice, withered in their thirties. And in the 1920s, the war still rumbled through Melbourne, as fathers died of wounds that never healed, and other men, still hearing the guns, screamed in the night and struck out at their families and themselves.

This was a world in which it was easy to be discarded, and the poor paid a high price for their frailties and failings. For all but a very few in the 1920s, unemployment or illness brought disaster, as well as the indignities of meanly measured doles. Then came the Depression. Australia's was savage: in 1933, the worst year of the decade, perhaps a quarter or a third of Melbourne's men were jobless. An even greater range of people were undermined and unsecured by a crisis that picked off skilled workers, independent women, and respectable clerks. The Depression blasted dreams and dented hopes, lengthened unemployment into years, and drew many into a cycle of rural relief work, tramping, sustenance, and slums that would be broken only by wartime mobilizations in the 1940s.

The COS inquiry officers worked in a welfare system still unsure of the most appropriate boundary between public and private responsibility, protective of the unquestionably deserving, such as the aged or the blind, yet neglectful of those whose problems were seen as more circumstantial and temporary. As historian John Murphy so aptly characterizes it, this form of welfare reflected a strong antipodean cultural tradition that "combined grudging commitments to any form of social provision, with a strong resistance to the idea that the poor had a claim upon the state."[2] In interwar Victoria, public elementary education was free, but free or sub-sidized medical treatment was reserved for the "truly needy," and wait-ing lists were long. There was no guaranteed unemployment benefit until 1930; when it came, it took the form of a miserly "sustenance" of grocer-ies and eventually coupons, overlaid with conditions and restrictions and not even available to young, unmarried men and women. As unemploy-ment peaked, there was government-funded public work on roads, dams, rivers, and monuments, which provided men with jobs but often took them away from their homes, leaving wives to try to support families as best they could.

There was no right to relief, no Poor Law like that of Britain; in Aus-tralia, it was important to maintain the argument—more in hope than in fact—that a new world without "real" poverty could get by without the instruments old worlds needed to manage destitution. In Melbourne, as in the United States, the poor were befriended, helped, and advised by a range of philanthropic agencies, which were just as crucial for those liv-ing on public pensions and benefits that barely covered the basic costs of living as they were for those who struggled along on low and intermit-tent wages. Private agencies distributed cash and goods, worked alongside and sometimes in competition with each other, and provided investigation and distribution services for public bodies. Governments relied on them to deliver and discriminate between those who should and should not re-ceive assistance. There were ladies' benevolent societies in most suburbs by 1900, and various churches set up missions. The stamp of early twenti-eth-century urban reform campaigns—the settlement house or the model tenement, for instance—was less obvious in Melbourne than in London or most American cities and was strongest in those services that focused on a new nation's next generation: free kindergartens and baby health centers, for instance. Nor was there much of the philanthropic interest in poverty amelioration that characterized the cities of the Northern Hemisphere; used to booms and busts, Victoria's rich preferred at this point to hold on to their money or to invest it in schools and other instruments promoting the privileges of their own class. Much was left to faith. Melbourne's sectarian boundaries were very strong, so Catholic women tended to work within the St. Vincent de Paul Society's local auxiliaries, and Jewish women in the Hebrew Ladies' Benevolent Society, but poor Melburnians were not always so interested in the niceties of sectarian logic. They used the Sal-vation Army or the Wesley Central Mission or "St. Vinnies," drawing as deeply from different wells as their circumstances demanded.

In this mix of public and private relief, the women of the Charity Or-ganisation Society certainly witnessed suffering. They heard some harrowing stories and met people in what must have seemed insurmountable circumstances. They helped organize appeals for wives and children left behind by accidents or by husbands killed at work. They sought gratuities for young men, army veterans mostly, whose parents couldn't afford to keep an adult son at home in the lean years of the 1920s. They interceded with creditors to protect families from repossession, and they helped people write applications for pensions and payments. With relatively little to give, they paid off gas and electric bills or paid for milk, eggs, and special diets, sometimes, I think, from their own purses. They watched some of their applicants recover, and they watched a few of them die.

In 1932 Melbourne's *Truth* newspaper, a tabloid mix of crime reporting, sports news, photographs, and "human interest" stories, published an article titled "Those Nine Women and Their Capable Director, Service, Sympathy and Efficiency."[3] It must have pleased Smith, who always felt that the dramas and the lessons of charity investigation merited wide publicity; in 1928 he had planned a "series of radio talks on interesting aspects of philanthropic work in Melbourne," and in 1925 he had secured the Executive Committee's approval for a "small quarterly Journal ... for educational and propaganda purposes," which was called the *Other Half*.[4] He wrote his own pieces, too; one daily newspaper, the *Herald*, printed his long article, "What We Do with Your Christmas Money" in December 1928. It reassured donors that "we sift every case and deal with it as it deserves."[5]

Calling the COS a "baby" that Smith had "tended with loving care," the *Truth* article noted that this "is not really a charity organisation in the sense as recognised as such in most other parts of the world." The author's next—and more grammatically adept—sentence captured something dear to Smith; his COS was "a centre of social service which is the epitome of efficiency" and "the centre-pin upon which a whole series of charitable—benevolent if you like—activities rests and draws inspiration."[6]

The "nine splendid women" whose case notes provide the material for these chapters were also featured in the article. Four of them—the assistant secretary and three "inspectors"—were pictured alongside Smith. In the photograph, they are well—though conservatively—dressed. They wear necklaces, though not, of course, earrings. Unused to posing for a camera, they look uncomfortable, in the way that almost everyone does in photographs of the 1930s.

I know so much and so little about them. I know their writing hands and turns of phrase, even puns they found amusing. I know what they would have said to applicants and how they would have said it. I know when they were hired and how long they stayed: Agnes Cutler was appointed in 1922 and resigned in 1943, the year in which the first ever married investigating officer, Meryl Wiseman, joined the society, and both Lillian Allen and Ethel Brown were rewarded for a quarter-century's service in 1948. I know what they were paid: in the early 1920s, inquiry officers earned £2/10 a week, which gave them an average wage for Australian women and about half the average wage for Australian men. They earned about as much as a male factory worker and rather more than any woman working in a manual occupation (Secretary Smith's annual salary was raised to £560 per year in 1925, a substantial sum). In 1930 they earned around £4 a week, but their weekly wage was cut by six shillings—about 8 percent—in 1931, a sum not restored until 1937. The secretary took a 10 percent cut in salary at the same time. In 1944 senior staff earned £5 a week, still less than the majority of working men.

In the 1920s they were not yet called social workers. They were inquiry officers or investigating officers; it was an important signal of what their work was meant to achieve. Their initiation into professional casework came from their senior colleagues; Celia Bedford, Agnes Cutler, and Lillian Allen spent a good many days training novices. What marked out the best inquiry officers was a combination of experience and a "special fitness" that, in Melbourne, remained somewhat undefined but was assumed to be particularly developed in women.[7] There was no formal training until the 1930s, when the Victorian Council for Social Training—which Smith had helped establish—developed a Diploma of Social Science, the practical component of which could be taken "on the job" at the COS. A university course wouldn't come for another decade. While acknowledging that "social work is an exceedingly difficult business," the *Other Half* also reported in 1930 that "the main body of social workers—professional and voluntary—still gain their training largely in the school of stern experience, which is subject to narrow limitations and carries with it the certainty of errors of judgement."[8] It was an uncertain endorsement.

Yet beyond that, there is mostly supposition. I can draw on the factors identified in studies of other Australian places, assuming that Melbourne had no reason to be different, and on the illuminating interviews with hospital almoners done in the 1970s by Laurie O'Brien, Cynthia Turner, and others.[9] Like them, the COS women made their choices from a mix of vocational calling, religious conviction, economic necessity, and the narrow occupational paths available to women of their social background. It was a satisfying and interesting career, straitened by constraints on women's public work but still fulfilling expectations of useful personal service that were forged in professional families and reinforced in Melbourne's powerful independent schools. There are more specific hints of their backgrounds in the case files: the trams they caught from home to the city, their meetings with other charity workers at weekend church socials, and even the insults some of the applicants hurled at them. Although they grew familiar with the streets and lanes of working-class Melbourne, they did not and would never live there. Some were the daughters of clergymen and schoolteachers, and others had fathers who owned shops. They attended "good" schools, perhaps with the help of a bursary or money from a grandparent. Some lived independently, probably in the small flats respectable Melburnians of restricted means could rent in South Yarra, East Melbourne, or Hawthorn, and others still lived in the family home. They were all Protestants. They came from and remained church people, and it was their churches that centered their lives outside of work. From the evidence of their convictions, homilies, and ideas and from their emphasis on service, they were Methodists and Presbyterians for the most part. They were not rich, and if they were comfortable it was probably because they could draw to some degree on family resources. They were not married when hired, and most were still unmarried when they resigned or retired.

For most, this was a life's work. It was important and demanding, and they assumed—as many men assumed—that it was work to which women like themselves should be well suited. As they met with and questioned the poor, they would have to find the balance between service, sympathy, and efficiency that inspired the idea of charity organization.

. . . .

CHAPTER 2

Mr. Smith and the Importance of Modern Casework

Agnes Cutler and her colleagues joined a society about to claim—courtesy of Stanley Greig Smith—a more important role in Melbourne's welfare network. Melbourne's Charity Organisation Society was founded in 1887. Like its British parent, and the similar bodies that were formed at that time in American, British, and European cities, it aimed to coordinate the activities of various benevolent groups and prevent the unthinking charity that was believed to encourage "pauperism" and "dependency." Rather than provide material aid, it would offer friendly and constructive advice to the poor and provide leadership to the jumble of alms-giving agencies in what was then both Australia's biggest city and one of the largest cities in the British Empire. Like its overseas counterparts, the Melbourne COS struggled through the severe depression of the 1890s; with coordination difficult to achieve, the survival of new agencies such as the COS depended to a significant extent on whether they took up other functions, particularly the provision of direct relief. The COS emerged from this first great depression still struggling to find its foothold.

Stanley Greig Smith moved from Scotland to a civil service position in London and then came to Australia in 1908. He took over as secretary of the COS in 1909 and served until 1957. The COS of the 1920s and 1930s was very much shaped by his strengths and aspirations and by his shortcomings. For good and bad, Smith's zeal for organization, and his determination to shape Melbourne's agencies into more efficient patterns, made Melbourne's COS a distinctly important—and sometimes rather fractious—molder of the city's charity network. Taking as his guide the "new social work" of New York's Community Service Society, and especially its emphasis on casework, Smith managed to construct "a picture of his profession from the sources available to him," despite his lack of formal education and training.[10] As Richard Kennedy observes, the COS had established "the outlines of casework method" by 1900, but it was Smith who made inquiry the society's central and most influential claim.[11]

Smith was a vociferous critic of what he called "indiscriminate benevolence," which could only be cured by careful oversight of all forms of relief so that assistance went only to the "truly needy": those whose initiative and effort ensured that temporary support would not become permanent. This in turn meant that all charitable bodies had to accept a system of rigorous record keeping, such as a central index or register, which listed each applicant's dealings with every private or public agency. Smith had the ordinary person's impatience with the oversympathetic foolishness of Melbourne's "better" classes. While attending a Combined Sports Day of the Associated Grammar Schools in 1931, for instance, he saw a man singing and begging in the grandstand. Having "identified him in the records" as a heavy drinker, Smith wrote to the headmasters of the schools so they "might use the incident as a text for a brief talk to the boys on the folly of indiscriminate giving."[12] As he had earlier warned in the *Other Half*: "Melbourne citizens spend annually in charitable gifts to individuals claiming to be in distress probably as much money as would keep all those who are genuinely in need in a state of luxury. But because so much of this expenditure goes to the clever cadger, and the plausible imposter, the worthy poor get less than they deserve and often less than they need."[13]

It was a brave claim, and it was intended to have an edge. By distinguishing

the COS approach from those who gave charity carelessly, he also tar-
geted organizations that were unwilling to accept "the spirit of coordination": the Salvation Army, policewomen (who were often delegated to
"welfare" cases by their male superiors), the ladies' benevolent societies,
and anything and anyone associated with the Catholic Church. In a report
prepared for the 1932 Victorian Parliamentary Committee on Social Services, Smith was highly critical of the opinion that "anyone can distrib-
ute relief—without experience, without adequate investigation, without
training and often without records."[14] While he was careful about inflam-
ing anti-Catholic feeling, he was comfortable lambasting the Salvation
Army and the benevolent ladies for their "poor case work," and his description of new ventures in public provision invariably talked of a ter-
ritory threatened by "a fresh army of workers" or "interfered with" by
inexpert outsiders. At the same time, the cases he chose for publicity purposes always included examples of "overlapping," including one in which
a "husband who drinks" had been assisted by "a ladies' benevolent society,
two spiritual missions, a clergyman and a policewoman."[15] A charity or-
ganizer could imagine nothing worse.

Smith's vision had its imperial—even imperious—overtones, but there
was no doubting his frustration. In 1930, as concern over the extent of suffering during the early part of the Depression generated new "charity ventures," the secretary reiterated his mission to "inspire a general desire to
get together in a common cause, to abandon the water-tight compartment
methods of the past, and to build up in unison a fine, long-visioned scheme
of adequate and appropriate relief for the genuinely needy that will reflect
credit on our city."[16]

He liked that metaphor. He'd used it before, in 1927, criticizing social
workers who were "happy to jog along in [their] own little water-tight
compartment."[17] He also liked the idea of unison; what rankled with others, of course, was that Smith always seemed to assume he should choose
both song and key.

Yet increased coordination and efficiency was not Smith's sole focus,
and it would not be the true measure of his impact. In many ways Smith
combined a nineteenth-century diagnosis of poverty, which emphasized
character and was rooted in a certainty that the worthy and unworthy
poor were real groups that could be distinguished from each other, with
a twentieth-century "casework" approach to its treatment. He was one
of the bridges that carried charity toward social work, and as his society
shifted into investigation, casework, and direct provision, it grew more
influential.

The 1923 annual report noted somewhat ruefully that the COS was now regarded as "a distinct and separate charity," restricted largely to "investigating causes of distress, planning schemes of practical aid, and securing whatever co-operation may be necessary to the carrying out of those plans."[18] Even in the 1950s, after the Charity Organisation Society had been renamed the Citizens Welfare Service (CWS), the rueful tone remained when it came to writing history: "[When] it found that there were a good many people in need for whom no appropriate agency existed, [the society] began, rather reluctantly, to develop a social work service of its own. With this development, [it] tended to become another social work agency, rather than a co-ordinating body."[19]

If Smith wrote this, it was self-deprecating. If he didn't, it measured his waning command over the CWS in the 1950s, when a new generation of university-trained social workers were steering it toward family therapy. In any event, this version of the past underplayed the important shift he had engineered. By developing a "social work service," and especially one that revolved around casework, the COS provided practical and useful leadership to Melbourne's welfare providers during the middle decades of the twentieth century. It was not perhaps all that Smith had wanted, and it did not exemplify the Christian faith expressed in a social work that was "set upon a fairer future ... [and] looking forward to the clear day of peace, and wisdom, tolerance and human fellowship."[20] But it made his organization significant.

The COS doled out the same shillings, meal tickets, and blankets as dozens of other benevolent societies and religious missions. What made it different was its dedication to the view that only "modern case work"—including "careful enquiry [and] the sifting of statements"—would "place the socially dependent back on a plane of self-dependence."[21] It wanted to ensure that only the worthy poor received assistance and that they were in some way changed by it. Before other agencies made decisions, COS investigations provided the evidence for sound conclusions; they drew the line between the deserving and the undeserving, with the truly needy or "decent poor" on one side and the "clever cadgers," "ingenious impostors," or "socially inadequate" on the other. Good casework defended the resources that were always too thinly spread to help everyone in need. It also defended the claim—which rested more on assumption than evidence—that at least some among the poor were cheats and liars.

In the 1920s and 1930s, around three-quarters of each year's new applicants were referred from other organizations. They were interviewed at the COS office, first in Flinders Lane and then in the society's new building on Exhibition Street, and initial judgments were recorded: "seems deserving," "not sure she is telling the truth," "a strange and complicated story." With the assistant secretary and secretary providing reception and initial examination, the inquiry officers then sallied forth to check each day's cases. They visited applicants in their homes; interviewed neighbors, teachers, police, and local shopkeepers; and carried out the investigations that helped identify "genuine" applicants for free medical and dental treatment, provident loans, or help from veterans organizations. As Smith assured anxious Melburnians in 1931, such investigation was even more important when the city was "riddled … with beggars and cadgers of all types" and "infested" with child impostors or men "much disfigured by disease" who were seeking charity they did not deserve.[22]

The society's focus on casework underpinned other aspects of its growing "popularity and authority" among Melbourne's first generation of social workers and among the networks of men and women "prominent in medicine, nursing, business, charitable work and in the University" that were so crucial in the interwar period.[23] With casework came the idea of regular caseworker discussions and conferences, introduced and maintained, at first falteringly, from 1925.[24] Because "the new social work" was based on learned method and judgment, the COS also took up a significant role in the training of workers for other agencies, including the hospital almoners introduced during the 1920s and 1930s, Presbyterian deaconesses, YWCA trainees, and the investigators who worked for the Sustenance Branch after 1932. Of these, perhaps the most important links were with the almoners, who had their own institute and, in Agnes Macintyre, who joined the Melbourne Hospital from London's St. Thomas Hospital in 1929, a strong and determined leader.

In Melbourne, medical social work—and British women and men—led the move toward the provision of training, with a course that involved a degree of general as well as almoner work, but the COS remained a close ally, and Smith took up yet more voluntary positions, such as honorary secretary of the Victorian Institute for Almoners and treasurer of the Victorian Council for Social Training. With the university deciding it was not equipped to provide a social work program, the council was formed in 1933 to provide a two-year course, mostly supervised by volunteers and dependent very much on the practical experience that could be gained in existing agencies. Each student spent the equivalent of three full-time months with the COS. Emphasizing its breadth and its nondenominationalism and claiming to bring students into "actual contact with working-class life" and arm them with rigorous casework methods, the COS accordingly played a crucial role in the emergence of professional social work in Melbourne.[25] As Smith suggested, "Australia has been dilatory in recognising the need for special education in social work"; his society was one of the most important in addressing that deficiency.[26]

The COS's role in Melbourne's welfare network certainly rested on Smith's immense energies and aspirations. He involved himself in everything. He prepared notes for the premier and others titled "The Problem of Unemployment," "Human Credulity and the Begging Imposter," and "The Problem of the Street Mendicant." He gave evidence to committees, from the Royal Commission on National Insurance in 1926 to the Victorian Slum Abolition Board in 1938 and the new Repatriation Commission in 1940. In 1930 he agreed that his staff would manage sustenance inquiries from hundreds of single women living away from their families. He secured a vital role for the COS in the 1928 United Unemployment Relief Committee (which the COS essentially brought into being), to which he was honorary secretary and for which the women inquiry officers created and checked hundreds of records. He was also the very energetic secretary of the Victorian Society for the Prevention of Cruelty to Children and the first president of the Victorian Association of Social Workers.[27]

Smith aspired to be an authority and a pedagogue. In a very important way—and in the absence of any formal qualifications—his fulfillment of those aims rested on COS casework. It provided the evidence of experience, and the stories that his inquiry officers generated always played a crucial role in his testimonies. On the evidence of his writings and reports, Smith was a competitive and earnest man who felt deeply the need to convince everyone that only what he termed the "more nearly perfect development of case investigation" would protect Melbourne from "armies" of "simulators."[28] He was sure of the need to dramatize the problem and the solution, and he saw the potential for casework to provide true and telling stories that, he wrote in 1928, are "terse with human interest, and stratified with pathos, dramatic situations and often a vein of humour."[29] Or, as he said more fulsomely: "Many strange experiences come the way of the social worker who visits the homes of the poor. Tales of tragedy and sacrifice, glaring incongruities, grim humour, startling contrasts— every note in the full gamut of human emotions and human relationships is struck at one time or another."[30]

Certainly, one outcome was to strengthen the claims of his society and attract more subscribers, but this was never just a matter of tactics in a competition for influence and resources. The need was more urgent than that. There were too many "ingenious" and "plausible" people and too many "soft-hearted ladies in suburban homes." Resources were too few to waste. So the "enlistment of public opinion, through press and other propaganda" was a matter of great importance, however difficult: "The sentimentality which does not see behind the sightless orbs or pitiful deformity, the outstretched hand and the silent appeal of the sub-normal to the normal, cannot easily or speedily be eradicated."[31]

In sum, the particular role played by the COS in Melbourne during the 1920s and 1930s, and the unusually significant degree of influence it sought and achieved, heightened its appreciation for the dramatic possibilities of case files. The COS was always, at least in part, a provider of stories about poverty, as well as resources to combat poverty, and its case files provided the raw materials for the public's education in the differences between those who should be helped and those who should be discouraged. Case files proved that rigorous investigation would reveal the truth. They reassured observers, and the secretary and workers of the COS, that their judgments rested on solid foundations. They also defended the COS against accusations of insensitive and indeed "inquisitorial" methods; in a retort to a Trades Hall Committee report on the COS's dealings with unemployed single women, Smith was able to list nine numbered cases of attempted imposition, impersonation, and deceit, including Case 46,122 (a young woman who said that "the only way to get any assistance was by telling lies") and Case 46,302 (in which the COS visitor "disturbed a drunken quarrel"). Whatever his attempts at proof, relations with unions and Trades Hall were never good; Smith was especially affronted by an article in *Labor Call* in 1932 that portrayed what might have happened to Jesus had he ever come before the COS. Mimicking the style of a case file—with an accuracy that almost suggests an inside job—the story concluded:

He asked officer to give up Charity Organisation Society work and to follow him, but refused to guarantee any stipend. Applicant appeared to believe in a Social Revolution, which should make the last first and the first last, but officer refused to waste time upon him. Applicant appeared before the committee, and was rebuked for his utter want of thrift, industry, temperance, and for the bad company he kept. He was offered a set of carpenter's tools by a lady if he would return to carpentry, but the Society refused to do anything for him, except recommend him to go to the infirmary, lunatic department, or else to live a more business-like and practical life.[32]

By the middle of the 1920s, the COS's collection of case files and the central index to which they were connected had taken on a particular significance. Each opened with a story, the details of which were tested by further investigation. The inquiry officers added letters from clients or other agencies and kept a detailed record of each conversation and encounter. The daily work of investigation was sometimes mundane. There were fruitless searches for misheard addresses, cases that never progressed beyond an initial application, and straightforward "character checks" for the Melbourne Hospital and benevolent trusts. Perhaps a third of the case files fell into this category. Another third narrated relatively straightforward investigations: perhaps a small loan to recover tools from pawn, a spinal brace for an invalid, or a positive report for the Legacy Club. But about a third involved repeat visits and encounters, sometimes over a year or several years. These brought in new characters and evidence, introduced unanticipated twists and connections, and sometimes revealed the client's secrets and fabrications.

For the inquiry officers, these most detailed case records told a story of professional accomplishment, ending in a client's gratitude or the successful detection of the slyly dependent. Casework visibly amassed the information that made decisions and judgments seem solid. Workers also rewrote case notes for discussion at the case conferences that brought together inquiry officers, almoners, and investigators from around Melbourne. As they rewrote, they sometimes added flourishes and colored the story by exaggerating the most significant moments. They suggested conclusions about "social types" and broader messages. Case notes were produced for audiences, and Smith was a particularly active interpreter. He interrupted some records with exclamations in red pen and underlining in pencil and produced shortened versions of the most "telling" cases for the society's Executive Committee, the newspapers, the *Other Half*, and the frequent reports, notes, and submissions.

Of course, there were Melburnians the COS never saw and would never see, because they drew from or contributed to other traditions of benevolence and care.[33] But they did see thousands, especially as the number of cases surged in the middle of the 1920s and again after 1930. And because the COS had such a major role among Melbourne's charity providers, many of whom it trained, the stories based on its cases were an authoritative part of Melbourne's public conversation about entitlement and welfare in the decades before and during the twentieth century's most profound economic and social crisis. The "successful" cases provide insights, and so do the unsuccessful, partial, and frustrated cases that were also—thankfully—saved for the archives. It is important to explore what they suggested was the accepted truth about poverty. Written by experienced investigators and shaped by pedagogical imperatives, the case files of the COS are a particularly interesting measure of what Melburnians who were not poor and not in need of welfare believed and wanted to say about those who were.

CHAPTER 3

Wise Discrimination

In a 1926 submission describing the practical work of the COS, Stanley Greig Smith emphasized "the sympathetic but thorough investigation of the circumstances, character, etc., of applicants for charitable aid."[34] Although a later article acknowledged that "social work is an exceedingly difficult business" and "is characterised by all sorts of complex problems," he was also sure that these could be overcome with "thoroughness" and "rigour."[35] Among the social worker's most important tools, he added in 1930, was "wise discrimination."[36]

To believe, as Smith clearly believed, that it is possible—and indeed worthwhile—to distinguish between the worthy and the unworthy poor, allowing you to assist the former and deter the latter, you must be confident about at least two things. First, you must believe that you can achieve the proper attribution of people into these groups; in other words, there must be a method for reliably distinguishing one from the other. Second, given that the unworthy poor are unlikely to freely divulge their deficiencies, this method must be able to make use of something other than the simple testimony of the applicants themselves.

The sorting of the poor into types is not the only possible approach to poverty. It is a choice among alternatives, and it is based on assumptions about poverty's origins and manifestations. As elsewhere in the 1920s and 1930s, in Melbourne there were alternative convictions. As John Murphy has shown, different Christian traditions have always had distinctive ways of imagining poor people, with an older Catholic emphasis on showing mercy and seeing the face of Christ in the poor at odds with an evangelical Protestant focus on sinfulness and the need for individual redemption as a precursor to any more general reform.

Of course, the distinction was never as sharp in practice as it might have seemed in doctrine; many Protestants "reconciled individual evangelism with social reform by framing the latter as a moral issue."[37] Protestant agencies could also disagree on the appropriate balance between sympathy and thoroughness. During the Victorian Parliament's Social Services Board of Inquiry in 1932, for example, Smith, who sat on the committee, had some sharp exchanges with leaders of the Victorian Association of Ladies' Benevolent Societies (LBS). LBS treasurer Jeffreson insisted that "if a family are starving today they must be helped no matter what they may have been in the past." Pressed on the advantages of the central registration of all cases, a cause célèbre of the COS that the LBS had always disliked, President Bleazby replied: "The people who come before the Benevolent Ladies' Societies are dealt with as people who are hungry and poor.... I do not like the idea of, in cold blood, looking up a record in regard to a person who formerly received help and had since made good. We do not want to make the poor and needy feel that somebody might be unkind enough to look up their records and to use the information against them." Pressed again, she said simply: "My concern is that people who, through no fault of their own, have to ask for help shall not have their feelings hurt. It may be that occasionally my sympathies carry me beyond my commonsense."[38]

The COS was unmoved. Their work, like the casework of their London parent, held firm to the conviction that applicants could and indeed must be sorted into the deserving and the undeserving. Rigorous casework tested the first impressions of sympathy on the harder foundations of evidence. Knowledge of rigor among the poor would also deter the potential mendicant or pauper, preserving relief for those who truly merited assistance. A statement Smith made in 1911 would serve just as well in 1930. Speaking of the need for coordination, he argued that "it is not a scheme with the object merely of establishing a sort of detective agency to unmask impostors, but one whose immediate object is the diversion of charitable relief from unworthy channels, with a view to rendering more possible than at present the adequate assistance of the deserving."[39]

In a sense, though, the COS's most obvious achievement was to become a "sort of detective agency," which carried the spirit of inquiry, so vital to nineteenth-century charity investigation, forward into the twentieth century. The focus of inquiry remained the moral character of the poor; as Murphy has so aptly put it, "Inquiry was a form of soul-searching."[40] Casework was the modern method that would better fulfill that search. It was a body of knowledge and practices that could be imported, somewhat refined for the temper and conditions of Australia, and transmitted through training and publicity to social workers and philanthropists of all kinds. Melbourne's charity leaders and workers drew on the new advances of Americans such as Mary Richmond or, in the 1930s, Charlotte Towle and Joanna Colcord, as well as British advocates of "scientific charity" such as Helen Bosanquet. Eager listeners to a transatlantic conversation about method, they followed British, American, and European trends with great care.

They always thought that there would be some local translation. Although they did not often set their unspoken assumptions into words, Smith and other Melbourne charity leaders seem to have regarded Australia as a newer, richer country in which poverty was less entrenched. Its distances and emptiness, and relatively high levels of personal mobility, also made it harder to be certain of people's true identities. Even if interwar Melbourne was no longer a frontier society, it was still a long way from the Northern Hemisphere center against which many of its citizens still measured its progress, and nineteenth-century anxieties about people in new and mobile societies pretending to be what they were not still rang true.[41] All of this tended to make Melbourne's charity investigators even more suspicious of the dependencies and inadequacies of Australia's poor and even more determined to find and reveal those who were simply "cadging," "simulating," and "imposing."

Even if they were certain of their target, their methods rested on some rather shaky suppositions. A phrase used by several investigators captures one of them: "They are not the type to ask for assistance," it was reported of the Ramseys in Flemington, "but deserve it."[42] At times this train of thought seemed even stronger: the fact of not asking for assistance somehow proved that it was deserved. With another applicant, Doris Richards, whose home "had such a neat and clean appearance that I did not make enquiries in the neighbourhood," the definitive point for Agnes Cutler was that "there is no doubt that she is quite unused to seeking assistance of any kind."[43] In several other cases, the fact that applicants had not asked for assistance, but had been referred by concerned relatives and neighbors, made their cases "obviously genuine." This was despite the fact that the refusal to seek assistance could sometimes cause real problems. In one 1932 case, a man's refusal to apply for sustenance despite his prolonged unemployment, coupled with his wife's anxiety about seeking help from the local ladies' benevolent society, meant that an ill daughter was seriously undernourished. But not seeking help was at the same time a sign of "bravery."[44]

This was an uncertain and at times inconsistent method of inquiry, one based on impressions and appearances. The clearly genuine and deserving client convinced without being convincing (a "very convincing way of speaking" always triggered distrust).[45] It was important to speak well and to avoid sounding "not genuine." One should not be "very secretive" or overly sensitive, but neither should one be "very talkative," especially by "playing on the 'I'm badly done by & have sacrificed my life' idea" which was "probably true [but] ... very prejudicing" in the case of a deserted Richmond mother pursuing her husband for maintenance arrears.[46] It was just as important to appear guileless and to not be "too knowing" about possible solutions, which indicated you had used charity before. But to feign ignorance, or "simulate simplicity," as did one rather hapless young man to Cutler in early 1931, caused its own suspicions. The COS eventually loaned the young man eight shillings so he could redeem his bag from a railway cloakroom; Cutler seems to have concluded that he was actually just "a remarkably simple fellow."[47] Not so fortunate was an overly "plausible woman" from inner-suburban Richmond; although "people in the street were not disposed to give any information," she was given no assistance to release some of her belonging from storage in order to furnish a new home.[48]

To be a COS applicant demanded very careful control over words. Every meeting carried the overtone of giving evidence, wittingly or unwittingly, of one's character and circumstances. Feelings had to be watched, and anger checked, and statements always had to be put carefully for fear of misunderstanding. For the inquiry officers, the practice of casework was just as difficult. The everyday work of listening, judging, and investigating was never straightforward. The complications of real people's lives always threatened to erode whatever self-assurance a worker might bring to each of her encounters and interviews. And they were in places and among people they mostly didn't know and wouldn't have encountered were it not for their vocation. In that situation, how did you find the truth?

Every conversation involved a difficult negotiation over the "true" predicament, as well as what would most effectively overcome or ameliorate it. There was a careful exchange of questions and answers in which workers struggled to unearth the truth from guarded applicants. As well as proving beyond a doubt that an applicant deserved help, the workers believed the most difficult problem was finding something solid on which to base that judgment. Workers probed for details, consulted the central index for possible aliases and links to existing known cases, asked local shopkeepers, or interviewed neighbors, the police, and local teachers. They listened and weighed the evidence, but they also knew words could be deceptive, especially when they were spun into stories. People could learn how to mimic the truly needy or try to confuse the inquiry officer. The real skill of the caseworker was to sort the merely plausible from the honest and the true and to know "false feeling" when she saw it. And although this sounded straightforward, it wasn't. It is not surprising, in a way, that inquiry officers sometimes seemed relieved to have discovered a falsehood: a lie was at least solid; it was a basis from which you could proceed with a degree of confidence.

Those judgments were further complicated by the assumption that even the worthy poor did not fully understand their own situations and could not know what they really needed. The investigators disliked applicants who had already identified the cures for their own ailments. Indeed, Agnes Cutler and the others could be scathing toward applicants; in a letter written to the State War Council, one applicant, a fireman, was criticized for being "rather inclined to fancy that he is the best judge of what should be done for him and how it should be done."[49]

In their determination to ensure that limited resources were spent wisely and in a way that would not create dependency, and sure that the applicants themselves could not identify the best way forward, the inquiry officers had to make very hard decisions. Even in the best circumstances, their methods were inexact. People were unreliable. They differed on details and seemed to forget things. They couldn't always understand what the inquiry officer was asking, or they tried to provide her with the kind of story she seemed to want. Rather than telling the truth, they said what they thought they should say. Sometimes they tried to hide things, such as the commercial artist, too ill to work, who was trying to take his overworked wife and daughter to live with his parents in Adelaide in September 1932. He was seeking thirty shillings for traveling expenses. Dorothy Macdonald acknowledged that the artist was "quite a nicely-spoken man," but she "was not impressed with him. He gave information that was asked for, but was careful not to give any more than what was necessary." In fact, she recognized him as an earlier case, from 1925; further inquiries revealed that he was a former drinker who had lost jobs—but not his family— during his struggle with alcoholism between 1924 and 1931. In the end, he was given his fare, though not without having to share that story once again with strangers while they picked over the traces of his history.[50]

Trained to listen, but also to doubt, and largely dealing with people who were not like them, the COS workers struggled to find answers to questions that never became easier. How could people be trusted? How could you tell if they hadn't simply rehearsed the script beforehand? Everyone had secrets, but which of those might be dangerous if undisturbed? The consequences were just as unnerving. If they gave, they feared creating dependency. If they trusted, they feared being taken in by liars and cheats. If they refused, they feared damning those who really needed their help. It was a delicate and demanding science. In 1929 an article in the *Other Half* perhaps said more than it knew. "Family welfare work," it said, "may not be properly classifiable as a 'dangerous occupation,' but it unquestionably involves a severe mental strain and the expenditure of much nervous energy."[51]

What could never be acknowledged, of course, was that the strain could never be relieved so long as charity first demanded distrust. As Melbourne's interwar charity investigators tried to identify and assist worthy sufferers, they knew the most needy might be suffering alone and in silence. They knew there were never enough resources to care for everyone. They developed their social work and their dramatic stories of poverty, and they struggled to identify the worthy by unmasking the unworthy. This success in turn rested on their capacity to identify the fraud and the "simulator." In this kind of social work, inquiry officers looked for lies and secrets and read people's bodies for the signs of falsehood. In that sense, Melbourne's interwar caseworkers couldn't afford to be benevolent carers, at least for most of their clients. They couldn't afford to be too trusting. Instead, they tended to imagine themselves rather differently. They were lady detectives, and they would hunt frauds and liars.

· ·

CHAPTER 4

Lady Detectives

In Melbourne during the 1920s and 1930s, the battle to define what should be done about poverty—on the small as well as the large scale—took place in the COS Executive Committee and in parliamentary inquiries and political debates. But it also took place in humble homes and the COS front office, in tearful admissions and arguments, in a more intimate, exacting, and exhausting war of words that was never as resolvable by "wise discrimination" as it might have seemed from the outside. Even a case deemed a suitable example of the COS method—that of Letitia Donaldson in 1932—held some ambivalent messages about the effectiveness of COS intervention. After twenty-nine visits in two days—including one to a sister-in-law "who told a story altogether different" to the applicant, eight to houses in two "poor" streets trying to track the woman's sons (three of whom were reported to be in jail), three to the local police station, and two to the local sustenance office, as well inquiries to a butcher, two grocers, four rental agents, a boot repairer, and a dairy—only one person who could shed any light on Mrs. Donaldson could be found, and all she could say for certain was that the person given as a reference by the applicant was probably living somewhere near Browning Street in South Yarra or at least had been at some point in the last several years. In any event, after two days, "further inquiries [were] impossible as case withdrawn by

Mrs D."[52] The case seems to have been regarded as exemplary for the rigor of its method; it might just as well be an example of exhausting futility in the face of real or feigned local ignorance and the sheer difficulty of finding an incontrovertible story.

Different COS workers came up with somewhat different solutions to the dilemmas of their casework method. A few took people at their word and trusted that their stories, if not absolutely accurate, indicated real problems. Among the inquiry officers, Lillian Allen always tended to have a somewhat softer heart than Agnes Cutler, for instance. Even as that meant her case notes sport more of Smith's underlinings and questions—"has this been checked?" "possibly former case?" and "drink involved, surely"— it also made her a more effective collaborator in several long-running cases. Others relied on a shorthand of easily defined "social types," especially as the caseload increased during the 1930s. Such rough-and-ready prediction ruled out able-bodied men, as well as young, single women, and counted only the elderly, mothers, and respectable people fallen on hard times among "the immediately deserving." Others based their decisions on shaky conclusions. "She did not impress me favourably, but I could not tell why" was the denouement to one 1931 case of a single woman who had come back to Melbourne from Camperdown and needed the government sustenance. Her form was neither signed nor returned.[53]

Detection was always the most satisfying version of casework. It also provided some of the most significant "signature stories" and raw material for the COS's broader attempts to teach Melbourne's charities and citizens about poverty. Detection meant testing applicants' stories and finding truth in the accuracy of the language and the "genuineness" of their telling. It was a delicate and demanding game. Too much skill was dangerous. "The woman struck me at first as being a woman who drank, but after speaking to her for some time, I came to the conclusion that she was of weak intellect" was Agnes Cutler's first impression of Ellen Robson, the wife of an unemployed laborer and hawker.[54] After another encounter, however, "she has a plausible manner and knows how to make her case appear needy." She had, in other words, learned the rules of the game and played them too well. She was given a small loan and a grocery order for two shillings and told to go to the Ladies' Benevolent Society. A woman who received nothing was also "very plausible and 'knows the ropes,'" according to Celia Bedford, who warned a church charity that "we are satisfied that she is of a most unreliable type, and one of those who take full advantage of the possibilities which exist in Melbourne for seeking and obtaining help from many sources."[55]

Words couldn't be trusted, but the body could. The most reassuring certainty came from knowing that however skillful and "plausible" the applicant who wanted something for nothing, or however inept a truly deserving person was at telling a tale, one's body would reveal the truth. Indeed, as workers struggled under mounting caseloads, the bodies and the gestures of applicants, as well as their clothes and furnishings, increasingly came to make the difference between relatively straightforward acceptance and further inquiry. In most of the cases that proceeded beyond routine or fruitless inquiry, how people looked, moved, stood, and appeared always played a role in determining their worth. In the same decades that enthusiasts promoted lie detectors as a universal solution to crime, and detective fiction, with its characteristic reliance on revelation and hidden clues, became ever more popular, some of the COS investigators were convinced they could also detect the physical signs of falsehood and deceit. The crucial distinction between the deserving and undeserving poor was visible to—and verifiable by—the well-trained investigator. Bodies revealed the truth that minds wanted to hide, so in case notes that sometimes took on the character of detective stories, inquiry officers showed their skill in the interpretation of gestures, expressions, dress, and physical surroundings. They looked for too much makeup or obvious nicotine stains or sensed the faint smell of alcohol on the breath. They looked at bodies that failed to bear out what the clients said. There were always clues.

The choreography of charity investigation was physical as much as verbal; applicants had to show the evidence of "genuine need" in their bodies and faces. This demanded an almost inhuman control over body and gesture, and people attracted suspicion for their "vague and smirking manner," their "furtive eyes," or their "evasive and deceptive" faces or merely because "her eyes flickered just a little."[56] Deception always left its traces: in bodies that were too strong and healthy, in teeth that were too white and well formed to support a story of consistent poverty, in clothes that spoke of frivolity rather than misery, in houses with a pianola or a gramophone, in rooms that smelled of perfume or cigarette smoke, or in a supposedly needy home with "cigarettes on the latch & bought cakes on a dish."[57]

Although it was rarely made explicit in their case files or the society's administrative records, there was always an assumption that women were especially suited to the tasks of welfare investigation. They were careful and considered in their actions, perhaps better listeners or more inquisitive. I think they regarded themselves as exacting and precise. Perhaps clients were seen as more likely to let down their guard to the soft-spoken questions of a woman. On the evidence of their stories about poverty, the COS inquiry officers drew from and contributed to a closer and closer linking between femininity and detection—and between femininity and the art of intrigue, for good and bad—that was played out more broadly in a popular genre of fiction and film. Here, it also informed a particular understanding of women's contribution to social work and poverty amelioration. Among some of its early Melbourne practitioners and proponents, social work was dramatized as women's work because women were more adept at the detective skills the work seemed to require. Women not only had sympathy and a capacity for care; they were also seen as more capable of spotting the liar and the fraud.

Agnes Cutler was the exemplar lady detective. By the early 1930s, the "general Depression" meant she, like the other inquiry officers, was handling dozens of cases at once. But she never lost her ability to identify and track down "the plausible impostor," a talent she had first shown in the 1920s.[58] Cutler prided herself on her forensic skills; indeed, in several of her case files, she added flourishes that were perhaps drawn from detective novels or films. In one, there was a mysteriously closed door, in others the faint smell of cigarette smoke in an empty room, a bed moved to block a doorway, and the careful probing of a story she knew was untrue. In Cutler's precise, detailed, and storylike notes, applicants "admit" and "confess." She could not "place any faith" in one 1924 applicant because "tho' her home is beautifully clean ... [she] looked uncomfortable when giving information, as if it was not quite truthful in every respect." This applicant was not working, she said, because she was upset over a son who had been put into a lunatic asylum five months before, "tho' she confessed that she was quite strong" and "admitted that she is very good at housework."[59] Nor would Miss Cutler accept refusal or evasion. A New Zealander achieved little, for instance, by barring her entry: he was "rather aggressive in manner and resented being questioned ... [and] kept the door well closed behind him and did not ask me into the house. . . . As it was impossible to extract any useful information from him, I made inquiries at a grocer's opposite."[60] One apartment house landlady refused to give information about her tenants, one of whom had received cheap treatment at the Melbourne Hospital. Visited a second time, she again refused:

[I told her that] this obvious evading of enquiries would most probably arouse some grave doubt about their case. I asked if both went to work of some kind, but was again faced with the landlady's quite pleasant but decided refusal to give any information. . . . Judging by the landlady's manner it is also most probable that they have warned her against giving any information, tho' she declared that she is no relation to them. She was smoking when she came to the door this morning. The case, generally, impressed me as a very doubtful one.[61]

Applicants were rarely left undisturbed. They "seem to be"—or "have the appearance of"—drinkers, unreliable workers, or "poor social types." They had feelings that had to be raised to the surface and made to play out in their gestures and faces. They had to be seen in context, in their informal surroundings, something that could be achieved by unannounced and unanticipated visits. In one 1931 case, an order for cheap spectacles was refused because a daughter seen at the door was "too well-dressed" to support the applicant's story and because a neighbor reported that the family was purchasing a pianola.[62] One man risked his claim because there was lipstick on a glass in his kitchen when he said he wasn't married. Another was fortunate to overcome a first surprise visit; the case of "a tall thin man with a strangely pink face" and his wife, "a much coarser type, with sallow complexion and lank brown hair," was almost undermined by Cutler "seeing an empty beer bottle in the yard." Luckily for them, after one neighbor—a stammering and "very stupid" man—had accused them of drunkenness, another, more "reliable" woman had said they were decent.[63]

Agnes Cutler could be forensic in her vigor. On more than one occasion, she inspected yards and alleys for bottles and cigarettes, once even digging through a garbage pile—I have always hoped she used her umbrella—before emerging triumphant with an empty beer bottle. Perfume always galvanized her, as did traces of men in places they were not supposed to be. In one 1931 case, Cutler put two and two together to make something a little more than four; suspicious of Ellen Goss, a widowed applicant for free dental treatment, she quizzed her on why she slept in a double bed while her two daughters shared a single, having "noticed a man's bag, boots, collars & ties about" and the girls "talking to some man whose voice I could hear." Mrs. Goss said that a man occasionally stayed with them and slept in a back room; the Dental Hospital was informed that she "was said to be decent," which was damning with faint praise.[64]

It mattered little if the supposition was wrong. June Chivers, a single waitress who had moved to Melbourne from Western Australia, was referred to the COS by the Sustenance Branch in 1932. June wanted to return home, where her sister kept a lodging house, and brought her friend Gloria Roberts to the interview. In this case, Ethel Brown took over from Agnes Cutler and reported that "both these girls strike one as of a type well able to take care of themselves. The air was thick with cheap perfume and they were much painted." Visiting their rooms, catching the landlady's young daughter referring to "Mrs. Chivers," and noticing "a young man coming down the stairs," Brown "asked if they were single and both said they were, although they looked rather sheepish about it. They were quite well dressed and very made up." A policewoman later confirmed that the man was June's married brother, also from Western Australia, who was living in the same house.[65] What would have indicated strong family bonds in one case became a reason for refusal in another.

Agnes Cutler had a particular knack for distinguishing between "true feelings" and "mere appearances." A father from Fitzroy, about to be evicted, was sent to the Ladies' Benevolent Society but "returned and sat on the [COS] steps nursing his head in his knees. He gave one the impression of deliberately working on his emotions for effect."[66] So did Freda Hamilton, a woman whose eldest child had died of meningitis in 1937; in debt from the funeral, she had approached the Society for the Prevention of Cruelty to Children for fifteen shillings to pay the rent. "Extremely plausible and smiling" was Cutler's opening summary; "it impressed me that she is quite able to work as her only complaint is varicose veins from which many other women who work are suffering. She is receiving no treatment for this and I had no faith in the very deliberate lame way that she walked in my presence. She impressed me as a very dangerous, cunning woman."[67]

Though she didn't always get her man (or woman), few clients evaded Agnes Cutler for long. In one case involving visits during 1932, 1933, and 1936, she struggled to get the "real story" of an unemployed man, Edward Wilson, whose wife and children had returned to England in 1931. He "impressed me most unfavourably," she wrote in her notes, "owing to a very unreliable way with him." His eyes were "extremely evasive." In what I think was a deliberate strategy and not a slip of the pen, she inverted their positions: "He interviewed me in his bedroom, leaning over the end of the bed and scarcely looking at me at all while he gave information and 'explanation' of his very strange attitude toward his wife and children in a vain endeavour to try to put himself in the right as far as my opinion of him was concerned." When challenged over part of his story, "he merely smiled in his unreliable way and did not deny [it]." Glimpsing an unfinished painting of a woman in a garden, which Wilson said was of a friend, Cutler "thought it probable that he has formed an association with some woman and that this is one of his reasons for not being eager to be with his wife and children." Her dislike of him was "instinctive"; during an unannounced home visit in 1933, "he was very well dressed, and had not the appearance, in any way, of a man who is suffering hardship." When he responded to a letter, prompted by a British agency inquiring on behalf of his wife, Wilson "was well dressed in a rather showy way and has a familiar manner, but this seemed to me to be a pose to hide his real feelings." Their last meeting was in 1936, when he needed dentures. Cutler knew he was a liar "for some vague reason that I can never define." He maintained "his peculiar and always unsatisfactory attitude of 'deep thinking and little speaking.'" He was denied assistance in part because "his case is one that I feel I can never fathom"; indeed, concluded Cutler in a letter to the hospital, "I feel that we must leave him to work out his own salvation."[68]

Agnes Cutler was a careful and meticulous investigator. She crossed and dotted what should be crossed and dotted, and she had, on the evidence, a remarkable memory. She was conscientious, and she was indefatigable. She also had two particular dislikes. One was anything that smacked of unionism or political radicalism. The wife of one unemployed laborer was denied assistance in 1933, for instance, when it was discovered that her husband refused to work for sustenance "with many others" and was in receipt of "what she calls 'strikers allowance.'" He had also been drinking and "associating with wharf labourers" (it was not clear which of these was the more damning sin).[69] The other dislike, which she shared with most of the women investigators, was "flighty girls." In December 1932, for example, a young unemployed waitress asked the COS to help her find a domestic position and board her eighteen-month-old son. Her husband was in Albury looking for work and may have deserted her. Her initial presentation at the COS desk aroused hostility. "Applicant was well dressed. I don't think I would trust her very far. Her fingers were very stained with nicotine." After a visit from COS inquiry officer Ethel Brown, the applicant returned; "when I interviewed [her] at her aunt's home, she impressed me quite favourably, but when she called here yesterday she was so much done up she looked like a different being." No help was provided.[70]

As inquiry officers assessed independent women applicants for sustenance, they grew more and more irritated at "girls" who were more interested in rouge, dances, and cigarettes than attending training classes or taking any work they could find. In 1931 Cutler tried to secure the return home of May Oates, an unemployed domestic servant; when visited, "she was very much 'done up' and a tray in the room was full of cigarette ashes and butts.... I considered it possible that applicant's trouble with her father (who does not drink) is due to her flighty ways, done up face and foolishly 'plucked' eyebrows, tho' she appears to be quite decent in many ways." Both May and her roommate "go out a good deal to dances with boy friends.... So far, [they] have done nothing to arouse any suspicion about their morals," though this was more by good luck than good management, in Cutler's view.[71] Nor was Ethel Brown of a mind to trust Irish migrant Mary Pearce, not so much because of her story, which was unconvincing, but because she was "particularly well dressed, with scarlet lips" and "fingers very much stained with nicotine."[72]

Most infuriating of all was Victoria Robinson, "smartly dressed and rather 'made up'" at her first visit, and Victoria's mother, who clashed with Cutler from the start. According to Cutler, "I asked her why she came from W.A. in April 1930, and she declared in a very resentful way that she was tired of being asked that 'silly' question. I remarked that it should be considered a most reasonable question, but she persisted in her arrogant attitude & would give me no satisfaction." When told that the COS would interview her daughter, Mrs. Robinson "insisted on interviewing the Secretary" and came to the office to do so. Victoria turned up later, and this meticulous description is in Ethel Brown's file note: "She was attired in a black satin dress with a lace front, a new blazer & a well-made top coat with a large bunch of boronia in her buttonhole. Her face was done up and her eyebrows plucked and blackened. She smelt strongly of perfume.... After she had left our room, she went outside and handed [Miss Garry] a ten shilling note which she asked her to change for her. When she opened her purse several other notes were seen inside. Both Mrs Robinson and her daughter struck me as being able to exist very well without sustenance." It seems they had come to that same decision themselves; no further inquiries were made, and it is just possible that the black satin display, and the ostentatious note changing, represented the Robinsons' final move in a game they had decided to abandon.[73]

The dislike of disrespectful "girls" or unionized men stemmed in part from their lack of gratitude—something the poor have always had to show—and in part from their unwillingness to accept that the COS investigators could and should judge their prospects and characters. Here, as ever, the gender, class, and generation of the social worker mattered; Melbourne's female inquiry officers were unimpressed by male bravado and trade union politics, and their encounter with undeferential younger women also worked to the latter's disadvantage.

The struggle to find and tell the truth about poverty in Melbourne in the 1920s and the early years of the Depression was one in which what most applicants said was mistrusted, tested, and found wanting. Surprisingly, perhaps, revelations of falsehood were not normally savage or triumphant. Indeed, many of the applicants characterized as untruthful or ignorant were still regarded as decent and given help. Nor did dissembling preclude sympathy and even friendliness; even tough investigators such as Agnes Cutler could understand why people wanted to keep some things secret. One man impressed her very unfavorably at first, as "his breath was heavy with cigarette smoking, and his lips stained with this, so he must have spent a good deal on cigarettes. He impressed as a rather 'spineless' type of man, but he seemed anxious for work, which was a point in his favour." But he grew in her estimation when she discovered that he married a woman with an illegitimate child: "Statements re his marriage were very contradictory & difficult to follow, but I learned the reason for this later and admired him for the manner in which he had shielded his wife."[74]

Such benign outcomes are puzzling, in a way. Of course, the rigorous testing and probing of applicants' stories were intended to prevent the misuse of funds, and checks of character and circumstance were meant to catch out those who were trying to exploit different sources of benevolence. The COS always had trouble with alcoholics, especially those whose problems were not yet obvious; it is clear that investigation prevented some of the money intended for benevolence being spent on cheap booze. Yet even by the COS's own account, fewer than 5 percent of the applicants they visited could be accused of any kind of imposture at all (and the COS applied a very broad definition of "imposture"). There were, of course, frauds and liars and pathetic attempts to garner a few shillings or even a few pounds for a drink or a nice dress. There were people who hid their errors and then suffered the shame of their revelation. But these were relatively minor in number.

Instead, these detective stories provided two forms of reassurance. One, I think, was that casework methods were deterring the imagined "armies" of beggars and "simulators" who kept appearing in the society's public statements. The war on "pauperism"—or, for that matter, the war on "welfare dependency" that became so popular in the late twentieth century—always assumed that but for such deterrence, the majority of the poor would make no effort whatsoever to change their situations. Another was the confirmation of a larger truth: that the poor, being poor, lacked the ability to really understand their circumstances. In these case files, and in the knowledge generalized from them and taken out into public discussion, the COS investigators and the secretary dramatized a more general truth: that when impoverished and "inferior" people spoke, their sense of what was wrong in the world—and of how it might be put right—was generally inaccurate and self-deceiving.

This attitude was most evident when applicants—and they were almost always men—were foolish enough to blame governments, mass unemployment, the system, the bosses, capitalism, or the class system, which led to the very few examples of COS workers humiliating or belittling people. One man who inquired about obtaining some boots in 1933 was asked why he had not managed to find regular work; perhaps reasonably, in a city where a quarter or a third of men were jobless, he suggested that it was "not unexpected." He was told in no uncertain terms that although "drifters and loafers" might not have work, anyone who wanted a job could find one.[75] Other men were described as "all too ready to blame other people and conditions for [their] misfortunes" or "full of arrogant notions about what is owed them" and "expecting far too much from others."[76]

With most applicants, the point was less direct. Women were generally too sensible to risk offending the inquiry officers with direct talk of injustice and inequality; what husbands and sons lost through grandstanding and empty vindication had to be regained through a careful and apologetic repair of the relationship. Instead of being described as wrong, they were often labeled "stupid" or "dull." They got their stories muddled and forgot the details. Most of all, they didn't really understand the world. They talked about vulnerability, said that luck and not character played the major part in their problems, or suggested that the rich were obliged to help the poor. It was at this point that they were reminded they were not the best judges of what should be done. It was then that they needed to make nodding agreement with the truth about character and reward and acknowledge that outside interpreters, and not impoverished people themselves, knew best.

In this light, it is particularly interesting to read the "ideal" cases circulated to subscribers and newspapers. Invariably, the applicant was a passive—and very grateful—recipient of a strategy and a remedy devised for them by the society. In a mid-1920s case list, there are "battlers who do all they can" or who have "a heart-breaking struggle to make ends meet," "a grateful deserted wife" who was being assisted by a "local relieving society"—the hapless, disorganized LBS, of course—"in a totally inadequate way," an amputee "fitted with the latest type of artificial hand," and a book salesman "made self-supporting." All were discovered, diagnosed, and remedied by the COS, and all were portrayed as waiting for someone to have an idea or make a plan that would change their situation. They were "bright and brave" and "sad and struggling" and "needed a friend." And their struggles were the outcome of individual circumstance and tragedies, not endemic or structural problems.[77]

For the Charity Organisation Society, assistance was always predicated on two more general beliefs. First, whatever the impoverished and inferior sometimes said, poverty could only ever be overcome by effort, a "wise strategy," and good character. Soul-searching preceded any remedy, and every remedy was individual. Second, the poor were not "the best judge" of their situations. Charity investigation stemmed from those beliefs, and the stories that it generated helped to reinforce those beliefs, at least before the severity and duration of the Depression began to undermine some of the assumptions that made them seem true. In the 1920s and early 1930s, though, what was taken out into Melbourne's streets and lanes, played out in case notes, and written up for an audience of subscribers as the "truth about poverty" was a broader conviction about the links between character, judgment, and fortune. If you held it to be true, there could be little doubt that while there might be remedies for poverty, it was the lady detectives of the COS, and not the poor themselves, who were "specially fitted" to describe and define them, as well as to unmask those who did not deserve them.

. . . .

CHAPTER 5

There Are Those Who Feel Their Position

There was another kind of social work. It was used much less often, and it was reserved for those whose capacity to feel shame about their need—as well as the signs their bodies gave of respectable character—marked them out as immediately deserving. This was the way to avoid investigation, even by Agnes Cutler. If you truly "felt your position"—and perhaps one in every thirty or forty cases was understood in this way—the normal rigor of inquiries was reduced or even suspended. In April 1931, for instance, the Melbourne Hospital almoner referred the wife of a failed shopkeeper. "Upset at having to come to the COS," she was "in a pitiably nervy condition and extremely sensitive about her position.... There is no doubt of the truth of her story." Indeed, Cutler did not even check her references; her primary fear was that "Mrs B and her husband would probably suffer much unnecessary hardship in preference to calling for assistance." The COS provided cash and, in July, arranged for the entire family to stay rent-free at the home of Cutler's friend. This was a generosity far and above what could normally be afforded applicants but, as Cutler wrote to the almoner, "it is a particularly distressing [case], because [they] are refined and sensitive people, and not at all of the dependent type which we so often encounter."[78]

It is an interesting and telling phrase, which goes to the heart of assumptions about obligation, entitlement, and the continuing importance of "character" in interwar Melbourne. There was a simple proof that the shopkeeper's wife could be trusted: as the case notes repeated three times, she "felt her position." She was ashamed of her dependency. She deserved help, in other words, because she was shamed by her need for it, so shamed that she could hardly bear to ask. This was a powerful logic in the work of the COS. The "truly deserving" hardly ever asked for help. They waited for it and were discovered. Refined and superior people felt their position even before asking, while the respectable and deserving poor felt it during the compulsory interview or during the home visit. Others, "coarser" or "rough," did not; on occasion, they were encouraged to "feel their position" or sent away to "consider their feelings about their position." Or it was presumed that such feelings were in some way beyond them. The capacity to feel shame—to feel one's position—more or less mirrored a social hierarchy the COS investigators assumed to be first and foremost a measure of character, worth, and truthfulness.

In the 1920s and 1930s, the inquiry officers developed a form of social work that took clients at their word, trusted them to interpret and understand their situations, and relied on them to carry out plans. But it was provided to a relatively narrow social band and to people like themselves: shopkeepers, professionals, educated men and women, salesmen, and the occasional "gentleperson" down on his or her luck. These people had documents and papers and other marks of respectability. They wore their status in "refined" faces, "gentle" expressions, and "upright" postures. They experienced "genuine" feelings. The poor were sometimes "unconvincing" or "strangely indifferent," but their social betters "suffered keenly." They were also more likely to seek help well before problems turned into catastrophes; this, to the COS investigators, simply confirmed the intelligence and refinement that made them deserving in the first place. These investigators fundamentally misunderstood the role that charity played in the lives of the poor—who invariably avoided asking until their need was desperate—but they understood the emotional and material dimensions of need among their own kind.

In 1925 there was a "refined and most reliable couple" from respectable Armadale, the husband "a very sensitive man [who] appears to feel most acutely the necessity for applying for assistance." Here, "as the case was so obviously genuine, and applicant showed me papers which confirmed his statements, I did not consider it necessary to bother him about references."[79] In 1931 another applicant, a car driver and homeowner, was "a very decent man—he was most emphatic that he does not wish C.O.S. assistance—if the Lodge decide to discontinue allowance he will then be grateful for C.O.S. to assist." Cutler "could not have [been] impressed more favourably.... As the case was such a genuine one, I did not care to ask many pertinent questions."[80]

Showing sensitivity could also guarantee relatively rapid service. In July 1933 one unemployed motor driver was given an order for free spectacles without investigation; "he has not asked for charitable assistance before and feels his position" was all that Lillian Allen felt the need to write. In the case of another "exceptionally decent family," Agnes Cutler agreed that forgoing their piano was too great a sacrifice and recommended the funding of a surgical belt, and Ethel Brown interceded with the organizers of training classes to plead the case of "a superior type of woman [who] feels her present position keenly."[81] The COS could do little for a down-at-the-heels professor of foreign languages or his wife, "a charming little English-woman, very well-educated and well-spoken." Elizabeth Cathie did report that "he is so exceedingly well-educated, speaking 9 languages. We chattered a bit in French & personally he appealed to me as very genuine."[82] He eventually went to work on Melbourne's Shrine of Remembrance along with hundreds of other unemployed men.

This confidence in the veracity of those who visibly "felt their position" was very strong. It spoke to the investigators' faith in the straightforward match between personal qualities and social position. As Karen Halttunen and Janet McCalman have shown so powerfully in their respective studies of nineteenth-century America and twentieth-century Australia, character is one of the most important possessions of refined people. Although wealth and material comforts matter, a superior character is what underpins middle-class self-distinction. As Agnes Cutler and Celia Bedford wrote stories about "refined" and trustworthy applicants, they described what made those people recognizable and made other, "rougher" types distant and even unknowable. They exaggerated the differences and sharpened the boundaries between those who could and could not be trusted, and they wrote about—and acted out—the sense of affinity they clearly felt. Their encounter with the poor was shaped by strong expectations of difference. Case files were a place in which those differences could be explained, dramatized, and perhaps even enjoyed. As such, they tell us something very important about the mix of capacities and values their writers saw as constituting membership of their class (their absence, of course, denying it to others). These included good character, Protestant faith, and the virtues of self-restraint, thrift, and self-denial. Superior people also shared the investigators' general assumptions about the ways of the world, not least that people generally deserved what they were given, barring occasional tragedy. Perhaps the key differences between superior and inferior people, however, were captured in the idea that only the former "felt their position" and wanted to be self-reliant and independent. As such, of course, they could be given help without "undue investigation."

This was a sturdy faith. It needed to be, as the evidence of their own experience should have weakened the investigators' confidence. In the more than a thousand case files I have read, there are perhaps fifty or sixty in which investigation revealed and halted attempts to defraud the COS or another agency, every case involving a small amount of money or goods. There are only fifteen cases in which the COS was the victim of some kind of deception involving more than a few shillings. In every one, the COS was defrauded not by "dependent types" but by "sensitive people" who seemed to "feel their positions" and displayed "refined suffering." In most cases, this was not because their dissembling was remarkably adept but because Cutler, Brown, and the other investigators refused to press for details or embarrass people who were so "obviously refined." In 1925, for instance, "a superior type of man" was helped into a farming job; Secretary Smith was a little embarrassed when he promptly forged one of his employer's checks and left for Sydney. Another "sensitive man," who so "felt his position" that he cried, was given £5. He disappeared and was also rumored to be in Sydney (Melbourne people always assumed that Sydney was the obvious destination for cheats and liars, just as Bostonians always tended to picture their frauds heading down the highway toward New York City).[83]

The supposition that "superior types" could be trusted left the COS exposed to more than financial embarrassment. In 1932 Roy Thompson was referred to the COS by a smaller agency. He was visited by Agnes Cutler, who saw "photographs of all members of the family, and they seem to be of an exceptionally fine type." Because "there is no doubt the case is a very genuine and pleasing one," Thompson received a daily pint of milk and a weekly ration of one dozen eggs. Returning to the office six months later to request secondhand boots, he casually dropped into the conversation the fact that he was married and expressed surprise that the COS visitor had not asked about such an obvious matter during the initial investigation. Cutler was upset that he had questioned her methods in front of Secretary Smith; visiting again, she met his wife, Gloria, with her "very good teeth" (always suspicious in applicants) and "very strange evasive eyes." There was strong dislike—"she had been lying down when I called and appeared to be of a very lazy, apathetic type"—and this was also now extended to the applicant: "He impressed me as a very weak character. He looks extremely pale and I think that he trades on this when calling at houses [for work]."

For the next seven years, various investigators tracked Roy Thompson through churches and relief agencies, to all of which he offered the reassurance that he was "known by the COS" or "personally known to Mr Greig Smith." Invariably, their warnings came too late. The exasperated Agnes Cutler or Lillian Allen would locate his most recent address, there to find a "cabinet wireless" (Smith underlined that in the file) or "well-clothed children" and the applicant, with his "very smiling, plausible way." Visiting again in 1935, Cutler noted: "On his wife's dressing table there was also a photograph of applicant in which he looked well dressed and quite good looking. When I remarked about this he said it had been taken only a month ago! The expense of this photograph is typical of his selfishness and conceit." Even aggression failed to dent Thompson's "begging propensities" or Gloria's "stupidity": in 1937 she was "as uncommunicative as ever, volunteering no information. As a visitor from the Jewish Women's Guild was appalled by the poverty of the home, I decided to try and get into one room at least. . . . [She] then took me into the bedroom. The room was quite decently furnished. . . . Told [her] that she had better try and induce her husband to stop his begging tactics or the Police would probably get hold of him."

This was a man, Cutler wrote, "of extraordinary audacity." Charged with an assault in the Myer Emporium on Bourke Street, he then approached the Myer family for charity. He also did odd jobs for a city firm that was sent tickets for a charity ball; "the morning after the ball, [the organizers] phoned to ask who was the dreadful person whom they had sent to represent the firm. It finally transpired that [Thompson] had taken the tickets, hired or borrowed an evening suit, and gone to the ball. . . . This is characteristic of the man's colossal impudence."[84] Another possible moral of the story—that charity investigation could do little to prevent truly resourceful "mendicancy"—was never acknowledged. Rigorous inquiry never deterred Roy Thompson or their other fraudsters, but this never led the lady detectives or the COS officials to wonder about their conviction that it should.

For some applicants, even deceptiveness could be ignored. Agnes Cutler took great interest in the "most pitiable" case of Dorothy Holmes, who was widowed in 1933. Dorothy's husband, a returned soldier, was working on a relief project when he was "assaulted by strikers and cut about the face. Double pneumonia set in and he died." From the inception, the future of this client was ruled by Cutler's determination to always give "sympathetic consideration" to a case in which the husband's death "was due to him being attacked by militant strikers." Dorothy told Cutler that she could not pay the rent. At Cutler's urging, Smith organized for several weeks of rent to be paid by the Sustenance Branch. This was a very generous gesture; if there was one thing every applicant wanted, it was rent, but it was something very few received. It soon emerged that Dorothy was already receiving rent assistance from the Sustenance Branch at the time of her first meeting with the COS, but had neither paid her rent nor informed Cutler. "Perhaps she does not know," wrote Cutler in the case file, concurring with the department's view that "she is not the type who would attempt to mislead in any way." It was amazing forbearance in the context of Cutler's other cases.

Cutler continued visiting and helping through 1934 and 1935. She organized hampers of food, clothing, shoes, and toys for Dorothy, her daughter, and her two sons. When the Sustenance Branch decided to stop paying rent assistance in January 1934, Cutler intervened, reminding their social worker that Holmes "is not a grasping type of woman." The rent was still being paid in August 1936; she "impressed me most favourably as usual when seen this morning, tho' her rather simple way makes her case a little confusing at times." Confusing was perhaps a little generous. On two other occasions in 1937 and 1938, Cutler discovered that Holmes had been "overlapping"; although "I told her today that I was very disappointed that she had done so as the COS had always done everything possible to assist her," interest and support continued until she could no longer be located in 1942.[85]

Agnes Cutler's nurturing and dedicated response to Dorothy Holmes formed a kind of constructive, supportive social work that only a few COS clients received. That kind of social work recognized that people in desperate situations weren't always completely truthful. They might be overcome by anxiety or too frightened by the prospect of destitution to refuse help from different quarters, even if the COS defined it as "overlapping." They had no desire to be "grasping" or "dependent." They were nervous and desperate, and sometimes they felt defeated. Once listened to, and known, they could be trusted and become involved in determining their own destiny.

CHAPTER 6

But Most Will Never Better Themselves

There were very few Dorothy Holmeses. By focusing on the problem of mendicants, liars, and "poor social types," the COS developed an approach to poverty—and a story about poverty's origins and solutions—that ruled out constructive social work for most of the people it saw. By being too occupied by a fear of fraud, waste, and inefficiency and by emphasizing the discovery of an elusive "truth" based on impressions, appearances, and detection, the COS and its workers undermined their own capacity to care. Their work was made less effective by the emphasis on mistrust, checking, and verification. And the evidence of occasional fraud suggests that the tools and methods of charity investigation didn't work particularly well anyway; if people really wanted to get something for nothing, the COS workers' own assumptions and prejudices about the virtues of "refined people" made them relatively easy targets for those who could mimic "feeling their position." As Karen Halttunen argues, the reliance on character, and the conviction that their own truly respectable and refined characters could not be simulated, has always made middle-class people particularly susceptible to the confidence man, the trickster, and the hypocrite.[86]

The secretary and the inquiry officers of the COS could have drawn a number of conclusions from their failures as well as from their successes. One was that they sometimes trusted and mistrusted the wrong people for the wrong reasons and that all the time and effort spent on detection— often, of course, at the behest of equally distrusting agencies—might have been better spent on fulfilling their ambitions of "modern social case work." Nothing in that precluded either reasonable investigation or stern responses to actual fraud or deception. But the COS, and especially its secretary and Executive Committee, always found it difficult to grasp the potential and actual contradiction between its service to subscribers who were not poor—"the skilled investigation of the circumstances of applicants"—and its commitment to appropriate and adequate aid for those who were.[87]

Charity investigation—like every other kind of welfare practice based on distrust—also tended to produce the very problems it feared. In the case of the COS, this was in part because the investigative process took so much time. As Margaret Baker or Dorothy Macdonald checked the details of individuals' stories, rang various agencies and charities, and located— or sometimes failed to locate—the applicant's house after a tram ride to Fitzroy or Richmond or North Melbourne, many of the clients accused of "overlapping" or "applying to multiple agencies" were simply trying to find a solution to pressing problems. Although the COS recognized this, and sometimes gave applicants grocery orders, old clothing, a blanket, or even a little cash, they nonetheless seemed to expect their applicants to then suspend all dealings with other agencies until details had been checked, advice given, and plans made. They seemed not to understand the ways in which people who lived close to the edge of penury could be tumbled over it by a small accident, a day's lost wages, a sick child, or a bad decision. They didn't grasp that poorer women, in particular, were often in need because they were undermined by the irregularity and insufficiency of men's earnings or by a man's unwillingness to provide.[88] They misunderstood the ways in which people vulnerable to poverty used and understood charity as one kind of temporary resource rather than their only option and the ways in which the desire for self-reliance could make people wait too long before seeking assistance. By assuming there was something different and inferior about the characters of the people they encountered, differences that would be "revealed" by their bodies and gestures if not by their words, most of the inquiry officers failed to understand what they shared with them. Exaggerated distance undermined the potential for care and especially collaboration.

The focus on dependency and falsehood had another outcome, too. It made people lie. Indeed, it drew out the very performances and "simulations" the COS most feared, and it ensured that most conversations were guarded and staged rather than honest and open. Because the inquiry agent's decision relied so much on a "science" of impressions, nuances, and inflections, applicants tried hard to give the right impression and "appear" to be deserving or honest or respectable. Welfare based on distrust always encourages people to portray themselves as strong, capable, and determined. It encourages them to hide part of the truth about their poverty. It brings forth stories about endurance, heroism, and undeserved suffering, keeping secret the complications that are part and parcel of lived deprivation and discouraging a more honest exchange about poverty's origins and effects. In Melbourne between the wars, charity organization focused attention on "imposture" rather than on the dependency that stemmed from frailty, confusion, weakness, and resignation. Most of all, it hid the fact that at least some of the people in the COS waiting room were probably not capable of independence, at least not there and then. They needed help, and perhaps they needed someone to just give them something. They were ill and felt defeated. Poverty had rubbed away their certainties and dimmed their hopes. They lacked the strength to fight. Some were consumed by grievances and demons they couldn't overcome. Others, I think, just wanted to talk and have someone listen, perhaps to feel, for just a few minutes, that they mattered. Too often, the fear that they might be considered liars or "useless" stilled their tongues. They had to be "bright and brave," as one inquiry officer put it, and "show some steel."[89] They had to be grateful and watch every word.

I think Agnes Cutler, Lillian Allen, Ethel Brown, and the other investigators wanted to help. They were trying to provide care in a difficult situation. Even if they weren't angels of mercy, it does them no justice to portray them simply as agents of denial. But their situation was made harder, not easier, by the task the COS had set itself and to which it clung, with some tenacity, through the 1930s. In the end, prejudices and assumptions put the brake on any aspirations for that "fine, long-visioned scheme of adequate and appropriate relief" Smith once shared with his readers in the *Other Half*.[90]

What is perhaps most striking about Melbourne's dramas, though, especially in comparison to the American examples that will follow, is the extent to which this was a dramatization of poverty in which the characters and the script remained fixed. Melbourne's theater was in that sense closer to London than Boston or Minneapolis. There were rough people and refined people, "battlers" and "beggars," those who were self-reliant and those who were feckless and grasping. On this stage, the actors' bodies, gestures, and possessions would always reveal their "true selves." Inferior people might cloak themselves in falsehood, and superior people might for a moment be unidentifiable in scruffy clothes, but trained inquiry— and "wise discrimination"—would soon separate the deserving from the undeserving.

The drama of charity investigation in Melbourne, at least until the 1930s, did not focus on change or uplift or transformation but on revelation and judgment. Certainly, the discovery of flaws might sometimes change behavior and lead to self-improvement, but this was not always true, and it was not in any event the core of the story. The triumphs in Melbourne's dramas about poverty were of truth revealed and pauperism prevented, not the sufferer transformed. It was sometimes possible to lessen the number of the "socially dependent," but "often, nothing better than palliative measures are practicable."[91] Reading these hundreds of case files as a shared and developing story about poverty, especially in light of the stories that were being written in Boston and Minneapolis, is to read about the need to protect respectable Melburnians from deficiencies that the poor might struggle against but could rarely overcome. In other words, the deficiencies of character were not only difficult to hide but just as difficult to change.

During the 1920s, the inquiry officers, agents, and visitors of Melbourne, London, Boston, Minneapolis, and Oregon would have agreed that the poor were inferior. In Melbourne, Boston, and Minneapolis, they would also have agreed that the poor had to change in ways that made them more like the caseworkers themselves. Where they differed was in analyzing the nature and means of that transformation. In the American cities, it was usually the "ignorance" or "race" of the poor that mattered, and by "race" Americans meant nationality and ethnicity; the agents and visitors tended to assume, however, that at least some of the poor could gain insight, even lose their "race," and become more American. In Melbourne, where a hierarchy of class based on character was the primary focus, few of the poor would or could ever better themselves. Whatever the debates about education, social improvement, and reform that had shaped social attitudes in Australia in the previous two or three generations, the dramatization of poverty in these case files tended to portray the poor as a class apart. It might be a class on the move, perhaps, and needing a good deal more investigation than was true in London, but apart nonetheless.

This made the Melbourne caseworkers less optimistic than their counterparts in Boston and Minneapolis, but it also softened the scale and nature of their interventions. Despite its emphasis on prevention and waging a war against mendicancy, the work of the COS was rarely directly punitive, and revelation of lies and secrets did not always preclude the provision of some help. Though the poor could change aspects of their behavior, and understand their positions more honestly, there seemed little point in expecting too much or anticipating that they could be easily rid of the faults that produced and explained their struggles. There are very few references to the kinds of techniques and interventions more common in the United States—a 1930 article supporting the referral of particular cases to "specialists in mental hygiene" was never reflected in practice—and there is no mention whatsoever of eugenic principles or ideas.[92] Even if eugenics enthused some of Melbourne's professional elite during the 1930s, it had little effect and influence on the daily business of social work.

In the minds of these Melbourne caseworkers, the origins of poverty could always be traced to some combination of character and circumstances. By the early 1930s, those circumstances were certainly worse, but the poor seemed more helpless and ungrateful too; a report from a caseworker conference in early 1931 noted general agreement that "a definite lowering of tone was noticeable in some industrial areas since the introduction of the Unemployment Relief Act," while there were also warnings of "a marked increase in imposition on benevolent citizens" and a "growing tide of dependency" in 1930 and 1932.[93] A 1931 article in the *Other Half* recognized that "the financial and industrial depression had brought many troubles in its train"; the one it highlighted was "a great increase in mendicancy [as] Melbourne is riddled these days with beggars and cadgers of all types and ages" and "infested" with begging children.[94] In the theater of poverty and inequality written by these Melbourne social workers, the flaws of the poor were not easily overcome, at least until the Depression began to disrupt the script.

· ·

CHAPTER 7

A Growing Sense of Justice

In March 1931, Stanley Greig Smith wrote an article for Melbourne's popular conservative newspaper, the *Argus*. "A Plea for the Workless" offered a solution to unemployment—"let men and women get back to work on whatever conditions industry claims to be able to offer"—that few in the labor movement would have found palatable. But his account of Melbourne's suffering was one of the strongest he had ever written:

Hundreds—nay, thousands—of the unemployed are not of the work-shirking, work-refusing, communistic, anti-social type. They are the decent, law-abiding, home building and church-going citizens with whom we all brush shoulders in trams and trains every day. Most of them are eager for work, which prevailing conditions deny to them, and they are passing through a vale of suffering and sorrow which, it is much to be feared, will have a serious effect upon social conditions for years to come. Government sustenance, relief works, and voluntary charity are powerless to stem the tide of hardship, eviction, and homelessness which is sweeping over Melbourne today.[95]

From a sense of profound crisis came further changes in the society's stories. In 1934 the *Other Half* approvingly reprinted a circular from the

New York State Department of Public Welfare that emphasized welfare's responsibility for people who were in need "through no fault of their own," reminded its workers to "let no trace of superiority or condescension creep into your manner or bearing ... [as] there is no disgrace in asking for help when it is needed," and concluded that "relief investigators are not detectives."[96] Most striking of all was a 1936 article that described sustenance as a "hurt to the soul" and noted "a growing sense of social justice" before dedicating social workers to "an earnest effort to ensure that the disasters which have happened to tens of thousands of citizens during the past six years will not continue to happen."[97] For an organization so devoted to highlighting flaws of character and behavior, it was an amazing statement. "Social justice" and "disaster": these were not words that the Charity Organisation Society would have used five or six years before. Even the distance between the "decent citizens" of 1931 and the simple "citizens" of 1934 tells us something of the journey it was making.

Two years later, in the middle of 1936, Stanley Greig Smith addressed the Charity Organisation Society Council in London. The council had recently discussed the theme "COS at the Crossroads," further strengthening a debate about the society's future that would continue into the next decade. Smith certainly listened, and he kept listening; by the early 1940s, his emerging plans for his own COS, which would in 1946 become the Citizens Welfare Service (CWS), closely followed those being suggested in London by Eileen Younghusband and others. In the middle of the 1930s, the Melbourne society was not yet canvassing its future in quite the same dramatic terms, but it was discussing novel ideas and words.

Like most Australians, whether or not they were born overseas, Smith was a close follower of trends in Britain and the United States, and he was especially influenced by the British debate about preserving the COS's particular contributions as governments more or less reluctantly accepted the call for greater public investment in welfare. Like some of his counterparts in London, he had begun to realize that "the matter [for] ... immediate and urgent consideration" was not how to prevent the growth of public welfare but "the clear definition of the respective spheres of public and voluntary agencies."[98] The relationship would demand vigilance. But Smith was certain that the COS, with its knowledge based on close experience with "the socially inadequate and inefficient," could provide new public bodies with the expertise and "skilled social workers" they would need.[99]

Yet the changes in the Charity Organisation Society were also led in part by the women with whom Smith worked, whose writing began to explore somewhat different genres as the Depression hardened. And they, in turn, were using words and concepts they had partly learned from the poor. The responses of these women to the economic disaster of the 1930s, and their proximity to its human costs, shifted how they wrote their stories. It wasn't all or nothing. The theater of poverty in Melbourne would continue to feature Agnes Cutler's detective dramas, and the COS continued to doubt the effectiveness of public relief and government intervention without a degree of investigation.[100] But just as they had played a particularly important role in developing a story about poverty based on character, the inquiry officers of the COS were equally as important in unraveling some of its threads and questioning some of its assumptions. As frontline workers in an agency that dealt with all kinds of difficulties and disasters, they found themselves in more and more situations that confronted rather than confirmed the comfortable division of the poor into deserving and undeserving. Perhaps their own vulnerabilities as female workers—symbolized in pay cuts and mounting caseloads—heightened their capacity for alternative stories and their willingness to listen to and even learn from poorer Melburnians, especially poorer women. It was hesitant. There was no sudden shift. But here, at the heart of scientific charity, and because women were listening to other women, what the poor actually said began to matter just a little more.

What the poor said hadn't changed that much. They stressed the central problem of uncertain wages and unemployment, as they had always. They talked about disaster and circumstance. They emphasized how hard it was to exist on the meager sustenance payments or the pension, and they emphasized the Depression's cruel combinations of joblessness, eviction, and never-ending anxiety. Whole families were without work, so grandparents struggled to help grandchildren, brothers tried to relieve the burdens on married sisters, men left home tramping for work, and people turned to whatever resources they could find. The COS workers heard things that shook them: pensioners who could not afford to light a fire and wanted a coat in which to sleep, or a couple who had sold all of their furniture save for one bed in order to pay the rent. And they listened.

In Melbourne, applicants had always struggled against the logic that in a new and vigorous society poverty signaled individual rather than collective failure. This was a long-established feature of Australian understandings of charity and welfare, in which visions of the "real" poverty of old-world Britain and even crowded immigrant America were deployed to refute the claim that Australia had any poverty of its own. In the 1920s, Melbourne applicants were defensive in their descriptions of poverty's causes and very careful to distinguish themselves from the unrespectable. Conscious of the Charity Organisation Society's reputation and mission, perhaps, they struggled to find words that would indicate need without appearing too needy. The theater of poverty in Melbourne was a particularly difficult and demanding one for the poor. They lacked powerful allies, and they faced a welfare system in which the protection of male breadwinners tended to impoverish the old, the infirm, and single women. The greater hesitancy of Melbourne's poor might also reflect the role the COS played in the city's welfare system; a bad reputation there could have serious ramifications in many other places, from government departments and the sustenance authorities to the hospital almoners and infant care nurses.

Still, the Depression changed what it was important—and perhaps possible—to say. Women emphasized the hardness of the persistent struggle and were more likely to question the interpretations and priorities of the inquiry officers. The mother of a young man suffering from encephalitis became very emotional during her 1931 interview, partly out of grief for her son and partly over being called "not very provident" by a hospital almoner; as she suggested to the COS visitor, her son had been ill for more than six years, and because her daughter's husband had lost his job they were also helping her with food and clothes for the three grandchildren. Her own husband, who had worked in the same job for thirty years, had been thrown out of work three weeks earlier. She tried to convey to visitor Margaret Baker, with some success, how hard it was to be "provident" when an entire extended family was leaning on you.[101]

Quietly, but persistently, impoverished women insisted on their own explanations. They tried to show their visitors that poverty was a disaster. They emphasized how their bodies, not their characters, had failed them. They showed the power of circumstances that were beyond control. They talked about bad luck, "broken time" at work, accidents that couldn't be predicted, and consequences that couldn't be managed. They emphasized that they were put off work with hundreds of others or related how all of Melbourne's clothing pieceworkers were dumped at the same time in 1931. They also talked about a social system that didn't keep its promises about effort, sacrifice, and reward. They talked about insecurity and how close they always were to trouble. They showed the workers how disadvantage accumulated: an injured husband, a son in an asylum, a daughter's child sick with the whooping cough, a landlord who wouldn't wait any longer for the rent. It was all very well to talk about the need for plans and independence, but with six children, an unemployed husband, and a tumbledown tenement, that would have to wait.

In the midst of a crisis no one seemed sure would end, women also continued to reject plans and strategies that offended their sense of obligation to others. They refused to share their homes with strangers or go out to work when children or invalids needed care. This determination had long been a feature of conflicts between inquiry officers and applicants. One woman was told to go to work because none of her children were babies, but she argued that she "could not look after her children properly while doing the half day's work she used to do." Nor did she want to take in a lodger.[102] Mavis Williams, a mother of two children with an ill and unemployed husband, was not keen to take on more work than the few days a week she did as a cleaner at a hotel. Agnes Cutler's view was clear: "It is clearly the wife's duty to do something to help her husband. She has no young children, and is a woman of very good appearance who would find no difficulty in getting a decent position. She admitted that she was quite strong in every way, and that her husband would not object to her working, but the idea of doing so has apparently no appeal to her, and I told her that no society would help her if she made no attempt to help herself and her husband in some way."[103]

Whether or not this view was reasonable, Mavis Williams and others were within their rights to be a little confused by the mixed messages that often came from agencies, public relief authorities, and benevolent visitors. A woman in the inner suburb of Richmond, for example, showed little interest in letting rooms, despite Lillian Allen's encouragement; the house had five rooms, but she had an invalid husband whose disability was not severe enough to qualify for the pension, a two-year-old son, and a "delicate" baby who, it later emerged, was suffering from serious spinal deformities.[104] One can imagine what another charity investigator might have thought of a woman with a seriously ill husband and child who was running a lodging business and taking strangers into the home.

Poor women also contrasted their own steadfastness and sense of principle with that of governments, the rich, and employers. They did not do this directly, in the way that men sometimes clumsily did, but by implication. They described the generosity of their neighbors and families, most of whom had very little, praising someone as "a 'well living woman' who was always willing to help a neighbour whenever she had anything to help with" and—it was hinted—not asking inappropriate and foolish questions first.[105] They insisted on the unquestioning nature of some forms of support, such as by parents for children or by Catholic agencies or the Salvation Army, contrasting this with the equivocal care of the state or the COS. Asked why she had already spent one grocery order, a Melbourne mother explained: "The baby's food had to be procured on the grocery order as she must have sufficient food, even if the parents have to go short."[106] In one long-running Melbourne case, COS workers were critical of a woman, Isabella Davis, who protected and shielded her alcoholic son because, as Agnes Cutler put it, "if he had to battle for himself a little more he would have to suffer hardships for the folly of his ways." Gerald Davis was "unemployable" by 1936, but his mother continued to give him a home, provide him with meals, and bring him back from the hospital. She died in 1938, and Gerald eventually joined the army and served in the Middle East; Isabella's thoughts were never recorded in the case file, but from the accounts given of her principles, she simply held that her son, whom she believed had been fated to alcoholism by his heavy-drinking father, had to be looked after. She refused to have him certified or committed. The file suggests that although Gerald found it difficult to keep a job, he was never violent or abusive and suffered a great deal of anguish at his mother's death. The COS focused on his "uselessness." Isabella focused on a simple fact: her only son needed her care.[107]

The evidence of the case files is that applicants were able to influence at least some of the inquiry officers who heard their explanations. We can't always know exactly what they said, but even if their words emerge only through the transforming prism of the worker's narrative, we can trace something of their imprint and their effect. By the late 1920s, and even more during the early 1930s, those working along the borders of class began to explore some relatively new ways of writing about inequality. Once the "hard economic times" of 1928 and 1929 turned into the "general depression" of the early 1930s, they were more drawn toward ideas about disaster and fate. Words such as "poverty," "helpless," "distressed," and "unfortunate" became more frequent, and terms common in the 1920s—such as "shiftless," "pauper," and "plausible"—were used less often. The idea that character or self-reliance was sufficient protection against disaster, an idea that the poor had always questioned, lost some of its reassuring persuasiveness.

Three responses were common. One was to take more of what poor people said at face value and to simply give them what they wanted. Rather than masking a desire for dependency, a request for firewood might simply be a request for firewood, born of actual need and able to be met immediately. As the number of cases increased, mothers, the elderly, and invalids usually received automatic help, especially if it was relatively cheap and straightforward. Another group—single men—were invariably given nothing, as the COS tried to move away from providing for the "drifters and wanderers," people the *Other Half* described in 1934 as "the bugbear of the social worker."[108] Rigorous investigation, costly in time and effort, was directed toward those who deserved some attention and might be redeemed.

A second response was more despondent. There was a growing sense that for a good many of the poor, little could be done and little expected.

As Lillian Allen said of one case in 1927, an invalid pensioner who "finds it hard to struggle along" and could not keep a job: "I explained to her [that] her position has been the same for years now and will never better itself."[109] During the 1920s, the most telling tales were sudden tragedies that began with the death of children or husbands or the continuing echoes of the First World War. It became more common in 1930 and 1931 for inquiry officers—even Agnes Cutler—to write of applicants having a "hard past" and to emphasize the long-term and more mundane suffering of people who "haven't had much chance in life."[110]

Increasingly, applicants were seen as the hapless victims of overwhelming forces, and there was a growing tendency to identify those forces in economic terms. Social work intervention could not by itself prevent dependency or disaster. In a way, this meant being more honest about the sheer weight of the world for vulnerable people. In 1931, to take one example, the COS began helping a couple with whom they would remain in contact for two decades, in large part because, by 1949, the Harrisons had eighteen children. The family survived various catastrophes—including the mother's frequent miscarriages, the loss of their belongings to thieves, and the father's chronic stomach troubles—and were also the recipients of some unhelpful government interventions, including an unworkable South Gippsland block of land through the Unemployed Land Settlement Scheme. They always needed blankets and bedding and, not surprisingly, children's clothing and footwear. The father worked when he could. As Agnes Cutler wrote, "One has only to talk to him for a while to realize that he is a man of decent character, good to his wife and children." And as Lillian Allen later commented, "They are quite decent but likely to be always more or less dependent on State and voluntary charity."[111] They were never really investigated; they, like another couple seen in 1933, were simply "average lower class working people suffering from the effects of the depression and thereby in need of our assistance."[112] In similar vein, Cutler reported of another "rather ignorant" woman whose husband had gone rabbit trapping despite his asthma and whose two children were ill with epilepsy and a thyroid complaint that "she appears to have had a very hard time" and was "looking old & worn for her years." The couple, she wrote, "appear to pull together as well as possible in their distressed circumstances."[113] In a very real way, this was not what the COS meant by expert casework. This was more like the humdrum work of material relief. But as the annual number of cases soared above two thousand, it was the work the COS found itself called on to do.

The third response was more akin to protective advocacy. It continued the kind of care and attention given to those who "felt their position," but it developed a somewhat more universal focus and a greater emphasis on seeing the world, at least in part, through the eyes of the applicant. This meant collaboration, taking people more at their word and placing some faith in clients' capacities. Those assisted in this way were always women—the female inquiry officers of Melbourne rarely forgave men for their failings—and usually either young single girls or mothers. In 1931 Agnes Cutler befriended a young woman, Gloria Simms, cut adrift from her family; although she was "a poor little waif and a girl with foolish ideas where men are concerned," Cutler also argued that "she seems, so far, to have had very little chance in life." The best Cutler could do was to ask a sympathetic landlady to "safeguard" Gloria, but she continued to check on her progress.[114] In several cases from the 1930s, COS inquiry officers acted as advocates for women being "harshly" or "unjustly" treated by their local sustenance authorities or private loan providers. Earlier that year, Ethel Brown was able to prove to the Sustenance Branch that a mother from Carlton was being unjustly charged with fraud; the department claimed her married son lived at home and contributed from his earnings as a butcher, but COS investigations showed he did neither.[115]

In the midst of so many cases and concerns, it is impressive that any applicant received such protective and prolonged advocacy. There was a different tone to some of these 1930s cases, which stemmed in part from the recognition that people's tangled lives and circumstances could make it almost impossible for them to make wise plans or good decisions. During 1932 Cutler counseled another young woman, Celia Stratton, who had run away from home; the North Melbourne police reported that "she had been quite justified in going away from her home as her parents were no good, the mother being a chronic drunkard and the father having been convicted of street betting, and each associating with people of ill-repute." Cutler investigated and found that Celia's "parents" were actually her aunt and uncle. Her father was dead, and her mother disappeared shortly after her birth. Neighbors reported that the uncle regularly beat his wife, who regularly beat Celia; with Secretary Smith's help, she was granted sustenance, but then used the freedom of a small income to attend "very common dances" at various halls in Swanston and Lygon Streets. Cutler intervened. Celia was reminded to seek healthy amusements, preferably through the Club for Workless Girls. Once she had found a job, working as a waitress in a Lonsdale Street café, she came into the COS office once a week to place part of her earnings into a savings account. But Cutler also defended Celia, especially when a landlady accused the girl of theft and being "mixed up with various men." Cutler argued that there was no evidence to sustain such a charge. Nine months after first coming to the attention of the COS,

Celia eventually took a job at the seaside town of Sorrento, and she did not appear again in their files. Cutler thought her a "strange character," but Celia's last letter suggests something of the care the older woman took: "I do not think at any time that one older than myself preaches to me, [as] I like to hear them speaking to me of things that they consider good for me. And I am always ready to hear what they have to say."[116]

Though the Depression picked off and hurt more of the people the COS workers could recognize as their own "type," Cutler, Brown, Allen, and the others also built a new kind of relationship with poorer and more vulnerable women. They were moved by something, and their sense of the injustices in the world was strengthened by what they heard. In these few cases, I think, lay their attempts to endorse a view of poverty as a form of vulnerability in which remedies might lie not just in the transformation of individuals but also in reforms to some of the general, structural problems that impoverished poor women. They never doubted that even these women needed their advice and their guidance, and they didn't necessarily rule out the need for further investigation. This was not yet a social work based on the client's perspective. But it was a social work that was beginning to take context and circumstance more seriously. Its exemplary stories began to speak of a disaster that must never be allowed to happen again.

Of course, they did not all head in one direction. Hindsight always make changes in understandings of poverty and need look sharper and more deliberate than they really were. In the midst of the Depression, these women struggled to identify explanations that would fit with their changing experiences. Some workers at most times and most workers at some times resorted to an explanation of inferiority being rooted in the bad characters of the poor; the faith in detection as a deterrent didn't disappear, though it became a less automatic supposition. Of course, advocacy had its clumsy moments. "A community which is seriously concerned with the uplift of its socially and industrially maladjusted units," suggested the *Other Half* in 1934, "should do something better for them than leave them to the precarious, haphazard and character-destroying doles of indiscriminate givers."[117] Even in 1939, with the miseries of the Depression lessened but by no means resolved, Smith's verbal report to his Executive Committee included the assessment that "the city was swarming with men who were besieging charitable agencies, missions and private citizens." Arguing that perhaps half of these men "were not genuine workers," he continued: "Those who were genuine were suffering from the actions of the unhelpables or unemployables who were exploiting the situation to the full."[118] There was also a kind of maudlin despair, best illustrated in an excerpt from "a social worker's notebook" in the *Other Half*: "Their names were given as Daphne, Rose and Violet. Their mother explained, with a vague, elusive smile that revealed faint traces of past attractiveness in her now apathetic face, that 'she used to love flowers when she was a girl.' If only she had been born with that intelligence that prevents so many brave-hearted women from sinking beneath the heavy load of long years of poverty and hardships, how fragrant and lovely could her own human flowers have been!"[119]

Writing up cases for publicity always carried the risk of bad prose. But it should not blind us to the fact that the conversation about poverty in Melbourne began to use or at least to grasp words and concepts that would never have been used in the 1920s, words and concepts that Melbourne's female inquiry officers and charity investigators had learned at least partly from the poor. Based in part on what some women said and what these other, professional women began to hear and understand, the theater laid out in the case record began to explore some different dénouements. Some workers dramatized unresolved problems and intractable dependencies. All were more accepting of the limits of investigation and intervention, more true to what poorer applicants said about the weight of the world. They portrayed empathy and advocacy. Most of all, they began to understand—and in some cases to insist—that character was no defense against disaster.

. . . .

CHAPTER 8

The Citizens' Welfare

The Charity Organisation Society seemed to be drifting by the 1930s, with no clear sense of where it was heading or even of how to consider and debate that question. Smith came back from London and followed with great interest British discussions about renaming and reorganizing. But a lack of money and the persistently high caseloads made it difficult for the COS to continue its publicity and propaganda work. The *Other Half* folded in early 1937. As the war began in 1939, Smith was anxious to grasp the opportunities war might afford, and he ensured the COS worked with the service welfare associations and the Repatriation Commission. He was also wary of possible challenges. As he reminded the Executive Committee, "Certain activities in Melbourne indicated the growth of a competitive tendency in the family case-work field," and there was a "need for watchfulness in the matter of new war activities."[120] But in 1940, even if there was no longer an old way, the new way remained very unclear.

For the COS, and for many of Melbourne's poor, world war changed everything. In Australia no less than in other combatant nations, the shock of war dramatically expanded the tasks people imagined governments could and should do, and it helped empower and fund governments to do them. The effects on private charities were dramatic; the COS took on more than 2,200 new cases in 1938–39, but only 1,389 in 1941–42, 832 in 1944–45, and 662 in 1946–47, when most were referrals from service organizations and connected to the temporary, if complicated, problems of demobilization. The COS played a key role in developing university training, but this shift also meant it would play less part in preparing the next generation of social workers. To Smith, the problem for the COS was where its future might lie after the balance between public welfare and private charity shifted decisively toward the former. A long-time critic of the poor standards of casework in public agencies, the COS would have to forge a new relationship with them in the postwar world.

Things also changed in Melbourne's streets and lanes. Just as the war created new versions of older problems—hasty marriages and desertions, inadequate child care for working women, and a severe shortage of housing—wartime mobilization and a relatively buoyant postwar economy washed away much unemployment and poverty. There were people of whom COS investigators had once despaired, the "unemployables," "chronic loafers," and families of whom "nothing much can be expected." Frequent visitors for assistance in the 1920s and 1930s, some of them becoming "almost like friends" through the regularity of their need, disappeared during the war. Investigators sometimes came upon them again during their visits to other clients in the 1940s and 1950s. They were no longer in need. They had decent, secure work. Their husbands had stopped tramping and were earning regular wages on the tramways or the railways. Their sons had been in the army and had learned to drive a truck or use electronic equipment and were working for the Postmaster-General's Department or in factories and warehouses. They'd moved into public housing or had rent control. Enjoying their greater distance from disaster, they didn't need help anymore, especially from a private charity.

There were still poor and vulnerable Melburnians, but they were often people the COS assumed should be the focus of other agencies. There were significant numbers of deserted mothers, as well as tenants "decanted" from condemned houses into temporary camps. As caseloads mounted again in the 1940s and 1950s, the most frequent cases were homeless alcoholic men, or the "workless," some with severe physical ailments and others with illnesses of the mind. By the early 1950s, they made up half the caseload, and in 1953, the Executive Committee ruled that no further help was to be given to "homeless, workless, single men."[121] But in deciding to leave aside its single largest group of clients, the agency raised new questions about its role and purpose in Melbourne.

During the war, the COS discussed a change of name. Smith first raised the idea in 1939, and it was discussed again in 1942. As was also true in London, "the common dislike of the word 'Charity'" was the trigger, but the shift was meant to signify more than that.[122] As mentioned in the previous chapter, in 1946 the COS renamed itself the Citizens Welfare Service, a name also mooted for the London body but rejected there in favor of the Family Welfare Association. The new service hoped to emphasize family counseling and situations in which "material aid, if necessary at all, may only be a minor factor."[123]

The discussions in 1945 and 1946 help us understand just what had been forged in the transition from detective work to advocacy and protection. The impact of wartime mobilization, full employment, and public provision in the 1940s convinced everyone that a different kind of welfare service was possible. By 1946 the Executive Committee—which had always seen change as risky—was insisting that "we should aim at even better case-work" and "should spend even more freely to achieve constructive ends."[124] Ever mindful of the possibilities for expansion, Smith was pushing the new service even further, recommending four functions in 1948 (delivering skilled casework, providing information, promoting cooperation, and developing student training), adding an "efficient migrant welfare service" in 1949 and, in 1950, suggesting close involvement with citizens advice bureaus and specialized child placement.[125]

There were new voices. Joyce Sambell was hired as field work supervisor in 1947, and a younger man arrived as an assistant and understudy to the secretary. Yet the CWS did not flourish. It struggled to find a place in the dramatically changed welfare landscape, at least until a new generation of social workers swept into and across Melbourne in the 1950s. For the CWS, a new role would be engineered by Leonard Tierney, the director of Social Work and Research from 1954 on, by social workers such as Kathleen Foley, and by new members of its executive branch, especially academic Ruth Hoban. Tierney, having advised the committee that "the old fashioned approach to families in need was not acceptable to modern thought," developed a focus on family work, research, and cooperation with other agencies, such as the Brotherhood of St. Laurence. Smith retired with a generous annuity in 1957. By the early 1960s, when it took advantage of new federal government funding to move squarely into marriage and family counseling, the CWS was no longer a dominant force in Melbourne's welfare debates. It became an important but smaller agency, specialized around a particular contribution.

There is more to be said about the changes that followed the 1930s, which reflected the impact of the war and relative prosperity on organizations such as the COS and the society's own shift, in the middle of the 1940s, to a rather different conception of its relationship to citizens and their welfare. The case files of those years exist, and they await their historians. So do other welfare traditions. Although the COS opens a window onto the lived history of class and welfare in twentieth-century Melbourne, there is much it doesn't show. It played a particular role among a particular group of Melbourne's disadvantaged citizens, and it saw them through a particular lens. It was Protestant in a city with many Catholics, and there are many conversations about class, inequality, and welfare we will never hear in its files. The point of my story is not that the COS was the only scriptwriter in Melbourne's theater of poverty and inequality. It wasn't. But if the period of the 1920s and 1930s represents a particularly pivotal time in the history of that theater, a time when what seemed solid crumbled in the face of crisis, it is significant that some of the first, hesitant whispers about injustice can be heard here, unexpectedly, in the home of detection and distrust.

Certainly, social workers in Boston and Minneapolis were moved and challenged by the Depression; the crisis in Minneapolis was perhaps as stark as in Melbourne, for instance. In London, where the slump was less dramatic and more associated with "outer England," Scotland, and Wales, the connection between poverty, vulnerability, and disaster was finally clarified by the war's assault on the city. Melbourne's workers moved farther than the Americans and earlier than the Londoners. This was partly because their economic whirlwind was stronger; however brave and successful the struggle seemed in memory some forty or fifty years later, people's accounts at the time make clear the bewildering speed and the terrible scope of the Depression's insecurities in Melbourne. But it was also because the emphasis on detection had left Melbourne's workers especially exposed. Their faith in the real and unshakable differences between the deserving and the undeserving and their belief that poverty's origins could always be found in the deficiencies of the poor were particularly unhelpful in the midst of a general economic crisis.

The women of the Charity Organisation Society had always struggled with difficult questions and dilemmas. They feared dependency but didn't realize that the great majority of the poor had no desire to be dependent or that sometimes people needed to be carried for a while before they could find their feet again. Theirs was a clumsy science. It was damaging for what it did to people in need. It was damaging as well for what it forced Melbourne's early welfare workers to do, for the care it undermined and the relationships it marred. Yet those women also showed an ability to listen to another way of talking about poverty, which some of their clients had always tried to share with them. Even though we can wonder at the tenacity with which a few held firm to failing explanations, we must also recognize the courage with which others began to question and even replace them.

Part Two

LONDON

CASE 2

Miss Hedges and the Stupid Client

Dramatis Personæ

DOROTHY HEDGES, a charity visitor
LILLIAN GOLDING, a pregnant housewife
ELSIE, her friend

· · · · · · · · · · · · · · DRAMA · · · · · · · · · · · · · ·

1 November 1935

This flat was almost impossible to find. Mrs. Golding is 28 years of age. Her husband is 25, and a porter at the markets, but has been out of work for over a year. There is a daughter, five years, a son, four years and currently in Fulham Hospital, and another son between two and three years of age. Mrs. Golding is pregnant and expecting to be confined early next year. One enters into a dreadful front room. A line of dreadful looking washing was hung across the street in the pouring rain. Mrs. Golding wants to redeem some bedclothes held in pawn, though it was hard to fathom why she had pawned them in the first place. She is a most untidy woman, obviously of very low mentality. She is quite haggard and very poor. I discussed the case with Miss Moore. The committee decided that the bedclothes can be redeemed but only if Mrs. Golding will go to the hospital for her confinement and agrees not to bring the boy aged four home from the hospital. She seems to have an unreasoning fear of hospitals & is really too stupid to invent a logical basis for it. She doesn't seem very happy with this conclusion.

Dorothy Hedges

"Elsie, what do you think? I didn't like the way she spoke to me at all. Not the first time, nor this time. First time she was all a-flutter. Couldn't find the place, she says. Directions weren't right, she says." Lillian Golding draws herself up in her chair and lifts her head so she can look down her nose at her neighbor. Pursing her lips and lifting her voice a few notes into a whine, she mimics the just-departed charity visitor. "I am afraid, Mrs. Golding, that my directions are not entirely exact, and I do not know the area exceedingly well."

Elsie chuckles and takes a sip from her tea. "Wonder what area she does know well, eh, Lil?"

"Not the Hammersmith Road, that's for certain." She shifts in the wooden chair and grimaces.

"You're looking tired, love. Put your feet up later, at least for a bit, do you good. It's not easy when you're carrying."

"It's a a kicker, this one. Must be another boy. They don't half kick, and that's the truth."

Elsie nods. "My Ernie just about kicked his way out, Lil. Couldn't wait to come. And he's been running ever since."

"And there's the worry about Jimmy, too, Elsie. I was down that hospital yesterday. His sheets had all come away, and they just don't feed 'em proper. Poor mite's hungry and wants his mum."

"Well of course he does, bless him." Elsie reaches over and pats Lillian's hand. "So why did she come back, Lil, that lady from the Charity? I didn't know you needed help, love. You should have told me."

"I needed a bit of money to get things out of pawn, Elsie, and I know you don't have lots of that. So I thought I'd ask at the Welfare Centre, and then the Charity turned up, like they did a couple of years ago. That was a nicer lady, that one. This new one, Miss Hedges is her name, comes around here, nose up in the air, I can tell you. I don't think she has much time for the likes of us, Elsie. Anyway, you know what this one told me? She says if I want the money for the pawnshop I have to go into hospital for me birth and promise not to bring Jimmy home."

"Hospital for your birth? You've never had no trouble before, have you? Your last one was fine. What do they want you to go to hospital for?"

Lillian shakes her head and sighs. Leaning over, she pulls across a rather battered tin and prises off its lid. "I don't have anything really nice, Elsie, but I've some digestives if you'd like one."

"No, that's fine, love. I'll be right till me supper."

"They want me in the hospital, Elsie, this is what she says, because babies should be born in hospital. Why, I said. She wouldn't tell me. Just looked at me like I'd said something stupid and said I just ought. Just told me I ought to. Told me I ought to. That's not a reason, is it?"

Elsie clucks her tongue. "And who's supposed to pay for that, then? Are they going to pay for that? I mean, just the doctor is two-and-six. What's having a baby in a hospital going to cost?"

"Oh, there was something about a payment or some such. But that's not the point, I told her. I just don't see why I should. I don't like hospitals. Can't abide 'em. They smell, and no one has a good word to say about 'em.

People die in hospitals, don't they? They go in, and they don't come out. I mean, if you're sick, if you're really sick, well, beggars can't be choosers, can they, but I don't hold with having a baby in one. I mean, that's why I need the money, ten bob, to get me sheets and the bedclothes out of pawn, so I'll have the bed ready here."

"And very sensible too, love. The shop on Hammersmith Broadway? I've got that candlestick in there. That brass one of me father's."

"Yeh, on the Broadway, Elsie. They're not bad in there."

"No, quite fair, I've found, quite fair."

"Anyway, she comes around Wednesday to check, and then she comes around this morning to tell me what the committee says. You can have the money if you go to hospital for your birth and don't bring Jimmy home until they tell you. I told her I don't want to go to no hospital. I told her I can't abide them. You know what she said then, Elsie? Just told me I ought to and said, 'You have nothing to fear, Mrs. Golding. There's no reason for you to be afraid of hospitals.' Afraid of hospitals, Elsie!"

"What a thing to say. And she'd know, I suppose. Miss, was she?"

"Yeh, Miss Hedges her name was. She'd know all about how to birth a baby, wouldn't she?"

"Not much, Lil."

"And I never said I was afraid, did I? What I said was, I don't like hospitals, and I'm not having a baby in one when I can do it at home in me own bed, with Margaret who's done me other three. And I'll take 'im to the infant welfare nurse, like with the first three. But they're not safe, those hospitals. I mean, if they could tell me why, Elsie, if they could tell me why I should go to hospital, that's the thing. Give me a reason. I'm not stupid. I just want a reason, that's all."

"Quite right too, love."

"I mean, I'll leave Jimmy there if that'll get him better. But the way the Charity wants it, you just do what you're told, don't you. Yes sir, no sir, three bags full sir."

"That's right. It's always the bloomin' same."

"I just want a reason. I know me own mind, and I don't like her saying do this or do that or else you won't get your money. I mean, that's what it boiled down to, Elsie, didn't it? Do what we tell you, or you'll get nothing. One minute it's 'what do you plan to do, Mrs. Golding,' and 'you'll need to make a decision, Mrs. Golding,' and the next it's 'do this or else.' I mean, who do they think they are?"

"Well, I hope you told her, Lil."

"She knew I wasn't happy, Elsie. But you have to watch yourself, don't you? I mean, you might need 'em again later. And they all talk to each other." She shakes her head. "There's not much you can do, is there? I mean, I told her I'd think about it, but she knew I was going to say no. I bet that'll go in her bloody book 'n all. Actually, Elsie," she says, laughing, "I don't think she'd know how to write what I actually wanted to say to her. I wanted to tell her to take her bloody pawn money and shove it. She probably don't use words like that, does she?"

"I bet she'd understand 'em though." They both laugh.

"Oh, it's a tonic, Elsie, a bit of a laugh. You're a bad one for making me laugh about Miss Hedges or Hedgehog or whatever her name was. I still haven't got no sheets, though. There's not much I can do, is there?"

"Well, I don't know about that, Lil. Do you know old Mary from over on Field Road?"

"I'm not sure, Elsie. Probably know her to see her."

"Well, she was saying just last week how she was thinking of moving because her house is too big with her husband gone. And she's only got her youngest there now, Evelyn, that's her name. Nice girl, was going out with Hettie's lad Robert a while ago. I'm not sure what happened there. I mean, he's not the brightest star in the sky, but he'd probably do all right by her. Quite nice-looking, too, especially when you think what his father's like. Anyway, old Mary was saying last week that she's not using her big bed anymore because it's too much trouble making it, what with her rheumatism, and she's just kipping in her chair by the fire. So she might have some sheets to spare, you see."

"Maybe I could borrow 'em if she wouldn't mind. Or give her something when I can."

"Oh, old Mary won't mind. Kind as kind, that one. Look, I'll pop over and see her now, before Len's home for his tea. Anyway, then you can tell Miss Charity Whats-It that you don't need her money, and she can go to hospital herself if she wants to."

She stands, moves behind Lillian, and gives her a brief hug around the shoulders. "Don't you mind, pet, we'll sort something out. Louisa up the street, her Bill's getting good money, and her Brian's just started in the Lyons cake factory up in Hammersmith. He's a smart boy, that one, and her Doreen's got work at the post office, so they're doing a bit better than the rest of us. She'll help if old Mary can't."

"Thanks, Elsie. It's just such a worry, and I need them sheets, but I'm not having that woman thinking I'm stupid and making me do things against me nature. It's not right. It's just not right."

· · · · · · · · · · · · · · RESOLUTION · · · · · · · · · · · ·

One of the most enduring characteristics of poor people's experience of charity is managing the bargain between loss and gain. Each gain—a little cash, a blanket, some used clothing, or perhaps some help applying for a pension or a payment—usually means a loss: of dignity, often, of privacy, almost always. In Britain, as in Australia and the United States, in the present and the past and more than likely in the future, the bargain is managed largely by women, who have to decide at what point the price they must pay for something they need becomes too large. For Lillian Golding, I think that point came when the ten bob she needed to redeem her bedclothes from pawn became hostage to a decision about hospital confinement she was not willing to accept.

Even from the relatively short description of this encounter in Lillian's case file, it seems clear that what she resented—and resisted—was that the success of her request for money became dependent on her compliance with the Fulham Committee's wishes about hospitalization. Dorothy Hedges saw her as stupid and unreasoning. A less dismissive understanding of Lillian's argument is that she did not see any reason to accept what she saw as the risk—and perhaps the cost—of a hospital birth without explanation or just because she was told to. Indeed, she seems to have regarded this as a threat to her independence and her self-reliance, the very attributes London's Charity Organisation Society regarded itself as encouraging among the poor. I can't know for sure, because Dorothy Hedges doesn't give us enough information about Lillian's point of view, but it is at least likely that Lillian felt well served by past arrangements, which probably involved some mix of a local midwife, a health visitor, and an infant welfare center. As Lara Marks has shown in her comprehensive study of maternal health in London during this period, growing numbers of women—in working- as well as middle-class districts—attended antenatal clinics and other services, and the number of hospitals in the capital meant that more London women delivered there than was true in provincial cities such as Birmingham or Manchester. But midwives remained very important for some women, especially those who lived in areas that lacked sufficient hospital beds or doctors, as well as for women who preferred to deliver at home. Lillian may also have been one of the women described in a 1934 London County Council report as less likely to use antenatal and hospital services "because she is a multipara who is bound by household ties and has lost her fear of the danger of childbirth."[1]

In attempting to give a voice to Lillian Golding and to say something of how she might have experienced this encounter, I do not want to belittle Dorothy Hedges or deny that her decisions were well meant. There may have been concerns for Lillian's health, especially because a previous COS visitor had described her as "haggard and worried." As Lara Marks shows, and as Janet McCalman so brilliantly demonstrates in her history of Melbourne's Royal Women's Hospital, the struggle to develop and deliver improved maternal health was never and nowhere a simple matter of imposition. Indeed, it often reflected poor women's own demands for improved care, as well as a professional desire to make childbirth safer for mothers and infants.[2] But this does not make the bargain proposed by Hedges or the Fulham Committee any less disrespectful. Hedges may have been making the point that a hospital birth would be safer or that Lillian's child was better off in a hospital bed than at home with a probably overworked and tired mother. She may have been too curt or clumsy or skipped over important details when summarizing her account. But that is not the tone of the writing, especially in light of what I know from reading dozens of similar files in London. Dorothy Hedges's tone is colored by disdain, and she was clearly exasperated by a poor woman's "unreasoning" fears about something people who were not "stupid" took for granted. Yet the file describes no attempt—or indicates any inclination—to explain why or to understand Lillian Golding's concerns about her pregnancy and her ill son as anything more than "stupid" and evidence of "low mentality." Dorothy Hedges may have been trying to do the best she could for Lillian Golding. But it seems to me that in deciding what was best, Hedges might have taken a little more care about understanding Lillian's fears about the worst.

This encounter introduces the chapters on London because it conveys very well the assumptions that the poor were ignorant and rather stupid, assumptions that had a particular strength—or at least a more open and automatic expression—in London. These helped make antagonism along class boundaries especially likely there. Charity visitors and their applicants in London—from Fulham and Hammersmith across to Shoreditch, Poplar, and Islington—were also likely to use a vocabulary of class difference when explaining each other's characters, decisions, and motivations. Conflict was less muted here than in Melbourne; in London, clients of the COS had a wider range of alternatives—including dense networks of neighborhood support and a thick layer of competing charitable, voluntary, and public enterprises—that afforded them more chance of saying no.

Lillian Golding and her family remained impoverished. Their Fulham street had been described as "poor" and "rough" in the second volume of

Charles Booth's survey of poverty in London, published in 1891, and it seems that little changed in the next forty years. In October 1937, with five children at home, Lillian was again visited by the COS; to this visitor, Marian Wilkinson, Lillian "seemed a decent sort of woman, but very poor" and "a very nice genuine sort of woman who seems discouraged by her continued misfortune." Lillian's husband—"rather a heavy, dull type of man"—called in to the district office in June 1938, and a report was sent to the Friends of the Poor: "They have had a great deal of help from charitable sources and are regarded in this whole neighbourhood as being quite unhelpable in a constructive sense." It was thought best to leave them to "the statutory authorities." We hear of Lillian once more in the summer of 1949, when the National Assistance Board approached the COS for help providing a nightgown, as Lillian was about to enter the hospital with serious bronchitis. Given her earlier misgivings, I hope Lillian's experience of hospitals had improved by then. In any event, it appears from her file that by then she had been rehoused, remained married, and kept her six children alive during the hard times of the 1930s and the horrors of London's war.

Poor and haggard she may have been. But I think that Marian Wilkinson's "decent" and "genuine" were probably closer to the mark than "stupid" and "unreasoning." And as the files of London's COS show, by the middle of the 1940s, with so many "dreadful" streets blasted by flying bombs and rockets, those who described London's poor saw something different again in Lillian Golding, something more like resilience, fortitude, and a just cause.

CHAPTER 9

The Man with the Repulsive Face

In the eyes of the Charity Organisation Society's visitors, London's poor were usually rather dim. Some were "ugly" and "misshapen," others "worn" yet "brave," but they were almost always mistaken about something. Even if Lillian Golding gained a little respect from the apparent honesty of her battles, others were written about—and perhaps spoken to—in a more dismissive tone. William Rowthorn was twenty-one years old when he first called in at the office of the South St. Pancras District in May 1935. His father was dead, and his mother was in the hospital, so he was living at the Rowton House near King's Cross. He wanted to ask about hospital treatment for what the visitor, Mildred Harding, described as his "repulsive" facial rash; she explained to him that the COS was not able to help. She tried to be patient and to "ram the idea of the PAC [Public Assistance Committee] into his head, but I fear with little success, and he shambled off." He returned a year later and was given a shilling; "he seems to have a pathetic reliance in our ability to help him although we have never done anything for him," and "he is not to be trusted." He came back again, about ten months later, having just been released from prison (for housebreaking, apparently); he was "quiet & friendly & seemed a little crushed." He wanted help finding a job. Nothing was done. By 1942 William was married to "a most attractive, charming, sensible young woman" and had a son aged three months—"he worships the baby," wrote the worker—and wanted overcoats. He didn't get them; "his face is a perfectly horrible sight ... [and] he seems even more defective than usual." He was seeking help from a variety of agencies, but "it was not so much cunning as lack of brain."[3]

In London's theater of poverty and inequality, people such as William Rowthorn were characters in a drama that first and foremost established how different they were from the charity visitors who heard their stories and tried to address at least a few of their problems. They faltered, and they failed. But it was to be expected. There was little here of the suspense that accompanied Melbourne's lady detectives, still less of the saving transformations described in Boston and Minneapolis. In London's theater, not much was surprising. Of course, one of the advantages of comparison is that it highlights such differences. It makes striking what seems less so in its own place and time. And what is striking about the dramatization of poverty in interwar London is the sense of unshakable difference that COS caseworkers expressed in their descriptions of the poor. London's case-workers watched the poor from a distance, sometimes with a sense of almost ironic detachment.

An annual report from the early 1920s contains this description of London's casework. The applicants, it argued, "appear to us only at intervals, so that we catch glimpses of their lives as one might see a film through an opening in a curtain, which closes before we learn what happens next. In fact we seldom see the ending of the story, happy or otherwise, but we often see snapshots of good and less good, of courage and weakness, of sorrow and bitterness, and sometimes of quite incredible stupidity, just like a popular film."[4] The image was repeated in the society's regular publication, the *Charity Organisation Quarterly*, in 1932, where "every member of a COS committee" was said to watch applicants "passing before her week by week like an endless cinema show or pageant of contemporary human life."[5] In London the poor were on a stage, but the caseworkers were not there with them, acting out stories of Australian detection or American transformation. They were in the seats, watching the flickering and momentary glimpses of other people's lives.

The Charity Organisation Society has loomed large in the history of modern London. This is fitting, for it laid the founding stone of a movement that would help transform charity in late Victorian Britain and beyond. The city that more than any other dominated the nineteenth-century world has been a place to study the changing dynamics of class and gender, as well as responses to the threats of poverty, inequality, and "degeneration" at the heart of the empire. Judgments about the COS are judgments about the nature of Victorian society and its legacy, and accounts of its leaders and its critics are accounts of some of the most important figures in British social, political, and economic thought. All of its historians have been talented, and most have been stringent. In the 1960s, Kathleen Wood-roofe suggested that the COS "inherited the inadequacies as well as the achievements of the particular period in which it was born," and Gareth Stedman Jones's assessment from the 1970s—"methodical investigation of individual cases combined with a lack of any real imaginative insights into the problems of the poor"—continues to ring true for anyone analyzing the society's case files.[6] Madeline Rooff is more measured in her centenary history, emphasizing the importance of the society's contribution to professional methods and casework theory; Gertrude Himmelfarb, while swatting away the insights of previous historians a little dismissively, also emphasizes the COS's achievement as "shaping both the idea of poverty and the conception of the problem of poverty" for an entire generation.[7] Alan J. Kidd points to the persistence of the charity organization movement's characteristic "views and vocations"—and its "tensions and contradictions"—in Manchester.[8] A. W. Vincent also takes issue with overly simplistic views of the society's social theory, arguing that in attempting to hold together two apparently contradictory ideas—the old idea of "character and the moral factor in destitution" and the modern idea of "the environmental root to much poverty and the necessary role of the state in eradicating it"—the COS "was only reflecting the confusions of the wider society."[9] For Vincent, COS stories about poverty become a little more representative than they have sometimes been assumed to be.

Later historians focused more attention on the dynamics of investigation and the COS's role in changing welfare methods, with Eileen Yeo arguing that its leadership "provided a harsh discourse which was in constant tension with some of the more generous feelings of the social workers."[10] In her comprehensive and compelling account of the society's influence over London's changing welfare landscape in the twentieth century, Jane Lewis emphasizes its faith in social casework as "the only sure way of securing desirable and permanent social change" and its inability, at least before the late 1930s, to understand that "individual casework could never play a large part in modern schemes of social security."[11] But in the most recent comprehensive account, Robert Humphreys describes the COS leaders as "a besieged idiosyncratic minority"; the society's important contributions to casework methods, he argues, were undermined by its unwillingness to embrace either environmental explanations for poverty or an important role for the state in its alleviation.[12] His final comment about the society in the 1940s is scathing: "[The COS] was but a distorted mirror of a bygone age. In the public's eyes it reflected the image of hardhearted, mean, pitiless, inflexible, class-based elderly fogies, judgemental of others. In its over-bearing confidence, the COS had misinterpreted for too long that public revulsion merely confirmed the validity of its own archaic principles."[13]

It is a harsh verdict, but dissenters within the society itself were hardly kind, whether during the 1920s and 1930s, when some of its workers made similar criticisms, or in the 1940s, when members of the Senior Secretaries Group suggested that "some members of committees still had the *de haut en bas* view of applicants" and were "unsympathetic, condemnatory and superficial" in their attitudes to the poor.[14] By then, of course, the COS was in the middle of a transition—similar to that of its Melbourne offshoot— that would change it into the Family Welfare Association and encourage a rather different interpretation of its role: "[T]he need now is to gain the co-operation of the client, and to foster his desire to help in the solution of his own problems. This he will want to do if he trusts in the worker's general desire to help from his own level, and realises that he is not merely being 'improved' from above."[15]

These chapters are not a history of the London Charity Organisation Society's policies and principles or of its role in the development of British social work. They do not need to be, because the fine scholarship described above has already covered that ground. By focusing on the case files, I ask some rather different questions, in particular about the understandings of poverty, entitlement, and inequality that the COS workers enacted in their dealings with the poor and dramatized in the stories they wrote about them. Relatively little use has been made of these files from the interwar period, in part because their survival was so haphazard. They are relatively few in number—just over a thousand are stored in the London Metropolitan Archives—and they mostly stem from several districts on the northern side of the Thames: Bethnal Green, Fulham, Hackney and Stoke Newington, Hammersmith, Holborn, City and Finsbury, North and South St. Pancras, Stepney and Mile End, and Shoreditch. There are just a few from Greenwich, Lewisham, and Wandsworth. We are lucky that some were kept, when so many were discarded and when still others were lost to the bombs of the 1940s. It is not completely clear why some files from these districts were kept while others were destroyed. There are relatively few of the short and mundane cases that made up perhaps a third of the files in Melbourne, and it seems these cases may have been retained for their potential educative value; for a history of what twentieth-century people have wanted to say about poverty, of course, the case files they saw as most representative of their work are particularly useful.

In London, as in Melbourne, COS case files open a window on empathy and its absence and on trust and distrust. They reveal what those who listened to the poor heard and misheard and what they then felt compelled to make the moral of their stories. In a society beset by critics, and sure that most other contributors to the debate about poverty were wrong, case files were an important source of "telling tales" and the conclusions about poverty that could be claimed only from experience. At one point in the 1930s the COS likened itself to Cock Robin: "the revealer and the symbol of the truth we most need to know."[16] Trying to shape wider perceptions of poverty and welfare was a serious business, especially when the number of competing charities willing to act as murderous sparrows seemed to be increasing.

Comparison makes particular words and choices stand out with special clarity. In London, applicants are always rather hapless, when they are at a distance, when they come close, or when they are tracked to where they live: behind things, under things, down the stairs, or surrounded by the debris of their hopeless lives. They "shamble" and "shuffle" on and off the stage, largely untouched by any attempt to help them, and are probably cheerful, apart from the odd teary moment. They are disfigured and disarrayed, too fat or too thin, and distant and different enough to warrant such terms as "repulsive." William Rowthorn's rash might have been worse than many, but he was not alone in attracting a rather offhand belittlement. As the COS faced its own crisis in the 1920s and 1930s, that version of the poor would hardly waver.

· ·

CHAPTER 10

We Are at a Crossroads

To examine the London COS in the 1920s and 1930s is to see leaders divided from visitors and unclear practices in increasing tension with confused principles. Insiders recognized that it was standing at a "parting of the ways," and outsiders imagined it might even be swept away by the tides of change.[17] This was a time of crisis in which the COS came close to anachronism before quickly reinventing itself to fit the shape of the postwar welfare state. Yet even as its council frothed and fulminated in ways that made it less and less likely to be welcomed as a serious contributor to Britain's deliberations about social policy, the COS remained an important producer of stories about poverty and an important campaigner in the verbal battles over welfare that took place in the metropolis and beyond. The intense conflicts of the 1920s, culminating in the 1926 General Strike, also rumbled through its meetings, conferences, and debates, with arguments over the abolition of the Poor Law system, the development of national insurance and unemployment assistance, and the future relationship between voluntary and local authority hospitals.[18] As Madeline Rooff has suggested, although the chief officers of the society seemed out of touch, "many of the Districts were in closer touch with reality."[19] The COS's journal, the *Charity Organisation Quarterly*, was a forum—at times a rather heated one—for the discussion of issues people saw as absolutely fundamental to Britain's future, and the annual conferences pro-

vided other opportunities for strenuous debate. The council and its committees remained a global center of sorts, attracting visitors and speakers
from around the world; in 1928, Joanna Colcord of Minneapolis addressed
a Secretaries Meeting, and in July 1936 Melbourne's Stanley Greig Smith
addressed the council.

The society was also conducting a lot of investigation. At the beginning
of the 1920s, its thirty-two metropolitan districts received about fourteen
thousand applications per year, including referrals from other agencies;
around half were approved for assistance. The early 1930s saw a rise—the
number of applications peaked at 17,722 in 1934—and there was a further
escalation in the first year of the Second World War, when 18,801 applications were made, mostly as a result of the confusions that accompanied
London's partial evacuation. In the 1920s, Islington and Camberwell were
the busiest districts, with Southwark and South Lambeth also topping one
thousand cases a year during the 1930s. Of the districts in which some case
files were saved, Hammersmith and Fulham received around five hundred
applications per year, and North St. Pancras around nine hundred, while
Chelsea and Shoreditch received perhaps two or three hundred. Within
each district, a secretary supervised a group of visitors, social workers, and
caseworkers (the terms were used somewhat loosely and interchangeably,
though I will use "visitor" here) and conducted the meetings of a district
committee. The Fulham records reveal that the committee discussed fi-
nances, correspondence, and administrative issues and considered perhaps
fifteen or twenty cases at each meeting. Its members included local subscribers and dignitaries, as well as workers from other local welfare organizations.[20] During these years, the district committees dealt with a wide
range of applicants, from returned servicemen and widowed women to
homeless children and the terminally ill. They took cases from borough
Tuberculosis Care committees, employment exchanges, the Friends of the
Poor, the Professional Classes Aid Council, and, in the 1930s, groups aiding Spanish refugees. They also sent cases—especially those in which difficulties became chronic despite "plucky effort"—to the local Public Assistance committees.[21]

In the 1920s and 1930s, the work of the London COS was increasingly
women's work. Women had always been important, but their visibility
increased as the society became more active in direct provision, casework,
and training and less influential in the public and political work that was
largely the province of men.[22] In 1918 twenty-five of the thirty-six district
committee representatives on the council were women (six were married,
eighteen were unmarried, and one was described as a "Lady"); there were

also four reverends and one "Sir." The society's nine organizing secretaries included three single women and a countess, and women made up two-thirds of the district secretaries. By the early 1920s, all but two of London's district secretaries were single women, a balance that remained roughly the same throughout the 1930s. The feminization of its workforce had a clear cost benefit for the COS. In 1919, for example, female secretaries earned between £120 and £150, and female district secretaries earned between £175 and £200; their male counterparts earned the higher of those figures at the beginning of their employment and gained an advantage of some £50 per annum within a few years.[23] Few men were recruited; the 1920 annual report lamented that "the young man is more difficult to attract ... [even though] a short term of years as a COS secretary would be no bad training for public life."[24] It was not until 1945 that the society applied the principle of equal pay for equal work, and only for new appointments; it also promptly installed a special "family allowance" of £75 per year for any man who had a child under the age of sixteen.

In London, as in Melbourne, while the generic client in social work's stories was sometimes—and rather inaccurately—described as "he," the visitor was always "she." Women did the bulk of the investigation, inquiry, and judgment, shaped the poor's immediate experience of charity, and carried out much of the everyday conversation about needs and entitlements. They also adapted casework in theory into casework in practice, and their certainties and uncertainties shaped the accounts recorded in their case files. In London, there was more of a mix of volunteers, temporary trainees, and paid social workers than in Melbourne, where all casework was salaried by the 1920s. As in other areas of British social, political, and welfare service, women often blurred the distinctions between paid and unpaid or amateur and professional. As historian Pat Thane suggests, many organizations depended on the work of educated women—whether unmarried or married—making whatever use they could of their skills and talents, sometimes paid but often unpaid.[25] Those organizations also shared a reliance—more often implied than stated—on the particular qualities and intuitions that women apparently brought to the tasks of investigation. An attempt to describe the personality required of the social worker in 1929 suggested "accuracy, poise, insight and discrimination, sense of responsibility, initiative and resource, capacity for team work and a sense of humour."[26] Even Elizabeth Macadam, one of the most important proponents of academic training in the 1930s, listed "inborn personal qualities" as "essential qualifications" for social work.[27] Vera Brittain and Ray Strachey included social work and especially hospital almoning among the more promising careers for the daughters of professional families, Brittain noting that "the sense of service is supposed to compensate for inadequate remuneration" and Strachey suggesting that social work "even more than nursing or teaching is undertaken in the vocational spirit."[28]

These women are less familiar to me than Agnes Cutler or Lillian Allen; drawing on a smaller and more scattered collection of files and records, I am less able to identify particular hands and identities. On the evidence, the London visitors were mostly drawn from the middle class and included large numbers of young women whose professional and vocational aspirations were forced into relatively narrow channels of opportunity. For women who did not want to teach school or undertake nursing, charity and social work was one of few remaining options. Few if any were upper-class "slummers" or "ladies bountiful"; they expected to work for a living, at least until marriage restricted their choices even further, and the longevity of most names in the Hammersmith, Fulham, and St. Pancras case files suggests that most did not marry. Their politics, like their backgrounds, were most likely from the mainstream of the English middle class, most of whom might have endorsed this description by COS student F. D. Meredith: "There are days when the mean streets of London seem places of unrelieved ugliness, and yet it is one of her charms that her slums are seldom entirely hideous, and beauty is the more lovely when it is unexpected."[29] Like Meredith, some COS visitors were undertaking university training, while others followed the pattern of Eileen Younghusband and similar pioneers by beginning with voluntary service and then going into paid work, training, and a salaried career.

By the 1920s, these women were also beginning to develop a sense of themselves as different from the earlier cohorts of COS volunteers and visitors. A more and more female leadership, at least in the districts, was one factor, while those who had learned and practiced casework assumed a more professional status. The newer kind of visitor "paid more attention to the physiognomy and the mental outlook" and "makes it her business to investigate further into the case, to find the root of the trouble and to help solve it."[30] Another factor was the continuing tension over the relationships between paid and volunteer visitors, with T. E. Lloyd at one point suggesting that the "inevitable result" of an "over-professionalised" service was that the poor became "so much case-fodder."[31] Also, although frictions within COS districts—or among the districts, the central office, and the council—were publicly focused around generational rather than gender issues, it was also clear by the late 1930s that the young women of the COS would be the most important and vigorous proponents of change. As the council heard increasing debate about crossroads and new roads and old roads, it was Miss Hill, Miss Lawrance, Miss Smith, and Miss Simey who rose to speak, and it was the district secretaries—mostly women—who made the most challenging criticisms of existing practice.

Women played a lesser role in public pronouncements. It was a troubled time. By the end of the First World War, the London COS, and especially its council, was likely to see itself as "the guardian of principle in the administration of assistance."[32] The society's "most important functions are of an educative and sometimes critical nature," suggested the writer of a 1917 occasional paper; during the 1920s, the desire to educate seemed frequently overcome by the need to hold the COS line against an increasing number of detractors.[33] There was at times a sense of hurt at the scale of this rejection, whether strikes and socialism or the specter of spreading "Poplarism." When the Poplar Borough Council's generous public assistance policies led to the disbanding of the COS's district committee, its secretary lamented: "We should not be devoting our time and means to this work if we were indifferent to the sufferings and anxieties of our fellows. We are in it because we have a passionate desire to understand and remove both. . . . We submit, further, that the more the struggle with these natural difficulties is taken away from the human beings concerned, the more the difficulties get the upper hand."[34] Few in the COS's upper reaches ever seemed to grasp the fact that the "naturalness" of difficulties such as poverty had been a matter of debate for some decades.

Troubles were internal, too. A committee appointed in 1918 "to consider the best way of making the Council and its work more effective" described "widespread dissatisfaction" with council discussions that were "monopolised by a small number of the older members." Proceedings, it charged, "are marked by an absence of reality" and "an insufficient appreciation of the younger generation's attitude towards social problems." The "work of the Society," it added, "is seriously prejudiced by the fact that its members belong to the same social class. It is an unfortunate fact that hitherto the Society has failed to win the confidence and active co-operation of the industrial classes."[35]

If it was hardly surprising that the industrial classes were unwelcoming, the COS seemed less prepared for the findings of another committee appointed to examine the question of "standardization." Canvassing opinion about the COS from clergy, almoners, visitors, and pension officials, the committee found that while they "generally appreciate both the methods and principles on which the Society works," they had pointed criticisms of the society's now mostly paid visitors: "lacking in helpfulness"; "the touch of humanity is wanting ... [and] principles sometimes press hardly"; "dislike of waiving routine in order to help"; and "the COS is more organizing than charity."[36]

The critics would have found little to change their opinions in the grumbling archaisms of annual reports, publications, and council meetings. Trying to "compress the spirit of the COS into one sentence," one 1921 contributor to the *Charity Organisation Quarterly* suggested this: "It was inspired by a passionate desire to prevent that most terrible of disasters, nay, crime, the manufacture of paupers—the manufacture, that is, of economic and often, alas! of moral imbeciles out of the raw material of men and women."[37] In 1923 district secretaries complained of a diminishing "reluctance to ask for relief," and a 1925 council discussion of unemployment included an observation that "the provision of educational facilities and so on might be made the excuse for neglecting the search for work." Stepney's Mr. Turnbull warned that "the children are likely to be the unemployed of the future and we should guard them from infection with the spirit of inertia."[38] And although the society enjoyed some authority due to its visitors' expertise in casework, its leaders, such as J. C. Pringle, also put a few shots across the bows of those suggesting new trends. In 1928, for instance, he suggested to a Secretaries Meeting that few of the agencies sharing "the rapidly developing interest in the psychiatrical side of social work ... will realise how vain this work is unless based upon methodical and scientific general family casework" rather than "sight-seeing in psychiatry."[39]

The sense of isolation only increased during the 1930s. As Jane Lewis notes, the society "only latched onto the new literature on casework in order to reaffirm its traditional practice."[40] COS leaders became ever more ardently fastened to the idea of casework as the only possible antidote to the failures of "mass action," while warning that the "weaning of the people away from the crude, unthinking collectivism of recent years will take time."[41] What is perhaps most amazing is the confidence that such a reversal was even possible. In April 1933, a memorandum written by eight of the district secretaries pondered the society's dilemma at length and in a way that captured very ably its increasing inability to see a way forward: "[There is] present demand for more advertisement and more rapid methods of finance. But the fact cannot be ignored that the COS, if it appeals truthfully, and in accordance with its principles, can never attract more than that small section of the public which it has succeeded in educating to appreciate its view and work."[42] It is not surprising that by 1936, two meetings of the council were occupied by discussion of "the COS at the crossroads." One district secretary argued that her committee "had drifted unconsciously into being the suppliers of spare parts" rather than "constructive case work," and another thought that "the Society stood at the parting of the ways, and one road was easy and well-trodden with all the familiarity of 60 years, the other was new, in parts roughly paved and in others quite unmade." She wanted the COS to take "the road of the future, and that of youth."[43] Other COS workers shared her frustrations, though most were less sanguine in regard to its prospects; one caseworker used the society's *Charity Organisation Quarterly* to criticize the "lust for indiscriminate investigation" as early as 1927, and in 1932 another worker, T. E. Lloyd, argued that district committees were "chiefly concerned in the task of finding out how not to help their applicants."[44] But those older members who dominated the council and wrote the annual reports were unconvinced of any need for change. That they preferred the old road is clear in a number of statements; the 1938 annual report, to take one example, included a report claiming that young unemployed people "are being degraded to an almost sub-human way of life ... [by] doles without end and without conditions." Indeed, the writer continued, "human nature cannot stand the strain of such an easy-going offer of unconditional maintenance by the State."[45]

Even though its council tended, like a cantankerous old man, to sputter that better days lay only in the past, the COS continued to play an important role in London's charity network. It suffered diminishing importance among legislators and policymakers but remained an important source of casework training and propaganda work. Annual reports featured accounts built on COS cases, while casework stories in the *Charity Organisation Quarterly* sometimes ran over several pages and, by the 1930s, included assessments, questions, and considerations about "what might have been done." In London, featured stories tended to highlight examples of successful planning and solutions that were rather less common in reality. The 1932 report reassured its audience: "It is true that no one can fail to be saddened by daily contact with sin, sorrow and suffering, much of it beyond human aid; but yet the Annual Reports make cheerful reading on the whole, showing as they do what courage and self-respect on the part of the applicant, supplemented by timely and intelligent help from those more fortunate, can accomplish even in these distressful days."[46] The cases included in the *Quarterly*, meanwhile, tended to show applicants as short-sighted and rather stupid, wanting immediate rather than lasting change. They also described forms of intense engagement, careful conferencing, and psychological assessment that may have been the definition of "ideal casework" but bore little resemblance to the casework being practiced in London's streets and lanes. By the early 1940s, however, reforming elements within the COS were suggesting that "the publicity given to the Society's work dealt almost exclusively with what they would term its repressive aspects"; in that sense, perhaps, the use of exemplary stories to impress subscribers with the COS's rigor had succeeded all too well.[47]

The London COS played a major role in the training of social workers. In 1930, 161 students worked in the district offices. Thirty-one came from the London School of Economics and twenty-one from Bedford College. Fifty-three were hospital almoners, and the others came from university settlements, other welfare associations, or the Battersea Polytechnic.[48] During the 1930s, students also came from Birmingham, Bristol, and Edinburgh. All but a few were young women; a special meeting of the district secretaries in 1931 was "painfully alive to the difficulties of employing inexperienced students in dealing with work which must be difficult, and is often quite unsuitable for girls with no experience of life."[49] A typical course at the London School of Economics included a first term of general survey, a second term with one day a week in lectures and four days a week in a COS office, and a third term of "Case Committee work" and three weeks of full-time service in one of the districts. In their second year, students divided their time equally between "practical work" and lectures and discussion classes in psychology.[50] From 1931 on, the Secretaries Committee also organized regular "case conferences" and case review meetings. These discussed summaries of cases on a relevant issue ("Faults of Character in Children," "Mental Instability in Parents," and "Public Assistance Difficulties," for example) sent in by district secretaries, organized sessions with other groups (in 1932, psychological social workers attached to clinics), or heard reports from conferences.[51]

At the eve of another war, London's welfare landscape was more complicated than it had been in 1900 or 1920, at least from the perspective of the Charity Organisation Society. While it managed increasing caseloads and training responsibilities, it was also facing a degree of marginalization its leaders failed to appreciate until the very end of the 1930s. Of all the agencies in this study, London's COS faced the most vigorous contest over its continuing role and relevance and the most obvious rejection of the values and ideals for which it claimed to stand. The blustering defensiveness of the council, with its fervent dislike of public provision—"an enormous administrative machine the purposes of which [the applicant] can never understand"—only confirmed that this was a group nearing not so much a crossroads as a choice between extinction and a new direction.[52]

Yet whatever wars the council was fighting, the local district secretaries and visitors were left to identify what the COS could actually do. It was a question, especially on the evidence of the case files, for which they found no ready answer. In that sense, as we look through their eyes, we are with people who seem to lack the certainties of either conservatism or reformism. Without any reliable faith in transformation or a larger mission, their casework most resembled a detached and almost disinterested description. In the same vein, their hopes for the poor amounted to little more than a somewhat clearer understanding of how fixed in their "grubby" stations most of them really were.

Reading these accounts, and examining the words visitors chose to use to describe the largely impoverished people they met, is not a means of holding them up for ridicule. It is to ask how they understood the world and what tools they brought to the task of listening to, comprehending, and addressing the problems of the poor. These were people whose work took them toward and onto a class boundary; their words accordingly open a window into how they imagined and acted out the differences in behavior, character, and prospects they thought defined that boundary. As the COS once put it, "Our maxim [is] that prosperity depends upon character."[53] It was as simple as that.

. . . .

CHAPTER 11

They Are Somewhere Down the Stairs

As it met criticisms of its methods and values, the Charity Organisation Society moved quickly to defend them. "The social worker," wrote N. M. O'Connor in 1917, "knows that relevant inquiries made with tact and sympathy are seldom resented, frequently reveal unexpected sources of help and throw light on many a seemingly hopeless case."[54] A 1921 contributor argued that the "exhaustive and scientific study of all the circumstances of each case" obviously involved questions, but the COS "asks no questions which any honest man or woman could justly regard as insulting or which it would not become them to answer."[55] The 1934 annual report tried to be lyrical:

The [caseworkers'] minds who mused upon these possibilities were looking into the sad, or lovely, or tired, or dull, or flashing eyes of living creatures. A word or an intonation in the wrong place, or an emphasis in the right place, brought at once a flag of distress, anger, warning or gratitude, into the answering eyes. . . . To the COS every detail of the antecedents and circumstances of a person are [sic] of infinite importance and interest. Might not one of them give a clue to the elusive mystery that lurked almost hidden behind those lustrous eyes?[56]

In practice, those mysteries often remained elusive, partly for want of trying. The London caseworkers lacked the rigor of Agnes Cutler, and they rarely approached the forceful and sometimes optimistic determination of the women who visited the poor in Boston or Minneapolis. The case notes from those other cities described rooms and streets with caustic intensity. There is rancid milk and decaying food. Torn curtains limply respond to a breeze; washing strains against jag-toothed pegs. Social workers grasped at clues, seized the moment, and stepped through partly barred doorways. In London the social worker was more detached, her progress less determined. London's poor were hard to find. They were "somewhere down the stairs" or marooned in "a horrible basement flat" or "down from the street and through a dank, dark passage." If Melbourne's investigator always found her man, Mildred Harding often just missed him or couldn't find the right block of the Peabody Buildings or the estate in which he lived. It didn't matter; he would probably shuffle back into the district office before long.

In London the poor remained rather hazy. In Melbourne and the American cities, caseworkers and inquiry officers also expressed a strong sense of social and moral distance from the poor and illustrated it with a series of markers: everyone utilized dirt, disorder, and decay, but female investigators also tended to emphasize furtiveness, dulled intellect, shaky stories, and poor people's inability to control their emotions. But the functions of casework in different places varied, especially in its actual application. In London it was neither a rigorous detection of pauperism, as was true in Melbourne and, to some extent, Oregon, nor a means of laying down the path by which at least some of the poor could transform themselves, as it was in Boston and Minneapolis. At least on the evidence of the case writing it generated, London's social work did attempt to dissuade the poor from wanting too much and making too many demands on a strained welfare system. But it was rarely as strenuous as Melbourne's or as vigorous as those of the American cities. There was simply less interest in pursuing and questioning the poor.

In one 1930s case, a Fulham visitor entered a supposedly unmarried woman's small flat to find that "the bedclothes were pulled back & showed that the bed had obviously been slept in by two people," and there "was also a man's as well as a woman's hairbrush on the dressing table."[57] I know what Agnes Cutler would have made of that or of another case in which a "pleasant, good-looking woman, but frightfully poor" kept the worker "at bay on the doorstep."[58] The London workers certainly noticed and mentioned the apparent evasions of the poor, such as evidence of "preparation" for their home visits or references who "had been primed to give as little away as possible."[59] London applicants could also be "quite obdurate," as was an elderly woman who refused to reveal how much she had in her savings or to show the worker her savings book: "She said it was her secret and nothing would persuade her to divulge it . . . and even her husband does not know how much she has (he sat meekly by during the argument & did not speak a word)."[60] But when confronted with such stubborn resistance to their inquiries, these visitors rarely pressed for more.

This was a kind of case writing based more on hurried impressions—verbal and behavioral as well as visual—that served most of all to confirm prior suppositions about the links between character, possessions, and economic fortunes. London visitors were much more likely than those in Melbourne to trust the evidence of a quick visit or a straightforward exchange; in one 1926 Hammersmith case, an applicant (and mother of ten children) was "most anxious for a home visit as she is very proud of her home." The visitor noted a piano and "a good looking suite of furniture" and declared the family "very respectable and hard working," an impression aided by the "two stag heads" that adorned the parlor.[61] Another Hammersmith applicant was "a very superior and straightforward man" and "quite different from the ordinary type of labourer" in part because he was "quite willing to give full particulars," while his wife "looked extremely honest and extremely affable."[62] Another "very neat superior woman" made an immediate impression because "she did not come to ask for charity, but for our help" and was "anxious to help with the necessary information."[63] So did a "superior sort of woman who prefaced her remarks with 'I haven't come here to plead poverty and don't want to ask for anything I can't pay for.'" Being so "forthright and forthcoming"—and "a very good type [who] is reluctant to ask for any help"—always helped secure assistance.[64]

Applicants who understood how to give a good impression and had the means to illustrate their claims to superiority always fared best. A Fulham violinist, his "delicate" wife, and their daughter, a dancer, were referred by the Musicians Benevolent Fund in 1938 because they wanted to "avoid charity places." He looked "very dour and wretched" and was immediately given thirty shillings and a promise to pay his telephone bill. The home was "large & comfortably furnished with piano, sofa, carpet etc & many pictures & ornaments." When the COS visitor insisted that the daughter apply to the Unemployment Assistance Board, the father replied that "she could not 'give up her art' & sacrifice her long training." He was, the visitor wrote, "rather inclined to be weak and sit down under his difficulties," but their superiority continued to bring rewards, including three further sums of five pounds each during June and July. These were large amounts of money compared to other cases.[65] An "above the average standard" family in Kentish Town received even more substantial help in the early 1940s, when the father was pensioned for a chronic illness. The North St. Pancras committee provided a permanent financial supplement of eight shillings per week, "as it would take some time for the family to adjust themselves to a lower standard of income." They also provided a school uniform for the couple's only child and helped the family again after their home was blasted by a flying bomb in 1944.[66]

This faith in impressions survived even its obvious disproving. A visitor in Shoreditch in 1937 felt some sympathy for an "ex–public school boy down on his luck," especially as he "appeared distressed during the interview . . . [and said] that he had never asked for charity before." Given small loans, he did not repay them, and the next visitor was more critical: "public school manner and voice, shifty eyes and thoroughly bad first impression." As late as 1947, however, he was presented as the old rogue: "He made me feel completely at home, as if I was making a social call. He told me a lot about his life story, how he had come down in the world, and that confidentially his wife was not quite his type. . . . [He] has the bearing of a soldier still, and has not lost his charm in telling stories."[67] Another man with a "superior manner & voice" was helped in Fulham, as it "seems sad that a man like him, obviously superior, should have come down in the world so much." He was helping himself as a pavement artist. As it happened, he was helping himself more than they knew: as a visitor some five years later learned, he made a habit of sitting beside "other people's pavement pictures" to beg for money.[68]

The Fulham Committee worked with Dora and William Sutton for more than three years. They were very much swayed by two facts: William had been in one of the guards regiments, and Dora had been a servant in a "good home." As their first visitor wrote, "I liked her and felt very sorry for her. She looks as if she had been a good young servant before her marriage. She has a quiet, gentle manner & seems to have made a plucky fight." In a letter seeking support from the regiment's welfare body, the COS reported that William "has a very superior home and a nice little wife who was in good service." Their rent was paid for several months in 1921, and fifteen shillings a week was given while William was unemployed. In early 1923, the couple decided to migrate to Canada with their three sons, and the Fulham Committee not only provided £20 toward their fares but also convinced the Emigration Committee to match the sum, while organizing and paying for medical checks and character references. At that point, and with the £40 apparently in their keeping, the Suttons left for Canada, their fares paid by a Canadian employer. They did not tell the COS. The committee, the visitor noted in the file, "was a little bit hurt."[69]

The worst case of fraud among the London case files reveals the frailties of impression and the ways in which only a rare "type" of applicant could succeed in real deception. A woman and her two sisters, "pleasant, superior women," came to the attention of the Fulham COS in 1922. They were refugees from the Bolshevik revolution in Russia—COS visitors were always highly sensitive toward those victimized by radical outrages—and "could not be grateful enough to the English Govt & people." Their sisters in Petrograd were "being commandeered for work of all sorts," and their brothers "looked of intellectual type" in photographs. The district secretary wrote letters and organized help from various quarters, including private school fees for the woman's thirteen-year-old nephew. A naturalized British subject, the woman was eventually granted £16 from the Relief Fund for British Refugees from Russia. The COS only noticed that they "appeared of superior class but were very lethargic & did not fall in readily with suggestions of work"; the Poor Law Guardians were more energetic in their inquiries and discovered that the family was receiving a weekly— and unadmitted—allowance from the General Council for the Assistance of the British Repatriated from Russia. They claimed to know no English, "and it is due to this that they have made false statements as regards income." It transpired that the sisters were living rent free in one flat while subletting two others for a tidy weekly profit. At that point, even the COS refused further help.[70] Such were the perils of first impressions.

. . . .

CHAPTER 12

Little People

For the bulk of applicants who could afford neither pianos nor private schools, London COS casework normally began and ended with, again, a rapid, rough-and-ready division between the "helpable" and the "unhelpable." The first described the "decent" and deserving poor, who were always grateful; one Camden Town man, whose wife and children were sent away on a country holiday in June 1939, "was very pleased to see the visitor & grinned from ear to ear.... Although he felt very humiliated at having to come to us at first he was now very glad & very, very grateful to us for giving them what he could never have given them."[71]

Humiliation and gratitude were the common stock of charity exchanges. But there was another and more distinctive feature of the helpable poor in London. They were always little. They included, for example, "a decent little man," "a very nervous little woman," "a thin-looking little woman," a "quite a nice little woman," "a poor little husband" bullied by his wife, "a nice little woman" with her "rather decent young husband," a "rather weedy looking" man who suffered from nerves," a "plucky little person," and one applicant who was both a "particularly friendly and decent little woman" and an "extremely pleasant little woman."[72] It is possible, though unlikely, that the COS's London applicants were without exception short and physically unprepossessing. Class differences shape people's bodies from birth. But "little" was, I think, more a description of how many of the poor appeared to the COS visitors. They were little in substance and presence. They didn't amount to much. They were even somewhat childlike in their "muddles" and confusions.

When the poor and the needy were little, their lies and deceits also seemed less significant. The "decent little man" from Hammersmith, who had epilepsy and was an amputee and returned serviceman, was also "tidy [and] well-washed up" but "possibly rather shifty." At first, and based on the report of his son's headmaster that he was "trying it on and could work if he would," he was denied free dentures from the West London Hospital. Seen again in 1928 and 1929, on the second occasion because his donkey had gone lame, he "did not give me the impression of being shifty but very muddle-headed," though it seems from the file he was using at least three different surnames, at one stage claiming that he could not remember his name because of a hitherto undisclosed wound to the head.[73] The family were denied assistance, but little was done to pursue his apparent deceptions.

Most of London's poor were viewed through a murky fog. They were small, often rather innocuous. Their bodies were disorganized; they shambled and shuffled, were too fat or too thin, and gave away their inferiority in gap-toothed grins, "repulsive" blemishes, and misshapen features. Once located—and sometimes this was only with some difficulty—they appeared as more or less engaging characters in a comedy of manners or a pathetic, drab, and rather sentimental drama. Drawn to type, they took their appointed positions on the stage. And the scripts changed little between 1920 and 1940; the COS annual reports mentioned the "distress due to unemployment" and "distressful days," but there were few references in the case notes themselves to changing patterns of need in the city, and these were made by the applicants rather than the visitors.[74] Although London's Depression-era joblessness lacked the double-digit scale and seeming permanency of the crisis in "outer" Britain, the economic and social miseries of the 1930s were real enough, but rarely interrupted the case files.[75]

Some of the poor also appeared in another kind of display, as exhibits in a museum of ethnic and class hierarchy. Some references were in passing—such as the King's Cross woman who was "very Irish but seemed a straightforward sort"—while others stemmed from frustration, including a wife who was "Irish and desperately tiresome," which included being "voluble and unreachable."[76] Although a couple of other so-called types did appear in the case files, including a "Romany" woman, "very dark-skinned, a gorgeous colour" and a man who may have been West Indian, the Irish were the most numerous of the exhibits.[77] Visitors used stories to display their acuity. One nurse was a "rather superior Irish woman," Miss Pelham wrote, adding later that she was of course "of the West Kensington class, superior, not a lady."[78] They were also impressed by the ability of some Irish to appear not Irish: "I liked her—she is one of the best types of Irish; in fact, I would not have known she was Irish had she not told me." Part of the proof of her refinement was that she was "touchingly grateful"; her husband, also Irish and also of a "high standard" appearance, did not "look at all a wild or reckless sort of man."[79]

The hierarchies of class also mattered, and their subtle manifestations did not escape the COS visitors; "a very unattractive low class sort of woman with very bad teeth" was one description of a 1936 applicant, a Catholic Spanish refugee referred by the Catholic Council for International Relations, and she was discussed later as "a rough sort of woman and I should think a very casual mother." This supposedly casual mother expended a great deal energy ensuring that the four of her seven children who were still in Liverpool arrived safely in London. The COS gave the generous amount of £20 for secondhand furniture; when the other four children arrived, however, their "low class" propensities were confirmed: "They are quite indifferent to the extreme overcrowding & shortage of beds which results."[80]

A Fulham family visited in 1934 was of "typical coster [hawker] type" and "very shabbily dressed"; one of the clearest signals of the husband's status was that he "did not take his cap off the whole time I was there," and the overall judgment—"he is definitely feebleminded"—seemed rather rapid. In fact, he later sought—and fully paid off within three months—a loan of two pounds and five shillings that enabled his wife and children to travel to Scotland to see her parents. In 1939 he repaid another loan of around four pounds, with which he moved the children to Scotland for safety due to the looming war, and in 1941 the committee decided—even though he was "rather truculent & stammering badly"—to give him his fare to Stirling so he could visit them before being called up.[81]

To the largely middle-class women who visited them, the poor were different and distant. Their emotions and feelings didn't match those of respectable and refined people. Faced with the exposure of a lie, they seemed to feel no shame. They became indignant over small things and spoke "in high dudgeon [anger]" but were strangely indifferent to rejection and denial. One woman, whose overstuffed house resembled "an inferior pawn shop" and whose husband was described as an "out and out grouser," accepted the third rejection of her appeal for assistance "quite philosophically" and in a way the worker clearly felt indicated a degree of coldness.[82] Other applicants were too emotional and bared too many of their feelings. One "bright little woman" had "waves of depression," which were perhaps related to a difficult pregnancy, a husband turned out of work by the bombing of his factory, and a committee decision not to assist because he should find part-time work. But strong emotions had no place in the COS office. "Any real sympathy I felt," wrote the worker, "would have sent her into floods of tears."[83] Other women "reacted strangely," and even men "became completely hysterical."

The poor were also likely to be rather stupid. This explained not only their problems, at least to some degree, but also why sensible planning often failed. One Stepney applicant was "a very ignorant woman & so dense she was quite unable to answer a question right out."[84] Of course, stupidity could also excuse their clumsy deceptiveness; one Fulham applicant was "decent," but it was "exceedingly difficult to obtain any really definite information from her," more because she was slow than because she was being "intentionally evasive."[85] This woman, as with so many of the people who appear in the London visitors' stories, would need to be told what to do, again and again.

There was another group in the case files: "characters" who bemused and amused the district secretaries and visitors. They were reported by other agencies as "rather cheeky" or truculent, but most behaved or spoke in the wrong way in the office or during a home visit.[86] Some were "taciturn [and] uncommunicative," "touchy," "very vague and elusive," and "rather shifty-eyed."[87] Others were "very neat and respectable but very talkative (the local health nurse concurred that this woman was 'rather specious').”[88] It was important not to seem too eager to share your story. Ellen Walker in Kentish Town, described as “an extremely pleasant woman ... [who] did not plead poverty” and had “sound sense” while in the North St. Pancras office, was “too willing” to give information when visited. The worker “had to listen to vivid details of ‘her operations.’ ... Her old [surgical belt] is worn out & to be as convincing as possible, she hoisted her skirts & there, sure enough, was a very old belt struggling against incredible odds to control a mountain of flesh.”[89] Ellen Walker received her belt, but only after playing a rather comic foil.

I think the interwar visitors rather liked “characters.” Though they couldn’t help her when her father’s death meant the end of her invalid mother’s £300 per year pension, the Fulham committee was rather taken with artist and manicurist Mary Ditchburn, “a large stout woman with reddish hair (dyed?) & too much powder.”[90] Even when showing great kindness, for instance toward lonely and sometimes unhinged old people, there was a touch of theatrical flair. In Fulham, widowed old-age pensioner Mrs. Dickinson was “quite mad & wild.... The room was full of photographs of King Edward VIII about whom she kept talking in the midst of her long talks about her troubles.”[91] Another applicant, a war widow who was also caring for her grandson, attracted a similar tone: she was “the most extraordinary looking woman” and earned money as an art collector (the auction house at Christies responded to a COS query and said she dealt in fakes). After one visit to the office, one worker wrote: “She is a very typical Chelsea inhabitant—draped in black silk of ancient pattern & an enormous high crowned black felt hat crushed down on her head, [and] brilliant henna-red hair.” The file concluded that she was “given odd clothing.” This usually meant the applicant was given a couple of items from the office’s stock of used clothing, most of it donated by subscribers. What it meant in this case was left tantalizingly unclear.[92]

In Hammersmith, Arthur Knight was “a very shifty customer [who] spoke very plausibly but unconvincingly” and was “very truculent,” and his mother was “a most loquacious lady, very buxom & not at all refined.” Arthur claimed to suffer from migraines “after being dropped on his head as a baby,” a story that was not believed. A hospital almoner’s inquiry in 1939 was answered “unfavourably known,” but “judging by the complacence and almost alacrity with which he accepted our intimation that we could not help him, I am inclined to think that he did not expect anything.” Arthur always interested the Hammersmith COS. It was partly his criminal record, though not so much his crimes—which ranged from drunkenness to housebreaking—as the fact that when he was charged with an unspecified misdemeanor during the General Strike in 1926, he was so "defiant" that he "arrived at the police court wearing spats and looking like the Magistrate." It was also because he didn't play his part properly; seen in 1942, "he was not at all shabbily-dressed but was wearing a loud looking brown and white jacket and gray and white striped trousers. The effect was 'flashy' in the extreme."[93]

Overall, whatever sympathy or understanding was achieved by COS visitors, there were few examples of empathy. The sense of distance and the matter-of-factness about the strong correlation between social position and talent and between prosperity and character made it very difficult for COS visitors to do much more. For people who were like them, and had fallen on hard times, there could be trust and vigorous support. Some were odd, even a little amusing, and from them the charity visitors often seemed to have derived a kind of comic relief. For most, though, there could be friendliness and kindness, but only when tempered by strong advice and what was once described—in a telling phrase—as "the duty of remonstrance."[94] If you assume the poor to be stupid and incapable, there is little point in really getting to know them. The problem, as Gareth Stedman Jones, Robert Humphrey, Jane Lewis, and other historians have recognized before, was the expectation that the poor were ignorant, that they could or would be deferential and independent at the same time, and that in seeking the means to survive—money, rent, or free medical treatment, for example—they also welcomed or indeed needed "intelligent help" and wise planning from those who knew little about poverty. To the dilemmas of unemployment, low wages, ill health, and constant struggle, most COS officials, secretaries, and workers could offer only patronization: "[Our work] is to lay before the man who must move a plan, and to be ready if necessary with some at least of the means of carrying it out, *but* using meantime all the skill, tact and wisdom in the world to ensure that the plan calls out all that is great in him and never panders to the *vis inertiae* that is in him and in all of us."[95]

There were moments when those associated with the COS explored other avenues, as in this remarkable statement from an unnamed COS secretary in 1925:

Can we find any encouragement as we look around on our shattered plans? Perhaps, from the very fact that so many of our applicants will *not* allow us to do what we like with them arises the consolation that, amidst all the harm we may have done, we have not taken away completely the independence of the poor. Revolt is, at least, a sign of life.... Some little encouragement we may [also] take from the thought that our standards of success may be all wrong. Seen from the viewpoint of our office the Smith family never made much of the art of living.... But it may be that, in some scheme of things, the Smiths' plan for their salvation *was* the better plan—at least it was their own and not imposed upon them from the outside.[96]

Gilbert Elliott, a former district secretary and a volunteer visitor, created a small storm in 1927 with an article titled "Who Should 'Scape Whipping?" He criticized the emphasis on character and the "vast amount of investigation" as "quite superfluous; and, if superfluous, then not merely and negatively useless, but positively harmful and mischievous." He continued: "At the bottom of the trouble lies this *idée fixe*, this veritable bugbear, of the 'undeserving' poor, and the exaggerated precautions which are necessary to bar their way into paradise.... 'Good case work' has come to mean with many nothing more than good, i.e. *'thorough'* investigation, indiscriminate investigation, investigating all cases on the same lines and to the same extent."[97] These were fighting words, and some COS subscribers and workers responded with vigor, mostly by suggesting that character could not be divorced from investigation. In the same vein, an article in the *Quarterly* argued that "our submission is that we have left behind the crude categories of 'fraud,' 'unwillingness to work,' and are in touch—as always in the relief committee room—with the complications of life."[98] Unfortunately, if we accept their writing as our guide, crude categories still shaped a good deal of the society's casework.

Yet even this debate lacked a little of the heat that it might have sparked elsewhere. Certainly, people within the society were raising questions about its methods and purposes even in the 1920s and well before the sense of crisis that enveloped the COS by the middle of the 1930s. Still, what is striking about these London case files is the way in which the visitors from Hammersmith and Fulham or St. Pancras and Shoreditch shared a sense of almost unbridgeable distance and incomprehension. In interwar London, class was fixed and solid, and class differences formed a bedrock that these particular observers confirmed rather than undermined. They went out looking for character, and they found both the deserving, decent, and largely ignorant poor and the ineffective, furtive, and undeserving poor that their assumptions about character told them they would find. The equation between class and character was one the Melbourne workers made as well, but never as confidently. What the workers in Melbourne strove constantly to prove, in part by emphasizing the poor's inability to either feel their position or acknowledge the truth, seemed in London, at the heart of the charity organization movement, to need hardly any demonstration at all.

CHAPTER 13

Dense and Low Grade, but Still He Builds Great Castles in the Air

Toward some of poor, the "unhelpables," the ungrateful, or the overly demanding, COS visitors were often disdainful and sometimes dismissive. This was especially likely if the applicants tried to claim some prerogative in explaining either the origins of their poverty or the best means of overcoming it. One of the clearest discussions of casework aims and methods, which appeared in the 1925 annual report, suggested that its best hope lay in "discovering a solid bit of personality or character upon which to build a more effective life." Of the notion that the cure for social ills might involve "slogans, Acts of Parliament, and the expenditure of public money," and especially that it could be accomplished without rigorous casework, the article's writer was scathing: "The whole process takes place in the realm of fantasy which it is the aim of the COS to get behind. The simplest illustration of this is a common saying among COS workers, 'You will never find in the end that what the applicant really needs is the thing he wishes for; just the opposite, or, at least, something quite different.'"[99] In practice, "getting behind" the applicants' fantasies more often than not meant insisting that they did not know what should be done to remedy their situations. It also meant insisting on uncovering the whole truth, or at least whatever the visitor could exact from applicants who didn't realize that needing help meant revealing all of their secrets.

At times, the COS could be desperately insensitive to the subtleties and complexities of the lives they glimpsed. In one Hammersmith family, the visitor reported the seventeen-year-old son to be "rotten," paralyzed and nearly blind with congenital syphilis; not surprisingly, "things seem to be very strained between father and son," the whole family was "difficult & quarrelsome," and the young man—who "didn't seem a bad boy, a bit wild around the eyes"—was "desperately resentful of his disease." He wanted a surgical boot, and perhaps some help finding work, but the visitor kept pressing for more details and joined in the stepmother's demands that he learn a trade. Eventually, the father and son did not "welcome any further assistance."[100] A family from Camden Town, referred by a local hospital, also met unwanted inquisition over the status of an adopted daughter who needed convalescent care for rheumatic endocarditis. They wanted to let the matter drop, but the visitor persisted. This prompted a letter from the girl's mother: "Dear Madam, [my husband] does not agree with you wishing to know any more questions he think's we have answered enough.... We are most grateful to you for all you have done for us but he feels he does not see why all these questions should be asked." The visitor eventually discovered that the daughter was in fact the father's illegitimate child. At that point came another letter: "I was willing to tell you all from the first and God knows I have suffered enough for it." The girl had already been away, and the family repaid its debt, perhaps pondering the cost of the revelations.[101]

Some interactions bordered on the aggressive, at least in the telling. Judgments about the supposed stupidity of some applicants prevented reasonable assistance and colored interpretations of everything they did. Those who demurred, who questioned advice, or who tried to assert different prerogatives often ended up as "stupid," "ignorant," "dense," "low grade," and "defective." The public face of home visiting—in which the COS "sits down with [the applicant] by the fireside and worries out his problems with him"—was not a particularly accurate description of some actual visits. The Hardemans, a family from Fulham, were assisted with a small allowance when the father died of lung disease at the age of thirty-nine. One of the daughters later came into the district office seeking help to find work; after checking with a former employer, the caseworker described the sixteen-year-old as needing "strict discipline" and as having been dismissed from her work on suspicion of thieving. On this and no other basis, the district arranged a place for the girl at a training home in Berkshire, into which the committee considered she should be "pressed" if she proved unwilling to go. The girl decided against it. In the same family, four years later, the committee determined that a twelve-year-old boy should be charged in the Children's Court and sent to an industrial school. The mother again said that in asking advice, she had not wanted such a draconian outcome. According to the report, "She does not want the boy treated as a Criminal ... and she seems to think the Case Committee could do something."[102]

Between 1928 and 1931, Beatrice Tennyson of the Hammersmith office had a long battle with Arthur Cook, whose wife ran off with another man—because, she later said, Arthur had been violent—and pawned all of their belongings. Cook had two sons; the older, just two years of age, was in the Barnardo's Home on Clapham High Street, but they would neither keep him nor accept the baby. Cook needed to find the boys a home. Tennyson first suggested the Children's Aid Society and a foster mother. Cook's response was unexpected: "To send my child to a woman on such conditions would only mean that the little chap will be pushed and buffeted from Foster Mother to workhouse and finish up heaven knows where." Eventually, the older boy went to a home in Plymouth, and the Home for Waifs and Strays in Bristol took the baby. Cook had to make regular payments, but stopped after ten months. Tennyson's letter was strident: "I am disgusted that you have not sent money," she wrote. "One has little respect or sympathy for a father who does not attempt to support his children, and there must be an end of it in your case. Do you realise that you have sent no money at all since May 13th and does that fact not fill you with shame. If it does not it most certainly ought to."

In Beatrice Tennyson's eyes, Cook, a rather rough sort of laborer, seemed to have none of the feelings for which one might hope in a parent; he would neither feel his situation nor fulfill his obligations. He wrote back, saying that he had been ill and out of work and would make more payments when he could. He added, "I wish there was a law to compel the creature that brought these children into the world to do her share towards their maintenance. But *no* women get off scot free." This began something of a war. Beatrice Tennyson wrote: "Your last letter does not fill me with any confidence or respect for you at all. You are just as much responsible for bringing the children into the world as the Mother and it is the part of the father to provide for his family not his wife's part." A few days later, having tried to find out—without much success—whether he was drawing illicit unemployment benefits for the children, she wrote again: "I am suggesting to my committee at their next meeting that immediate steps should be taken to bring you to a proper sense of your responsibility." In another letter, this one to one of the homes caring for his sons, she described what she wanted to do: "We ought to advise that the children be deposited on his door step and if he cannot support them he must go into the House with them." There was another letter to Cook but no response. Another letter from Tennyson brought this reply from Cook: "Perhaps you have noticed by the paper that there is an increasing army of unemployed."[103]

While Tennyson wrote increasingly damning reports, it is clear even from the file that Cook tried to maintain the payments owed to the homes, despite irregular employment and frequent illness, until he was jailed in 1931. During that year, Mildred Harding encouraged his parents to take both of the children, but no account of her success and failure is provided. We know the youngest boy was back in London by 1939, because he was then evacuated, and we also know that he had returned by 1942. We know that his father was jailed again but that the older brother had disappeared, perhaps into adoption. A dozen years after the family first began to disintegrate, propelled outward by whatever forces had destroyed the relationship between the parents, its members were so far apart that they could no longer find each other.

This case exemplifies the sense of distance that characterized many of the relationships between COS visitors and applicants in the 1920s and 1930s. The applicant was aggressive and possibly violent. He was angry, and he ended up in jail for housebreaking. But at least for the three years between 1928 and 1931, on the evidence of the file, he did attempt to fulfill his financial obligations to the homes that had taken in his sons. He made payments, albeit irregular ones, and despite the worker's suspicions, nothing ever suggested that he was gaining illicit benefits or that his account of irregular employment and illness should be doubted.

Arthur Cook didn't play the game that the worker thought should be played. She was sympathetic at first, and her suggestions and decisions helped secure a place for both of the children. But her reactions to his failings—real or imagined—exemplify several of the conflicts and contradictions that characterized COS casework in London. Cook was meant to be independent and to face up to his responsibilities, but he was not allowed to fail and struggle. To lose work in the uncertain metropolitan labor market of the late 1920s was to invite suggestions that he wasn't trying hard enough and was looking to evade his responsibilities. Cook was also meant to feel ashamed by his inability to care for his sons, however desperate his circumstances and however uncertain he was about their best prospects. To insist on what he saw—for good or bad reasons—as a "proper home" and not a foster mother was to express prerogatives that he, as a poor man, did not have. To be needy one had to be ashamed; to not show shame was to invite the suspicion that he was like the other "coarse," "rough," and "indifferent" types of "unhelpables," a man who did not, in some fundamental way, feel and suffer like his more "refined" betters.

Cook made another mistake, too. It's one he shouldn't have made, but it's one that a welfare practice focused more on understanding needs than policing entitlements and building character might have forgiven him. Cook was ungrateful. He became angry. He failed the test of necessary patience, the kind of patience that is frequently demanded from the poor but is all too readily denied to them in turn. He failed a test of character that so many applicants—perhaps especially men without mastery—had failed before.

In their confrontation with the stupidity of the poor, COS visitors also made a point of discrediting and demolishing fanciful aspirations. This meant showing the impracticality of Dora Houston's "vague plan of letting unfurnished rooms," for instance.[104] It also meant, when providing details about a man who was considering emigration and needed help from his service organization and the National Association for the Employment of Ex-Soldiers, writing that "he is just a labourer," and "I am afraid he is only an unskilled labourer." Several years later, in fact, this man "looks very different from the ordinary type of labourer" and seemed "a very superior and straightforward man."[105]

Walter Collins, a hospital orderly, approached the COS in 1921 seeking general help while he was temporarily unable to work. Although he had a small weekly pension from his military service, he wanted assistance to change his family's circumstances. He was "full of talk about the way he had been sent from pillar to post" and wanted to "end 'all this charity business.'" The visitor was suspicious: "He seemed rather too much used to saying that." She continued in this vein when writing up her notes on the home visit: "He evidently builds great castles in the air as to the shop he will keep.... [He] seems to think anyone with any brains can make a shop pay, & then he won't let his wife and daughter go out to work." It made no sense to encourage him in such aspirations, especially when he was so disparaging about the ease of proprietorship. Making applicants realize the narrow ambit of their abilities and prospects was one version of "thorough planning." It emphasized the fixity of people's class positions and circumstances. But it seems now—and it seemed to some of the COS's own workers then—a deflated and even defeated version of "social work."[106]

Applicants were also frustrated by what they saw as a mismatch between intrusive questioning and actual results. Visiting the Godfrey family in 1939, one visitor "felt a very strong atmosphere of antagonism as soon as I went into the room and it turned out that Mrs G had worked herself up into the most tremendous indignation against us for asking so many questions."[107] Skilled working men were particularly incensed by inquiry, though it was the view of COS visitors that their attitudes stemmed from "an entirely wrong opinion of the Society and what it stands for."[108] Charlie Davis was "very bitter" about his past record of imprisonment—for the theft of a bottle of whiskey—being brought up in his 1934 investigation. At one encounter, "he said if he still stole now he would get better beds for his children"; in 1937, denied help with moving to a new flat, he "was not best pleased & rambled on in an aimless fashion about the wrongs suffered by the working man."[109] Some applicants also wondered about the wisdom of their interrogators. Beatrice Wilson was referred to the Stepney COS shortly after her husband's imprisonment in order to get shoes for five children aged under thirteen: "[I] spent some time trying to explain the value of saving 1/- per week towards the next pair of shoes. This [she] was quite willing to do, but [she] couldn't see what good one shilling would do when all the children need so much."[110]

With a greater range of options than impoverished people in Melbourne, and in a city where the power and influence of the COS was diminishing and the range of public provision was expanding, London's poor had less to lose by pointing out the limits of what a "charity organisation" was able to achieve. On the evidence of these case files, they also had access to a stronger language and tradition of class confrontation and were more prepared to use that particular weapon in their dealings with charity investigators. Conflict was certainly not the most common experience, but it was more common in London than in Melbourne or Oregon. It was also more common here than in Boston and Minneapolis, where the emphasis on transformation and faith seemed to have buoyed the relationship between workers and applicants even when aspirations went unfulfilled.

The story of poverty told by London's COS visitors not only measured their frustration with poor people who couldn't accept their limitations but also reflected a growing sense of their own powerlessness. This was not so much because economic circumstances prevented real change in people's fortunes, as was more commonly recognized in Melbourne, but because the people in question—whether through stupidity or carelessness or incompetence—were "quite unhelpable in a constructive sense."[111] Of course, the COS's official doctrines and documents spoke of plans and directions and of supporting "the plucky, self-reliant fellow who scorned to be dependent."[112] In effect, however, if applicants were not already self-reliant and capable of overcoming their problems, the local district visitors found few reasons to feel confident about cajoling or producing real improvements in people's prospects. They looked at the "raw material" and found it difficult to imagine into what other shapes it might be molded.

In the 1920s and especially by the 1930s, the secretaries, committees, and visitors in these London districts were carrying out the routines of an investigative practice even they had begun to doubt would lead to much more than palliation. This was partly a matter of changing context. In 1918 the COS was said to attach "chief importance to the hope of permanent improvement."[113] But by 1932, the annual report noted the rising amount of "distress due to unemployment" and added that "unfortunately, it is seldom that anything constructive can be done in such cases, the real need being work, which no one can provide."[114] It was a reasonable conclusion, perhaps, but it was also clear that some in the society were beginning to despair of the poor in particular and the "industrial classes" in general. Indeed, the 1938 annual report suggested, "We know, of course, that the long-term remedy is to see that our young workers have both better parents and a better start in the industrial world."[115] It seems a rather deflated version of social work, let alone hopes of "permanent improvement."

This sense of decreasing ability was mirrored in the daily work of the districts and helped nourish the sense—which was especially strong among younger and female workers—that the COS was, like an unmoored boat, drifting somewhat aimlessly into the future. The Hammersmith secretary, Miss Hill, told a 1936 meeting of the council that her committee had become "the suppliers of spare parts ... [and] opportunities for constructive casework were considerably restricted."[116] By the early 1940s, the pressure for change was growing; as another district secretary, Miss Simey, remarked in an interview, "The whole philosophy of the COS was based on individualism, whilst the trend of modern thought was towards socialism. The Society tended to criticize any move towards socialism and this made it appear reactionary."[117]

As part of the self-reflection that took up much of the early years of the war, a special committee examining the future of the COS interviewed Eileen Younghusband. Younghusband was already well known as an advocate and innovator in social work training and professionalism and within a few years would lead national surveys and publish influential books (including, of course, *The Education and Training of Social Workers*). Her work in social settlements and as a social worker in Bermondsey and Stepney had preceded her professional training at the London School of Economics, something that was true for a number of the COS visitors. But Younghusband had gained from her social work an appreciation for the resilience and abilities of the poor, as well as for the continuing importance of private and voluntary societies, even in an expanding welfare state. In the report of her interview, Younghusband echoed the criticisms that were also being made by the society's own workers: "Most people criticised the rigidity of the enquiries made by the COS and expressed the view that these enquiries were directed more to finding reasons for refusing an application than for helping people. She thought that the general impression was that the COS was more concerned with character than with need, that they took a quiet delight in discovering that a man was a fraud." The COS, she said, "had not kept pace with the social outlook of the community."[118] Younghusband and hospital almoner Margaret Roxburgh, who reported that she and her colleagues were growing frustrated with the COS's emphasis on "deserved rather than needed assistance," concurred that the society's most important role might be training the many social workers who would be needed for state services.[119] In their conviction that an unreformed COS might find itself an unwanted anachronism, these critics were in one way echoing a conclusion already made by many of its clients, many of whom would have expressed less regret at its possible passing.

CHAPTER 14

Nightmare Days

In July 1944, the Charity Organisation Society's annual report made a simple statement: these "nightmare summer days," when for two months flying bombs killed Londoners in their hundreds, changed its work "overnight."[120] Here, it seems, was a moment of compelling truth.

As for most Britons, debates about the future became frequent during the war, quickening even more once the dark days of possible defeat had given way to some faith in ultimate victory. By 1943 the role of COS workers and officials in planning postwar reconstruction and securing a place for "personal service" agencies began to appear in the annual reports. The Central Committee for Aims and Policy explored ways forward, while the district secretaries circulated ideas for reform, including a change of name to the Citizen's Aid Society or the Citizen's Welfare Association (in the end, the name chosen was the Family Welfare Association). As Jane Lewis has shown, the war years saw a significant rethinking of purpose and future relationships with a new set of state social services, especially when eligibility for assistance—at least in some forms—would be unshackled from the Poor Law system's focus on deterrence.[121] The COS sponsored a conference in Oxford on social reconstruction in 1941 and, more generally, "moved firmly away from a casework practice that was designed both to educate and to categorise for purposes of relief" and toward one based on "adjusting the individual to his environment."[122] By 1949 the new association's Aims and Policy Committee had agreed that its functions should include "a family case work service in the London area," "pioneer work in the field of social service"—which would include initiating new services and advocating "social improvements on a national scale"—and training family caseworkers for universities and other organizations.[123]

The breath of optimism and ideas about a definite and energetic role in the changed landscape of British welfare had set the renamed society on a new path. This was to be a "service" agency, in the new meaning of that term. And by the early 1950s, one member of the Central Committee could even go on record as saying that "we should be ready to take more risks in trusting clients" and that "a community must be able to carry people who are unable to accept responsibility."[124] It was not something that the COS council would ever have said.

Many of those arguments had first been made out in the districts, especially by younger women who had come into the COS as trainees and new workers during the 1930s. Some of them, at least, were prepared to seize the rudder and try to steer the COS back toward the main currents of social thought. Of course, the prejudices and convictions that had dampened any sense of optimism about the poor during the 1920s and 1930s did not disappear in 1940, and it was still possible for the new Family Welfare Association's social workers to echo after the war some of the negative sentiments that were common in the years before it. But during the war years, the case files started to reflect something that would not have been expected, perhaps especially here, at the starting point of the Charity Organisation Society. They started to reflect different kinds of ideas and philosophies about welfare and social work. Moreover, they began to reflect what social workers heard when they actually listened to the poor, especially, I think, when women began to listen to women across the barriers of class and social position. Sometimes, this meant the COS visitors listening to other women working in welfare, such as almoners and public assistance workers, and to probation officers, policewomen, and nurses. But in some of the words they wrote in their case files, and in some of the arguments and points they put to the committees and working groups, women listening to women helped drag the COS out of distrusting investigation and onto the "road of future and of youth."[125]

It is, of course, a truism that the war remade what it was possible to think, do, and argue about poverty, inequality, and need in Britain. The emphasis on sacrifice and its rewards remade the social and political landscape, and the debates that changed the Charity Organisation Society into the Family Welfare Association transformed a whole range of institutions. This was change on the large scale and at a rapid pace; wars, and especially the people's wars that were fought in the twentieth century, stir up the societies that fight them, and many things once taken for granted can no longer stay the same. And at the same time that this war proved democracies could prevail, it also made clear that the people who had won the war expected democracy and equality to mean something once it was over.

But that statement about "nightmare summer days" also tells us something about the impact of the war on Londoners and about the ways in which convictions about character, hierarchy, and poverty were actually challenged and changed, especially in 1944. London's ordeal in 1940 and 1941 had certainly established the resilience of its people, as COS visitors made their way through bombed streets in sometimes vain attempts to find applicants. The impact was direct, too: the Southwark office was destroyed in 1940 and with it the district's records and files. A new kind of description entered the files. After visiting one Hammersmith woman, whose flat "showed signs of a struggle to make the best of a low income," a visitor wrote, "I like her very much, she seems to me to be a real Londoner with a backbone."[126] She would need to be resilient, because in August 1944 she would be injured and made homeless by one of Hammersmith's most serious flying bomb incidents, at Blaxland House in the White City Estate.

COS visitors witnessed the impact of the war at very close hand. At first, I think, this impact could be explained or at least accommodated without abandoning older ideas about character, pluck, gratitude, and position. The applicants came across as "poor things," including an elderly woman from Greyhound Road in Fulham, who spent a terrifying period trapped on her stairs after a land mine explosion and was evacuated to Cornwall, and a girl of sixteen from St. Pancras, who became hysterical during the heavy April raid in 1941; the great raid of May 10, 1941, "made her even worse & she shakes all the time & cannot eat & is looking pale & frightened."[127] Her uncle wanted her to be evacuated and to join his wife and children in Hampshire; he had himself been injured by a bomb at work, but said that he would not mind the bombings so long as there was no one to worry about at home. The flying bomb attacks in the summer of 1944 generated an even greater level of anxiety; a couple in Kentish Town had to be called out of the shelter to meet their visitor at the end of June, and a long-established St. Pancras couple, first visited in 1921, were much affected, the wife writing a letter to the district secretary to apologize for missing the visitor because "my nerves won't allow me to come & see you, you see I have to keep near the Shelter, that's the only Way I can Control myself a Bit."[128]

For the first time, though, COS visitors began to write about how problems piled up and could overwhelm you. They noted the Shoreditch woman bombed out in 1941 and then "dehoused" again by a V-2 rocket in the hard winter of 1945 and how exhausted and defeated she was by what had happened.[129] They listened to their other applicants bombed out in 1940 or "blasted" by flying bombs in 1944, and they recognized that one aspect of the raids no one had anticipated was their impact on London's housing and the great problems that losing a house could cause to vulnerable people. They saw—and felt themselves—the stress of living on edge and in constant anxiety.

It is important to remember how rapid and horrifying was London's transition in 1944, from the seeming safety of June's first ten days, including the relief at the invasion of Normandy, to the terrors of its next two weeks. On the first Saturday of the attacks, June 17, St. Mary Abbott's Hospital was hit, and sixteen patients and nurses died; the next day more than a hundred people died at the Guards Chapel of Wellington Barracks near Buckingham Palace, with dozens more dead in Putney, Battersea, Fulham, Finsbury, and Hackney and at the West End Hospital in St. Pancras. More than thirty people died in Whitfield Street and Tottenham Court Road on Monday June 19, the same day fifty were killed in the warehouses, workshops, and offices around Southwark's Union Street, and there were similar death tolls at Highbury Corner and Lambeth's Acre Lane in the next week.

By now, of course, London was being evacuated again, and dozens of COS applicants were asking for help to leave the city. On Friday, June 30, more than fifty people were killed in the curve of Aldwych near Bush House, and another fifty died along Tottenham Court Road and in Howland Street at the western edge of Bloomsbury. On the first day of July, twenty people were killed in Earsby Street and Lisgar Terrace in the Fulham COS district. Two days later, a flying bomb killed more than sixty billeted American soldiers—and a dozen local residents—as it shredded the facades from buildings in Sloane Court in Chelsea, and another destroyed much of Princes Gate Mews just north of the Victoria and Albert Museum. On July 6 a shelter in Hawley Road, St. Pancras, was blown apart, and two dozen people died. The bombs kept coming through July and August, killing dozens of people in shopping streets at Lewisham, Camberwell, Willesden, and Kensington; hospital patients in Finsbury; and residents of charity dwellings in Marylebone and Stepney. From September would come a mix of occasional flying bombs and the long-range rockets, which arrived without warning and dissolved houses, flats, and shops into dust even before the noise of their explosion arrived.

I want to suggest that what the COS workers saw, especially in 1944 and 1945, as the bombs of the Blitz gave way to flying bombs and rockets, was vivid confirmation of things the poor had always said about the dangers of the world. This also helps explain why it was the nightmare summer days of 1944, and not the bleak and terrible Blitz winter of 1940 and 1941, that the COS regarded as its turning point. In part, of course, this reflected the way in which the political context had changed. But it also reflects, I think, the particular impact of the flying bombs on those who endured them. There could be few more dramatic demonstrations of the suddenness—or the randomness—of disaster than their sudden arrival and terrifying explosion. And those demonstrations were not of the night, but of the day, and the worst incidents occurred in highly public places and at institutions such as hospitals, often in the parts of London the COS workers knew well. Even more than the Blitz winter, the "nightmare summer days" made what the poor said seem more true and more compelling. It was perhaps more possible to accept that people were made vulnerable by forces they couldn't control and that individuals could find themselves suddenly exposed, suddenly hurt, and suddenly stripped of every possession and every defense. Most of all, I think, the COS workers were able to grasp something of what the poor had always known and some of the poor had tried to explain: that the strengths or flaws of character mattered little in the face of disaster.

Of course, the idea that poverty was a disaster or that the vulnerabilities caused by inequality were a matter for public attention did not suddenly and irrevocably replace an older faith in the strong links between character and reward. Indeed, they would prove more resilient than the people of 1944 and 1945 might have imagined. As Ross McKibbin has suggested, while "the conventional wisdoms of public life became for once the wisdoms of the left," the "stereotypes of the working class remained as powerful as ever; they were just believed by fewer people."[130] But change there was.

These are hints and speculations, advanced with the modesty that a few sources must demand. But I think, for a time at least, the theater of poverty in London changed. To say that also does justice, as historian Seth Koven argues we must, to the fact that even if some of these visitors and social workers expressed their distance from and distaste for the poor, they all had made a commitment to "look closely at the human face of poverty and find ways to redress the injuries of class."[131] Koven is describing an earlier generation, who built institutions of social investigation and reform—including, of course, the COS—during the 1880s and 1890s; in the somewhat different atmosphere of the 1920s and 1930s, the COS case files also show the importance of reestablishing and redramatizing the differences and ideal relationships between classes. But there is change here, too, change in the understanding of those differences and relationships, change that reminds us, as Koven shows so well, that whatever the difficulties of class privilege, the dynamics of sympathy and respect were rarely as straightforward as their caricatures might make out, especially among women.[132]

In these files lies the evidence of a revelation of sorts, which rested to some degree on women listening to women. They changed poverty's story, even if not forever and even if only for some rather than for all. From one in which the feckless poor shambled across the stage at a distance too great to really hear what they said, it became one in which audiences and actors shared something of the weight of the world and understood—haltingly and fleetingly, perhaps—that in a time of sudden disaster, it might be best to make entitlement and reward rest on something more sturdy than the more or less expert categorization of "character." What can be advanced most confidently, perhaps, is that these "nightmare summer days" showed in London what the Depression showed in Melbourne: all of the tools that refined and superior people brought with them into the 1930s would be tested, and some of them would be broken. If it is important to focus on those times and places when the distance between the poor and others is forged and defended, it is just as important and interesting to look at those moments when that distance lessens and the assumptions that underpin it begin to fail.

Part Three

BOSTON

Miss Wells and the Boy Who Wanted to Be an American

Dramatis Personæ

LAURA WELLS, an agent for the Boston Children's Aid Association
JERZY (GEORGE) KOZIOREK, a young Polish American man

· · · · · · · · · · · · · · DRAMA · · · · · · · · · · · · · ·

She had been told it was a "good speaking story," one the Boston Children's Aid Association could use in its publicity material and when training new workers.

The client was baptized as Jerzy, though he now insists on being called George. He is twenty-three years old, and, Laura Wells thinks as she looks across her desk, those impossibly blue eyes take him most of the way to handsome. Jerzy-George has just completed the discharge interview, and it will be his last contact with the agency. He is wearing the suit his foster parents bought him for his twenty-first birthday, but he is going home to change before starting his job in the produce market on Boylston Street in Brookline.

When Jerzy's case began in 1925, Laura Wells was yet to graduate as a social worker. Ten years on, it is her job to write the final entry and close the case. The file for Case 9127 was thick, though far from the thickest she'd seen. She had read it earlier and was quick to see the shape of the story. Jerzy was American born. His father worked in a woolen mill, and his mother looked after seven children. Jerzy was the second child and eldest boy. Reported as truant and "stubborn," he kept running away and sleeping out "like a hobo." His teacher had seen "none of the peculiarities of a delinquent boy" or any evidence of "anti-social conduct," despite his "complete indifference to any method of discipline."

When questioned as a thirteen-year-old, the boy had refused to say anything. He was sullen and uncooperative. In time, though, came the hints. His mind was "filled with the movies," the first CAA visitor had written. He was "restless and excited," told of his father beating his mother, and was ashamedly ignorant about "the common decencies of household life." He said he wasn't sure about how to keep himself clean or be "a good American boy." The parents spoke only Polish, and the father was, at best, "a very slack, irresponsible kind of person."

For two weeks in 1925, Jerzy lived at the boys' home in Framingham. He was examined at the Judge Baker Guidance Center, one of Boston's most important clinics for the diagnosis of troubled children. From the center came a report recommending the "drastic action" of placing the boy in a foster home. Only this, the center suggested, would tackle the real problem, which was "a combination of dislike for his home on account of his suppression and Americanized aspects and his abundant energy." The center was also pleased to report that their client had developed a "fearful respect" for the CAA.

"You were in some trouble back then, George," Laura said to the young man sitting across from her. She could hear him shuffling his feet under the desk, and he was spinning his cap between his fingers.

He looked back at her and smiled, "Yes, ma'am. I was in much trouble all the time then."

She glanced back at the now opened file. In 1927 Jerzy was returned to his family, having spent two years in a foster home in Dedham. Within a week, he had run away and gone back to his foster parents' "American family." His father, he said, was making moonshine, and his mother was encouraging him to steal. The house was dirty. The CAA visitor agreed that his mother was "obviously abnormal," but the agency then moved Jerzy back and forth between the foster home and his parents for three more years. He maintained his "horror of going home" to his immigrant family, called his mother a "pig," and always talked about their dirtiness. Admonished for smoking by one of the visitors in 1929, seventeen-year-old Jerzy begged her to tell only his foster parents because they wouldn't beat him the way his father would. He wept at the prospect of another return to his family; "he wants to grow up to be an American and not a 'Polack.'" A year later, at eighteen, he left high school and began a job at a local store. They liked him there; the boy they knew as "George" was a good, steady worker. George also moved back in—for the last time—with his foster parents. They were still sharing their home with him now, at the time of his discharge and five years since he last left his parents.

George is still fiddling with his cap and making a show of being interested, but he clearly wants to leave.

"Well, George, I need you to sign the discharge form."

She gives it to him, and he leans over, writing with the flourish of a young man still excited by the idea of having his own signature.

"Good luck, George. I'm sure you'll do well. You stick to your path."

He stands up, straightens himself, and flashes a smile. "OK, Miss Wells. I promise I'll be good."

Putting his cap on with great care, George turns and walks toward the door of the office, pausing to give her another smile.

As he opens the door, he turns back, touches his finger to his cap, and says, "Be seein' ya."

For a moment, she thinks he is going to say "toots" or some other term he has picked up from the movies. He's probably been to see one recently, perhaps last night. If he is aiming for Jimmy Cagney, it isn't quite hitting the mark. Before she can answer, though, he turns away.

He closes the door too loudly; Wells guesses that George does many things too loudly.

Rereading the file, Laura Wells smiles at some of Jerzy-George's antics. He wasn't above using smiles and tears, and some of those stories about dirt were perhaps a little too minute in their details. Yet she is reminded of some of her own cases with the children of other immigrants, the Italians and Russian Jews in the North End and the Portuguese in New Bedford. There, too, the story is about potential and about transformation. These boys and girls can have a hard time of it. Theirs is a quiet and sometimes not-so-quiet resistance against immigrant parents who might be citizens but would always be estranged in some way from their new home. The struggle to imagine and then make a future couldn't be made with Old World ideas.

From the age of thirteen, Wells thinks, Jerzy had been trying to become an American. With the long-term help of the CAA, he has succeeded, she thinks: twenty-three years old, a good job, and decent prospects, even in the hard times of 1935. And he had a tailored suit, as he told her, "just like the men in the movies."

Laura Wells writes a last sentence for her summary. It is another year of growing caseloads. There are two more discharges to handle tomorrow, and she has clients to visit in Roxbury and Jamaica Plain before the day is through.

She closes the file, bringing back to the top the now slightly torn and faded first sheet for "Case 9127, Jerzy Koziorek." She takes up the pen and draws two neat lines through Jerzy. Above it she writes "George." Jerzy isn't erased, nor, she thinks, should he be. But he should give way to George, the new American.

Jerzy is also smiling as he leaves the office on Mount Vernon Street. He hasn't been to the CAA offices in Beacon Hill for a long time, so he takes a wrong turn at Bowdoin Street and has to retrace his steps to get to South Station.

He is a bit distracted. He is thinking about his date tomorrow and how he is almost ready to ask Rose if she will marry him. He has a steady job at the store, and his foster parents say they will keep helping him. The suit was a kind of down payment, they said. They are good folks, and he will always be grateful for what they have done.

But that isn't the most important thing right now. He isn't heading for Boylston Street, because he always has Wednesday afternoons off. He has to get to Dorchester for the weekly dinner with his parents. It is his father's birthday, so his brothers Steven and Willy are coming, and his sister Franciszka is bringing her new baby, Clara.

South Station is as crowded as ever. But he loves the crowds. He loves feeling part of something bigger, one of the people moving here and there, into work, back home, downtown. It's America.

Ashmont Station is still a few stops away. Turning his cap in his fingers, Jerzy rides with the trolley car, shifting his feet and bracing with each turn and rumble. He smiles as he thinks of the way his mother will deliberately get her sons' American names wrong, accenting the wrong syllable or twisting the sound. Franciszka likes her Polish name, even though she's married a German. But Stefan and Boleslaw, like Jerzy, made their names American. Matka still pretends to chide them for being too American. "Polski, polski," she'll say. "Too many American chłopcy!"

It is ten years since he left home. Ten years since the school reported him and he was sent away for being uncontrollable. When you're twenty-three, ten years is a long time. He'd done bad things. But he has also been given things not known to a lot of the boys he grew up with.

Even five years is a long time, Jerzy thinks, to be living away from home. Still, he has never been alone. Mama and Tata have always known where he is and where he will be going.

· · · · · · · · · · · · RESOLUTION · · · · · · · · · · · ·

In writing Jerzy's story, Laura Wells made some interesting choices. While she pictured his life in terms of a redemptive transformation, she was less willing to acknowledge how Jerzy himself had helped ensure that the CAA's visitors would accept this story as the basis of his diagnosis and treatment. There is little acknowledgment in her side of the story of Jerzy as at least partly an agent in his own fortune. His desire to be rescued from "suppression" was probably real enough, but choosing Americanization as the dynamic of his story earned him a level of support and resources that was never awarded to other "stubborn" or "defiant" teenagers. His life was clearly regarded by the CAA as ideal testimony for one of the "speaking stories" that generated interest and funds among the association's supporters. In its twists and turns, it also reflects many of the characteristic ways in which Boston's welfare workers wrote about poverty, ethnicity, and class.

There is much to ask, only some of which can be known. How active were Jerzy and his family in that transformation and "rescue"? How much of what was written about him did Jerzy help to script? There is a vital clue contained in the file but rather tellingly omitted from the Children's Aid Association's "good speaking story." In the speaking story, Jerzy is his immigrant family's victim. He is returned to them but each time runs away, back to his American family, and it is with them that he is eventually allowed to settle. In fact, things were a little different. A 1929 note in the file makes clear that Jerzy's parents were paying a weekly board directly to his foster parents. As far as I can tell from the record, this commenced in 1927—at the same time that he "ran away" from his "abnormal" family life—and continued until 1930, when he left high school and began full-time work. It seems an unlikely gesture for parents rejected as "backward" and "irresponsible." The file suggests that it was voluntary. On the evidence of the other files preserved in the archives, it was also rare. Courts could and did impose maintenance orders, but this appears to have been an arrangement between Jerzy's birth and foster parents in which the Children's Aid Association played no part other than to record the fact.

It is possible to argue, I think, that Jerzy helped the CAA write the story of his life. He shaped it around a theme he increasingly understood as one they found interesting and affirming. Yes, he wanted to be an American. But this was hardly something he wanted only by himself or for himself. Jerzy's transition into an American young man, with good prospects and a movie-star suit, is best understood as a process his parents at some point decided to fund, perhaps even from the beginning. On the evidence of other places and times, this was not particularly unusual. In the midst of difficult situations and choices, working-class and immigrant parents sometimes see fostering, institutional care, and even reformatories in strategic terms. These places not only assist in controlling unruly children but also offer training, education, and a form of social mobility. Like apprenticeships or domestic service, they can be a way of locating a child—perhaps a troublesome one, but perhaps also an ambitious and clever one—in a place where opportunities are more likely to come their way. In that sense, Jerzy and his parents had been able to call on a particular kind of American bargain, which doled out possibilities in return for what must have been a sometimes painful rejection of "Old World" faith, values, and standards. It carried a cost, for it meant their eldest son living with relative strangers, at least for a time. It was also an uncertain future, a gamble. But in a new world, immigrants knew that uncertainty and risk were sometimes the price of better fortunes.

As Laura Wells understood, I think, Jerzy's characterizations of his irretrievably immigrant family were sometimes a little too exacting in their detail. What she was less willing or able to grasp was that they may have been caricatures, in part prompted and sketched by the association's own visitors with whom Jerzy had built his own "good speaking story." Jerzy's discovery by the child rescue and welfare system may or may not have been something in which his parents had a hand. It may have been an unexpected and threatening intervention into their lives. Yet once Jerzy and perhaps Jerzy's parents discovered how eagerly American child-savers invested in the stories of immigrant backwardness, they were perhaps even more compliant—and complicit—in their telling and retelling.

Certainly, we can wonder how much those supposedly ignorant, backward, and "very Polish" parents understood their responsibilities in playing out the script of an Americanized "delinquent." On the evidence, I doubt it was something they actually initiated. But once it had started, and their oldest boy was enmeshed in a new country's child welfare system, they clearly found a way of keeping him close and supporting him while letting him benefit from the kindness of strangers. Jerzy's stories about moonshine and backwardness and ignorance were a little too dramatic. Perhaps that was in part because they were aided and abetted—even dramatically enacted—by parents who were cast in roles they understood all too well and who were making the best they could of a bad situation. In that sense, they did always know where Jerzy was, and they just as consistently tried to shape where George was going.

Changing Jerzy

In Boston, no less than in Melbourne and London, agents and investigators heard and misheard, and they understood and misunderstood. They made decisions—and mistakes—about the lives they examined, and they participated in a performance that wasn't always under their total direction. The Massachusetts Society for the Prevention of Cruelty to Children (MSPCC), the larger agency with which the Children's Aid Association (CAA) worked closely during the 1920s and 1930s, described its approach as "friendly [and] sympathetic," carried out by agents with a "keen appreciation of life, an ability to work with people [and] a desire to serve."[1] But the broader perils of "defective citizenship, with all its attendant evils and burdens" could make relationships with clients dictatorial and even punitive.[2] In one 1928 case, agent Eleanor Graham, warned by neighbors that "it would be hazardous to visit" one family, took pride in her ability to so "greatly unnerve" both the mother and the father that they agreed to improve their "unclean" home. In fact, for fear of another visit, they moved from Brockton to Dorchester.[3]

In these Boston agencies, rescuing children and finding a cure for their parents' problems justified the application of remedies that may or may not have made any sense to the clients. There were moments of sympathy and of the befriending that still carried benevolent volunteers into charity and continued to form an important part of paid workers' vocation as well. At the same time, there were moments of hectoring and triumphant confrontation, careless attribution, and overly rapid judgments that turned out to be wrong. Compared with the women (and a few men) who worked in more general "family casework" in Minneapolis, "child welfare" in Oregon, or "charity investigation" in Melbourne and London, Boston's agents were just as dismissive of "abnormal," "inferior," and "backward" people, especially if they tried to assert their own prerogatives and values. They were sure of their own self-evident superiority, which needed no explanation, and just as sure of the need to call the poor, the marginal, and the disorderly to account for their deficiencies.

Yet these hundreds of case files also show Americans concerned with social problems and "social work" drawing on somewhat different resources when understanding their clients as well as themselves. They struck a rather different bargain with the poor, a bargain that emphasized the importance of changing at least some of those clients into what they could be if they were to abandon their old ways. Although their dismay about the imprint that cultural and social inferiority left on individual character and the collective future was just as strong, their confidence in the capacity for change distinguishes their stories from those most commonly told in Melbourne or London. In Boston—and to an extent Minneapolis—the problem that investigation, inquiry, and social work struggled to address was less likely to be pauperism, fraud, or intractable stupidity. The problem here was a failure to transform, and the struggle was ensuring that clients remained committed to the idea and the goal of remaking themselves in the image of their "visitors." Whereas Agnes Cutler and the other inquiry officers in Melbourne wrote themselves leading roles in tales of detection and investigation, and those in London developed an intricate and somewhat ironic theater of "inferior types," the agents of Boston's child-focused charities cast themselves in rather different dramas. During the 1920s and into the hard times of the 1930s, they wrote more optimistic stories about transformation, which emphasized some clients' capacity to make themselves into "better" people. They showed more interest in the idiosyncrasies of personal paths and more trust in people's willingness to reveal "the most minute details" of their histories that would help plot their reinvention.[4]

They were also quicker to offer protection from the small and large disasters that affected the poor because they had a greater faith in their applicants' ability to envisage and even carry out a sensible journey into the future. At the same time, they were quicker to intervene and more likely to offer counsel that seemed to clients little removed from lecturing. The very faith in uplift that characterized their approach to the needy and the delinquent made them more impatient with irresponsibility and indolence; they were more willing to punish and police the poor because they expected them to change. Yet in the stories they told about their clients in case files and case conferences, hope was a more common motif than mistrust. They were fascinated less by the detection of lies and secrets than by the discovery of suffering's remedy, and they assumed that some clients, at least, could be trusted to achieve self-improvement.

This is not the most common way of describing American social work or even child protection in the 1920s. Historians examining the surface of social work—its prescriptions, annual reports, and policies—have found little to celebrate in the period between the pioneering work of the settlements and surveys and the transforming revolution of the 1930s. They are more likely to emphasize the increasing focus on casework and individual culpability, to the detriment of advocacy and social reform; its inadequacies thrown into sharp relief by the new deals that followed, the welfare work of the 1920s retreats from progressive promise along a narrow and increasingly psychological path.[5]

Historians exploring the everyday world of welfare in case files have been more circumspect because the record of these more intimate encounters suggests that the shifts taking place below the level of prescription and policy were more complicated and contradictory. Little of the everyday welfare work of agencies such as the MSPCC incorporated psychiatric methods and theories, for instance; the impact of new ideas and training took a while to be felt in organizations where many older workers lacked college qualifications and newer ones found psychiatric and especially psychoanalytical theory difficult to turn into social work practice. Rather than seeing great change or progress, these historians view the 1920s as a period when social work wavered; much of it still resembled scientific charity more than psychological therapy, as Daniel Walkowitz argues.[6] It was also a period, as Regina Kunzel puts it, when the new social workers increasingly saw clients as "untrustworthy interpreters of their own experience" or, as Karen Tice suggests, when "tales of detection" and "adversarial relationships" were still more common than "tales of protection" and collaborative accomplishment.[7]

American welfare work, like British or Australian welfare work, was never entirely one thing or the other, especially in the complicated interactions between real workers and real clients in the many different places that made up the United States. In Boston itself, strong traditions of social obligation, activism, and reform had created an unusually dense network of Progressive institutions and clubs, even if the 1920s, Charles Trout argues, "had taken a toll on social activism" and activist reformers formed a smaller cadre than twenty or thirty years before.[8] As Susan Traverso shows, welfare agencies, policies, and programs were also being transformed by "social conflict, cultural dissimilarities, and antagonistic politics" in a city in which first- and second-generation immigrants—mostly Catholic or Jewish—were about to become a majority and increasingly challenged Yankee elite ideas about entitlement, relief, and public responsibility for the poor.[9] The records of the MSPCC and the CAA take us into only one part of Boston's welfare network. It is an important part, and the MSPCC's files bulge with the letters, reports, and notes it exchanged with both longstanding Protestant organizations and the increasingly important representatives of other traditions, from the Associated Jewish Philanthrophies and the Society of St. Vincent de Paul to the Salvation Army. Still, as late as the 1930s, the heads of most charitable bodies belonged to the city's Protestant and comfortable minority, as did most of the visitors and agents whose stories about poverty are traced in this book.[10] As Linda Gordon argues, the MSPCC was "the quintessential upper-class charity in Boston."[11]

The work of Boston's welfare and charity organizations was powerfully shaped by the city's fortunes during the uncertain years of the 1920s and the economic crisis of the 1930s. In his comprehensive history of these decades, Trout suggests that Boston's boosterish nickname of "the Hub" provides a rough idea of the city's strengths and weaknesses. More diversified and commercial than the industrial cities of the Midwest, Boston's economy would falter less quickly after 1929, but its reliance on trade and finance also meant that its recovery had to wait for the return of prosperity elsewhere. Boston was a union town, at least relative to other large American cities, and its Overseers of the Public Welfare reflected the legacy of a long-standing Commonwealth commitment to tax-supported relief for the indigent poor and, by the end of the 1920s, mothers with dependent children and the aged. Trout's assessment remains accurate: Boston's overseers "supervized a welfare system no more shaped by traditional outlooks than any other," and "the city's commitment to aiding the poor was stronger than in most of urban America."[12] At the same time, Boston's elites tended to assume that their city's traditional advantages should stave off the worst of the Depression; they "clung tenaciously to voluntary efforts," while "acute political rivalries" made significant public works almost impossible to implement.[13] Even with a first New Deal and then another, Boston's Depression was severe and lasting.

Yet we are left still with the differences in Boston's stories. Stories about transformation are perhaps not unexpected in agencies dedicated to the rescue and reform of children. Different missions generated different styles of case writing, different dramatizations of poverty and inequality. Yet these differences might also reflect the shape of local life, especially the fact that when welfare's providers in Boston looked across the class boundary, they saw immigrants and could imagine some of them as potential Americans. Or perhaps there is something here again of women listening to the poor—sometimes other women but also immigrant children and teenagers—even if those cross-class conversations about poverty were as halting and difficult in Boston as they were everywhere else.[14] When compared with their counterparts in Melbourne and London, the female visitors of Boston were particularly likely to allow their clients greater authority over their own stories and to invest greater hope in their ability to change their lives. It was often patronizing, but from their vantage point on the borders of class, these American workers narrated distinctive dramas of inferiority and superiority, in large part, I think, because their clients—poor women or immigrant children such as Jerzy—shaped those dramas too. The social workers' idea of America, expressed in their stories, emphasized their capacity to take up the raw clay of European heritage and mold it into American patterns. That may have differed from their clients' idea of America. But in the end, the fact that they didn't listen to everything didn't mean they hadn't listened to something. And even if those dramas became more hesitant in the 1930s, the faith in transformation would still give these Americans a different place to stand once the Depression came.

· ·

CHAPTER 16

Closed Mouths and Wise Guys

For the Massachusetts Society for the Prevention of Cruelty to Children, redeeming what its forty-second annual report termed "the pain-wracked, neglected citizen of the future" meant dealing with around five thousand complaints of neglect, cruelty, or delinquency a year during the 1920s.[15] The Children's Aid Association was much less busy, but its cases tended toward greater complexity of supervision and long-term placement, and it often took over such children from the MSPCC.

The MSPCC, founded in 1878, was one of the most significant products of the moral reform movement in which Boston's elite women and men cooperated in the two decades after the Civil War. The society devoted itself at first to "awakening interest" and encouraging legislation. Yet for all of the energy of its first generation of leaders and volunteers, during the 1890s the MSPCC "fell behind the leading edge of social work activity" and struggled for both funds and influence.[16] Between 1910 and 1920, under the leadership of Carl C. Carstens from the New York Charity Organization Society, and with Theodore A. Lothrop as the general secretary, the MSPCC recovered its standing as one of the nation's leading child protection agencies, in part because it gradually shifted its work toward prevention and casework with parents rather than the rescue and removal of children. The society also built strong links with other child- and youth-focused initiatives, including the Judge Baker Guidance Center, one of the first clinics to diagnose and treat "disturbed" children.

Beginning with New Bedford in 1908, the MSPCC opened more than two dozen offices in towns outside Boston. In 1907 there were five paid agents, all men, but the society had thirty-nine agents by 1920, most of them women. More than a third of the MSPCC's total cases originated in Boston; to conduct these two thousand investigations in 1922, the Boston office had a supervisor (Edward H. Cavin), an assistant supervisor (Frances Marley), and nineteen agents (twelve women and seven men). During the next decade, the MSPCC maintained the growth and professionalizing trend that Carstens had instigated. By 1932 the society dealt with more than seven thousand families; Frances Marley was now the supervisor, with Catherine Mullowney as her assistant, and twenty-four of the society's forty-four agents worked in Boston.[17]

The society had always emphasized publicity and advocacy, using photography as well as "speaking stories" as ways of illustrating the transformations it wrought, but during the 1920s its work became increasingly "civic" as well as humanitarian, with the aim of "building up a better community for the coming years."[18] This was important, demanding work and needed "specialized knowledge and equipment."[19] Under Carstens's stewardship, the society emphasized training and standards, with professional staff supervising the volunteers and an increasing proportion of the visits and casework being performed by paid staff, with particular people beginning to focus on specific issues, such as sexual assault. There was a greater stress on keeping comprehensive case records, and case conferences were held weekly starting in 1928. In addition, each agent took turns in presenting cases to the regular meetings of the Executive Committee. By the 1930s, newer agents were mostly college trained. While the 1928 annual report advised that agents "must have some experience in other fields of social work, or must be a graduate of a professional school of social work, or must go through a very intensive course of training in our own office, which takes from one to two years," the descriptions of those hired between 1928 and 1936 reveal few without a college degree and some with advanced degrees in theology and law, as well as social work.

Agents came to the MSPCC from New York (city and state), New Hampshire, Maine, and Pennsylvania, as well as Boston and its surrounding towns. Evelyn Morris had "several year's experience in child welfare and mental hygiene work," and Virginia Faulkner had three years in psychiatric social work. Thomas McNulty had been doing probation work in New York City, Walter Taylor had a "strong business background," and Eugene Irwin completed a master of laws at Boston University.[20] Throughout the 1920s and 1930s, about two-thirds of the agents were women, all but one or two unmarried. All of the agents were white, and few—as far as their names suggest—were less than two generations American; most had enjoyed advantages for which few of their clients could have realistically even wished. The MSPCC and Boston CAA workers had smaller caseloads and more education than their counterparts in Melbourne or London. They also earned more. In 1922 male and female agents were paid the same salaries (about $1,500 a year); their salaries rose to between $1,800 and $2,500 per year, depending on seniority, by 1930. It was a narrow base from which to assess the pressures and problems of child neglect in Boston, especially when the single most important shared characteristic of their clients was poverty.

Linda Gordon's incisive analysis of these agencies' case files shows a clear shift from moralistic to environmental explanations of family problems after 1910. However, although caseworkers now identified poverty, unemployment, and illness as causes in their own right, rather than as the symptoms of some deeper malaise, Gordon argues that "understanding environmental stresses did not lessen the racism and class bias" they applied in their diagnoses.[21] Karen Tice, in her just as intricate dissection of caseworkers' narratives, agrees: "Notions of benevolent femininity," she argues, "always camouflaged class power and privilege ... and notions of racial superiority."[22] As was true then—and is indeed true now—an environmental or circumstantial explanation of poverty does not rule out assumptions about behavioral, cultural, and moral inferiority, at least for some of the poor. Environment might be seen as influencing "bad," "dependent," and "undeserving" types, but the idea that existing flaws of character or culture somehow cause poverty and inequality dies hard, at least in the United States, Britain, and Australia. So, of course, does the logical conclusion that poverty's solutions must also lie in changing behavior, character, and culture.

Certainly, caseworkers were apt to write terrible things about some of the people they met. Even if we leave aside for the moment their ideas about race, we see that MSPCC agents occasionally used the emerging rhetoric of eugenics and "breeding." A thirteen-year-old girl committed to the Girls' Reformatory at Lancaster in 1922 had "poor heredity," and a mother was from a "trashy tribe," while a family first seen in 1922 was described to the Red Cross in 1937 as a "branch of the W—— clan ... [from which] have sprung degenerates, thieves, drunkards, and all sorts of misfits."[23] A similarly long-term relationship with another family—which covered at least three unlawful marriages and ten illegitimate children, all of whom ended up in public care, industrial schools, or reformatories— ended in 1930 with the lament that "this is a terribly sad and pathetic situation. It is evident that the woman is mentally deficient, and altho' she realizes that the situation is morally wrong and bad for all concerned, she does not want it made public, nor any trouble made."[24]

The agents could also be hasty and dismissive, especially when people tried to evade investigation or refused to provide information. They regarded some "types"—men fathering alone, single mothers taking in boarders, any Irish Catholic who drank (or just Irish Catholics because all were presumed to drink)—as disasters waiting to happen. And they endured some angry meetings: "[Mo. in office] very indignant and demanded to know the complainant. She threatened agt by saying that she would get a lawyer after him if he did not produce the name of the complainant. She talked on at length and said she gave children best of care and was a good woman etc. She also raved on about how bad the neighbors were. She left the office in a huff."[25]

But a comparative perspective shows Boston's child protection workers to be somewhat more ready to dramatize poverty and other social problems in environmental and circumstantial terms. They seemed more ready to recognize that much of what they saw reflected the harshness of people's lives and the restricted opportunities they had enjoyed. Compared with the general family caseworkers in the other cities, they also seemed more willing to understand the difficult situations in which parents found themselves and to defend their clients against clumsy misinterpretations. This was true of both female and male workers, suggesting that it was at least in part the nature of their work that softened some of the prejudices produced by class and cultural distance.

In 1922 a family who lived in Revere was reported to the MSPCC by a school nurse, who said the ten-year-old son "impresses everyone as seriously abused and neglected." Both mother and father were of Irish background; the mother told agent William Proctor that she, not the father, chastised the children. She was "rather co-operative with Agt. saying she wished he would call around again some time." Call again he did, as the case was reopened three months later, following a phone call from the same school nurse; again no evidence of neglect was found. Four years later, the Children's Hospital asked for an investigation of neglect in the case of a younger daughter, then thirteen years old, stricken with diabetes mellitus. This time, the hospital claimed, living conditions were "atrocious," and the "continually apologetic" mother was being "domineered over" by the father, who was "very plausible and very unreliable in statements and promises." In 1927 and 1928, there were further investigations on behalf of the Massachusetts General Hospital. This time, agent William

Bronson visited the home, the father's workplace, and even the restaurant at which he ate lunch, where he "made enquiries of the waitress."

Proctor and Bronson both disliked the father, who was a "wise guy" and "a glib talker." But "with it all," wrote Bronson, "I could not help feeling fa[ther] was sincere and had lost the hold on himself and was trying to regain it." The mother, meanwhile, "asked agt. if her house and her children looked any different from hundreds of other houses and chn. and the agent told her no." On a subsequent visit, Proctor echoed the mother's observation: the father had earned very little as a bus driver in the last few months, and the home was sparsely furnished, but it "was no better or worse than many another house within a stone's throw." By 1929, when the father finally managed to get more regular work, and the eldest son (then seventeen) left school and began earning a wage, reports of "disorder" and neglect ceased. They were doing "much better." What is particularly telling in this case is that both agents had every opportunity to intervene more strenuously. Here was a man who "told agt. frankly that he did not want him or anybody else sneaking around his place" and a woman who challenged each agent to show how her situation differed from hundreds of others. They did not, instead choosing to see the sense in what both were saying.[26]

In other cases, MSPCC agents urged family members to see the roots of their problems in money and privation, rather than morals and character. One Italian family in Cambridge was being torn apart by conflicts between a widow and two teenage daughters who were convinced that their mother was trying to "turn us out, give up this house, and go back to the North End." Caught in the middle of a family row, with "mother and daughters hurling invectives, profanity and abusive language at each other," the agent, Joanna Clapham, wrote that the mother was "a good, decent, hard-working, respectable woman" and maintained that "money matters were the source of all the trouble."[27] Whether she convinced the warring family of that remains unclear.

The agents could also find themselves defending clients from the aggressive dismissals and suspicions of other welfare bodies. After a nurse complained of "serious neglect" by a mother who "refused to follow instruction" regarding her baby's hygiene, agent Elizabeth Carter was disinclined to act on discovering a domestic idyll "immaculate with several luxuries of life." Small luxuries were an important signal of self-improvement in Boston and in this case served to overrule the suspicions of the nurse. On the whole, investigators in both Boston and Minneapolis allowed their clients more of life's pleasures than was true in Melbourne and London, where, as we saw earlier, the possession of objects—and even aspirations—above your allotted station in life generated suspicion rather than encouragement. Carter continued her story, describing "little home touches of cretonne hangings and plants in the window." Overall, the mother "impressed agt. as being a capable housewife, with the responsibility of her little home [which] will probably show that she is much more capable than she was thought to be."[28] Carter was often impressed by curtains; in another case a month later, although a supposedly neglectful mother from Charlestown was inexperienced and a "decided mental problem," the fact that she "did the very best she was capable of doing" was in part established by "little cretonne curtains at [the] door."[29] Another agent, Clara Weaver, was pleased to see "nice clean curtains in evidence" on her second visit to a house in Cambridge.[30] Female agents were more likely than men to be swayed by signs of care, perhaps because they knew at least something of the hard grind of responsibility for cleaning, cooking, and laundry.

In 1928 an eleven-year-old boy was reported by a school superintendent; allegedly given liquor by his Italian parents, he was falling asleep in school and "in danger of becoming delinquent." A teacher reported that the entire family was "of rather low mentality." The agent, Theodore Mercer, preferred to discuss the problem with the parents and discovered that they thought the boy might be nearsighted. He was examined at the Eye and Ear Infirmary and given glasses.[31] In 1928 a Portuguese family reported by a police officer were praised for "giving the best care possible."[32] The Marchettis—mother, father, and six children—were reported by neighbors in 1931 because the children were being abused. Caroline Cheshire "did not believe [the seven-year-old boy] was chastised more than any boy in an Italian family that did not behave." The problem, she said, was that "they are very loud spoken and that may account for the neighbors thinking they quarrel." Mrs. Marchetti was reported again in 1934 for beating her fifteen-year-old daughter, whom the agent, Bronson, found "very sophisticated"; the girl denied the charge and said that the family "tended to argue very loudly," especially when it came to matters of the girls' reputations.[33] A worker at the college settlement, Denison House, found in a Syrian family that "sleeping arrangements were most promiscuous, men's clothes were mixed in with the clothing of the family, men's boots being found under large double bed." But Virginia Faulkner preferred to keep track of the woman being charged with neglect, eventually discovering that despite some apparent irregularities in the marriage, the woman's in-laws were purchasing a house for them in Somerville and that there was no need for drastic intervention.[34]

This willingness to defend clients, even in unlikely situations, continued into the 1930s. In a 1935 case involving a recently widowed father, MSPCC agent Dorothy Putnam had reports of suspicious relationships and deplorable conditions from a health nurse and a school principal. The local Board of Public Welfare insisted that the man was "quite clever in knowing how to get aid and looking out for his own interests" and warned Putnam that the city's "Italian section" had "given fa[ther] an idea of our suspicions," so caution would be needed in "attaining evidence." Putnam disagreed and wrote her story in a much more heroic vein, about the mother's death in childbirth and the father's struggle to do his duty and make the best life he could for his two daughters. Visited again in 1936, "he said he was doing the best he could for the chn. and though admitting a mo[ther]'s care was more desirable did not want to break up his home." The Board of Public Welfare argued that the case should remain open because "eventually a crisis would develop." Putnam disagreed, and the case was closed, never to open again.[35]

Of course, the MSPCC's agents were not always so careful or so trusting of what their clients told them. Some were self-righteous and unforgiving. They hectored and even bullied people over whom they possessed decided advantages of power and privilege. They condemned and could be blinded by presumption and prejudice. They were patronizing, diminishing others with words and inflections that betrayed profound disdain. They could move too quickly to the conviction that a client was unfit, mentally "deficient," irresponsible, or "stubborn," sometimes because they couldn't understand the agent's words and sometimes because they couldn't understand the agent's language.

But in child rescue, it seems that such aggressiveness was always tempered by the particular difficulties agents encountered in establishing the truth. For a start, they were conscious of the potentially terrible consequences of getting it wrong. Some of the children they saw were in great danger, but some of the parents they confronted had done nothing but earn the enmity of a neighbor or an anonymous informant and genuinely cared for their children. About a tenth of the case files I read contained accusations and reports that agents suspected were unfounded or malicious, and they were usually right. More than once, landlords laid complaints against tenants they wanted to evict or who were late with their rent. One Irish mother from the South End was accused of drinking and "going motoring" with numerous men, of illicit sexual relations, and of being "irreligious." As agent Stanford Johnson found, the case was clearly one part of her former husband's revenge, orchestrated by his mother and two of her neighbors.[36] First husbands were very prone to report ex-wives, who were accused of illicit sex, sending children out to buy liquor, turning daughters into prostitutes, and causing sons to masturbate, steal, commit arson, and run away.[37] There was also the problem, of course, of parents seeking help with unruly children; in anger, mothers and fathers sometimes sought to have children declared "stubborn" and uncontrollable, only to retract later and keep the child away from court.[38]

When little was clearly black or undeniably white, agents made difficult judgments. What impresses the reader of their case files eighty or ninety years on is not how cavalier they were, but how difficult it was to know the truth. People lied, sometimes because the truth was too hard to bear. They exaggerated and used "the Cruelty" against unruly neighbors. Nurses in infant health care made true reports and false statements. Schools helped the MSPCC save some children from abuse and condemned some families to months and even years of suspicion and surveillance. Respectable people made wrong assumptions and false accusations, while disrespectable people told the truth about awful abuse and violence. It was sometimes the case—as in a boarding [foster] mother accused by the parents of giving their three-year-old son a concussion—that "true facts have not been unearthed" and the agent was "helpless to go any further."[39]

Of course, some agents could conclude from all of this that no one could be trusted. But that wasn't the most common response, on the evidence of their case writing. Instead, compared with their counterparts in "scientific charity" or family welfare, the MSPCC agents were more likely to weigh competing claims in the full knowledge that, as Virginia Faulkner wrote of one complicated family situation, "much of the talk made was untrue."[40] They weren't as confident that truth would be reflected in the demeanor, dress, or gestures of the people they met because situations were too easily misrepresented or misinterpreted. Family conflicts could be savage, disrupting expected patterns and scripts and producing unwanted revelations, lies, and secrets. Mothers accused of drunkenness and cruelty could seem suspicious or, like one woman who worked as an usher, be "a neatly clad, pretty young Polish woman [who] created a favorable impression" and "was very much surprised at any complaint having been made."[41] In another incident, the police and a worker from another agency were pressing for the removal of "dirty and ragged children," but Evelyn Marks found that although the children looked dirty, "on closer examination by agt had clean clothes on and were clean underneath their clothes."[42] Later that year, Marks handled another case, this one in which a nine-year-old boy was reported as "terribly beaten" by his stepmother; "while mother was out of the room for a minute agt asked [the stepdaughter] if stepmother was good or bad to her and she said laughingly that stepmother was very good to all of them."[43]

The twists and turns of some cases must have seemed formidable. One case opened in 1922 was finally closed in 1930 with five children committed to good homes and the mother in a psychological hospital; here, the father and mother warred for eight years, accusing each other of bootlegging, theft, violence, and drinking.[44] Another case from 1922 provides a good illustration. The agent, Jean Stoneham, responded to a police report that a widowed father, who worked for the city of Boston, drank heavily and beat his two children, a boy aged fourteen and a girl aged thirteen. Her initial impression in March was that both children were "very much afraid of him." She continued: "In order to talk with ch. alone agt. asked to look at the apartment which was vacant in the next house, pretending it was wanted for a friend and fa. allowed the boy to show agt. this apartment. Agt. then asked boy if everything was all right at home, and he was just as close mouthed as fa., not even willing to give agt. his name, but said there was no truth in the comp[laint] and everything was satisfactory." Stoneham was unsure. The local policeman did not believe the complaint, though there was evidence of occasional inebriation, and the father had been in jail for drunkenness. In April the father's probation officer reported that he "goes about the house in a nude condition" and took his daughter into his bed, as well as sent her to buy liquor. Both children were taken into custody, but the daughter promptly recanted her claims. When the father visited his daughter at the MSPCC office, he was "well-dressed, neat and in good order [and] did not look like a dissipated man." He "grilled" his daughter, who again recanted most of the things she'd said, but when he left, she "burst into tears and begged [agent] not to be returned to her fa. as she was in mortal terror of him." The children were judged neglected and put in the custody of the MSPCC, who found them a home with relatives. Within two months, both the son and the daughter had returned to live with their father, with the daughter telling Stoneham that her father was doing very well and had stopped drinking. There were renewed reports of drinking in January 1923. The father then died of pneumonia in March 1923, and both children went to live with relatives in Jamaica Plain.[45]

Such difficulties in making judgments and decisions were by no means unusual. On the evidence, too, the women social workers of the MSPCC were particularly likely to expect the truth to emerge only slowly and through effort. Although, as Linda Gordon contends, the feminization of child protection work did not "create feminist policies" or practices that quickly or completely reduced the distance between agents and client, female agents were more likely to seek out and to trust the complicating views of mothers and children.[46] They found that women and children talked more easily to them, but they also encouraged this talk in a way less true of male agents, who were more likely to speak to—and speak up for—fathers. This may also have reflected the female agents' keener sense that a woman was much more easily blackened by unprovable accusations of immorality than a man.

In any event, disentangling truth, half-truth, mistakes, misinterpretations, and lies was difficult for every agent, especially when the outcome of bad decisions could be so injurious to parents and children alike. In 1922 MSPCC president Grafton D. Cushing argued that "our work seems to begin where the work of other social agencies leaves off."[47] That view also captured the way in which the agency's caseworkers seem to have imagined and written up the dramas in which they found themselves. They sometimes felt abandoned by the police and other agencies. Looking in on situations that could be absolutely frightful, they took seriously the tasks of rescuing children and observing the injunction "to know, to understand the family in all its aspects" as best they could.[48] They did this, too, in the conviction that they were the last best hope for the people they saw, for suffering children, and for the broken or disintegrating families they sometimes visited.

One outcome of this effort, at least for some workers, was a greater willingness to accept that every story had its tactics and strategies, and some recognition—made with more or less discomfort—that certainty was both crucial and elusive. There were wise guys and closed mouths, liars and people who shared everything. Some were defensive, but others turned against agents in fury and rage. Nurses and doctors and teachers laid terrible charges against some who were innocent and completely ignored the hidden crimes of some who were guilty. For the MSPCC agents, I suspect that "truthful feeling" was always a more unstable concept and that the kind of confidence COS investigators in Melbourne and London placed in the links between appearances and truth was much harder to preserve.

In an immigrant city, the nature of their work and its dilemmas encouraged a rather different way for agents to dramatize themselves, their clients, and their role in overcoming poverty and social problems. Instead of the supposed infallibilities of scientific detection or the expert judgment of character that bolstered the confidence of charity investigators elsewhere, Boston's agents focused their most compelling stories around the dramas of self-improvement. Theirs were not so much dramas of discovery and uncovering, of fraud discouraged and dependency avoided. Nor were they the dramas of children rescued, abusers jailed, and cruelty exposed that had been so important to the first generation of agents. Instead, they valued their ability to oversee personal transformations, and they were increasingly drawn to the idea of social work as one engine—and perhaps the most crucial engine—of America's future. They weren't really detectives. They were the magicians of Americanization.

· ·

CHAPTER 17

She Has Found Herself, and He Will Make a Good American

Zillah Nelson and Annie Lee of the Children's Aid Association were used to long relationships with clients and to writing up their case notes in ways that conveyed something of their significance and drama. In June 1925, Nelson was approached by a young man, Patrick, who wanted to marry "his girl," Mary. She was seventeen, he told her, and in "solitary confinement" at the hospital for being stubborn and uncooperative. "They are going to send her to an insane asylum," he said. He was responsible for the pregnancy, and he wanted to marry her before the child arrived in August. Mary was well known to the CAA and the MSPCC because she had been in foster care. Nelson began with hard realities: "We have spent all we intend to spend on her," she told Patrick, giving him "the [money] figures for both foster home and hospital care." He insisted that they were going to marry. Nelson "acquainted him with reasons for not acceding at once to his wishes—youth of girl and himself, unfortunate background of girl, many of the domestic problems that make for trouble in families—but he was unshaken." Patrick's mother also supported the decision to marry, though "she is apparently a little shaken by some of the information given her."

Unable to marry before the birth without CAA approval, the couple remained committed to their plan, even when Patrick "went to the South" in search of work in April 1926. Mary was by then in a boarding home and given household chores "so she will not be demoralized by idleness." But Nelson was warming to her. Mary was taken out to buy a hat and shoes—she was "very sensible and practical in her choice"—and then was taken out again to buy a dress for the wedding. There was a setback to love's true course; Patrick stayed away, making money, and Mary, now in a foster home, became restless. Nelson saw her, but she was "in very defiant mood." "I will leave at once and if you do not take me away I will behave so badly that the foster mother will not be willing to keep me" was Mary's only statement. Kept in the home, she then took up with another young man, a sharp character, big on words and promises but not to be trusted, the kind of boy who might drag her down again. Failure seemed certain. But Patrick returned, flourishing a ring and a proposal and driving off his smoother, slicker, and younger rival. They were married, and Nelson finished with this description: he is "a crude young chap but makes a rather good impression on me. He is evidently devoted to Mary and insists he is never going to let her go out to work." The file closes; given the assiduousness with which CAA workers kept track of all their Marys and Patricks, it is a reasonable assumption that they and their baby son lived peaceably ever after.[49]

Perhaps Zillah Nelson shared some stories with Annie Lee. Perhaps Lee suggested the idea of taking Mary out shopping, as she used that tactic herself with one of her most difficult clients, Carrie. Carrie was referred to the CAA by the police in 1925 when, at sixteen, she had been assaulted by a man who boarded in her parents' home. She had left the house to escape her father and was assaulted during a visit. Her family background was checkered: her mother and her aunt were known to the MSPCC and other welfare societies, her father had been diagnosed insane, and Carrie's file was thick with reports and tests. A Homeopathic Hospital report from 1929 found examples of repeated forced intercourse, and a Judge Baker Foundation (JBF) report labeled her "normal although she has a bad history and heredity." A case conference in 1929 agreed that Carrie "has been all right morally" and "seems to be very earnest and sincere in her desire to live a decent life." Indeed, her history, in Lee's telling of it, was one of repeated attempts to free herself from bad situations; at sixteen, she had answered an ad and taken a live-in domestic position, she consistently accepted guidance from both the MSPCC and the CAA, and she was attempting to assist her twin and a younger sister, both of whom had been boarded out in Maine. Her mother, "a respectable appearing woman," was very happy about Carrie's supervision.

As Lee wrote up the notes for a case conference in 1930, she decided to suggest this as a "publicity case" of a "girl pulling herself out of an immoral situation." Her confidence rested on the events of the previous month, when Carrie, now twenty-one and living in a country home, had come shopping. She had told Lee about a young man she was seeing. Lee promptly arranged a lunch at Filene's department store; he "seems a very straightforward, decent sort of chap," she reported to the case conference.

Unfortunately for the publicity case, Carrie's story did not have a happy ending. Having broken up with the decent chap, she took up with an older man and became "restless, difficult, unreasonable" and a "struggle." Lee investigated the new beau and discovered that he had three convictions for larceny and had been diagnosed as a delinquent at the Psychopathic Hospital. He was also already married. In a scene worthy of Hollywood drama—and perhaps slightly staged in its style—Lee confronted Carrie and the man. In a tearful scene, Carrie agreed that marriage was out of the question, and the man was forced to admit his past. Though she became "her old sweet docile self" once again, by the time Carrie was discharged in 1930, Lee was unsure: "She does not express any appreciation for all that CAA has done for her. Had become reconciled with all the different members of her family and seemed ready to accept their standards of living. Had been going around for several months with an Irish laborer whom she admitted had at one time made improper proposals to her and who was also more or less given to drinking." In the end, unlike the situation with Patrick and Mary, the shadows of Carrie's past had claimed her future.[50]

Case files were stories in which workers explored and revealed their understandings of social problems, both at the intimate scale of the client and the broader scale of the society. These Boston agents were more likely than those in other cities to emphasize capacities for advancement and change and to render as poignant those clients who proved unable to sustain or complete their transformations. Their most careful casework—and their most dramatic narratives—focused on redemption as well as detection. Love and careful guidance didn't always triumph, and devotion and effort could not always overcome the burdens of the past. Girls could still fall for the wrong men, and boys could go off track and run away. But there was a chance that some fortunes could change. Agents always anticipated transformation while dramatizing its difficulties.

Dramas of transformation involved Americans as well as newcomers, because some Americans were as "held back" by their pasts and their parents as immigrants from Europe. Whatever their clients' backgrounds and occasional failures, and however strong their own misgivings, these workers regarded more of their clients as redeemable. As Karen Tice shows so well, caseworkers often "embellished the plots of case stories to capture the human interest of social work situations."[51] The worth of comparative perspective is what counted for "human interest" in different places and times; in Boston it revolved around a struggle for change in which progress—and sometimes triumph—were considered much more possible. In the 1920s, impoverished people could rarely turn themselves into the equals of MSPCC agents, and it was no good to simply "dream of the possibilities of occupying some other position."[52] Their transformations were supervised, guided, and cajoled by people who felt themselves to be superior and assumed that inferior people needed to be reformed. There is little doubt that American social work developed a "dual interest in engendering the adjustment of the client toward society and protecting society from the client."[53] But in this agency at least, there was a strong and consistent emphasis that immigrant and second-generation clients could turn themselves into good Americans, with the aspirations and commitments to hard work that entailed.

This might at first seem obvious. Many of these stories involved children and teenagers, and it is self-evident that they change as they mature. But the shift toward environmental rather than moral interpretations, and toward casework rather than benevolent rescue, changed the types of cases that agencies identified as "good publicity" and, I think, that workers found most challenging and pertinent to their sense of professional accomplishment. Rescuing waifs gave way to making good citizens out of the "hopeless" and good Americans out of "Old World stock." It was adolescents and young adults, not children, who appeared in the most telling stories of the 1920s. The speaking story didn't focus on the baby, the child musician, or the street Arab; it showed Boston the teenager Jerzy, with his desperate zeal to be an American boy.

Of course, rescue remained an important theme, and stories in which agents saved children from Old World parenting continued into the 1930s. Agent Thomas Sherman's management of a difficult 1932 case involved estranged Italian parents and their twelve-year-old lame son. Sherman was told by teachers and policemen that the boy's mother was in an immoral relationship with her landlord, but the boy's father was more concerned about securing medical treatment; in fact, he did not believe the charges against his wife and believed the landlord was simply making trouble. Sherman found the father "an illiterate sort of person"—the mother, he said, was "fresh, smooth, cocky"—but he was impressed with "the apparent sincerity of the father's desire ... and with the fairness with which he urged agt. in consideration of the case." The mother regarded her son's lameness as untreatable, and it was with some difficulty that the child was eventually hospitalized. Sherman conducted a good deal of careful negotiation but then used the threat of a neglect complaint to force the mother's hand after she had tried to seize the boy from the Children's Hospital, sparking an "Italian family brawl."[54]

In stories such as these, children remained essentially passive. They were the subjects of rescue and played little part in shaping the outcome. A rather different kind of story—emphasizing the struggle to change and pitting teenagers and young adults against immigrant parents or Amer-

icans against "bad heredity"—grew in frequency and especially significance during the 1920s and into the first half of the 1930s. One family
from upstate New York was visited when a boy refused to go home. His
stepmother "would not let him have any fun or go anywhere with other
boys."[55] For the immigrant parents of Boston, these dramas were particularly intense; "immigrants," Linda Gordon astutely remarks, "experienced
adolescence in particularly concentrated form," and the strains of a new
form of friendship based on dating, mass-produced goods, and public en-
tertainment were particularly strong for them.[56] Italian family conflicts remained a common setting; in a 1935 case, the mother of a fifteen-year-old
Italian girl who had run off with a married man was described as "a very
good, motherly type of woman yet entirely European in her ways of disciplining children." The girl "frankly acknowledged" driving around with
men and boys and within a week of the first incident, "came rushing into
the office [and] claimed that she could not stand her family any longer and
refused to stay at home." She was taken for a mental exam, but the worker,
Eleanor Graham, saw negotiated removal as the best solution. After the girl
moved in with her married sister, all problems seem to have ceased.[57]

Desires for upward social mobility always garnered support, and there
were several long-term cases dramatizing these journeys. Not all were
successful because some clients strayed too easily from what the agents
considered "reasonable plans." Anna, a young woman of Swedish background referred by the Lynn probation officer in 1925, puzzled Leonora
Spencer at first. She had contracted gonorrhea, but made "a good impression [and] doesn't seem sophisticated." The Judge Baker Foundation found
her "somewhat supernormal" but added that "it is difficult to know just
exactly what this girl's problem is, in particular whether she is subject to a
good deal of sex ideation or stress." The JBF always took particular note
of "sex ideation," especially among young women. The JBF's report, summarized at length in Spencer's case notes, also claimed that Anna "has a
very ambitious plan, but it is very doubtful whether she can carry it out.
[She] wants to save and get a commercial education." Spencer noted Anna's "strong pleasure-loving tendencies" and the fact that she was a heavy
smoker. Spencer also believed that the most important contribution she
could make, as the JBF put it, was to help Anna realize her ambitions
through a "good plan for both work and recreation."

Anna's ambitions were realized, though not in the way Spencer's "plan
of recreation" had envisaged. By the end of 1925, Anna had "fallen in with
a rather fast set," including "a number of Harvard boys." Harvard boys
had their attractions: in 1926 Anna married a Harvard student who was
working in one of Boston's settlement houses. Harvard men also had their

drawbacks: a follow-up study in 1935 revealed that Anna's husband, unemployed and unhappy, had deserted her in 1933. There were no children, and Anna was working in an office doing typing and shorthand; in all, the file concluded, she "seems to have made a good adjustment to her situation."[58] Her case did not become a speaking story, however, perhaps for fear of encouraging other immigrant girls to pursue the limited number of Harvard boys.

Anna's story also showed how the female agents of the CAA and the MSPCC understood the changing lives of girls. Just as the male agents took particular responsibility for developing immigrant or troubled boys into young American men—a struggle I trace in part 6 of this book—their female colleagues took the task of forming immigrant and migrant girls into young American women. In immigrant families, in particular, the female workers understood the sensitivities but always endorsed the struggle for a degree of freedom from Old World ideas about women's prospects and possibilities. Among American girls, the struggle against tradition was less vital, but here, too, agents such as Jean Stoneham, Leonora Spencer, and Dorothy Putnam always emphasized "both work and recreation" before marriage and highlighted the possibility of paid work even after marriage. In a high proportion of the cases involving young women and female agents, one of the crucial signs of success, or at least of movement toward a desired goal, was the acquisition of a good job, a skill, or a chance at a qualification. Agents were thrilled by girls who became nurses, who stayed in school and gained certificates, or who went to secretarial colleges to learn shorthand, typing, and bookkeeping.

Women's work was always something of a dilemma for interwar social workers. Poor women were often confronted—and affronted—by a contradictory demand that they give their children full-time care while doing whatever they could to earn an income. As Susan Kleinberg's comparative study of three American cities shows, the coming of widows' pensions and anxiety over employment as a distraction from women's maternal priorities did not mean that widows were somehow exempt from the expectation of self-help, especially in a state such as Massachusetts, where low-paid work for married women in textiles or shoes had a long history.[59] In the case of these younger Boston clients, the agents of the MSPCC arrived at a rather different if still somewhat ambivalent position. As working women themselves, they were most likely to endorse and to model a version of womanhood in which it was important for girls to gain and then retain some form of self-reliance through paid work. Anna and other clients might marry and have children, but their ambitions were best safeguarded by an occupation and a sensible plan for self-support. They should neither see work as a last resort nor think only of turning domestic labor into money as laundresses, cleaners, or lodging housekeepers. The precise balance between paid work, housework, and child care was never made clear—perhaps because these unmarried agents had not yet confronted those issues squarely in their own lives—but they certainly proposed a new kind of relationship between work, self-reliance, and female security among poorer women.

No one believed that transformation was straightforward or would come without a cost, for girls or for boys. One of the most dramatic struggles for Americanization was traced in a long-running CAA case that commenced in 1925. At the center of what the CAA always described as "a very important case" were two boys from a North End Italian family of nine children. For more than a decade, Antonio and Marco Pinelli were moved in and out of foster homes, industrial schools, and reformatories as a series of agents tried to detach them from their "miserable street life and home conditions." Here were two brothers, two long histories, but each with a different denouement. Antonio, born in 1918, could not overcome his heritage. Marco, born in 1919, was by 1932 a "great success" and "entirely Americanized." At the age of seven, Antonio was described as "a swarthy youngster," and the Judge Baker Foundation report manifested—even for them—an unusual degree of aggressiveness: he was a truant, a beggar, a masturbator, a smoker, and a coffee drinker, and "as one might expect [he] has already been approached by homosexuals." His story was "well concocted," and he told of "having sex relations with numerous little girls." He spoke of this "in a very sophisticated way [and] uses extremely vulgar and adult expressions." The remedy, they said, was "urgent placement, re-education and habit formation." In 1927 the CAA visitor took him to lunch and noted that he "has apparently had some training because he removed his hat upon entering the bldg. & during the meal held his fork correctly and masticated with his lips closed." The JBF was less impressed and insisted that Antonio was a liar. He needed, they urged, comprehensive reeducation. If that didn't work, said the JBF doctor, "a good thrashing would be the best thing."

Antonio's story was one of constant failure and lack of accomplishment. In 1931 he was committed to the Lyman School for Boys, a reformatory, for the first time, and he spent further periods there and in the Shirley Reformatory between 1932 and 1936, at one time being found guilty of breaking and entering. Agent Calvin Fletcher scolded him for that and other misdemeanors. Antonio's parents are rarely mentioned in the file; the struggle, in a very important way, was with their ethnic and even genetic influence, rather than anything they actually did. There was, Fletcher reported, "considerable affection in this family. Mother is a good enough sort of woman, in a way, [though] ignorant and very superstitious." Her failure was that her son had "never developed any inhibitions." But it is not at all clear what the problem of this family actually was. Antonio was "pulled back to Boston" by "movies and street life" in 1931, and in 1932 his "breakdown seemed occasioned by the influence of the proximity of the city, the old craving for street life and excitement coming over him and causing his downfall." A case conference in 1936 reviewed Antonio's file; "it is dubious whether present arrangement is constructive." At age eighteen, his story simply ends.

When one reads the file without knowing its ending, Marco seems a carbon copy of his slightly older brother. But his story comes to a very different conclusion because the agents writing it see in these two brothers the greater dilemma of what they are trying to achieve: "Perhaps we do ask too much from these Italian boys & try to fit them into patterns which are of our own making.... We may well question whether at this age there is not a conflict of loyalty, a feeling on the part of the child that he is making a choice between an environment and relations to which he was committed by birth & early conditioning & an artificial environment & relations which have been imposed on him." Fletcher's insight did not prevent him, however, from consistently—and apprehensively—confusing actual delinquent behavior with a rather vague version of an "uninhibited" and "backward" street culture that beckoned Marco just as surely as his older brother. Marco, however, was pulled free and "entirely Americanized"; by the age of thirteen, "he would impress one as being a very normal little American boy [and] no one would guess his Italian parentage."

On the evidence of the file, Marco and Antonio seem to have very few differences. Both were found delinquent, and both participated in a series of negotiations with CAA agents over acceptable outcomes. When they were together and when they were apart, they used misbehavior and the threat of "downfall"—even at the risk of punishment—to express their own choices. They preferred some foster families to others and on at least four occasions ran away in order to force a new placement; in 1932, Antonio used a period in the Lyman School—no picnic, by all accounts—as a means of escaping one foster home and being reunited with his brother in a foster home both had enjoyed in the past. There were other instances of strategic stealing, insubordination, and smoking by both boys and an acceptance of censure as a necessary evil in order to win either removal or sufficient freedom to effect an escape to Boston. Both also readily admitted—and it seems rather enjoyed—the fact that they had been "an immense expense" and boys for whom "a great deal has been done."

Perhaps Marco was more pliable. The JBF called Antonio "swarthy" and "unmanaged," whereas Marco was "a very shy little boy with many fears." Perhaps the slightly gentler tone that characterized the JBF report described a less troubled and troublesome boy. Marco was endangered by his background and environment. Having done very well in his stint in a foster home, he was allowed to return to his parents in 1930 but "speedily went down hill." Antonio was presented more as a contributor to the bad neighborhood than its victim. Mario, on the other hand, seemed to be doing all right by the time of his discharge. He had never quite overcome "bad habits"; in 1937, at age eighteen, he had been convicted of larceny in the Chelsea court. But he began working later that year, and in 1938 he moved to New York City in search of a better job. Again, it would have been possible for Calvin Fletcher to conclude that here were two bad seeds, not one. In the end, though, two life stories that seemed little different on the surface were written to divergent ends. Marco's story was one of Americanization, while Antonio's could only track the power of Old World deficiencies, even in the New World.[60]

Transformations didn't always succeed. Bad environments and bad "stock" took their toll. Some of the people the agents met were weak and ineffectual. Some were of such "low mentality" that little could be expected. Some were hurting and even destroying the people they were pledged to love. But others were struggling to become "good citizens" and "good Americans" in the mold of the superior people most of the caseworkers assumed themselves to be. What made Boston's workers different in the 1920s and—to a lesser extent—the 1930s was not their conviction that all such barriers could be surmounted but their confidence that some of the young people they met could overcome their disadvantages and become citizens of the future. They understood and dramatized what they heard and saw in terms of a distinctive focus, which emphasized the difficulties and importance of journeys. Of course, some of those so-called disadvantages stemmed from "Old World" beliefs, superstitions, and culture. Casework was sometimes haphazard and always patronizing. But at the same time that Boston's child welfare workers could find fault with immigrant parents, their focus on opportunity, mobility, and motivation could lead them toward different conclusions in which it was possible to give people a better future. It may not have been the exact future those people themselves desired, but in some cases at least, it seems to have been a future shaped by a degree of agreement, negotiation, and trust between agent and client.

Boston's agents turned Americanization into their chief and most public drama because that was the struggle they saw and that was the achievement their expertise could accelerate. It is a choice explained in part by the nature of their work—the questioning, aiding, and supervision of children and teenagers—but also its context: a city becoming more and more shaped by its immigrants, even as the Immigration Acts checked the stream from Europe. As Boston's caseworkers of the 1920s looked at the borders of class, they saw boundaries that had been complicated and transformed by that just-staunched tide of immigrants. In a very important way, immigrants changed the nature and meaning of inferiority because, by their very mobility, they established the appetite of some lower-class people for change. They—and especially their American-born children—were undeniably but not irredeemably inferior.

· ·

CHAPTER 18

The Primitive Becoming More and More Dominant

"Awfully abusive." "A little bit of a thing and a very smooth talker." A file transferred from a female to a male worker "in case of trouble." A confrontation, a health inspector, the bringing of a policeman, and forced admission. Runaway children, a son dead in an industrial accident, a daughter pregnant with no husband. The mother in court for assault and battery on a neighbor's child. "General complaining," "it is obvious he is mental," "she is somewhat like father in profuse flow of language," the family's "wordy battle." And this neatly typed letter from the father: "My home heretofore has not been a gallery of observation and curios.... I was born in America, and have all the respectful feelings of an American. Each American is so trained that they are home only in their own homes. There are conditions in every home of the Americans that are not always put on exhibition to the general public." This request for dignity seems to have done little good. As agent Derrick Henderson wrote in the file after one episode, "Quite a scene ensued, the primitive negro becoming more and more dominant."[61]

In Boston, race was the overpowering barrier, and African Americans were never part of a drama about transformation. They were more like the London poor, though the stories about them were less forgiving and more savage. Here, case files provide a particular window into the forms of difference that are seen as mutable and immutable in different places and times. In Melbourne and London, where class divided and organized the world, it was difficult for charity investigators to imagine doing anything more than detective work or small-scale charity with the inferior orders. In Boston, while some immigrants and poorer white Americans could be imagined as having "good potential," African Americans were almost entirely irredeemable; the most significant division there was based squarely on race. Cases involving African American clients were relatively rare in Boston—there were certainly six and possibly several more—but very consistent in tone. In Minneapolis, the Family Welfare Association employed a specialized "colored visitor" from 1922 on. As far as I can tell, no such provision was made by the MSPCC or the CAA before 1950. During the 1920s and 1930s, the MSPCC's annual report, a model of clarity, transparency, and careful discussion of social work and child protection trends, also contained crude jokes about the "antics" of "our colored friends." Of course, what seems jarring now in the twenty-first century is often one of our best ways of understanding just what used to be taken for granted and said in public.

It mattered little if African American clients were educated or employed or locally born. All of the traits and decisions that drew forth positive responses when they were made by immigrants did nothing to change the often careless aggressiveness that characterized the treatment of African American families before the middle of the 1930s. Rosa Jackson of Medford approached the CAA in 1925 to request a temporary placement for her baby daughter because her husband had left her. Her husband was "no good," according to his probation officer, but she was "neatly dressed in rather good taste" and "gives impression of being [of] high grade colored family." Later, despite Rosa's desire to use friends and family to care for the child while she worked in domestic service, the CAA insisted on placing the baby in a home, with the mother having to pay for the full expense ($6 of her $10 weekly wage), while the CAA visitor "tried to impress his responsibility of his family" on the father.

For nearly three years, Rosa Jackson paid $5 or $6 a week to the foster parents of her child, sometimes with the help of the father and sometimes not. She frequently visited her daughter and consistently refused to sign her over to the care of the state "because she cannot bear to think of it." Visitors pressed the issue, and "she cried and said she was doing the very best she knew how." Agent Millicent Terry even thought that Rosa "probably does not work very easily with people as she speaks constantly [of] how she has been 'walked upon' by various employers." The child's first foster mother "tho' kind, [was] not particularly intelligent," and she was transferred to a second home in Revere. Rosa remained concerned, and another agent, Bertha Ricketts, was sent to give a report. Rosa's daughter, now three years old, was "very poor material, stubborn, shows very little initiative in walking and playing [and] is apparently quite backward in everything." The child was discharged to the mother at the end of 1928. A 1929 case conference concluded that the first visitor had shown "poor judgment," but also suggested that the "mother [was] impossible to work with." In 1935 the CAA did a major follow-up study of this and other closed cases. Rosa's daughter was seen in her Medford school, just before the break for the summer. She had earned the "best possible grade for conduct" and "does good work"; she was "well cared for, always clean, one of the best behaved in the room ... pleasant, answers easily, seems normal & happy." At least the agency had the grace to not claim credit for the child's "improvement."[62]

Nor did MSPCC and CAA visitors show much interest in defending African American children against the accusations and aggressions of police, teachers, principals, and nurses. In a 1928 case, an eleven-year-old girl from Jamaica Plain was reported by police as the leader of a group "practising sex indecencies." No grounds were found for prosecution or further action. In 1931 she was reported as "wayward" by the school principal because she was "distributing sexual information to other girls." Indeed, he suggested, she was probably "a recruiter for a house of ill-fame [as] she seems to be very much attracted to certain of the lighter colored and better looking Negro girls in the school." Mary McGuire visited the girl's home, which was "just as clean and orderly as could be." Her mother "impressed me as sincere and anxious for [the girl's] welfare." She was examined at a psychological clinic and found to be "rather of a flighty type [and] greatly imbued with the spirit of romance and love." Nevertheless, the report endorsed the principal's suggestion that the girl needed "institutional care and training," though it is not clear that anything more was attempted.[63] All of the sample cases involving African American clients were characterized by this same degree of carelessness and a willingness to proceed from unfounded and often bizarre assumptions about their "normal" behavior. It is a small number, but every case shows the same degree of disdain.

Those who were neither European nor African American were treated with a similar degree of ambivalence. One 1922 case involved a Chinese family. The police reported that the father, a laundryman, was beating his twelve-year-old son and tying him up by his hands. The father, "a very honest, agreeable Chinaman [who] was extremely courteous to agt. throughout the interview," reported that his son was very disobedient and was often brought home by policemen. The local police agreed that the boy would "become a delinquent and certainly not a good citizen" unless paternal authority was restored. The boy himself did not repeat to the agent, Stanford Johnson, the stories of "great brutality" he had shared with neighbors, saying only that the main problem was that "he wants to play baseball after school and not work in the laundry." Johnson could report only that the "father seems like a decent sort of fellow but mother has a very ugly countenance." Nothing was done to, for, or about the potential delinquent; no other authorities—such as schoolteachers, principals, storekeepers, or nurses—were consulted; and no particular interest was shown in following the case.[64] It was written and recorded as a kind of curiosity.

Such was the dismissal accorded those who were too different to be included among the changeable. They were forever enfeebled by their heritage—genetic or cultural—in the way that most white Bostonians assumed was not true of other immigrant groups that had made—or at least commenced—the transition to "whiteness." In a way, of course, the dismissal of "nonwhite" clients makes even clearer the welcoming of a desire for transformation among white ones. It highlights even more what the agents and caseworkers wanted to achieve and thought was possible. At this particular moment, when Boston was an immigrant city but not yet a black one, those who wanted to bear witness to the capacities of some of the poor could invest and believe in the possibility of their transformation, in part by emphasizing the utter inferiority of others. Once immigrants—or at least some immigrants—had become "white," they could also be encouraged to become Americans. For others, a future that looked bleak enough in the 1920s was about to darken even more.

. . . .

CHAPTER 19

More Sinned Against Than Sinning

That faith in transformation would be shaken during the 1930s. Compared with the charity organization societies in London and Melbourne, the Boston agencies—and those in Minneapolis—were less committed to a politics of pauperism and policing, and they were more able to accept the fact and the advantages of a public entitlement to relief. But their faith in realizing potential also faltered in the face of an increasing focus on poverty, neglect, and material hardship. Rather than the successes of Americanization, they began to emphasize the impact and complications of long-term hardship, with as yet few means of imagining any confident way forward. Indeed, by the end of the 1930s, it seemed that Boston's child welfare workers had begun to segregate clients in a rather different way, which relegated more of them to a category of "unhelpables" who might not bear responsibility for their condition but from whom little progress could be expected.

For the MSPCC, the 1930s brought increasing caseloads—they peaked at more than seven thousand families in 1932, with a growing proportion from Boston rather than the mill towns—and "a period of trial" that raised real possibilities of "permanent scars on American society."[65] Agents' salaries were reduced by between 5 and 10 percent in 1932; the cuts were restored in 1934, but the society's financial problems remained acute. The MSPCC was very grateful for a decrease in caseload in 1933 due to "increased social service given by the boards of public welfare."[66] Just as the New Deal helped save some Americans, it also helped cushion some of the private agencies from the continuing impact of the economic crisis.

Accounts of social work during the Depression emphasize the changing dynamics of entitlement and the impact of the New Deal; while an increasing sense of public responsibility and a focus on poverty as a cause rather than a symptom of social problems helped revitalize American social work's reforming impulses, there was also, as Beverly Stadum points out, concern that a "developing social work philosophy would be drowned in the swelling tide of public relief."[67] During the 1930s, the idea that social work might focus more on its "cause"—advocating social reform—and less on its "function"—individual casework—certainly gained ground. But at the same time, it is to the Depression and the increasing availability of public support that some scholars point in explaining social work's failure to fully align itself with social justice. "Despite the clear public mandate that social work received in the first decades of the century to be the profession responsible for the poor," argue Gary Lowe and Nelson Reid, "the profession could not embrace this responsibility as central to its identity."[68] At the very least, as Daniel Walkowitz shows, the changing nature of social work, and the changing social profile of its clients, profoundly challenged the ways in which workers thought about who they were and what they were doing.[69]

Child protectors' response to the Depression also emphasized physical neglect and deprivation, in part because in the 1930s, "the entire population, including social workers, was conscious of the stresses of poverty and quick to blame it for other problems."[70] But there was a cost to this focus on economic need and class inequality; in defining child neglect "as an epiphenomenon of poverty," Linda Gordon suggests, caseworkers tended to downplay other equally structural causes rooted in sexual inequality and "contributed to a well-warranted skepticism about their own ... ability to help."[71]

Gordon's point is crucial to understanding the changed ways in which these files dramatized poverty and inequality in Boston during the 1930s. In my view, and following her lead, the challenge of the Depression was reflected in two related shifts: there was a stronger emphasis on the hard facts of poverty and a decreasing sense that some clients, especially the very poor, could ever in fact become the masters of their own fortunes. The focus on class and economic inequality, in other words, tended to decrease workers' willingness to hope for—or insist on—fundamental or lasting change. There was also a tendency to divide clients more rapidly into those who could and could not achieve success.

As Walkowitz says, the Depression made more palatable to middle-class social workers a diagnosis of poverty that stressed social conditions rather than client pathology. In these child welfare agencies, it also changed their sense of what was possible, especially when their earlier explanations of inadequacy were rooted not so much in pathology as in stalled or frustrated assimilation. They began to doubt, at least to some extent, the role that they and even their profession could play in the drama of Americanization, something they had always seen as a long-term, complicated but vital process that would shape their society's future. The advantage of comparison is the highlighting of how strong a shift this was. Compared with Melbourne's investigators, who had never placed transformation at the center of their dramas and for whom the idea of poverty's origins in circumstance was more novel, Boston's agents had a different starting point for experiencing the shock of the Depression. But they would end with a more similar understanding of what they could and could not achieve. For them, it threw into sharper relief the difficulty of the task they and their clients were attempting; granting more weight to prior disadvantage and compounding problems, they, too, began to demand less and forgive more, and they also resorted to more automatic assumptions about the class and racial "types" of poor people who increasingly seemed destined to remain trapped on relief.

In part, this could mean workers taking a more realistic and pragmatic view of their dealings with the poor, and it could also mean a form of casework dedicated to realizing the more mundane ambitions of clients. It is not incidental, either, that the few MSPCC agents whose names suggest an immigrant background—Frances Ziskind, Julius Markert, and Madeleine Hoagland, for instance—seem to have been particularly drawn in this direction.[72] For them, the primary issues were securing relief to which families were entitled and protecting children as best they could from the forces rupturing the economy. More than their native-born and often elite colleagues, they focused on incapacity and prior debility and accepted the need for long-term and possibly permanent support.

By the end of the 1930s, even in the work of child protection, there seems to have been a growing belief that strenuous casework was best reserved for a smaller group of clients who had some chance of achieving fundamental change or, as the language shifted, "readjustment." In a way, they heard only part of what their poorer clients were trying to tell them: people could be derailed and needed unconditional help when they were, but that didn't mean they could or should be left alone forever. As London and Melbourne workers floundered in the wake of failure or joined in a push to make their agencies part of a modern form of social advocacy and service, those in Boston were coming to see casework as something best saved for those not already damaged by their poverty, with the rest referred back to the public relief created by the New Deal. And that meant coming closer to the idea of poverty as a kind of culture that fixed people in place.

This tendency was partly a matter of workers frustrated by the poverty of their clients when they knew that real treatment might bring results. It was, after all, something of an advance to recognize people's circumstances rather than their obstinacy as the barrier to change. But it also tended to mean leaving clients to what agents knew were inadequate outcomes. In one achingly sad case from 1936, a fourteen-year-old boy who had been rejected by his mother "needs a great deal of therapy on a very deep level and over a long period of time, and it would probably be necessary to make a psychoanalytical type of treatment. This treatment is not available for this boy, and without it the attempt to make an adjustment in foster homes seems useless. . . . Since he cannot receive the type of psychoanalytical therapy that he needs the attempt to socialize him through strict discipline in Shirley [Reformatory] is the next best procedure."[73]

For others, the issue was simply one of incapacity. The Powells, first seen in 1928, exemplify the kind of long-running and difficult cases the MSPCC and the public relief authorities shunted back and forth during the 1930s. Selina Powell was referred by her mother, who refused to be responsible for any more of Selina's children; Selina, whose husband was in the Concord Reformatory on a larceny charge, denied that she was pregnant, but her mother said she had been delinquent since the age of ten and was "mentally weak." The baby was born in August but was dead within a month; "mo. is absolutely irresponsible and unfit to be at large in the community," reported agent Dorothy Lynch, "but the Court refuses to interfere as the girl is living at home with her parents." Within the next few years, Selina would take out complaints against her husband and be the subject of allegations herself. A premature baby died in December 1929; in 1933, Public Welfare asked for another investigation, during which agent Catherine Macdonnell found "a very tiny frail looking ch, flies were all around ... found [two-year-old] girl asleep under a bundle of rags, no mattress, a dirty crib." Selina "seemed to treat agt's visit as a huge joke." Selina's husband had gonorrhea but was "working every time he has an opportunity." But in 1935, with the family now living in Watertown, and a third child dead from whooping cough, the children were committed to the Department of Public Welfare, and Selina, now diagnosed as feeble-minded, was found guilty of lewd conduct and committed to the Reformatory for Women at Framingham. At the end of the case, in 1942, two of Selina's children were in the state school for the feebleminded, and her husband was begging the MSPCC for something to be done. Selina was committed to the Boston State Hospital, and all of her younger children were taken to the Chardon Street Home and permanently committed to the care of the state.[74]

The MSPCC agents had always seen sordid and depressing cases, but their sense of possibility seemed dimmed by the Depression. One young father, reported in 1931 because his children were running wild and defecating in the yard, impressed agent Joseph Donnell with a "firm but sincere conviction to follow out any plans or suggestions which agent might make" and was "probably the victim of hard luck and unemployment, anxious and willing to improve the situation," but the addendum—"as much as lies within his power"—was telling. Nor could the agent suggest any remedy for the fact that, as the father pointed out, their fit-to-be-condemned tenement contained only one lavatory for ten families and more than thirty children.[75] There was a greater sense of detachment and even futility in the face of such forces so that clients seemed fated to fail. Agent Benson Swift certainly intervened in the O'Brien family's dispute in late 1936, which pitted a wife—"a bleached blonde with dissipated face" who was "oversexed and probably intemperate"—against an estranged husband she accused of molesting their seventeen-year-old daughter. Swift spoke strongly to the father; he "told him frankly that appearances were against him & stories were disturbing & it would require great deal of explaining shd matter research his place of employment." Though Swift was able to achieve a small

victory—eighteen-year-old Patrick O'Brien went to a Civilian Conserva-
tion Corps camp in Vermont in 1938—he seemed unsurprised when closing the case to say that the O'Briens' daughter had been arrested, "virtually
prostitute," and committed to a reformatory.[76]

Even more telling were those long-running cases in which the MSPCC
agents regarded their role as one of "case management," with the aim of
moving clients into long-term and probably permanent public relief. The
Buckleys were one such couple, though they were perhaps less immediately strange than their landlady, "a large extremely buxom type who has
bleached hair and who was known to agt several years ago. . . . Sometime
ago she was interested in boxing and now she is well-known for her mo-
torcycle. She usually wears a sombrero and a sort of cowboy blouse." The
police, the public relief authorities, and a Works Progress Administration housekeeper reported Alma Buckley for neglect at various times between 1939 and 1942, though most recognized that her problems were ill
health and "constant childbearing," and Laura Wells "congratulated her
on her perseverance." Though another agent considered her a "glib, facile-
tongued woman who talks readily about what she wants to reveal in an
effort to obscure facts she believed agt wanted to secure," there was little
attempt to provide what the society might call transforming or even interventionist casework; instead, the aim was to resolve Alma's situation by
having her obtain a divorce and apply for assistance from the Aid to Dependent Children (ADC) program. The MSPCC agents battled the supervisor of the Department of Public Welfare, rejecting as "simply absurd" a
demand that Alma furnish her home properly before ADC support could
be approved and finally, in a sharp exchange with the department social
worker, reminding her that "private agencies felt that they had particular areas of need to cover and that basic needs should be covered by public funds."[77]

The MSPCC agents were right, in a way. They were now able to direct
some cases to a public relief structure much improved from its rudimentary and chronically underfunded inadequacies of the 1920s. And part of
what they were recognizing was the importance of stable earnings, decent
housing, and adequate medical services; as a good many of their clients had
tried to tell them, it was very difficult to be recognized as a good parent
when the standards being applied bore no relation to the financial means
that allowed you to realize them. The Depression, if anything, seems to
have emboldened the people visited by the MSPCC; with a more general appreciation of the nature and impact of poverty, Boston's poor were
more willing to risk confronting workers with the contradictions of their

requests, especially in terms of housing. On several occasions, tenants suggested that complaints about garbage and dilapidation might better be directed at their landlords or asked aloud how a family was meant to stay decent in a tumbledown tenement or shack.

Part of the problem was that what really mattered was a form of financial stability and certainty that the agencies themselves were not able to deliver or even influence. What mattered was a resolution to family conflict, as when Thea King finally realized her aim of gaining custody over her thirteen-year-old brother Frank in 1933; despite MSPCC objections and claims she would be a "worse influence" than their neglectful mother, she was able to give Frank a stable home. A follow-up call seven years later revealed that Frank was about to finish high school—the first in his family to achieve this feat—and had joined the National Guard.[78] What counted was secure work. In a long-running relationship with the Edisons, whose wars with each other, their landladies, the MSPCC, the Department of Public Welfare, and the Division of Child Guardianship spanned the years between 1931 and 1938, there were periods of relative calm and independence in what the public relief authorities claimed "would always be a welfare case." In 1935, 1937, and 1938, the family was off welfare, there was "definite improvement," and the home was "immaculate." The final visit in 1938 was caused by a malicious complaint from a landlady (who alleged the usual and telling triumvirate of sins that people knew would attract MSPCC attention: the father was drinking, the children were starving, and the mother was out working). In fact, as the oldest daughter reported, there was no neglect because her father now had a stable and secure job as a motor mechanic.[79]

In a way, what these Boston workers allowed the Depression to teach them was the limit of their powers and influence. As Linda Gordon suggests, the ethics and practices of the MSPCC would be changed again by the war, but like her I sense a complicated, incomplete, and yet significant shift in these files during the 1930s. In their dramatization of inequality and poverty, the files reveal a changing sense of what was possible. As the cases described above show, the faith in transformation wasn't abandoned, but real effort would more and more be directed only at those who had the material and social means to afford it and whose problems were something other than money, resources, and housing. As social work became more sophisticated, it left many of its potential participants behind. There seemed little point in applying sophisticated social work remedies to those mired in long-term poverty. Rather than seeing their specialized social services as something they could contribute in a broader push for social justice—which I think was the position at which at some Melburnians and Londoners arrived—these American workers saw public and private agencies managing increasingly distinct populations.

This shift coincided with another, which began to soften the color line that had seemed so hard and fast in the 1920s and 1930s. The caricatures and jokes directed at African American clients were less frequent after 1932 and, although the fact that a few clients were "colored" was always in the front of white social workers' minds, they were less likely to focus on this and only this in their dramatizations of problems. In an even longer view, the change was evident in the case of a Roxbury woman, Beryl Farmer, first visited in 1941 when her daughter was placed in MSPCC custody. In 1942 Beryl married, and no further neglect was expected, as she was "getting along exceptionally well." Beryl continued to attract reports of neglect, especially in 1948, when her husband deserted her, and in 1952 and 1953. Despite suspicions from police and the ADC worker, Beryl always impressed the MSPCC visitors; she was, agent Kathleen Walters wrote in 1948, "more sinned against than sinning," and in 1953 agent Sonia Moller was sharply critical of the ADC worker for accepting stories about parties and unsupervised children. Instead, Moller agreed that Beryl Farmer was the victim of persecution by her landlord; "worker assured mo. that after another talk with the ADC visitor, we would be closing our contact, since, in our opinion, there was no neglect."[80]

In one of the most insightful studies of American "poverty knowledge," Alice O'Connor identifies a shift toward cultural explanations of poverty during the 1930s, with concerns for the "deeper recesses of psychological and social identity" as well as the obvious fact of economic deprivation.[81] She notes that this was not yet the idea of a "culture of poverty" that became so dominant in the 1950s and that notions of pathology were routinely applied only to the supposed deficiencies of African American culture and family life. Yet in these files, perhaps, are some of the first, unsteady signals of the way in which Boston's poor—and perhaps America's poor more broadly—would be redivided in the wake of the Depression. One group, almost entirely white and often temporarily fallen on hard times, had problems that could be resolved through adjustment and rehabilitation. Those problems were often deep and troubling, but they were psychological rather than financial. Another group, which contained almost all African Americans, "failed" immigrants, and a white American residuum "trapped" in poverty, drew together those from whom little could be expected because the damage of inequality and impoverishment had been too great. The drama of American poverty portrayed in these case files began to turn on a link between inferiority and more or less entrenched dependency. That inferiority had become, in a way, both more understandable and forgivable because it was the outcome of larger structural forces. But it had also become more intractable and best left to the more or less tender mercies of public relief programs.

These are hints and speculations, and like anyone who uses even relatively numerous case files, I must not advance too far. But it is possible to make suggestions. In them, perhaps, we can see that the poor had won something—the minimal but still significant entitlement and guarantee represented by the New Deal principle of social security—and at the same time were losing something that a good many of them had actually wanted: effective outside care and help to solve, rather than simply "manage," the problems that so damaged their own lives and the prospects of their children. As Linda Gordon is so careful to point out in relation to family violence, and I must just as carefully argue about poverty, it is not true that the victims of an unequal society don't want help and intervention. They want something of the care and investment that constitutes "social work." Poor women, in particular, have always wanted and needed resources with which to secure the future and do their work as mothers. They may not have wanted patronizing Americanization, but that doesn't mean they had no interest in—and desire for—the means and support that might help them fulfill their aspirations.

Boston's child protection agents had taken for themselves a key role in the fundamental drama of American transformation. They could be clumsy and belittling, and they often failed to understand the supporting role their clients played in shaping that drama to their own ends. The Depression then narrowed the scale of their ambition. It forged a greater sense of realism and a surer understanding of the role that large structural forces played in people's lives. But it also wove class and race together in a new kind of way, widening the gap between those who were worthy of interventions and those who were not. Struggling to care and to transform, Boston's child protectors had listened, and they had not listened.

Part Four

MINNEAPOLIS

Miss Lindstrom and the Fried Potatoes

Dramatis Personæ

ELSA LINDSTROM, a visitor for the Family Welfare Association
ANNA ARNESEN, a mother
OLE ARNESEN, her husband

· · · · · · · · · · · · · DRAMA · · · · · · · · · · · ·

Even if it had ever been a case needing her skills, it is no longer. The public relief authorities can take on the Arnesens. The Family Welfare Association provides service and casework, not relief for people who aren't about to try and find remedies for their problems. Elsa Lindstrom is glad of her notepad and pen so she can use the time on the streetcar to write down the details of what she has just heard and said. Fried potatoes, mind. Fried potatoes. The streetcar is slow through downtown. Slow and full, but Lindstrom remains focused on her notes. She wishes she'd found something to say at the end that was more effective, something more triumphant and crushing. She isn't sure that Ole Arnesen will feel as bad as he ought.

There is nothing else for it, so long as Anna Arnesen protects her husband in his delinquencies. Lindstrom can't understand why she does. Ole is forty-five and Anna only thirty-three. They'd married in Iowa when she was just twenty and lived out of state before coming to Minneapolis nine years ago. There are six children, three boys and three girls, the oldest eleven and the youngest a tiny baby. Ole has been in America for twenty years, but he still speaks Norwegian occasionally, and he still likes his *akevitt* as well as his beer. He is a painter, but he never seems able to keep a steady job. His last boss said his drinking was excessive; Ole denies it, but Lindstrom remembers that when she interviewed him he tried to evade the issue and did not want to admit that he was a drinking man. He said that it was his word against the other man's and that the other man was a troublemaker. But he simply won't accept that he is refusing to take real responsibility for his family. Today was the worst, she thinks, raising her pen as the streetcar jolts, presses forward, and then slows to a crawl along Hennepin Avenue.

Anna is just as difficult. She had been told that unless Ole was willing to acknowledge his need for help and accept that help, the association could do nothing. But Anna could not understand. Elsa Lindstrom had first seen her more than a year ago, in January 1925, because the family had run up a huge grocery bill. Anna giggled throughout the interview and continually played with her hair. Lindstrom also remembers Anna's silly remark, that the grocery store owner had plenty of money and didn't need theirs. It is just the kind of thing she says. She doesn't doubt that particular silliness came from Ole. She had tried to convince Anna that the grocer having money wasn't the point. The point was that the money was due him. What is owed is owed. It goes around, and it comes around. It is like talking to a child at times.

As soon as the weather turned cold, Anna turned up again. It was just before Thanksgiving. She looked very queer because of that strange hat she wears. The family was in crisis. Lindstrom asked her why she had waited until the very last minute to ask for help with planning their budget. At least she'd not giggled. It was then that Elsa Lindstrom made her decision. It was time to confront Ole with his irresponsibility. He had been called into the office, and Lindstrom well remembered what she had to say to him. It was up to him to make the arrangements for taking care of the family. It was not right for him to send his wife on such errands that were embarrassing for him to face, and he should not push them on to her. He'd said she was right. He'd said that he had been too ashamed to admit their need for help.

Today is the last straw. She is so angry. The notepad is back in her pocketbook as she steps down from the streetcar at Sixth Avenue. "Imagine," she says. She means to speak to herself, but it is louder than that, and the young man on the sidewalk ahead of her turns his head. "Fried potatoes. Fried potatoes." Puzzled—especially as Lindstrom is now punctuating each word with a finger pointed at an imagined person in front of her—he steps out of her way as she strides forward.

She goes back over it in her mind. Today there had been a chance for definite change. Had she been close to achieving it? Or was Anna too stupid and indefinite and uncooperative to see what had to be done?

She goes back to its beginning. She was seeing other clients on Fifth Street South and thought it would be interesting to visit the Arnesens. Anna is at home with the three children who aren't yet in school, but Ole is out. Sigrid and Hilda are the little girls, though she has to ask Anna for their names. The little boy, Anders, is just a month old and is fast asleep in a rather put-together baby carriage. The house is very bare, and the children's clothes are worn and dirty. She has interrupted Anna doing laundry, but after greeting her visitor, Anna starts to prepare food for the children.

She is cutting potatoes while Sigrid and Hilda sit on the floor beneath the table playing patty-cake. Miss Lindstrom starts to discuss her situation and urges her to take action.

"Things aren't so bad, Miss Lindstrom." Anna laughs nervously. "Really, things aren't so bad."

"But he is not taking responsibility. He has to accept his responsibilities, Mrs. Arnesen. You probably won't know it, but you can sue a husband for nonsupport."

"I don't know what that means, Miss Lindstrom."

"It means that you can have him charged for not fulfilling his responsibilities to provide for you and the children."

"But what would happen to him then?" Anna turns, cleans her hands on a dish towel, and takes hold of a frying pan.

"Well, he would be forced to support you. Or he'd go to jail."

"But what would be the point of that, Miss Lindstrom? It's hard for him. He tries to get work."

"Don't protect him so, Anna. The more you protect him, the less he'll do."

There is no reply this time. Anna has turned around and is at the stove. It is quiet. Anna has stiffened, and her shoulders are set and square. The girls have stopped playing patty-cake and are looking up at Miss Lindstrom from beneath the table.

"I know he drinks, Mrs. Arnesen. He won't admit it, but you know he drinks."

"He drinks, Miss Lindstrom. All men drink. He drinks, but he doesn't get into trouble. It doesn't seem much to charge a man with." Anna's back is still turned, so it is hard to know how she is really reacting to the conversation. From the other room come the sounds of the baby waking up. There's a half cry, a cry not yet sure of how loud it needs to be to gain attention. "What good will having Ole in jail do?" She turns now to get the pieces of potato, and she looks impatient. "He's told you. He finds it hard to ask for help."

"He seems to find it not so hard to make you ask for help."

"Well, be that as it may, Miss Lindstrom. He's proud. Proud like most men. And anyways, maybe I like keeping these things in my hands. Maybe it's easier for me to go and ask for a little help. Maybe I know what we need."

"But what about the future, Mrs. Arnesen? Do you want to just keep things this way?"

"Miss Lindstrom, it's just not as easy as you make out. It's all very well fixing to make trouble, but I just don't see how it helps us. Or helps me or these little ones. I'd rather have their father and no regular wage than no father for them at all."

"Well, Mrs. Arnesen, I think something more dramatic might be a better idea. Like suing him for nonsupport. You can do it, you know. I'll help you."

"We need help getting by. We need a few things sometimes. It doesn't mean he doesn't try. He does try. He just doesn't like you or anybody else bringing it up all the time. I'll see the Poor Department if I need anything, Miss Lindstrom. I just need a few groceries now and then or some wood."

As she finishes, Anna looks intently at Ole Arnesen, who has appeared in the doorway. He is smoothing the wispy hair of the baby in his arms, and his eyes are hard.

"I am looking after my family all right. What business is it of yours?"

"Ole, leave it." Anna nods at him and tries to propel him back out of the doorway with her eyes. Anna then looks at Elsa Lindstrom, more in exasperation than anything. "I'll see you out, Miss Lindstrom. Thanks for dropping by. Without being asked," she emphasizes, her eyes turned again on her husband.

But Lindstrom is angry, angry at Ole, angry at people who won't face the truth, angry at men who let their wives bear the heaviest load.

"I can't leave yet, Mrs. Arnesen. You'll probably need some grocery tickets, won't you?" She reaches inside her pocketbook, takes one out, and places it on the table so that it faces Ole.

"I heard what you said. No one can arrest me for not supporting. I am taking care of my family all right. We don't need you."

Lindstrom takes out another grocery ticket and places it next to the first.

"How many will you need this time, Mrs. Arnesen? Three? Four?"

"Miss Lindstrom, I didn't ask for those. I'll go to the Poor Department. Please, let me see you out. The children need their lunch." She picks up the tickets and offers them to the visitor. When she doesn't respond, Anna presses them into the still-open pocketbook. "Take them back, please. I will go to the Poor Department when I need them."

Ole cuts across his wife. "I am taking care of my family all right."

"Really, Mr. Arnesen? Really? Is your family all right and being actually taken care of? Is your family really all right when your children have only fried potatoes for lunch?"

Ole's expression is as dark as he can make it. Anna looks at him, holding him with her eyes. "I think you should leave, Miss Lindstrom."

"Are you taking care of the children, Mr. Arnesen? From where I'm standing, you haven't shown the right responsibility for your family all along. Sending your wife on your errands. Losing your job for drinking. Do you call this caring for your family? Fried potatoes for lunch? Fried potatoes?"

The question hangs in the air. Everyone is quiet: Elsa Lindstrom, because she isn't sure that what she's said is strong enough; Anna, because she doesn't want to hear any more; Ole, because he doesn't want to have heard what he fears he will say. The children are quiet, too, because children always know when silence is better, when what's already been said doesn't lead you anywhere but worse.

· · · · · · · · · · · · RESOLUTION · · · · · · · · · · · ·

We know what Ole Arnesen said: "I am taking care of my family all right." We know that among the challenges Elsa Lindstrom then laid at Ole's door was this: did he think his family was all right and being actually taken care of when his children "have only fried potatoes for lunch"? She said other things too. She probably mentioned the earlier exchange about his wife taking on the "embarrassing" task of asking for relief and the job she suspected he lost because of drinking, though that had clearly been Ole's word against his employer's. It seems Ole and Anna Arnesen fell silent. Lindstrom may have waited. Was there a sense of a dramatic denouement, or have I just imagined there must have been? In any event, Miss Lindstrom then left, and the Family Welfare Association (FWA) didn't see Ole again.

I'm not sure if Lindstrom took out two or three grocery tickets from her pocketbook. I included it here because the gesture seemed to capture her exasperation with the Arnesens, an exasperation built over time, and caused by Ole's unwillingness to discuss or perhaps even acknowledge his limited command over his family's future, by Anna's failure to cooperate, and by Lindstrom's assumptions about how couples and families ought to manage their struggle against poverty. Her suggestions to Anna Arnesen about nonsupport, like her several attempts to confront Ole with his responsibilities, were intended to dislodge this family from a path that the Family Welfare Association's visitors always found irritating. It was the Arnesens' unwillingness—or perhaps refusal—to "understand [the] visitor's mission" that most annoyed Lindstrom. They were "indefinite" and "uncooperative." Anna "protected" Ole in "his delinquencies" and left all her appeals for help "until the very last minute."

Lindstrom's desires were always a little contradictory, on the evidence of the file. She was frustrated by Ole's inability to live up to the responsi-

bilities of married fatherhood and by his lack of independence, and she was
frustrated by Anna's protective unwillingness to expose her husband to the
proper consequences of that failure. For a number of reasons, Lindstrom
wanted Ole to pay a price, and she could never understand why the couple
found "making plans" an unconvincing response to their compounding
woes. Lindstrom wanted the Arnesens to function as a couple, but only in
ways that accorded with her own definitions of what that meant. Whatever their capabilities and their means, and however frequently their plans
might have been interrupted by the births and illnesses of their children
or Ole's unstable employment history, they were meant to develop an approach to their lives that they didn't seem to understand and of which
they had little experience or knowledge. If not in her image, they—and
perhaps especially Anna—were meant to become the kind of person Elsa
Lindstrom thought she was: self-aware, in control, and able to plan. Nowhere in her conversations with the Arnesens does she show any sense of
imagining the world from Anna's point of view or of trying to understand
how her help and advice—however well meant it assuredly was—might
have sounded to a similarly young woman who just didn't share her faith
in the possibility of self-reliance.

Other agencies would help the Arnesens with groceries and coal or
clothing for their still-growing family. The Salvation Army would make
occasional donations of blankets. There would be other scraps of help and
hand-me-downs. Lindstrom always failed to understand this; she couldn't
comprehend why Anna Arnesen preferred last-minute parcels to well-laid
plans, the small coins of charity to the satisfaction of the banked dollars
you couldn't see. To Lindstrom, this was a symptom of Anna's silliness and
perhaps stupidity; even if Anna had good reasons for being poor, in Lindstrom's eyes she had less justification for staying so. Elsa Lindstrom could
understand her client as deficient and downcast, but never as simply and
justifiably dependent, at least for a time. Nor could Lindstrom understand
Anna's sense of entitlement, captured in her remark that "the grocery-
man had plenty of money and did not need to take theirs." In Anna's eyes,
her entitlement stemmed from a simple fact: there were children to be
fed, clothed, and shoed, and their needs were more important than whatever might be owed to a richer man. Anna "giggled" and "continually
played with her hair" during that interview. Another visitor, Catherine
Overshaw, described Anna as "laughing nervously" in order to "cover her
confusion." Perhaps she was confused, even unintelligent. More likely, I
think, Anna simply didn't know what she was meant to say, in the face of
their criticisms, to people who clearly thought they were acting in her best
interests but just as clearly didn't understand the way the world worked for

a poor woman, her husband, and her children. Here, my reading of this encounter relies on the work of Beverly Stadum, the best of the historians chronicling the city's responses to poverty in the first half of the twentieth century. As Stadum argues, the FWA's agents were not unsympathetic and were often helpful, but they were always quick—often very quick—to give forceful advice.[1]

It may not have been a "good speaking story," but the case of Ole and Anna Arnesen was in many ways a testament to the difficulties of casework in Minneapolis in the 1920s. In the conflicts Lindstrom had with the Arnesens, there is also something of the increasing tensions that would characterize relationships between FWA visitors and clients in the harder decade to come. FWA visitors would hear more of that sense of entitlement, that preference for cash and real things over and above the intangibles of wise plans. They would discover more clients asking why the needs of "the grocery-man" should prevail over those of their own children and hear more about the not-so-hidden injuries of class. They would confront solidarities they could not understand and find fewer people willing to say that misfortune was only ever delinquency's companion.

Within a few years, though, perhaps Elsa Lindstrom herself had cause to doubt the possibility of plans. In the hard December of 1929, when everyone was asking for wood and coal, when there was a growing stream of applicants, and when the FWA's new general secretary was talking to the Division of Public Relief about the cases the FWA could handle and those it would have to pass on, perhaps there was a little more doubt. Anna Arnesen turned up that December. Ole has bronchitis and had lost his job. A few months later, a neighbor reported them as destitute, so the case was reopened. Anna was "rather demanding in her attitude" this time. She was sent to the Board of Public Welfare (BPW), though Lindstrom also gave her two grocery tickets. After all, there were two more babies to feed. But it seems Lindstrom saw little point in trying anything further with the Arnesens. Perhaps she thought that they would always be destitute and that Ole was a hopeless and feckless man. Perhaps she assumed they weren't going to change because they had no real drive to succeed and couldn't see that hard work and effort would actually change the situation for good and for the better. Perhaps she'd said what needed to be said, and that was that.

But if there had been a sense of victory over Ole Arnesen's "delinquencies"—and it is clear that he was a difficult and frustrating man—I wonder how fried potatoes for lunch might have seemed to Elsa Lindstrom by the end of 1929. By then, there were new faces in the FWA office, brought in by lost jobs and reduced wages. There were some union men,

bitter and proud, and some women, typists and stenographers mostly, respectable and with no idea what happened next. They would have seemed
stunned and nervous about what might happen. Some would be unsure
what they were supposed to do or how they were supposed to look or
carry themselves. The board of directors talked about providing casework
only to families with children, families that hadn't been on relief before,
and single women who came in through the Gateway Bureau. The board
wanted their caseworkers to focus on providing services, not grocery orders and cash. It would have been difficult to see how, at the end of 1929.
It must have been difficult to talk with people about wise plans and long-
term improvements when they didn't have jobs and needed to keep warm
or when it looked like they might lose their house. It would have looked
liked a hard, long winter. And it was going to get worse.

CHAPTER 20

The Discovery and the Remedy

In 1922, just before it changed its name to the Family Welfare Association, the Associated Charities (AC) of Minneapolis produced a short history, which included this description of their work: "The present ideal of case-work ... is that the need which drives people to ask for assistance or advice can be discovered and by careful attention or correlation of resource can usually be cured and the task of casework is to make this discovery and apply the remedy."[2] In its change of name, and by directing its visitors to discover needs and apply cures, the FWA was signaling its persistent intention to distinguish itself from public and private relief agencies dispensing material aid. As early as 1915, the AC had identified itself as an agency dedicated less to relief and more to understanding poverty's causes "in the individual and in the social environment." Furthermore, "it must show in every way that it is sincerely concerned not only to relieve the condition of those who are now in poverty in Minneapolis, but also to save those who are not yet in poverty and misery from getting worse." That might mean taking "courageous and positive positions on vital questions ... which may arouse the antagonism of certain classes in the community, e.g. regarding the question of living wages, exploitation of the labor of women and children, unwise philanthropy [and] official inefficiency." And no one could claim its larger objectives lacked grandeur: "to save citizens from unnecessary misery, inefficiency and death; [and] to keep Minneapolis as safe as possible from slums, from vice and crime, and from pauperism."[3]

Although it focused on Minneapolis, the FWA certainly gained a national reputation and influence; Frank Bruno, who steered its transition from the AC to the FWA, was a significant pioneer in social work education and casework practice well into the 1950s, and Joanna Colcord, general secretary between 1925 and 1928, had worked in New York's Charity Organization Society and returned there to head the Charity Organization Division of the Russell Sage Foundation.

As was ever the case in the fields of scientific charity and charity organization, though, ends were easier to define than means. The growth of public welfare required one set of adjustments; after the Minnesota legislature authorized the first payments of monthly allowances to dependent families in 1913, for instance, the AC acknowledged that "the public agencies will doubtless take upon themselves the care of the better established groups of dependents, leaving the groups harder to classify and requiring more elasticity of treatment to the private societies."[4]

Thereafter, the AC-FWA tried to reduce its long-term relief and illness cases in order to focus on investigative, preventive, and "elastic" casework. In 1917 its visiting nurses were moved into a separate organization, and in 1918 the Tuberculosis Committee was also made independent. The Confidential Exchange, against which all organizations were meant to check clients' names and details, was one of the most important legacies of the AC's focus on registration, cooperation, and "correlation," but its limitations in practice tended to reduce its significance in the overall work of the agency. In 1921 an interagency conference established that there was still "a considerable degree of contradictory effort," with some clients being seen by two, three, and even four agencies; with groups such as the Salvation Army uninterested in correlation, such duplication seemed inevitable.[5]

Instead, the AC-FWA sought to contain its responsibilities for material relief. During 1922 Colcord held a series of meetings with the city's Board of Public Welfare, which led to an agreement that the BPW "would not interfere in the treatment of any family known to" the FWA and would "take over the care and entire responsibility of families in which the major problem was the unemployment of the breadwinner."[6] Later that year, the BPW also took over "old women and old couples awaiting county allowance unless work other than mere money relief seemed desirable," and homeless men were dispatched—along with an FWA worker—to the Union City Mission.[7] At the same time, the association developed new strategies to bring into its orbit groups and problems untouched by other agencies. In 1922 the FWA hired its first two "colored workers" (though it discontinued its "psychiatric social worker" in 1923), and in 1924 the board of directors decided to hire a male worker. The AC had employed one or two men between 1915 and 1922, but from 1924 until 1935 this new policy meant that there was always at least one man among the FWA's fifteen or twenty visitors.[8] In 1927 the FWA also set up its "Gateway Bureau" to assist "unadjusted older single women," and throughout the 1920s, despite occasional protests from the Department of Public Welfare, it continued to assist people who did not have legal residence rights in Hennepin County, especially when their rights had been lost on what the FWA workers considered technicalities.[9]

The FWA never lost its links with direct material relief. Indeed, the amount spent on relief soared to $130,000 in 1924, more than three times the total in 1918; in 1924 the amount of relief expended on a case averaged nearly $60, when in 1918 it had been less than $20.[10] Caseloads also increased. The number of "major cases," which involved some degree of detailed investigation, grew from 1,118 in 1918 to 1,411 in 1920 before rising sharply to 2,475 in 1922 and 3,411 in 1925. There was a slight drop thereafter, to 2,714 major cases in 1928.[11] Accordingly, while cutbacks and referrals of particular kinds of clients to public agencies reduced the average amount of relief per case to $41.60 by 1928, the total amount spent on relief increased to $186,000.[12] However much its directors wanted the FWA to become a distinctive kind of casework provider, it always dispensed relief along with advice and guidance, and it always maintained a strong element of investigation in its work. As late as 1938, a report on the agency concluded that it "is still rather generally known as a relief agency in the community ... [and] its case work service program is less understood and utilized."[13]

The focus on relief in part reflected the desperate circumstances of many local people. The economic mainstays of Minneapolis—flour, lumber, and freight—had been declining in the 1920s, though not as fast as Minnesota's small mining and farming towns; by the end of the decade, the city's mills and rail yards and factories were shedding jobs by the hundreds and even the thousands. The homeless and the jobless filled the parks, lined the streets, and queued for food. During the 1930s, Minnesota would see a series of struggles between business and unions; in Minneapolis, long kept "nonunion" by its Citizen's Alliance, the battle would be long and hard, culminating in the Minneapolis Teamsters' Strike in May 1934. These were hard days of police and pickets and fears of revolution, of blacklisting and street battles and brute force.[14] For the city's welfare agencies, it sometimes must have seemed that all of working-class Minneapolis was out of a job or on strike.

The historian of poverty and charity in Minneapolis can rely to a very great extent on previous scholarship, especially, as mentioned earlier, Beverly Stadum's meticulous and insightful study of three hundred cases, *Poor Women and Their Families*. My study covers a smaller sample—107 cases in all—and confirms Stadum's main arguments about the difficulties the FWA's clients faced in living up to the association's faith in economic self-sufficiency. Stadum's study also reveals the complexities of the relationships between agents and their largely female clients, insisting in the end that the lives of poor women were characterized more by a strong desire for independence than by the easy welfare dependency with which they were—and are—so often charged.

The comparative dimension is also helpful. The FWA provided material relief and had the same direct links to the charity organization movement as the Melbourne COS; its case files could be expected to feature similar dramas of detective investigation and a similar concern with truth, secrets, and lies. Certainly, both are present, as is an occasional focus on dress and gesture, but in Minneapolis everyone got at least something that they wanted, and workers there were less likely than their counterparts in Melbourne and especially London to focus on the ingrained deficiencies of lower-class people. Compared with the Boston agencies, meanwhile, there were fewer stories about rescue and the difficulties of becoming American. The Minneapolis caseworkers mostly met Norwegians, Swedes, and Germans, and on the evidence of their names, a good quarter of the visitors were themselves the daughters and sons—or perhaps the grandchildren— of Minnesota's great waves of Scandinavian and German settlers. On the whole, it seems they were less impressed by or interested in the struggle to assimilate.

Nor did the FWA workers regularly confront racial boundaries, despite the policy of maintaining a "colored worker." Of the sampled cases between 1920 and 1937, only two involved African American clients. The first, in 1922, was "a typical Southern family ... with a decided Southern accent [who] were very respectful, neat and clean" and moved to St. Louis for work before any relief was provided.[15] The second file tracked a difficult relationship between the FWA and the Jackson family; in the first instance, in 1924, Belle Jackson rang for assistance in looking after her two grandsons, whose mother had just died. The FWA's black worker, Ella Kirby, was confused because the woman "opened the door somewhat suspiciously" and would not let her in; one of the children "was extremely reticent about relating their back history," and other tenants in the building "seemed to be so suspicious of visitor's mission that they would give no information but simply advised her to knock on all the doors." Later, Kirby discovered that the problem had arisen in part because they were confused about her identity: "If they had known that [I] had been colored they would have told her 'where to get off.' This statement was later retracted [by Belle Jackson] and she stated that they did not exactly use that expression but were so certain that [I] was white that they had tried to be cordial and very nice. She agreed that they should be courteous and respectful with anybody regardless of their racial identities."

The Jacksons were engaged in a series of battles, with both Belle and her daughters attempting to make her son take her in. Nephews and sons-in-law provided financial assistance, and a grandson—"tall, attractive, courteous, and quite manly," reported Ella Kirby—also helped with the rent, but Belle Jackson was determined to make her "good for nothing" son responsible for her support. Another visitor suggested she enter a county home, but Jackson "insisted vehemently that she would hang herself before she would go.... She had gotten along all her life and she was not going to submit to anything so disgraceful now." By 1930, when the new "colored worker," Lillian Robinson, tried to solve the impasse, she had little success: "[I] attempted to find out something about the family situation but they refused to discuss it, saying there were some things about a family's life that just could not be mentioned. It was explained to them that this made it impossible for Visitor to work out a plan for them." Within a couple of months, Belle Jackson was found to have tuberculosis and was committed to the Glen Lake Sanatorium. Belle was seventy-one years old at that time, and it seems likely that she died there.[16]

In Minneapolis, the assimilation of different races and cultures was an uncommon template for social workers' stories. Instead, the story told by most case files was of the poor being drawn to and pulled away from pauperization. The phrase that seems to have been most important to Minneapolis charity agents was "making plans." This may seem a little unheroic, but it stemmed from a significant shared observation—and claim—about the nature of advantage, class, and inequality in 1920s and 1930s Minneapolis and, in the minds of the FWA caseworkers, "middle America" more broadly. If case files provide a window into the perceptions of people who are concerned about social problems and their solutions, those problems took on a particular hue in Minneapolis. Agents made less of fraud and deviousness, but more of dependency. They were most pleased by clients such as one "beautiful little woman" who was "very pleasant" to Esther Morwell. "It is very refreshing," Morwell wrote, "to find a family who was as self-sufficient as they evidently were."[17] But that family regained self-sufficiency largely because the husband's lodge granted him a weekly payment of $4.50. By retaining always that faith in a cure, the FWA workers also insisted on the possibility of uplift based on individual effort. They dramatized an explanation of inequality that highlighted the importance of making plans, the dangers of dependency, and the wisdom of middle-class self-sufficiency. This was a theater in which the poor had much to learn from the social workers with whom they shared the stage, even if what relieved their poverty was often fortuitous circumstances, a change of luck, or the gradual lessening of their vulnerabilities as children aged or husbands found work.

For these daughters and granddaughters—and a few sons and grandsons—of migrants from America's eastern states and from Europe, the best advice could be drawn from their own successful journeys. They endorsed a desire to rise, but they also made light of the hurdles that the poor confronted, and they ignored the fact that most of their clients simply wanted limited and temporary help so that they could eventually carry forward their own decisions and aspirations. In this way, the Minneapolis workers shared with those in the other cities a mistaken belief that a moment of need was always about to topple over into a lifetime of neediness. They may have focused less on detection and the detached observation of the poor, but they carried into their dramatizations of poverty's origins and solutions a similar—and just as unrealistic—insistence on self-reliance. Here, too, the poor had to be warned away from fatalism and undue reliance on others, recognizing in the process that the cure to their problems lay in emulating those who had adjusted better to the world's opportunities and challenges. It was a way of understanding inequality and poverty that remained consistent into the hard years of the Depression. It was a choice and one that made sure the FWA's workers heard only part of what the people they visited were trying to say. It was a choice, too, that would leave their agency, by the 1930s, with a sense that it had not so much overcome dependency as created it.

. . . .

CHAPTER 21

He Is Too Willing for Us to Assume Responsibility

If people approached the FWA without a sincere desire to make plans for change, they could expect little beyond a few dollars and a referral to the public relief authorities. The most significant work of welfare did not lie in changing material circumstances—something that could be left to the residual and "mere money relief" operations of the public departments—but in changing, "adjusting," and guiding clients' directions. Accordingly, dramas of rejection in the FWA tended to focus on a lack of planning and an unwillingness to change, rather than fraud; the real or potential pauper was not so much a mendicant as an unwilling partner in "necessary adjustments" or, as in the 1932 case of a man who requested shoes for his children, "too willing for FWA to assume family responsibility."[18]

In this case, there were other grounds for rejection. The husband was "dissipated and somewhat listless" (and a musician to boot), while his wife, who at one stage "bought rouge and lip stick, powder and golden-glow rinse for her hair" instead of groceries and was reported as "dressed in new clothing of the latest mode," did not always tell the truth. But here, and on similar occasions, the FWA workers were generally impressed neither by the fumbles of their clients' bodies nor by the details of their makeup and attire. When Leontine Kirkham interviewed a reputed prostitute who was suspected of having syphilis and gonorrhea, the applicant was "heavily rouged" and "clad in [a] kimono and apparently had practically no clothing on underneath." This was duly noted, but Kirkham was more impressed that the woman's statements "had the appearance of being truthful, willingly given, and complete. She apparently held back nothing." The financial difficulties of her older male "friend" had led her to seek more work from the Big Sisters movement, and the FWA provided some assistance until she secured a job as a maid at a downtown hotel.[19] For the FWA, finding and agreeing to a plan could excuse many things.

Even outright lies, shams, and evasions caused relatively few concerns for the FWA visitors in the 1920s and beyond. Helga Riegel tried to locate one applicant—described by his landlord as "ambitious, industrious and anxious to get along without help"—who proceeded to write the following letter to downtown businessmen: "You have perhaps many times donated a small sum, to some charitable organization, hoping that somewhere, someone would derive a bit of happiness from this. Wouldn't you get a more personal satisfaction if you actually knew, to whom you are giving a helping hand?"[20]

It was a daring subversion, but he was never tracked down and confronted. Ilsa Kaufman did trap one man in a lie during a 1931 investigation. When describing his elopement and marriage he "stammered dreadfully"; Kaufman told him that there was no record of his marriage and that "if there was something that they were both concealing it was well at this time to tell visitor the true facts." One can imagine Agnes Cutler's reaction. But Kaufman listened to the man's explanation and his statement that he "was very happy that visitor had come to this matter as he had been keeping it a secret for so long and it bothered him dreadfully." Because he "seemed very sincere" and "showed no tendency to want to desert his family," he was referred on for assistance.[21] In similar vein, a "dramatic hypochondriac" who feigned illnesses and had "persecution delusions"—and also had "some education and natural refinement"—was nonetheless given money for board and assisted into a nursemaid job in 1934.[22]

FWA workers directed their exasperation mostly toward those who refused to make plans, especially when they were considered to have the means and the capacity to do so. Better-off clients fallen on hard times could attract strong condemnation. In 1929 visitor Margaret Murray listened to a tale of woe from a man charged with embezzling $500; he had "no well defined plan," she wrote, and her response was prickly: "In his mannerisms [he is] a typical salesman. He affected a low confidential voice … [and] had the habit of saying 'see' after each remark." He was out of work again in 1930; the family was given coal, but another visitor, Cornelia Duchene, had sharp words for his mother, who was staying with them: "The very fact [was] that every time he had needed any assistance someone had been there to assist him, and help him out. Whereas if he had been made to stand on his own feet and make his own living and make his own complaints and get his own relief he probably would be a much better man than he was at the present time." She then told the man's wife that "they need not think that FWA was going to take care of them entirely." At this point, "both wife and husband's mother seemed to feel that FWA should step in and take care of them immediately and they were very hostile." For all that, the family received provisions and fuel through 1931 and 1932, when the FWA transferred all of its cases in which the sole problem was male unemployment to the Department of Public Relief.[23]

This absence of wise planning was the common factor in most explanations of poverty, destitution, and dependency in the decade before and even during the Depression. The reasons for its absence varied, but if clients failed to develop plans, whatever the difficulties of their circumstances, they faced rejection and even hostility from the FWA's workers. The Larues, a highly troubled family who moved to Minneapolis from Wisconsin in 1921, were referred over the years to various agencies in search of an effective diagnosis and plan of action. In 1924 Calvin Larue was unemployed and accused by a local shopkeeper of mistreating his six-year-old son; the conflict seemed to the FWA to involve husband and wife, "who quarreled and indulged in free-for-all fights," in part over his drinking. The couple had already lost one son, who died at age two from a fall, and in late 1924 a baby boy died of measles and pneumonia. The first worker attached to the case, Rose Grinter, noted that "his speaking voice and the English which he uses indicate that he is decidedly above the manual labor class [but he is] probably totally lacking stability." For the Larues, diagnoses remained "probable" and partial. In 1928, when the police declared them destitute, no cause could be found, and in 1929 the "erect" and "brisk" Mr. Larue became "stooped" and "limped" after a difficult interview. In 1930 he had become "emotionally unstable and a sex pervert." In 1931 the Big Brothers considered him "to be looking for sympathy" and "a bad mental type to be guiding a growing boy" but not "pauperized," but a case summary by FWA visitor Jane Gale in 1932 concluded that the entire family was "extremely pauperized. They asked for anything they could possibly need and when they did not get it they stirred up community feeling against the FWA."[24]

By 1935 the case was closed. Mary Larue had died before her thirty-sixth birthday, perhaps of tuberculosis, and her husband had entered the Rochester State Hospital. The worker closing the case reflected that he "had stood in his own way because his one besotting sin was women. He was not promiscuous but he was oversexed." The youngest child, a girl, was in state care, and the surviving son, seventeen years old but already suffering from tuberculosis, had left high school and gone to a farm in North Dakota. One worker suggested that "the children might have to be taken care of," but in order to force the issue, "the parents [could be] left to shift for themselves if they did not turn over a new leaf." Mary Larue once asked why the FWA workers were "discourteous and snippy and distrust[ed] and disbelieve[d] her." The file does not record a reply. Throughout, workers urged work and planning on the Larues when all of the evidence—and their own conversations with the family—suggested that their troubles ran very deep indeed and were unlikely to be overcome through the application of "wise plans."[25] This same inability to accept the idea that clients might be right about their situations was evident in several other cases involving tuberculosis and other debilitating illnesses from the 1920s and 1930s.

In dramatizing the issues in another 1924 case, FWA visitor Caroline Ewing made her own significant choices. The Hiltons, husband and wife, were both characterized as unreasonable and unwilling to accept the forming of plans. Alma Hilton was "a religious fanatic" with "constitutional psychopathic inferiority." She was "very difficult to deal with because she demanded relief and service of all kinds as her due as a 'servant of the Lord.'" Ewing was particularly incensed that the family was being helped by a rich benefactor, especially because Alma believed that as the benefactor "had plenty of people to take care of her and plenty of money . . . there was no reason why she shouldn't share it with client." Ewing consistently told Alma Hilton that "her self-respect depended on her doing the best herself that she possibly could" and was infuriated because "she did not feel it necessary to make strenuous efforts to adjust the situation, as the adjustment would be made with no effort if the Lord wished it so." Indeed, "no amount of reasoning could convince that the Lord helps those who help themselves." Ewing was just as dismissive of William Hilton, who was nearly sixty. He "lacks initiative [and is] slow," she wrote on their first meeting; on their second, he became "rather incompetent and inefficient," and on their third, he made a great mistake "by again blaming politics, economic conditions, and high rents for his inability to support his family."

Ewing's account of her closing conversation with the Hiltons recorded an unusually aggressive exchange: "She [Alma Hilton] was disgruntled and pugilistic. . . . She was most unreasonable and sarcastic and would not admit that they ought to help themselves before depending on someone else [and] that they would ask for help and they would expect to get it since it was the business of the city to give it to them."[26]

On the whole, the Minneapolis clients were rather prone to sarcasm, and they grew more so once entitlements to public relief became more secure in the 1930s. The women of Minneapolis were particularly likely to speak out and take the risk of earning criticism from the FWA. One who was in her fifties and at one stage considered a possible "dope addict" and "a reprehensible character" was none too happy with inquiries in 1934: "[She] gave visitor a most withering look and talked for more than an hour with a most scorching tongue. She talked fluently about the absolutely tactless methods which the FWA used in crushing people's pride. . . . She wanted to know what else was afoot to make her feel mortified. She thought that since she was being cooperative with the FWA that they ought to tell her exactly what was being done. She demanded to know what visitor had written and to whom she had written." The visitor explained the FWA's methods and need for "sufficient background." The client "launched upon one of her monologues about the injustices she had suffered at everyone's hands."[27]

But if they wanted relief, clients needed to hold their tongues. They had to avoid expectations of assistance or claims that something might be owed them by right, and workers often reminded clients that self-help—not some rudimentary form of social justice or some attempt to blame one's fortunes on structures—was the only way forward. As in Melbourne, welfare workers in Minneapolis warned clients against "developing a rather demanding attitude" and referred on to less scrupulous agencies—such as the Salvation Army—families who were "very strong-headed," who refused "some definite effort not to have help come in all directions," and who were "inclined to lean too heavily on anyone they can find."[28] They also disliked "needy" clients, like an "Indian woman" seen in 1925 who was "not interested in changing or bringing about much change . . . but would like the attention she would get from a social agency."[29] More likely to be helped was the couple of Norwegian stock who "gave the impression of dignity and independence," "talked frankly and openly," and were "extremely modest about asking for anything" or the elderly Swedish man who "was grateful for the help given, and tears came to his eyes when he thanked visitor."[30]

The world these FWA workers wanted to establish in clients' minds was one in which effort, energy, and planning would overcome most obstacles and in which your social position measured not the weight of earned or fortuitous advantages but your ability to master your own fate. One divorced woman was sent away from the office with nothing because "she did not want any help in planning, just financial assistance." With a $13-a-week job at a store, a child to raise, two rooms costing $23.50 a month, and unpaid child maintenance from a runaway husband stretching back ten months, the client had a point.[31] Few clients escaped an examination of their views, "tendencies," and positions on the crucial question of "wise planning," and few of those who expressed anger, bitterness, or vaguely radical misgivings about just returns for effort were allowed to participate in "service" rather than "mere relief." This was a version of the world—and an understanding of class, inequality, and mobility—that these workers clearly held to be true and that they honestly believed would improve their clients' lives. Yet it was also a version about which they seemed to need some reassurance. They insisted on relating failure to an absence of wise plans, and they were determined to reveal and suppress the telltale signs of "pauperization," if necessary by shaming, challenging, or confronting the people who had come to them for help. Though they rarely denied people some kind of help, they could be amazingly unforgiving. And, as Beverly Stadum shows so well, they often fundamentally misunderstood the careful ways in which the poor women of Minneapolis made their way "through and to myriad resources" the city offered, a task that demanded its own kind of planning and its own intelligence.[32]

They also tended to see women in terms of family responsibilities, almost to the exclusion of every other consideration. The focus on family welfare included making sure that women remained part of existing, potential, or temporarily fractured family units, and all planning took place within a framework of women's maternal and marital obligations. Where these clashed with practical circumstances, however, the FWA's female agents struggled to identify how poor women were actually meant to form "wise plans" that would combine self-sufficiency and what they defined as adequate mothering. In 1922, for instance, young mother Hanna Lindner was referred to the FWA by her sister-in-law. There were two children, four and eleven months, and her husband had just deserted her. They'd only come to Minneapolis from Sioux Falls in 1921 so he could look for better work, and now he was gone. Neighbors reported "frightful quarreling," some blaming her and some blaming the husband, but everyone agreed that he had hit her. The owner of the house they were buying was trying to foreclose, but her husband's family was anxious to help her and would finish the house so it could be sold. The FWA agreed to provide some cash and groceries.

Hanna Lindner, wrote visitor Rose Grinter, "lacks ambition and has a disagreeable disposition." She was "very elusive on the subject of work," and on her first visit into the FWA office, when chided by Grinter for spending too much money on children's clothes, "she became a little angry when I suggested that she talk over future expenditures." The FWA urged her to come up with a plan, and like other deserted mothers, Lindner was expected to find paid work. Somewhat against her own inclinations, she agreed to place the children in a nursery and work as a waitress. Grinter found her a room in a furnished apartment building.

It was at this point that the story turned to Hanna Lindner's disadvantage. She moved into the room, with the FWA paying some of the rent, and then moved out of it after only a few days. There were mice and bedbugs, she said, and the men of the house gathered downstairs to drink. Grinter "told her she did not approve of this arrangement [and] did not like her moving without consulting the FWA." Furthermore, she "told her it seemed entirely possible for her to do a great deal better for herself. She was very evidently averse to doing anything in the way of self-support which would cause any exertion on her own part." As a final word, the visitor "told her that she must begin to make plans for herself."

Lindner eventually found work as a dishwasher and then as a hospital cleaner; this, along with Children's Aid, allowed her to keep her daughter and son at home, though Grinter hadn't trusted her "very maternal sounding plea to be left with her children." The student who next visited noted that the room was untidy and the furniture shabby; when she visited again two months later, she reported "new furniture in the rooms, victrola and center table and other not absolutely necessary pieces, all evidently new." By 1923 Hanna Lindner was "a very good talker and ... perhaps not reliable," and when met on the street in 1924, all visitor Mary Kennan could add to the file was the point that she was "much rouged and powdered." According to the last entry in the file, Children's Aid was still being provided in 1931, but the family had been kept together without maintenance from the husband and without any record of neglect or inadequate care.[33] Hanna Lindner was dependent because the kind of self-sufficiency praised by her FWA visitors was simply impossible; she was a single mother whose parents had no money; whose best hope of work was unskilled domestic labor in hotels, hospitals, and laundries; and who had been left with two children to see through infancy and school, all the while having no access to adequate child care. Like hundreds of other women in her situation, she worked when and where she could and accepted aid as a means of keeping her children. One version of her story might emphasize the strength of her obligations to them and portray social workers' struggle to protect it. But the FWA visitors rarely wrote those kinds of stories in the 1920s and early 1930s.[34] Unwilling to see poverty as something that might cause—rather than stem from—dependency, and unable to come up with versions of womanhood that accommodated the real dilemmas of poor women's lives, they suspected many clients from the first and trapped themselves in too many relationships that wavered between vague suspicion and outright antagonism.

· ·

CHAPTER 22

His Attitude of Helplessness Is Exasperating

Although the importance of self-help, guidance, and "adjustment" was consistently made clear to the impoverished people of interwar Minneapolis, the visitors of the FWA would have struggled to show many cases in which "wise planning" had moved clients out of poverty. Certainly, the FWA's help was crucial for some of its recipients. In general, though, what mattered was a sufficient amount of material relief given over a long enough period. Success was also more common in the early 1930s, when the FWA could more easily refer people to material relief providers and had been freed by public agencies of its former responsibilities for the unemployed. With those duties largely taken over by the Department of Public Relief, the FWA could take up cases in which unemployment was complicated by other kinds of misfortunes and problems.

In a 1932 case, for instance, a family where the father was on probation for stealing from his employer was most effectively assisted by the provision of work relief for the eldest son, who was twenty-three. This allowed them to keep a younger boy of sixteen in school and to continue fostering a ten-year-old boy for whom they had been caring since he was nine months old. Ten months later, the family was in crisis because the father was seriously injured in a car accident. Inge Bergson called in the eldest son and told him that "with his father incapacitated, he must assume the head of the household" and form "plans towards helping the family out of their present situation." She saw him again during a home visit, when he and friends were playing cards in a room "full of smoke." His plans involved material relief for the family and work for himself until his father was able to earn again. After six months of relief, the case was closed because the family was "financially independent."[35] A similar outcome was achieved by the Hellstroms, a young couple who, one visitor reported, "were making a real effort to get away from the pattern of their parents' lives." Though both were from "relief families" of "chronic complainers," and the husband had spent a year in jail for juvenile delinquency, the visitor "was encouraged to see the clean and the co-operative attitude that the young couple were assuming and believes that there are possibilities of greater improvement for them." The key for the Hellstroms was the same: after several months of unemployment and small amounts of material relief, the husband secured a steady job.[36]

Such cases provided more evidence of the need for supplemental assistance than organized "cures" based on plans and confirmed that the compounded problems of the poor were best addressed through long-term material support. A sixty-one-year-old man with a military pension, for instance, approached the FWA in the winter of 1933. His pension had been reduced from $50 to $37.50 a month. His wife had a hernia and would soon enter the hospital for an operation. Both of his daughters were married, but with their husbands unemployed, neither could assist. During his visit to the office, "he said he disliked to ask for help, but he simply could not get along without some relief." He was given cash for food and clothing, and occasional relief was provided through the spring and early summer of 1934 until his pension was restored in July.[37] In another case two brothers, aged twenty-four and twenty-two, came to the FWA office in January 1934. They came from Altoona, Pennsylvania, but had "bummed" for three years. They were sharing a furnished room and were canvassing house to house, but their "clothes were tattered in appearance and they were anxious to be able to make a presentable appearance." As Ursula Dittmar wrote, they "seemed to be putting up a fight to maintain their respect, morale and spirits," and the older brother wanted to go to the university so he could be an engineer. There was little the FWA could do for aspirations such as those, nor was there any long-term support that could be offered to able-bodied young men who were simply among the thousands of unemployed drifters. They received clothing.[38]

But FWA visitors never really accepted that straightforward relief and practical assistance, and especially providing people with what they said they needed, was the best predictor of longer-term success. Instead, what they tended to do was to create a reliance on outside advice and intervention—which ending up looking a lot like dependency—in situations where they had little power to actually do anything about the problems they identified. Dilemmas such as these were sprinkled through the case files in the 1920s and 1930s. What was Vida Johnson to do, for instance, with the "very nervous and emotional" Mary McLeod, first seen in 1923? Having endured a "sexually abusive" second husband who had now taken up with another woman "on a farm outside the city" and a first husband who served time in jail for "selling liquor to the Indians," she wanted help in securing a separation. Her family had been broken apart by her husband's violence, but all Johnson could give was a dollar bill and a suggestion that she see the city attorney. Mary McLeod wanted Vida Johnson to become her investigator and friend, but all Johnson could do was keep telling her that "it is a legal case." McLeod came to FWA attention again in 1929; her daughter had been hit by a car, one of her two sons was in jail for murder, and the other was in Superior, Wisconsin, looking for work. The new visitor, Carrie Kennedy, refused to endorse McLeod's "insinuation that the law was not just where poor people were concerned." McLeod's teeth were also very bad, but she was very reluctant to go to the dental clinic; Kennedy discovered that her reluctance stemmed from the fact that she could not read and write and feared being exposed in a public clinic. The daughter then developed pulmonary tuberculosis and went to the Glen Lake Sanatorium, but died within three months. Illness, illiteracy, accident, and perhaps injustice; Carrie Kennedy agreed it was "hardly possible for her to do anything to help herself at the present time" and simply referred the McLeods to the Department of Public Relief.[39]

In another family of six children, the Bergsons, the father was described as manic depressive. He was released from the insane asylum in 1926, at which point his wife was referred to the FWA. The FWA, following advice from a doctor, tried to compel the man to work and support his family, while at the same time trying to make him "keep exact account of every cent that he earned and how he spent it." The visitor also told him that "the FWA expected him to cooperate. He then stated in a very boastful manner that he had plenty of money to feed his family. He did not need any assistance." The FWA consistently tried to assist the family by making a more or less unbalanced man work and accept full responsibility. By 1929, visitors, including Margaret Murray, were embroiled in several ferocious arguments between the Bergsons. Because the husband was troubled by disorder, they tried to force the wife to "improve her housekeeping," and because the wife wanted her husband to be forced to work, they continued to spark and then attempt to quell the disputes that always followed. At the same time, they often thought they "could do nothing ... since visitor could only talk and that weapon had been tried so many years to no avail." The situation became rather worse in late 1929, when the husband seized and read his FWA file at the hospital to which he'd been referred; from then on, "he had good reason for not trusting FWA." Relief was provided sporadically through 1930 and 1931, with more cash, groceries, medicines, and shoes granted in 1932. As Bergson traversed "calm," "rage," and "agitation," the FWA paid the family's rent in 1934 and 1935. A case evaluation was made in 1936: "Neither he nor she recognize the problems involved.... Any plan must come from FWA, as she is incapable of looking ahead [and] she is unable to realize conditions that lead to the delinquency of her children and so cannot help to prevent them getting into difficulty." After nine years of contact, the FWA concluded that "this is a family that will need relief for many years." The Bergsons were finally transferred to public agencies.[40]

Gestures toward independence and self-reliance were of little help to many of the FWA's clients, especially given the extremity of their situations. One woman, the wife of a drunkard and drug addict who was eventually hospitalized, was urged to "try a new plan of becoming financially independent of husband" in 1924. She wanted to take in roomers, which would allow her to continue caring for a two-year-old daughter as well as a ten-year-old son. A series of smaller and larger calamities continued until 1930, including the woman's prolonged illness, during which her son twice ran away from a boarding house, first to Chicago and then—for reasons the file doesn't explain—to Leavenworth in Kansas. By the middle of 1930, he was in a juvenile home for theft, and a year later, at the age of seventeen, he was dead, killed in a train accident. The only problem on which FWA visitor Hilda Lower focused, however, was urging and finally forcing the woman to work. As Lower reported, "She did not see why she should have to work. She was told that she would have to change her attitude." Eventually, the "case was closed as there seemed no other way to make the relatives assume their responsibility ... and to force [her] to find work."[41]

Some of the cases undertaken by the FWA in the early 1930s suggest that their increasingly interventionist approach ended up creating the very helplessness of which they were most critical. In one 1935 case, the agency agreed with the former employer of a man now on public relief on the best outcome: the employer "would supervise the expenditure of [the client's] wages, and would see that [he] spent it only for the living expenses and not foolishly." The client left the office, preferring to continue with the Department of Public Relief.[42]

In another case, the Mitchells had moved to Minneapolis from South

Dakota in 1931. By 1934 Earl and June Mitchell had two sons under four years of age, and Earl, selling on commission, was forced to seek aid. They had experienced a run of bad luck, including the loss of two thousand dollars in a bank failure. Earl was "quite embarrassed at necessity for asking"; June, when visited by Hilda Bakke, "seemed overcome with embarrassment at asking for aid and thanked worker several times." They received coal, cash, and groceries, and they were "assured that many families who had always been independent were now in straitened circumstances through forces for which they were not responsible." Bakke was also pleased that the Mitchells were attempting to secure custody of Earl's ten-year-old daughter from his first marriage.

As was often true in 1934, when caseloads surged again after a temporary lull, the Mitchells were then passed on to another worker, in this case Joan Benson. At this point the story of an unlucky, brave, and grateful young couple turned into a different drama. June Mitchell spent $1.15 on a present for a neighbor's baby shower; Earl was rebuked and told that the "FWA could not sanction the family spending the money in such a manner when it was needed for real necessities and that since FWA was supplementing his income it really meant that FWA had given the baby shower gift. He did not answer." Nor did Earl respond when he was rebuked again a little later because he had gone to the water department to protest at the water being cut off. Benson "pointed out to him that people seldom were given any consideration when they yelled at the top of their voices and swore at the persons from whom they expected the favor." This thirty-seven-year-old man was told he had to pay the $2 reconnection fee "as a matter of discipline."

Benson moved on—I think to Earl's great relief—and was replaced by Ingrid Neilsen. At the first home visit, she found June "well poised and pleasant," but noticed that "she talked so hurriedly it was almost as if she feared visitor would break in with something that she might not care to answer. In discussing her dread of relief she was asked if she would like to give some service in return for what they received. She was thrilled with this idea and was told of the possibility of doing sewing." Earl visited the office, where Neilsen told him that she "appreciated his efforts to provide for himself." Although "he seemed pleased with this praise . . . he was very white and kept closing his eyes and taking long breaths. He was asked if he were ill, and at that show of kindness he suddenly broke down and began to cry."

Earl's explanation was that "he had been under constant worry for so long that he could not continue that way for much longer." But in the turn his story then takes, it seems Neilsen wanted to intervene more directly;

for the last six months of 1934, Earl was bringing in written statements accounting for his income and expenses every two weeks. On the visit after he wept, he "seemed as usual crushed and pathetic," when he had never been so described before. Four weeks later, he was "as usual very shy and quiet, giving the impression that having to ask for help pained him almost unbearably.... His attitude of helplessness was rather exasperating." In late 1934, Earl secured a temporary job in Sioux Falls, South Dakota, and asked if the FWA could continue providing a small amount of relief to his wife during his absence. They did, but the file also noted that "he seemed to feel that now he had secured work he could ask for what he wanted and the FWA would be willing to accept his terms." In February 1935, Earl found a job in a haberdashery store, and the family never approached the FWA again.[43]

Another couple, the Glenns, experienced a similar journey between 1934 and 1935. Myra Glenn was at first a "young, good looking and modest appearing woman ... [and] seemed most sincere in her statements," but during the home visit Hilda Bakke found her "evasive" because she "did not stick to one subject when discussing her needs." They would receive fuel, but the FWA "would expect entire cooperation from the family in keeping accounts and making an effort to keep expenses as low as possible." Steven Glenn "seemed genuinely moved as, with tears in his eyes, he told how he had never needed help before now" and was told that "visitor appreciated his sincere desire to be independent." Within a few months, however, all relief was discontinued, apparently because Myra's sister and brother-in-law had moved in with them and were paying $2 a week in rent.

When Myra Glenn next approached the FWA, a male visitor, Vernon Hull, informed her that any future help "would have to be on a different basis than it had been in the past." He explained: "All income or sources of assistance would have to be told to the visitor and dishonesty, such as she had shown in the past, would no longer be tolerated.... [Visitor] pointed out that if the family were receiving any assistance from FWA it would be necessary for them to conform to the standard of living of FWA clients." During a subsequent home visit, Myra, "dressed in a dirty blouse and an old pair of trousers which supposedly belonged to her husband" did not "make apologies about her appearance"; convinced that the Glenns had no interest in "cooperative planning," the FWA closed the case. Myra tried one more time, in September 1935; she "became very upset and cried and said that she wished to know if somebody else could manage better than she could on her $15." She was told no help would be provided unless "her husband's salary would be turned over to FWA and ... she would have to follow exactly the plans that were worked out for her." Steven, "very antagonistic," came into the office four days later. Bakke "tried to show him that FWA did not wish to be spying on a household but they did expect when assisting in a household to have the family be perfectly free and frank and discuss with them." There was, she concluded, "no service that FWA could render the family."[44]

As Earl Mitchell and the Glenns found out, independence had a very narrow meaning to most of the FWA visitors. It is difficult to know, at least on the evidence of the file, what they were meant to do. Action on their own behalf, albeit sometimes clumsy and ineffective, earned them rebukes, questions about their accounts and priorities, and financial penalties. Many of these encounters shared a common outcome of clients confused about what to say, what to do, and even how to hold themselves. Just as Melbourne's poor faced the stern examinations of "feeling their position, those in Minneapolis struggled just as much to identify and retain the slightly different physical and verbal characteristics that the FWA's workers wanted to see. Here, the most important task was maintaining the appearance of independence, a dread of relief and "pauperism" that mostly showed itself in your control over strong emotions while you participated in making plans. Dread without despair, shame without helplessness, self-reliance but not assuming or doing too much, especially without first consulting the visitor: as ever, managing poverty, whether temporary or entrenched, was hard and exacting work.

Confronting the often compounded difficulties of the unemployed, the redundant, and the despairing, or dealing with mental illness, prolonged physical debility, and serious health problems, the FWA's visitors struggled to match a method that insisted on change with the recognition that change was very unlikely, at least for some. Accordingly, they often found themselves mired in long-term and difficult relationships that had no clear ending. Dorothy McRae, "utterly crushed" by her husband's betrayal and desertion in 1936, was given mental tests—one worker described her as "obviously feeble-minded," another as "not actually feeble-minded, merely a little slow in her reactions and willing and ready to plan"—and a good deal of advice, but in the end was just "a pathetic looking person" left without any real service. The FWA did manage a more effective intervention with Dorothy's twelve-year-old son, who had been put into special classes, whipped, and labeled "insane" by his school principal before being sent to another school at the behest of the FWA visitor.[45]

The visitors' relationship with Hanna Elfman was also typical of this frustrating inability to create change. Hanna was first referred by the Department of Public Relief in 1933 as "casework was indicated to prevent her from becoming a future dependent." She had been married at thirteen, then divorced, and then was in a bigamous marriage. She married again in 1935, divorced in 1936, and married another man in 1937; Hanna saw her problem as one of finding employment. The worker, Myra Kemmler, thought otherwise: "The client appeared to be an inadequate person, incapable of earning a living or contributing in any way to the community." Hanna "sought her own means of breaking the monotony of drab and dependent existence by occasional flights into matrimony." She was "unresponsive, dull and lived on a level of primitive comfort and satisfaction," and it was too late; "if she had been taken 'under the wing' of the right social agency as a young girl, more might have been done." Hanna simply kept repeating the defense she had always used: she did not spend her relief money on anything it should not be spent on, and she preferred direct material relief because she did not think the plans identified for her were realistic or achievable.[46]

Yet when the only alternative was turning such people over to "mere material relief" agencies, some visitors struggled to identify a means of being effective and even provoking some kind of transformation. In the process, however, what they often oversaw was the achievement not of self-reliance but of new forms of helplessness, along with an increasing uncertainty—for both workers and clients—about the practical meaning of self-sufficiency in the midst of entrenched unemployment and steady decreases in people's wages and living standards. It was not so much that independence was impossible, because some of their clients achieved it, usually those better placed to move or advantaged in earning power by their skills, sex, or freedom from family responsibilities. It was more that dependency was so suspicious in any quantity, in any form, and in whatever was the changing context of a city hard hit by the larger economic crisis. The FWA's workers heard about the desire for self-reliance and change that always characterized how the poor described their condition and their hopes. What they often failed to hear was poor women's much more realistic assessment of what would be needed to create lasting change and real self-sufficiency, especially when times were so bad.

In fact, when the visitors did hear, they were able to effect real change and provide real support for people who were desperate. Older women appeared a great deal in the work of the 1930s, in part due to the Gateway Bureau. At times, I think, some of the female visitors were especially helpful to them because as unmarried women themselves they could understand the kinds of insecurity that age, infirmity, and unemployment might bring. One woman, nearly seventy years old in 1935 and a former grade school teacher, had to be coaxed into accepting relief and was too "economical with herself." According to the report, "She had expected the 'investigator' would go through her bureau drawers and closets in the course of duty.... It was always difficult for her to accept relief, but it helped her to have it in cash and from an office where she knew her affairs were kept confidential." She was able, eventually, to accept the fact—and the justice—of dependency on a pension as part of a "more universal" system and came to see FWA worker Betty Graham as "a sort of protector."[47] In 1934 a couple in their fifties who had come to Minneapolis from rural Minnesota in 1926 received a similar degree of helpful support. They suggested that their greatest need was securing employment for the husband; Hilda Bakke agreed and helped him secure work at a garage.[48] In another long-running case, Dolores Penney, deserted by her husband in 1931, finally revealed in 1934 that she could not live with him again because of his sexual insensitivity. She "pleaded with visitor to give her an opportunity to get on her own feet and be self-sustaining, and get rid of him as best she could." A "very deserving person," Dolores gained regular employment in 1934 but continued to receive small financial contributions during layoffs and holidays, in part so that her "intelligent and artistic son" could remain in high school.[49]

The Minneapolis FWA may have moved away from its origins in "scientific charity," but its emphasis on "wise plans" and "cures" that would somehow supplant "mere material relief" rested on a misapprehension of poverty's origins and solutions that was just as profound. The dramas described in its case files focused on the idea that Minneapolis could be protected from poverty by changing the outlook, habits, and plans of its poor people rather than the decisions and forces to which they were vulnerable. It was an undoubtedly well-meaning counsel, but it sought to transform people's lives by changing their plans rather than their circumstances.

As such, the casework of the FWA also dramatized the differences between the providers and recipients of that counsel. As several clients were told, poverty or inequality were not inevitable and could be overcome. Superiority and financial power stemmed from fair, defensible advantages; the landlord, the grocer, the employer—and, indeed, the Family Welfare Association visitor—had earned their position and their rights and to suggest otherwise was to advance a palpably incorrect version of the world's workings. Again and again in these files, clients had to show their willingness to accept two highly controversial propositions. The first was that security and material comfort derived largely from individual effort and "wise plans" rather than, as some suggested, economic structures, unjust advantages, or good luck. In other words, they had to accept that inequalities largely reflected the inadequate adjustments, ideas, and skills of individuals. The second was that the charity visitors were best placed—either by training or superior knowledge of the world—to show clients the most effective means of understanding and then overcoming their problems.

In comparison to their counterparts in Melbourne and London, the caseworkers of Minneapolis were more confident that people could battle and perhaps even overcome their deficiencies. They were, on balance, less swayed by the imperfections of the poor and more certain that individual transformation and mobility were possible. But the other side of that confidence was an insistence on the obligations of poor people to make serious attempts at change and a tendency to belittle and punish—in deed as well as in word—those who were seen to have failed the implied test. There was faith, but faith disappointed could be punitive. Of course, it is best to be wary in ascribing such differences to national characteristics. But in the twentieth century's sweep of charity, welfare, and welfare reform, there seems to an outsider something very persistent about that misconception of poverty and something defiantly American about that faith, its disappointment, and the assault on supposed dependency it helped justify.

• •

CHAPTER 23

An Insecurity of Terrifying Proportions

The above title was one worker's description of an anxious, debilitated, and fearful client in 1936.[50] Such applicants weren't unusual. From 1931 on, despite efforts to shift clients over to the Department of Public Relief, FWA caseloads soared. By 1933 more than nine thousand cases were handled in one year, and in 1931 alone the agency spent more than four hundred thousand dollars on direct relief.[51] Only 1933's Emergency Relief Act finally stemmed the tide, in part because the Hennepin County relief department grew from seven to three hundred and fifty workers between 1933 and 1935. In 1928 unemployment and insufficient earnings affected 14 percent of the FWA's clients. By 1932 the main breadwinner was unemployed in 39 percent of the families seen by the FWA, some measure of Minneapolis's Depression suffering. Laborers and casual workers had been joined in vulnerability by truck and taxi drivers, teamsters, construction workers, janitors, painters, and mechanics. Nor did white collars offer much protection, with teachers, clerks, and salesmen also common among the jobless. The FWA could also see "an appalling, consistent and increasing decline in weekly wages earned by employed men," and its special work with single females gave its workers particular insight into the often more hidden struggles of Minneapolis's working women.[52] And Minneapolis's Depression dragged on; the Division of Public Relief argued in 1944 that joblessness reached its peak in the Twin Cities not in 1930 or 1932, or even during the tumultuous truckers strike of 1934, but in 1939, when perhaps forty thousand of the city's citizens were on direct relief.[53]

Although the case files of the 1930s often manifest the same convictions as those of the 1920s, there was also a greater degree of conflict and confusion. Clients spoke back more frequently, probably because, as mentioned earlier, they had more secure guarantees of public relief and could risk angering the FWA. Invited to describe their problems and possible solutions, clients were also confronted by differences among workers in an agency that was struggling to develop plans but increasingly, it seems, unsure how those might be achieved. Older and newer visitors disagreed over diagnoses and treatments, and clients were sometimes given very different responses to the same issues. The relationship between several visitors and Angela Cross, a forty-year-old woman with tuberculosis, was a good example. One visitor, Anna Carr, saw the client's problems as a lack of moral standards and feelings of resentment and loneliness. The client simply pointed to her tuberculosis, which made it very hard for her to hold down jobs. Myra Kemmler criticized her "coarse features," "very blonde, possibly peroxide" hair, "incongruously dowdy pair of low heeled shoes," and "bovine placidity" in late 1936. But another worker, Cora Boehm, who met the client in 1937, described a woman who "radiated animation and life." Lent small amounts of money to help her back on her feet, the client repaid everything she owed by 1940; "as she left the office she threw her arms around worker in an exuberance of good feeling." By 1946, after several years of working for the United States Army, Angela had developed encephalomyelitis (which was probably multiple sclerosis). A new worker, Patricia Griffiths, arranged a "particular investigator" at the Division of Public Relief to ensure she would be "handled quite carefully."[54]

Whatever was and wasn't understood as a result of the Depression, the future of the FWA would lie in a rather different direction. After 1940 it would see itself much more as a personal and family service agency, dedicated to helping those "who want assistance with problems that stand in the way of their happiness or their family's well-being" and fostering "sound and wholesome family life in the community."[55] The association also examined its past with a good deal of honesty. In 1938 the Minneapolis Council of Social Agencies undertook a survey of social and health work in the city. Its agency report on the FWA was highly critical. The agency's workers earned low salaries, and six of the fifteen had no professional qualifications. The workers "assume too much authority for making plans or decisions for the client," and the report also criticized "the administration of relief on a basis which tended to increase ... dependence" and spoke of workers who "lectured and moralized." The survey tended to blame "the supervisory and case work staff," who "were lacking in the amount of professional training necessary to equip them to assume the responsibility for a Case Work service program." Indeed, it charged, initial contacts "do *not* set the agency-client relationship on a basis which would insure [*sic*] the client's participation and be constructive to the treatment of his problem." The workers did not grasp "the significance of some of the client's story and attitudes," and in some cases they tried to "fit a client's problems into patterns of certain types rather than to adapt the agency's service to the client's actual needs." The future, the survey's writers insisted, would rest on an understanding of the "essential emotional problems underlying the client's difficulties."[56]

The FWA gave a response, apparently written by General Secretary Geraldine Lamb. There were "definite mis-statements" and inaccurate interpretations of case records, but the point was taken. By the middle of the 1940s, the FWA had completed its transition. Casework supervisor Thelma Dorroh's "A Caseworker's Notebook" from 1943 made clear that the association would from now on focus on family and relationship counseling.[57] Its case files would feature new dramas: of pathology, emotional problems, and clients "lacking insight," who would need to understand their emotional deficiencies before any needs could be met. The signs had been there in the second half of the 1930s in some of the case notes and summaries of the younger social workers; problems stemmed from clients' "inability to analyze thoroughly" or "recognize the full force of her emotional conflict," and solutions—such as finding secure employment—would only follow the emotional adjustment that came from professional casework.[58] There would be talk of "libidinal drives," "intense psychiatric treatment," or "extreme narcissism and blocking off of unpleasant experiences in the unconscious."[59] Another long-term client was "immature, primitive and punitive" and "probably [has] a high masochistic component," but these factors were "perhaps intensified by the pressure of the reality situation."[60] Even if all of this occasionally surprised clients who might find themselves asked about their relationships with their mothers when they wanted a little cash or an order of wood for a cold winter, it also made for a much stronger focus on long-term needs and support.

In the 1930s, though few could really miss the point that individual effort and "wise plans" had their limits, the FWA's workers were rather slow to canvas alternatives. Confronted with the fact that the bulk of "dependency" stemmed not from the unwillingness to make plans but the inability to sustain those plans in the face of disaster, they struggled to identify another story about poverty. To those two brothers from Altoona who had "bummed" from Pennsylvania and "seemed to be putting up a fight to maintain their respect, morale and spirits," the FWA could give only old clothing and a cheery hope that they "might be able to work it out yet."[61] It wouldn't have seemed like much of an offer to the clients or probably to the worker.

The problem was not a lack of professional qualification, but the adequacy of the approach to their clients that these women—and a few men—felt bound to uphold. Nor was the problem inadequate attention to psychology and emotional conflicts. As it moved toward the kind of psychiatric social work that became so dominant in private welfare during the 1940s and 1950s, the FWA, which became Family and Children's Services in 1942, undoubtedly did much good work. But it also left behind most of the larger ambitions it once had. Helping some people better understand their emotional deficiencies was a long way from helping the poor of Minneapolis better their circumstances or helping Minneapolis avoid slums and poverty. As agencies such as the FWA floundered in the Depression's wake, ideas about the origins of inferiority and poverty—and ideas about the origins of superiority and comfort that were their inevitable accompaniment—proved very tenacious. It could hardly be otherwise, in a way. Left a script that was proving less and less realistic, the players played on as best they could, bringing new dramas of mind and emotion to the center of the stage and pushing back into the wings what had once seemed their most important mission.

Part Five

OREGON

Miss Perry and the Boy Who Knew Numbers

Dramatis Personæ

EDITH PERRY, a Child Welfare Commission visitor
FRANKLIN SPILLER, a deserted father

· · · · · · · · · · · · · · DRAMA · · · · · · · · · · · · · ·

The whole mess has fallen into her lap. If there were more visitors to handle the cases, Edith Perry thinks, there might be fewer people accusing the Child Welfare Commission of everything from undue haste to tardy neglect. But there aren't, so she will deal with Franklin Spiller herself.

It has been some months since her first meeting with Franklin, the father of the boy in question. Back then, he hadn't wanted to sit. He was clumsy and uncertain, running the rim of his hat between his fingers and looking at the floor.

"I just don't think my boy should be in the Feeble Home, Miss Perry. And I don't think all this being in homes and boarding is doing him any good. They were saying things about him that I've never seen no reason for."

Mr. Spiller's fourteen-year-old son, Earl, had been in the State Institution for the Feeble-Minded in Salem. She'd asked him to give her just a minute as she read through a thin sheaf of letters and file notes.

"He just shouldn't be there, ma'am. There's all kinds of people there."

"Well, there seems to be a problem, Mr. Spiller."

She remembered looking back down at the reports. Earl's mother had deserted over a year ago, and there were two other sons, aged twelve and nine. After his mother's desertion, perhaps because Franklin couldn't cope, Earl had been boarded out, but the boarding home mother reported that "he masturbates continually and has a licentious mind." He had been expelled from school for "viciousness," and a local doctor in Yamhill County had committed him to the State Institution for the Feeble-Minded. The grounds for the decision aren't quite clear from the letter. Epilepsy, perhaps. Or potential perversion tendencies. The valleys aren't that far from Portland, but they seemed just as full of religious fanatics, moonshiners, and degenerates as the backwoods or the far coast.

"It scares him, Miss Perry. He's not like them people there."

"Is that why you took Earl out of Salem, Mr. Spiller?"

"It's not doing him any good, Miss Perry. I put him with the nuns."

"At St. Mary's? In Beaverton?"

"Yes, ma'am. It's better there. But I don't want to just leave him there, Miss Perry. I've been thinking about things."

He had paused and looked at her.

"I've been thinking about things and what I might do. The boy is sick, not sick in the head like in the Feeble Home. But there is something wrong with him, Miss Perry. Something like the sleeping sickness. The doctor said something about it. Did he write that down, Miss Perry?"

"It's not here, Mr. Spiller. I'm sure if there was a diagnosis it would be here."

"Well, I don't know why it isn't. The doctors should try something else. There must be a cure for it if the boy can catch it. He wasn't born bad in the head, Miss Perry, never was bad until this year. The boy's not sick in the head; the doctors should try something else."

He had rushed on. "I want to get us a housekeeper, perhaps get some charity help, Miss Perry. I was thinking that the Child Welfare could help me, help me get all three boys home."

"I don't know if that's possible, Mr. Spiller. Earl's not right, is he? The doctors have told you that."

"They need to look at the boy again, that's all I'm saying."

"But the doctor in Yamhill, is he a good doctor? Wouldn't he have Earl's best interests at heart? Do you think he would really send a young boy to an institution unless it was the best possible thing?"

"But he's not feebleminded, Miss Perry. Wouldn't that come on gradual? Wouldn't that be there from when he was born?"

"Well, I'm not a doctor, Mr. Spiller. But you're not a doctor either. I work here in the Child Welfare Commission, and I see a lot of cases of children needing to spend some time in the Institution for the Feeble-Minded or in the industrial school or the Hospital for Incurables. It's for the best sometimes, Mr. Spiller. Sometimes you're not the best person to judge when it's a disease or a condition that might need to be controlled. Earl might be in danger, Mr. Spiller. We see children who become immoral, who become delinquent, who end up in county jails. And for those kinds of problems, Earl's going to get much more help from the doctors at Salem than from the nuns at St. Mary's. Can you really help him at home? Can you really be sure?"

He had chewed his lip, shifting his eyes between the floor and the picture of Yellowstone she'd clipped from a magazine to brighten up the wall above her desk. He was hostile. But he was uncertain, too. It was likely that things hadn't been explained to him properly. Or that he hadn't really understood them. He is a rough laborer. Not quite a backwoodsman, she had thought, but the trappings of civilization probably didn't sit too well with him either.

The commission's job—her job—was to sort out the best plan. But it was difficult to know. The reports suggested that Earl was one of the seeming scores of feebleminded children being discovered around the state. Perry was aware that some of Oregon's charities and doctors were enthusiastic about the rehabilitative prospects of the Institution for the Feeble-Minded. Some were even advocating sterilization of the more difficult inmates.

He had mumbled something, looked her in the eye, turned away, and said he'd have to make plans. He clearly cared for the boy. But he was torn.

A week later, she called Salem for another case; Earl had been returned.

That was last December. On her return from her summer break just two weeks ago, Edith Perry found another letter from the Institution for the Feeble-Minded; Franklin Spiller had taken Earl away again in June. Also among the mail was a letter from Franklin. He was still seeking her help to organize a housekeeper or perhaps to have the boy boarded out by the county. Another doctor had pronounced Earl as incurable, but Franklin was sticking to his guns: "I have to do something with the boy, and Lord only knows he is such a care." But he wanted the boy close by, and he wanted him cured of what he insisted was a disease and not a "damage." He proposed to seek out another doctor and wrote: "I wonder if the Doctors would take him to experment on." She winced at his spelling, but there was no denying Franklin Spiller's interest in his boy. There weren't many deserted fathers among her commission cases, and there were fewer still trying to face and not evade their responsibilities.

The other visitors and the case supervisor agreed with her growing apprehension that a confinement to the feebleminded home should wait, at least until Franklin had a chance to seek the new diagnosis. In the meantime, Yamhill County should board the boy. She wrote a careful letter to the county authorities: "We really believe that under present conditions the child is going through an inconceivable amount of trial and suffering and we feel that in this enlightened generation, there is enough heart in any community to prevent that." She came back to that sentence and underlined "enlightened." She was pleased with it. It did Franklin Spiller justice.

Then, finally, there was a definite diagnosis. It was either lethargic encephalitis, the sleeping sickness, which the doctors at the Institution for the Feeble-Minded said was incurable and inexorable and had already rendered the boy subnormal. Or it was a severe form of epilepsy that had made him feebleminded. Earl would get worse, and there was no point his father thinking any differently. Earl would have to go back to Salem because either way his mind would give out. The commission's final decision was that he would be compulsorily transferred to the institution at the end of November.

Franklin made one more try, just a week before the committal. He wrote another letter; "I hear he is to be railroaded to Salem. I had rather he would dy on oppration table can the Dr opprate with any hope, tell them to try it." She read it and put it into the file.

Today, of all days, he has turned up at the office. She is surprised to see him. He has brought some letters from the home and from the nuns at St. Mary's. "I know all these letters might be important, Miss Perry, so I thought you should have them. They probably have evidence."

He is apologetic about their condition.

"I'm sorry, Miss Perry. The boy's done some drawings and writings on the back of these letters. If he wasn't so sick I would have larruped him good, Miss Perry, don't you worry."

"It's fine, Mr. Spiller. Just give them to me for the records. You were right to bring them in. It's best for it all to be together."

She takes them, puts them in the file, and closes it. She knows he wants to stay and ask something. Rather than heading toward the door, he shuffles sideways and looks at the wall behind her head. She considers but then decides against asking him what he wants. It's a difficult decision, but it has been made, and Franklin Spiller just has to understand that.

He looks at the file and then up into her eyes.

"Is that the end of it, Miss Perry? What about opprations?"

"I don't think there are any operations, Mr. Spiller."

"I want to give my boy a chance, is all. Can the Child Welfare tell them to opprate? He's not subnormal, he's not feebleminded. He's sick, is all."

"But remember the diagnosis, Mr. Spiller. I know it's very hard, and I've been wanting to tell you how much I've appreciated your concern for Earl. You've tried everything. You've gone down every road. But I don't think there's a lot more that can be done now."

He blinks, and blinks again.

"There are so many cases of the sleeping sickness and of severe epilepsy, Mr. Spiller. Earl is already damaged by his disease. He can't really manage very well in the world, and he will be better in the home."

"But that's it, Miss Perry. He doesn't seem very damaged, not from where I'm looking. He's a clever enough boy, you know. He had trouble at school, but I don't think that was all his fault."

"But it will get worse, Mr. Spiller. And as it does, he's better off where there are doctors and treatment, don't you think? You can't provide any of that, can you?"

He leaves, deflated and despondent. She puts the drawings and writings into the file and puts the file onto the top of her desk. She returns to the Boyd case and the calls she has to make to the St. Agnes Home.

More than two months later, Edith Perry finally manages to sort through some of her dormant cases. She comes to Earl Spiller's. There has been no word from Salem, so Earl's final compulsory committal has obviously taken place. There doesn't seem much point keeping the case open. She brings the folder into the middle of her desk. Franklin's last letter is on top. Below it are the letters he gave her, with drawings and writings on the other side. Earl's drawings and writings. Childish scribbles, more than likely. She unfolds a sheet and turns it over. She unfolds another. As she realizes what is there, she feels her hand at her mouth, and her fingers press down on her lips. Her eyes fill with tears.

· · · · · · · · · · · · · RESOLUTION · · · · · · · · · · · ·

Earl Spiller was good at many things. As he sat in his father's house one day in 1922, perhaps told to amuse himself, he used the only paper there was on hand. I wonder which of his pages Edith Perry turned over first, if she ever did. Perhaps it was his list of all the children in his small Yamhill County town, eighty or so names, apparently written from memory. On the same sheet, there's another list, "My Girls," of those he especially liked. There's a poem about driving a car. Perhaps it was the sheet with his drawings of detailed geometric shapes, some of them labeled. I imagine it might have been the one covered in complicated multiplications; in some, Earl had to write down the number he carried, but most he seems to have done in his head. And then there is the sheet on which he completed a mental long division of two eight-digit numbers without making any other calculations. He must have been pleased, for next to it he wrote "Ha!"

Of all the people who lived in the past, children stretch perhaps the flimsiest threads into the future. We know things about Earl Spiller: his deterioration, what doctors and boarding mothers thought of him, and what was written about his condition and his prognosis. Those words make him hapless and half-witted, perverse and stubborn. Those few remnants of his words and drawings, accidentally saved because they backed onto something considered worth keeping, suggest intelligence, wit, and whimsy. Perhaps he was eccentric and difficult. Perhaps the circumstances of his mother's leaving had made him angry or despairing. There is no doubt he was ill. But I wonder what might have been his fate had he come from what the Child Welfare Commission called a "superior home" or a "good family." I wonder what might then have been found for his care.

At fifteen, Earl Spiller entered the Oregon State Institution for the Feeble-Minded at Salem. As far as I can tell, it was for the last time. Perhaps his father took him out again and left the county or even the state. Perhaps they went somewhere there wasn't a history and a case file to damn them. Or perhaps Franklin accepted the final verdict and the argument that his oldest son would be better off living in an institution for the rest of his life. Whether Earl had encephalitis or epilepsy, the evidence of other cases suggests Earl was probably sterilized.

I don't know whether Edith Perry ever saw the drawings, lists, and computations she collected from Earl's father. This is the point at which what might have happened diverges from what we know did. Did she unfold a sheet and turn it over? Did she ever realize what was there? If she looked, I think those drawings and writings might have been enough to give her pause and to make her wonder whether a home for incurables and so-called imbeciles was Earl's last or best hope. Were there no other options? Certainly, they might have been difficult to achieve, and Franklin's plans for his son were more than likely unrealistic. The sleeping sickness baffled and unnerved everyone in the 1920s; if that is what he had, Earl Spiller was one of millions to endure its stilling grip. Yet Earl's incarceration reminds us that these were years in which different conditions were tangled together in a vague diagnosis of "feebleminded" that could in turn justify all manner of cruelties, even in the name of kindness. Edith Perry struggled to help Franklin Spiller care for his son. But in the end, she trusted neither Franklin nor herself with the responsibility of giving him a future.

There is a real woman here, whom I've turned into Edith Perry. I don't know much about her beyond the glimpses she left in her files. But I think she might have cried had she found what I found as I turned over the pages in the Oregon State Archives in Salem. I wanted to say something about people like Earl and Franklin Spiller, but in doing that I don't want to belittle this woman, who had courage and sympathy and other qualities besides. I can't and won't blame her, because we still ask all of the people who do her job to make terrible decisions without any of the resources that might allow them to explore real alternatives. Perhaps Earl had an incurable disease. Perhaps he needed an operation or long-term convalescence.

In a welfare system obsessed with spending as little as possible, Edith Perry was never given the opportunity to find out.

There is something else I don't know. Earl's real name was blacked out before I could see the photocopied file, so I can't find him anywhere. People became separated from their names and identities in twentieth-century institutions. And by the end of that century, nervous governments made sure that historians couldn't connect them again. Protecting Earl's privacy means covering over the rest of his story. Fiction might tell you what happened, reassure you, even make it seem all right. But history cannot. History can't give you the comfort of a neat resolution or a conclusion that explains everything. Worse, Earl is denied the justice of an ending and the disquiet that we should still feel on his behalf. It means that he is, and will forever stay, lost.

CHAPTER 24

Policing Relief

In December 1914, Thomas Markham visited the Associated Charities (AC) office in Portland. He had arrived three days earlier. With his pregnant wife, Carrie, he owned a small wagon, a horse, and a cow, but he could not get work. He was given groceries and wood three times in 1915 and put to work cutting wood. In May 1916, Carrie, again pregnant, was given a fare to Arlington so she and their daughter could go to a farm on which Thomas had found laboring work. They were back in Portland in October, and the police reported them destitute just before Christmas, but Multnomah County refused to help them because they had forfeited residence rights by moving to Arlington. Like the COS in Melbourne and London, the AC aimed to prevent duplication and waste among Portland's charities. Its worker described Carrie as "a neat housekeeper but not at all opposed to accepting charity" and authorized wood, groceries, and rent. They were supported until February 1917, when the AC paid their moving expenses to a farm. In early 1919, they came back to Portland in order for Thomas to have a hernia operation. The new Public Welfare Bureau (PWB) gave fuel, and the AC gave food sporadically until the end of the year. There was little reason to check details, the AC worker wrote, as Carrie was "a very refined, neat looking woman. Family belongs to middle class."

In 1923 the Markhams were again referred to the Public Welfare Bureau, on this occasion by the county commissioners, because Thomas was in poor health and jobless. This time the visitor became suspicious—for reasons she did not record in her case notes—that the family had a boarder and had not declared the income. The county agent shared Helena Atkinson's suspicions and had "informed [Carrie] that if they expected county relief they would have to be frank and truthful in all statements." Atkinson found the boarder at home; he was a relative of Carrie's, he said, and became "very antagonistic. Criticized Bureau, stating that visitor was going entirely too far." The case was closed, with the "family very uncooperative and untruthful." In 1927 Atkinson met Thomas Markham in the street; in these smaller cities in the 1920s and 1930s, it wasn't that hard to meet old clients as new ones were being visited. The family now owned a farm in the city limits. Jack, their eleven-year-old, was dying of a tubercular spine, but they wanted nothing from the PWB.

Another seven years on, Carrie Markham returned to the PWB. Thomas, now fifty-nine, had suffered another hernia and was in the hospital. Daughter Millie was "very nervous." On the word of a local grocer, who reported them as "very reliable and of high type," the Markhams received aid for three months, until Thomas was reemployed by the city. In March 1935, Thomas had a stroke. He would never recover. Millie, "very thin and anaemic," found work as a stenographer, but the bureau provided rent and groceries until August. Yet when Carrie Markham called in during late August of 1935, another worker—Hiram Lyell—told her to wait for the regular visitor because "[I] had been warned by [him] that the family were somewhat prone to chiseling," and "in his opinion there is other money coming into the home." Two months later, a "very nervous and excited" Carrie asked for help to supplement her daughter's earnings; "with tears in her eyes she related how she disliked asking for assistance." No answer was recorded, no reason provided; the case was closed and not reviewed.[1]

The scattered and somewhat disordered files from three Oregon agencies—the Public Welfare Bureau, the Associated Charities, and the Child Welfare Commission (CWC)—reveal the mix of public and private relief that characterized many Americans' experience of charity and social work before 1930. Because they span different agencies and record much of their conversation with other charitable institutions, these Oregon files also afford a more detailed glimpse of the occasionally combative relationships among state, county, and private relief officials and of the changes that state programs—especially in the area of child protection—and then federal New Deal legislation brought to both relief agencies and understandings of entitlement among citizens. In their focus on investigation, "plausible" clients, and "chisellers" and in their abrupt endings and half-realized investigations, we also witness the capricious results of the poor communication, overwork, and limited resources that have long plagued the administration of public relief in America.

The relationship between the Markham family and the Associated Charities, the Multnomah County Public Welfare Bureau, and new state and federal agencies established in the wake of the Depression stretched from 1914 to 1935. Such long-running encounters were not unusual for public relief clients, given the regularity with which illness, insecurity, and unemployment punctured ordinary fortunes, and neither were the unnerving shifts they experienced in their treatment and reputations. The public agencies with which they dealt had a particularly rapid turnover of workers, along with heavier caseloads, an emphasis on establishing entitlement, and a primary concern with preserving the correct demarcations between county and state responsibility. Much depended on the all-too-rapid—and sometimes clearly prejudicial—judgments of people whose words and assumptions reveal little empathy for the impoverished.

A young woman from Minneapolis experienced a quicker-than-usual change of identity in 1924. Divorced from her husband, who had taken their two sons back to a former home in Montana, she had recently left the hospital and wanted assistance; that day's visitor found her "very honest and sincere and to [my] impression very deserving of some aid." Indeed, "she feels bad that she has to call upon PWB." The next day, however, brought a different visitor, a different judgment, and a different outcome: "a very complaining sort of person, and one who is very anxious to play upon the sympathies of anyone who will listen to her." She was "uncooperative and unreliable," Ellen Stimson wrote, adding, "[I] told her that visitor was very much disgusted with her because of attitude she had taken. ... Visitor told her she had said everything to her that she was going to say and until she was willing to comply with visitor's request [to have a full physical examination] did not care to spend any more time going over it." Refused aid, the woman took a job as a housekeeper and never approached the PWB again.[2]

At times the pressures of work defeated good or bad intentions. It was not uncommon, especially in 1932 and 1933, for cases to simply lie untouched in the public agencies. A father who came to the PWB office in April 1933, for instance, was told to use the five dollars in cash he already had to buy medicines for a sick baby. As he tried to explain that he also owed sixteen dollars for rent, he was "advised that the cash should carry him practically two weeks with groceries if he was careful" and was promised a visit. Four months later, the worker closed the file: "Client made no contact after application. Because of overload visit was not made promptly [in fact, it was never made at all]. Client not making further appeal, it was deemed sensible to not disturb the situation."[3] More than a third of the cases opened during these years involved long delays.

On the evidence of its workers' files, the Child Welfare Committee, which was established by Oregon's legislative assembly in 1913, did not have a better situation. The committee, founded amid the national enthusiasm for child saving, was superseded by the Child Welfare Commission in 1919. As well as inspecting and supervising private and public children's homes and agencies and making decisions on the provision of state aid for dependent children, the CWC seemingly functioned as a kind of clearinghouse for complaints and public suspicions. This in part reflected the findings of an inquiry that emphasized the need for greater cooperation between Oregon's nearly two dozen private and public institutions, as well as the urgings of the National Congress of Mothers and Parent-Teacher Associations.[4] But attracting complaints also saw its visitors becoming embroiled in local, family, and marital conflicts. Neighbors, estranged spouses, local boards of health, the Red Cross, doctors, police, and a range of informants reported abuse, neglect, and moral endangerment among parents and "the appearance of delinquency" or immorality among children and teenagers.[5] In cases where no immediate danger seemed present or where the families lived well outside Portland and Salem, the CWC sent letters threatening investigation and prosecution. Some went to parents who failed to carry out doctors' orders or provide children with glasses, walking aids, or medicines. Others, such as this letter to a mother accused of abusing a three-year-old, struck an ominous tone: "A little investigation on our part has revealed the fact that there are some grounds for this charge. We do not feel like taking any drastic action in this particular case until we have given you a chance to present your side of the matter or to turn over a new leaf with regard to the care of the child. Any further reports concerning the mistreatment of your child will be thoroughly investigated."[6]

In other cases, and especially where accusations involved sexual delinquency or severe assault, the CWC would send its own visitors (who were renamed "social workers" during the early 1930s) or arrange for inspections by local authorities. As ever, the work of child saving was fraught with difficulties. Eager to offer effective protection, the CWC labored under the disadvantages of distance and the perilous origins of its evidence. One man in the small town of Richmond was told of "many complaints regarding your children ... [who] literally 'run wild' in the neighborhood"; the alleged neglecter wrote back in protest to say that the complainant was the real culprit and that her children were "vicious and destructive."[7] As in other cases when they inflamed local passions, the CWC then simply withdrew, leaving behind whatever conflicts they'd stirred up.

In 1923 a Portland woman was reported by her neighbor for cruelty and profane language. The neighbor "hate[d] to stir up a quarell [sic] with people of this type" but could be trusted because she and all the other people interviewed "owned their houses." The children were "neat and clean, the babe immaculately so," but the mother "seems of very evasive type of personality—neither refined nor intellectual, tho' she spoke to the children in a moderate tone it was obviously not her ordinary manner toward them." For all that, the visitor "did not find evidence on which to base a complaint" and could only suggest that "a 'friendly' visitor might accomplish something."[8] All too easily, the commission's workers found themselves in the murky space between suspicion and proof, propelled there by conflicts they struggled to comprehend. Husbands and wives were no less willing to draw the CWC into their often protracted disputes.

In one 1927 case, set in the small town of Central Point, a minister from Portland, who was a member of the CWC, first reported a family with a father who had tuberculosis and a mother who was "absolutely worthless and immoral, chasing around to dances with men of questionable character" and allowing "men of the same stripe" into her home. The children— a boy of nine and two girls aged seven and three—should be taken away as a matter of urgency. A day later, another letter came into Portland: not only was the family the target of unwarranted accusations and desperately needed assistance, but "I wish you could interview some of the people here as I have done and actually learn at first hand just what malicious gossip can do. It seems that some people thrive on such stuff." Whatever the reverend may have learned, the worker in charge of the case tried to organize a temporary commitment of the children to protect them from their father's disease—a reasonable precaution—and "their mother's possible moral failings." The mother refused the offer of three separate homes for her children "as it would be impossible for me to visit them often scattered apart in that way, and work too." She was directed to bring them to Portland for placement, but the file suggests she did not comply.[9]

The CWC also found itself wrapped up in people's disputes with other agencies. Having been to the Public Welfare Bureau in 1922, for instance, one widow referred herself to the CWC because she wanted to have her two youngest children—a girl aged ten and a boy aged six—cared for so she could work. With her wages and the earnings of her two older sons, aged eighteen and fifteen, she planned to support the family and save money to buy a house. She "resents the PWB attitude who she claims are anxious to make a pauper out of her; very resentful against their personal visits and recommendations." A CWC "contact" reported her to be "above average for charity cases" and was "personally convinced of her sincerity," so the CWC stepped in, organizing a home (at least for the girl), against the advice of the PWB worker, so that the mother "could get on her feet."[10]

Two years earlier, the CWC had been drawn into a scandal at the State Institution for the Feeble-Minded when the relative of an inmate reported her being sexually abused by one of the doctors. Given its obligations, the Child Welfare Commission could hardly ignore his charges. Given its limitations, it could do little to investigate them. As far as I can tell, its letter to the girl's relative followed one telephone call to the home's director: "[We] appreciate that a great wrong was done and sympathize with you in your interest in the matter, but your evidence seems altogether insufficient...."

While we realize that our information is inadequate as compared to yours, we would not feel like making [the director's] burdens heavier, for although his administration may be, as of course it is, imperfect, we would not be sure of finding a man who should do as well as he does to succeed him." The man reiterated his claim that the CWC, like the home, simply wanted the problem—and the girl—to vanish. That may have been harsh, but the commission certainly seems to have done little to try to make her visible or to undertake some kind of investigation of the possible broader implications of the charge.[11]

The Oregon visitors were also very conscious of cost. Part of their reason for constructing accurate and highly detailed family histories was, of course, the need to determine legal residence and the financial responsibility for county welfare that flowed from it. But it went further. Oregon's public and private social workers were very likely to reflect on the cost of dependency and to remind clients about the financial burden they created. In one 1925 case, for example, the CWC asked the Red Cross in Bend to investigate why a father of three had not paid anything toward the cost of his three boarded-out children. "In view of the fact that the state has been put to the expense of nearly $750.00 for their support," the commission wrote, "he needs some sort of a jolt to arouse him to a sense of duty to his offspring."[12] An undated report on another case focused entirely on the "savings effected" by thorough investigation. Faced with a court recommendation that four children be taken into state care, the CWC, at the mother's request, supported the father's desire "to keep his home together." Their "cooperation" over nonadmission created a "saving of $64 per month to the state" or "$384 over six months."[13] It didn't quite get down to nickels and dimes, but it wasn't far off.

Of course, the CWC and the PWB lacked the recourse private agencies had to a last resort; they were the last resort, and three hundred dollars saved could mean better support for other desperate people. Yet in their urge to dampen expectations of entitlement and ensure that potential paupers were left in no doubt about Oregon's firmness, both agencies' workers could find themselves more or less willingly assuming the role of debt collectors as well as detectives. One such case involved a father of six children, the oldest twelve and the youngest two. His wife died of pneumonia in 1925, and by the middle of 1927, his attempts to keep the family together had faltered. The CWC felt bound to demand contributions to the children's care, threatening permanent placement if he failed to comply. He took the two youngest with him to Twin Falls, Idaho, where he was working on a newspaper. A relative in Illinois offered to take two other children, but the CWC refused on the grounds that they were too young to be taken from their father.

In January 1932, a new visitor reopened the case, though it is unclear why. The father, Thelma Lineker wrote, "is extremely selfish and only uses his children for the sympathy he can arouse in others.... He is decidedly unstable." He was sent a letter: "It is high time these children were taken off state support.... I would suggest that you make a desperate effort to have the various relatives take these children ... as a last resort." In one sense, the commission succeeded: the five youngest children were all removed from state support by the end of May 1932, with only the oldest boy at St. Mary's Home in Beaverton. But their strategy for convincing him was to suggest that his total burden on the state amounted to $3,304, an amount that could not then be used for other and more needy children. The assumption seemed to be that if feckless public clients would not respond to morals or shame, they would at least respond to relatively blunt demands for cash.[14]

In addition to indicating strenuous policing of entitlement, these files feature a level of aggression from clients that was less common in Boston or Minneapolis. Perhaps because the potential outcomes of investigation were so dire, and because these were unavoidable agencies of government rather than church or philanthropy, clients were quicker to express a sense of resistance. The heat increased during the 1930s as ideas about entitlement were challenged and changed by the debates about the Depression and the New Deal. A 1933 case of an unemployed laborer ended with a refusal of help; the man was "not very ambitious or sensible," but he had a sense of change. Perhaps excited by Roosevelt's November election, "he stated he would have Washington make Oregon take care of them." This was a man of "decidedly radical" attitudes.[15] One man, "bolshevistic in attitude," was obviously not poor in 1932 because he had "tomatoes, mayonnaise, also bacon" for breakfast; his wife at one point "came to visitor's home and created a very disagreeable scene on the porch" and later "came up to the interviewer's desk and began a long tirade that she did not come in to be abused."[16] Another client, when told to reduce his expenses, questioned the workers' judgments and was "very insistent on learning how visitors obtain their jobs," and a PWB applicant in 1933 attended the office "accompanied by about eighteen members of the Communist party" in support of his wish to have a water bill paid.[17] Some pliable applicants were radicalized by the "women in the sewing room" who were working for their relief—the perils of collective forced labor, it seems—or by contact with the Workers Alliance, and others "want the best and think they should have it."[18] One worker was at least reassured that although a man was "not very conservative or cooperative," he was "not the communistic type."[19]

This was the welfare of last resort or, in the case of the Child Welfare Commission, a place where people battled over the future of families and children. The struggle was more intense, and the outcomes more final, than in private agencies. Here, the public met its government and in a good many cases discovered that its government was distrusting, investigative, and querulous. These Oregon encounters, and the dramatic stories they produced, were as much warfare as welfare.

· ·

CHAPTER 25

Evasive Types and Plausible Women

Relying on far-flung or anonymous informants, lacking the resources for careful investigation, and emphasizing the need to police and constrain people's claims on assistance, the workers of the Child Welfare Commission and the Public Welfare Bureau developed a form of detective visiting even more insistent on exposing paupers than the Melbourne and London Charity Organisation Societies. While their responsibilities for public money made them even more nervous about their clients' histories, they exemplify just as well the anxieties about entitlement, proof, and lies that made scientific charity such a difficult business for those who had to carry it out in practice.

Here, too, the weight of work—and perhaps the even greater burden of protecting public funds—led many visitors to adopt a rough-and-ready shorthand of types and surfaces. A "very evasive type," for instance, deserved close attention and no assistance in 1923, and "pleasing personalities, full of energy ... [and] anxious to obtain work" received $2.50 a week, grocery orders, and assistance in securing employment with the Civil Works Administration in early 1934.[20] A woman who was "coarse and without much ambition" received little attention in June 1934.[21] A deserted mother, at first denied help in 1933 because one visitor "did not feel that she had done all that she could have done and is a bit suspicious," later received a twice-weekly grocery order for four months because another visitor determined she was "ambitious and seems to make every effort to assist herself and her child."[22] Another family was "very ready to take relief at slightest excuse" in 1935; a year later, the mother was described as "prone to be very dependent," with this worker adding a further clarification of the client's problem: "It is suggested that she is over-indulgent with the children and attempts to set their standards too high for the family's situation."[23]

The preoccupation with overly plausible and possibly rehearsed stories that so concerned charity workers elsewhere was also evident. In 1923 a "very plausible" woman in the town of Bend lost unofficial custody of a two-year-old girl because her nineteen-year-old son had been charged with contributing to the delinquency of a minor; the issue was not the protection of the girl, but "since she had met with such little success in raising her own boy, we are certainly not apt to feel justified in allowing her to make [another] attempt."[24] Another woman inquiring after her two grandchildren received little help after her daughter, the boys' mother, was recorded as "putting up a very smooth story."[25]

The choreography of charity was just as exacting in Oregon, and visitors struggled to correctly link gestures, words, and possessions to their class origins. The Firths, longshoreman Patrick, waitress Ellen, and three children from Patrick's first marriage, came to the attention of the State Relief Committee in February 1931. Ellen, although "giggly, apparently indifferent to everything going on ... [and] very simple and foolish," was given cash and food relief for most of 1931. No home visit was made until April 1932. In June the couple's first baby died of meningitis. In February 1933, regular relief was again provided, though the visitor was perturbed by the possession of a "goat and an unlicensed 1928 car." Though the Firths "have always been quite friendly towards the present Visitor, husb is quite reticent as the amount of work received." Patrick was blacklisted during the longshoreman's strike of 1934; a case summary in July that year noted only that "a new electrical refrigerator which they have not explained satisfactorily has been instaled." Clearly, "the family [is] none too trustworthy."[26]

Some clients might have had cause to wonder what they had done wrong. A male visitor for the State Relief Committee not only disliked the "demanding tone of voice" of one client but became "quite suspicious ... due to the fact that they have requested nothing for groceries which is not reasonable for a family whose head insists that he is not working." Requesting too little could be as dangerous as requesting too much. This client was told that the family "could pick hops or cucumbers" and that "if this opportunity was not accepted further relief would not be forthcoming."[27] Another "pushing young man" who lived with his wife and child on a farm outside Portland saw his case closed in September 1933; "there was some friction between client and visitor as client usually came for grocery orders in a car.... He did not own a car, and always had some reason why he did have one at this particular time."[28]

As was true in Melbourne and London, the workers in Portland and other Oregon towns certainly met liars, dissemblers, and frauds. The workers' problem was not so much their desire to protect their resources—and the interests of the vast majority of honest clients—as the inadequacy of the methods they were encouraged to use. There can be few more damning critiques of the detective focus, and indeed of the entire assumption of an easily provable boundary between the deserving and the undeserving, than the fact that it just didn't work. Impressions were often deceptive, but they continued to serve as the foundations for judgments that could mean the difference between relief and no relief. In many examples, impressions—and misinterpretations—led to denial, delay, and significant deteriorations in the relationship between workers and clients. Sometimes, of course, it could cut the other way. A Public Welfare Bureau visit to an unemployed family in June 1933, for instance, showed a "house nicely furnished with artistic curtains and entire family impressed visitor as very intelligent and neat and not at all used to asking other people for assistance." Although the man had "no definite plans for the future," and despite the fact that he had two sons of working age, one of whom was "out in the county cutting wood," he was given $3 for groceries and further sums of money, along with fuel. Within two months, the family had moved on.

The purpose and intent of rigorously policing entitlements is even harder to fathom when relatively clear evidence of fraudulent intent did not lead to any consequences, while uncertain and often misconceived "facts" were used to deter those whose only sin was to perform their poverty improperly. The Crichton family, with whom both the Associated Charities and the PWB had dealings between 1913 and 1922, is a case in point. Married in eastern Oregon in 1908, Hannah and George Crichton were in Portland by 1912. Heavily pregnant with their third child, Hannah asked for a layette, but no visit was made, and it is unclear whether anything was provided. In 1915 George was unemployed, and they were given clothing despite the visitor discovering that the family had "a very bad reputation in neighborhood. Mrs C considered a professional beggar and Mr C a non-worker of the most pronounced type." The family received wood and groceries again in 1916.

George Crichton died in the great influenza pandemic in 1919. His dying wish was that his widow should marry his elder brother, Calvin, but this deprived her of the widow's pension, bringing her back to the PWB. Her landlady called Hannah "a terrible woman" and said she was selling the wood given to her by a local Catholic charity. It took some months for the PWB visitor to find her because, having left Calvin, she then moved in with a younger brother, Robert, taking with her the child she and Calvin had conceived. The visitor was convinced the pair was about to marry, having seen him "thru the opening [of the door] lying in the bed Mrs C called hers." Yet rent, groceries, and fuel continued to come into the house, and a month later another visitor heaped praise on "a very well behaved, happy, loving, little family."

In February 1921, yet another visitor was "very much impressed," but this time "with the fact that she can look a person so square in the eye and profess such extreme innocence and such straightforwardness in her conduct." A month later, "she greeted visitor pleasantly and expressed hope that visitor was not doing investigating because that was unpleasant for all concerned." It was already clear—and it is just as evident reading the file—that the Crichtons were visiting every charitable agency in Portland. There is a sense of growing excitement in the case notes as one worker, Mavis Branston, fixed on the case. Because "she would not tell the truth about the most trivial thing," and because all agencies confirm she is "the greatest liar they have ever met," Branston and a colleague from another welfare group decided to "confront her with many conflicting stories."

They tried to catch her out, trip her up, or perhaps shame her into admission and acknowledgment. It seems to have had little effect; on a subsequent visit, when Hannah guided Branston outside into the sunshine—and away from the kitchen in which "men's voices" could be heard—she was "very docile in her attitude, lying beautifully." The local grocer reported that she bought the "most expensive cuts of meat and fancy canned goods" (perhaps another reason for keeping Branston out of the kitchen). Hannah Crichton's response was to talk "long and smoothly." Mavis Branston tried to interview Robert, but Hannah stayed close, and "when he attempted to say anything she would interrupt and finish [the] sentence [the] way she thought sentence should end." In the same interview, in May 1921, she declared herself "tired of being investigated [because] PWB never helped, only promised." Because rent and groceries were still being provided, it was a statement of breathtaking gall.

Mavis Branston's response was equally astonishing, in a way: "If we give her enough rope she would hang herself sooner or later." Whatever faith Branston's supervisors or committee put in that statement, the Crichtons would never actually pay any price for a relationship with public and private charities that was at best adventurous and at worst deliberately deceitful. Contact was lost during the summer of 1921; by February 1922, as the police reported them to be destitute, they left Portland, having used up "$225 of relief from PWB and more than $100 from other agencies." They were in Seattle by the end of 1923; the last word was a report from San Jose, California, in July 1930, that Hannah had left several young children with a family and disappeared.

The best explanation for Hannah's ability to secure overentitlements is the very smoothness and alacrity of her lying. To stumblingly deceive was to invite denial as well as suspicion. Brazen lies generated a kind of fascination: "This woman's smoothness of tongue and her rather unusual confidence in dealing with people not well acquainted with her type made her a subject of great interest to all who met her." Yet acquaintance with "her type" did little to protect the PWB's resources. If an emphasis on detection and the policing of public welfare could not overcome a really determined liar and cheat, what, then, was its point? It is little wonder, really, that the more daring clients more or less audibly questioned the intent and integrity of the visitors' investigations.[29]

Yet in Oregon, as in other places and times, the struggle to care could override preoccupations with sorting lies from truth. Here, too, charity visitors could listen for and bear witness to stories about need and suffering that moved away from relatively ad hoc judgments about entitlement and highlighted the possibilities and importance of trust. Theirs were often contradictory impulses: to apply the letter of the law or the benefit of the doubt or to build or block the hopes of those who turned to them for help. In a 1923 case, for instance, a CWC worker engaged in a protracted correspondence with the state welfare department in Lansing, Michigan. Millie Dawson, who was living in Portland, applied for custody of her son, who was a ward of the state in Michigan. The Dawsons were known to the Public Welfare Bureau, and their worker described the family in one sentence as "lazy, pauperized, absolutely unfit, mother alleged subnormal, a low-grade family throughout." The next sentence described Millie's father as "a fairly good sort of man, not sub-normal, fond of his children, very neat and clean for a chimney sweep" and her sister—already known to the CWC because her husband had deserted—as "not feebleminded nor even subnormal."

The CWC worker, Lisbeth Berry, also met a former landlady—at a "tumble down shack of a place"—who alleged that Millie's father was a drunk and that Millie herself "ran around with other men" and also drank, though she "admits she never actually saw her intoxicated." Here were all the materials for doubt and denial. But the worker's account undermined the landlady: "she alleged," "she admitted," and "she did not know for sure." While acknowledging that the father's statement that he had never lived in the house was probably untrue, the worker described him as "clean-shaven as usual and talked with his customary cooperation." And the worker listened hard to Millie's story about her illegitimate child: "[Millie] is not as efficient as the others [in the family and] is scared to talk. . . . [She] seems to feel he will be the only child she will ever have and seems to have brooded over his absence. [She] is fond of the boy, and if she had proper supervision and some man to keep track of her like her father, would probably be an average caretaker, would not abuse him but might not give very scientific care." Perhaps the decision was clinched when Millie's father bought a house in August 1923 "in order to provide a better home" and by the obvious faith the worker and probably her supervisor placed in paternal direction. But Berry's willingness to support Millie's case remained vital. She wrote to Michigan, "She perhaps is not the most competent person in the world but it does seem that it might be advisable to give her an opportunity to carry out her plans in regard to her boy." The child came to Portland in October 1923. From the first to the last case note, "the child" became "her boy." It is an apt symbol for the change of heart.[30]

Heart characterized another CWC worker in 1928. A streetcar motorman, Eugene Groener, was referred by the Red Cross. He was making $120 a month, but owed more than $50 for groceries and a similar amount in arrears for furniture. The furniture company was threatening to have his wages garnished, and he feared losing his job. He lived with his wife, who was deaf, his eight-year-old son, and his three-year-old daughter. According to the file, the boy had a tubercular spine "and will not live long," and Groener was "a very nice looking young man [who] wept bitterly when he talked of his son." On top of his debts, he was buying medicines and drugs.

Spinal tuberculosis buckles and hunches a child's back, opening abscesses below the infection that can erupt through the skin or sometimes break into and drain through the rectum. The child loses control of the bladder and bowel. The collapsing spine compresses the spinal cord, causing terrible pain and eventually paralyzing the feet and legs.

The Groeners were given a loan of $68. As far as I can tell from the file, the worker who opened the case—I think it was Jane Lynn—asked no questions of Eugene's employer, undertook no home visits, and did not press him for details. The history is unclear, but it seems Eugene was given more money in April and perhaps another payment later in the year to cover medicines. In January 1929, a year after his initial inquiry, he wrote in to report that he and his wife had just watched their child die.

Heart-full, and then heartless. A week after the letter, another PWB investigator took the file. He or she—I can't be sure—sent Eugene a reminder that he owed the bureau "at least $68" for drugs, medicines, and debt payments. Perhaps that investigator had never seen a child inexorably consumed by tuberculosis. Or perhaps that investigator considered a week time enough to grieve, at least for the likes of the Groeners.[31]

· ·

CHAPTER 26

Into the Backwoods

The history of social welfare and social work in Oregon needs a larger canvas than I provide here. The distinctive features of Oregon's Progressive enthusiasms, including the focus on labor law and child welfare reforms, Portland's Community Chest in the 1920s, the longshoremen and timber workers' strikes, changes in "Indian policy," and the mixed reactions to the New Deal, are particularly important.[32] Yet I hope the telling of that larger story can be assisted through an examination of Oregon's casework dramas, which in Portland focused largely on establishing entitlement and policing the state's first child welfare laws. As these caseworkers looked farther out, however, into a disordered flux of people they labeled as fanatics, hunchbacks, and half-breeds, their dramas traced degeneration, and at a scale that justified urgent measures. Fearful of a still-threatening backwoods, Oregon's child savers and relief agents were more likely to imagine and implement removal, institutionalization, and even sterilization than the Americanization and wise planning so crucial in Boston and Minneapolis. Theirs was another kind of American transformation, a more radical intervention in the prospects of the disabled and disordered that, if anything, grew more rather than less aggressive as the Depression and then the New Deal arrived. If too much of the history of welfare stays in cities, we lose sight of the conflicts that shaped the story of poverty outside them.

Oregon's cities attracted their share of bad characters. By the 1920s, caseworkers and informants could claim—sometimes, it seems, with a degree of pride—that Portland now contained some of the urban degenerates who were exercising the minds of concerned citizens back east. The father of one Public Welfare Bureau family came from Austria; a machinist and a man of "independent, strong personality," he "rebelled against having [a] life plan made for him" and became "a Bolshevik" and "an industrial misfit."[33] A mother hailing from somewhere east of the Rockies was accused by a foster mother of taking a baby to dances. "The infant is not well enough to stand the 'jazz life' to which it is subjected," wrote the worker.[34] A woman grocer told another visitor of a pair of state wards who "run around with old men." One, she said, was close to becoming an invalid from "too much wild life."[35] Another teenage girl was reported as "addicted to the use of cigarettes, intoxicants, and drugs," and the CWC described a woman referred to the Court of Domestic Relations as a "mentally incompetent dope fiend."[36] Another report of improper supervision, this time by a neighbor, drew forth a more rapid response once "dope fiend" was added to the normal accusations about a mother being "either insane or feeble-minded."[37]

Bolshevik men and female dope fiends were relatively common features of American urban nightmares in the 1920s. Assumptions about working-class men's inability to withstand radicalism's lure, and women's inability to resist the intoxications of whatever stimulant might come to hand, gave the city a recognizable cast of characters. Yet most of Portland's problems were regarded as having arrived from the outside. Even its more local bad characters—such as the Dodges, "whom [the] visitor recognized ... to be the type usually classified as hopeless, requiring forbearance, much patience, and combined treatment"—moved around between cities rather than emanating from Portland itself.[38] As was true in the eugenic family case studies compiled and analyzed by Nicole Rafter, Oregon's charity investigators and welfare visitors tended not to locate degeneracy in the city's back alleys.[39] However wretched its basements and however attractive it proved to itinerant low life, Portland was more threatened than threatening. As Robert Johnston argues, Portland was home to an "uncommonly uniform populace."[40] Oregon's nightmares—and the perils that both generated and justified a greater level of aggressive intent than was true in Minneapolis and Boston—grew not from the turmoil of city life but from the undisturbed layers of the backcountry, the hills, and the wild coast. They lay in what had not been changed, in the stagnant pools too long undisturbed by the refreshing currents of migration, and in racial rather than ethnic "backwardness."

If the line between civilization and backwoods could be drawn anywhere, it marked out those places in which men and women, parents and children, offended the boundaries of normal family and sexual relation-

ships. There were clear-cut cases of rape and incest and desperate teenage
brides, like the nineteen-year-old from rural Columbia County who married in order to escape a "profane and irreligious home" and a grandfather
and uncle who had forced her into repeated intercourse, only to be in-
fected with gonorrhea by her new husband.[41] Yet the sufferings of women
and children at the hands of men or parents were not simply noticed or po-
liced for their own sake. Instead, family conflicts were interpreted through
the lens of genetic decline, at least when they emerged from the country.
A Wasco County girl, shuttled back and forth between a mother, a stepmother, and the State Institution for the Feebleminded despite the fact that
all medical and mental examinations showed her to be completely normal,
was returned again to the institution because the "family has married cous-
ins for three generations."[42]

Disorderly backwoods women held a particular fascination for the male
and female workers in the Child Welfare Commission and the Public Welfare Bureau. Out there, age, generation, and even time took on different
meanings. In 1927 a sixteen-year-old girl was sent from a small town in
Jackson County to a private home in Portland because she was being "besieged by an elderly man, perhaps 43 or 44 years old, and was almost per-
suaded to marry him."[43] Out there were all kinds of fascinating, depraved,
and even dangerous characters: the "'lumber-jack' type of man" who was
moving to Portland with two sons for whom he seemed at least to have
"a genuine regard"; the "grass widow" from Monmouth, for whom the
CWC worker tried to organize a visit by a "socially minded" local woman;
the "cow-like creature, probably feeble-minded," married to a farmer who
was himself "rotten from top to toe"; and the "crazy bean" poor farmer
from Clackamas County who found three of his eleven children and step-
children (boys of seventeen, thirteen, and twelve) sent to reform schools or
relatives for writing "vulgar words" on county buildings, while another—
a boy of fifteen—was "seen" and, it seems, beaten by a county judge.[44] In
some investigations, workers added detailed scenes, such as the "dejected"
scene of a man, wife, and five children in Baker, where "it was necessary to
step very carefully outside of the door in order not to be submerged with
barnyard refuse" and in which the family had managed to create "typical
tenement conditions" in a rural town.[45]

Some of the reports stemming from rural and small-town Oregon—
and some of the forays to which they led—concerned criminal behavior,
especially incest and sexual assault. Yet here workers faced even greater
difficulties in judging real from false accusations. Although it was settled
amicably, a 1925 family dispute sparked by a sixteen-year-old girl was ex-
acerbated by allegations she knew would create a stir; the girl's family, the

investigator wrote, are "the typical, poor, hardworking type. They do not look at all dissipated and the girl's alleged statement that they are bootleggers seems rather farfetched."[46] In a 1923 case from Marion County, an investigator from the Boys and Girls Association had "interviewed the gossips instead of the substantial citizens" and had committed four girls into care. In the ensuing tussle over custody, the CWC chairman became involved in securing statements and was telephoned and told that "any of the Klan officials [will] cooperate" in any resolution.[47] In another small town, a woman reporting a case "received a letter (said to be from the Ku Klux Klan) warning her to keep her hands off the case at the risk of being tarred and feathered."[48]

A citizen from a town in Grant County wrote to the state governor in 1924; writing on behalf of a fifteen-year-old boy, he reported that the boy's father was "debauching" five younger siblings aged between five and twelve. The CWC consulted the local district attorney but received no reply. The original source then wrote back to say that the sheriff and district attorney were in league with the father, who was a moonshiner. Although he assured the CWC that he wrote not from spite or self-interest "but only citizenship, good education, and the betterment of humane conditions in this county, and the purity of our homes," no further investigation was done. A later addition to the file indicates the boy's sixteen-year-old sister had become pregnant and was taken into the Salvation Army Home in Portland; she was subsequently sterilized because she was "without question an institutional case."[49]

Small-town officials also felt the need to remind Portland-based workers that their worlds were somewhat different; the mayor of a town between Salem and Eugene reported of one reported neglectful father: "[He] is a very poor man in a way and has a large family 7 or 8 children all small and works at the Paper Mill to support them and you know what that means. His children do run barefoot lots of the time as dozens of other boys around town do up here mostly out of choice. . . . While he cannot dress his children as well as some of his neighbors I am sure he loves his family and is doing the best he can for them."[50] For the most part, though, the Portland- and Salem-based investigators saw what happened "up here" as revealing more than the quaint olden days of shoeless Huckleberrys. Like other stories in the emerging "white trash" genre, these were thrilling tales of another America, an America at once strangely distant and perilously close. It was an America of fanaticism and fornication in the suspicious shadows. It was a Polk County Mormon mother who worked "at men's work" as a logger, who "asks nothing of the public except to leave her alone."[51] It was a Grants Pass "fortune teller" creating turmoil in her family, a man tied to a "divine healing church" who tried to kidnap his daughter and take her to West Virginia, and a couple who had ended up in Seattle, having "wandered purposelessly from city to city" and were possibly "fanatics . . . along religious lines."[52]

The racial frontier was just as troubling. One supposedly insane woman in Yamhill County, "very dark—might have Indian blood," was recommended for medical examination even though her main problem seemed to be that the father of her four children had failed to pay her any support whatsoever and was now refusing to give any money unless it was administered by an organization.[53] The degree of Indianness was more exact in another case, a girl born in 1912 who had lived with her family and in the St. Agnes Home and was a "quarter breed Indian, although she may have more white blood than that"; for another and younger boy in 1934, when a foster home refused placement because "he is an Indian and she does not know enough about him," the only option was an Indian institution even though he was not "full blooded."[54]

Most disturbing of all to interwar Oregonians, however, was the mental and physical degeneration occurring along the frontier. Little evidence was needed to confirm suspicions of an epidemic of physical deterioration and feeblemindedness; in one 1921 case, a doctor reported that a "crippled, pathetic hunchbacked boy" was "an idiot and no operation would benefit," even though he had never actually examined the child and even though another child labeled as "feebleminded" was in fact not yet able to talk because of enlarged tonsils and a burn injury to his mouth.[55] A girl committed to Salem in 1923 was called a "physical and mental wreck," feebleminded, and "undoubtedly a menace if left at large" even though the diagnosis was based on a written report from another agency and not an independent investigation.[56] Children also had to be shielded from parents whose bad genes had caused the problem in the first place. In 1922, for instance, the CWC reported on a runaway teenager placed in foster care whose mother had written asking for news and pleading to make contact. "I guess the child thinks that I am dead," she wrote. The CWC visitor replied that they did not know where he was. That was untrue, but the mother—and the boy's half-sister, who was also trying to find him—never tried again.[57]

Responses hardened in the decade of the Depression, as can be seen in long-running cases. A fourteen-year-old girl and victim of a sexual attack was first referred to the CWC by the Red Cross in 1921. In all likelihood, and based on the various strands of evidence in the file, the parents were "criminally negligent," and the stepfather may have been the perpetrator. But to the local authorities the greater crime was their "subnormal type," and its solution was rescue: "[She] told her story piecemeal. She has no future in view except that of a 'buckaroo cow girl' ... [whereas] we believe that she is a most unusual and remarkable child and that if she can be rightly placed now she will be a power in the world.... She is beautiful in anything but the peasant type that we see about here.... She should be in a fine private home, where they will appreciate her remarkable qualities and help her find herself." She and one of her brothers were removed and boarded out by the Pacific Coast Rescue and Protective Society.

For the same family, nine years later, there was less hope and more intervention. Between 1930 and 1931, the four youngest children were sent to training schools, farms, the Boys and Girls Aid Society, and the Children's Farm Home. Conditions were undoubtedly poor—the family was living in a converted chicken coop—and the father, now deserted by his wife, was "defiant" and "talked in a rambling way which visitor could not understand," giving "every indication of being mentally unbalanced." He had found work for two of the boys on nearby ranches; categorized as "insane" by the CWC visitor, Alexandra Holton, he surrendered custody of all the children to the county court at the end of 1931. In one of the last entries in the file, the two youngest sons expressed a desire to see their siblings and their father; "I was rather impressed by [the] family affection that seems to exist," wrote the visitor. The impression did this family little good.[58]

In Oregon's interwar public welfare agencies, casework could become a kind of preemptive prevention against which misguided affection or sympathy would not be allowed to prevail. It was not pedagogical; it was concerned with protecting America from the disordered and degenerate people that civilization had pushed to its edges. The outcomes often involved removal and incarceration, with release back into America dependent on a supervised and dramatic intervention. There was still a desire to free people who might be trapped by their ancestries, but in Oregon, as in much of the American West, the increasing faith in eugenic solutions also reflected the sense that the ancestries there were both harder to shake and more damaging to people's prospects. People were pulled down by racial mixing, cousin marriage, and the poor genes of feebleminded forebears. They were sexually precocious and mentally and socially inadequate, and their reproduction, especially in states with still relatively small "pure American" populations, was a grave threat. They had to be removed and institutionalized and, in some cases, sterilized.

During the 1930s, this faith in dramatic interventions appears in many of the Oregon case files. A long and complicated welfare relationship with the Watson family, to take one example, was punctuated by attempts to remove two children from a "moderately hypermaniac [mother] with some paranoidal tendencies" who had become a divorcee and "psychopathic case" by 1937. The daughter, Velma, was "definitely mental," and "from the record we would judge that the parents and paternal grandparents are all more or less mentally unsound." The son, George, remained with his mother and at one point asked a family agency to inquire after his sister, of whom he "speaks wistfully ... [as] he has been separated [from her] most of the time since he was five." In 1941 George went to California to be with his father and joined the navy. Velma, having visited her mother and her father, fell in love with a young man in Seattle; the CWC reported that "she undoubtedly wishes to be independent and at the same time to belong to someone who would be interested in her." But she was returned to Portland and institutionalized again until 1942, when, at the age of eighteen, she also moved to California.[59]

Sorting out the genetic refuse could be very complicated. The Coles family had trailed across the plains of Illinois and Missouri, scaled the mountains to Montana, headed south to Texas, and shuffled back up to Kansas before finally following the sweep of other Americans toward California. They were tramps and seasonal workers, and the drifting soils of north Texas had proved genetically unproductive, according to the Oregon authorities, leaving them with four feebleminded children. In total, there were perhaps a dozen Coles children scattered across the Great Plains, the Rockies, and the Pacific coast. To the Child Welfare Commission fell the herculean task of assigning them all to their respective jurisdictions. In 1930 the father—who had been accused of prostituting one of his daughters—turned up at the Pacific Coast Protection Society with $92 and a plan: he wanted to move to Spokane with the seven children aged eighteen and under and set up housekeeping for them. The CWC organized a court hearing; some children became wards, others were permanently relinquished, and three were consigned to the State Institution for the Feeble-Minded for sterilization, one of whom was then to be released into his father's custody. One of the older children was "last seen heading for Portland," and a four-year-old girl was sent to California to live with her older brother. The Coles family were assuredly the cause of some trouble to themselves and to those around them; to the CWC, however, the main issue was that "while it undoubtedly needed attention, there was no reason why Oregon should be permanently saddled with this kind of non-resident humanity." In 1938 one of the Coles children came to the office of Catholic Charities. His youngest sister, born in 1923, was in the Louise Home for Girls, and he and his wife wanted to board her at their home in Philomath, where he was working in a sawmill. "He has evidently improved, he is self-supporting, appears to be healthy and strong," they wrote to the CWC. Despite this living evidence of improvement, no conclusions were drawn about the possibility that this "non-resident humanity" might have been suffering from poverty more than anything else.[60]

One of the longest and strangest cases for the Child Welfare Commission included many of the fears and fantasies associated with the backwoods while also revealing their very great dangers as a basis for decisions. The Dysons were reported on by various agencies between 1929 and 1937. At first, Mary Dyson was "something of a religious fanatic," and her eldest daughter was "a most peculiar looking person and undoubtedly has negro blood." The case became more exciting and lurid every year. One of the daughters had a child whose father was a "hermaphrodite," seven of the eleven children were illegitimate, and every member of the family was guilty of "sordid sex indiscretions." There was manic depression, car wrecks, psychosis, religious mania, and bootlegging. Children ended up in farm homes, boarding homes, and hospitals. There was also, in 1937, a report from a doctor at the State Hospital: most of the reports, she wrote, were "scandalous [and] unverified," and the family "has been outraged and very unfairly treated." Another worker confirmed that Mary Dyson's stories were "really theatrical material. She speaks quite intelligently, has a rather extensive vocabulary, and is extremely shrewd." She also claimed that her incarceration in the State Hospital was part of a frame-up. It was only when her story was "taken" for the first time in full in 1937 that someone realized that she had largely and perhaps entirely invented it.[61]

Because degeneration was the expected truth behind most stories, Oregon's welfare workers sometimes stumbled too quickly into attempts to control the "feebleminded menace" they played a part in inventing and publicizing. They also had to step in to try to solve the unintended outcomes of a focus on heritage, as when adoptive parents were reported to continually beat and harass a girl, telling her that "her parents were not fit people [and] that she had bad ancestors" and keeping out an eagle eye for "manifestations of degeneracy."[62] The CWC also found itself resisting the full logic of removal and sterilization. In a remarkable and dramatic case from 1924, for instance, the commission's workers acted with great care to protect a girl, Harriet Wild, labeled an "incorrigible moron with dementia praecox" by the agents of the Boys and Girls Aid Society, who were insisting on her institutionalization and sterilization. Harriet pleaded her case to the CWC in a letter—"there is nothing wrong with my head"—and had attempted suicide. Her sister "recited their family history in an earnest, convincing manner, which impressed us with her truthfulness. So far as she could learn, there is nothing at all wrong with her family, except for the misfortune of being poor." The CWC visitor wrote to the hospital: "We do not wish you to perform ANY operation upon the girl.... I do not agree that she is either feebleminded, delinquent or insane. She is simply a pitiful victim of unfortunate circumstances and our very defective social system and we believe she will prove well worthy of humane assistance and encouragement.... I feel certain that you are as anxious as we are to prevent injustice being done to any human being." Bravely, Harriet also made a deposition, charging that in her mental exam, the doctor did not write down what she said. This might explain the ritualized aspects of her supposed history, which listed her father as a drunkard aged seventy-six (he was actually a sober fifty-two), described her brother as being in a reform school (the two sisters were the only children), and detailed her sexual delinquencies (she had never had sex with anyone). The CWC prevailed, and Harriet was paroled to her older sister.[63]

Not everyone caught in such situations had an articulate older sister or a vigorous defender. The case files of the Oregon Child Welfare Commission and Public Welfare Bureau not only show us some desperate situations, with people determined to attack and harm each other, but are even more revealing of how unforgiving and strenuous solutions, based largely on eugenic pessimism, always threatened to create new forms of injustice. They show how most of the poor and the indigent were seen as victims of their heritage, not a "defective social system." And they suggest just how much the fear of "bad genes" had permeated social welfare, social work, and child protection in some parts of the American West by the 1920s.

In the end, of course, these are only glimpses of a larger and perhaps more complicated picture. But there is something in this picture of welfare in Oregon, however suggestive and partial it remains, that reminds us that here the frontier of degeneracy, "half-breeds," and morons seemed much closer than in Boston or Minneapolis. As in other places where the imprint of civilization seemed less fixed and solid, the threat of a re-erupting human backwardness was felt more keenly. The strenuousness of eugenics and other interventions in states such as Oregon reflected a fear of the possibility that civilization had not won its war and might yet lose it in places that felt in some way close to the edge. As Boston's social workers were transforming immigrants into Americans, and as the Family Welfare Association visitors in Minneapolis struggled to turn disorganized citizens into wise planners, their counterparts in Oregon were expected to hold back the menacing flux of feeblemindedness and depravity. They were also expected to do it cheaply. Even as we can wonder at some of their clumsiness, the tenor of some of their assumptions, and the fact that fervor made victims of boys such as Earl Spiller, we might also recognize the difficulties they faced in fighting such impossible crusades; sometimes, as in the case of Harriet Wild, they found a way of following their better instincts rather than their worst fears.

.

Part Six

MEN IN
SOCIAL WORK

Mr. O'Neill and the Seductive Client

Dramatis Personæ

MICHAEL O'NEILL, a child protection agent
MARY FLYNN, a women accused of neglect

· · · · · · · · · · · · · · · DRAMA · · · · · · · · · · · · · · ·

Home visits aren't meant to end up like this. He'd been ushered through the Flynns' door twenty minutes earlier, and now he isn't sure how to make it back out again. What is this woman doing?

Agent Michael O'Neill had studied the case carefully and read the file. In the first entry, made back in 1945, agent Thomas McNulty had described Mrs. Flynn as "sarcastic" and "childlike in her change of moods." Agent McNulty had recorded his insistence on a higher standard of cleanliness in the home. Mrs. Flynn's husband, he'd written, was "a very small man, ineffectual looking," and the house was "extremely filthy and disorderly." Mrs. Flynn had grown more compliant and "did not show resentment" when another agent, Foster Derrick, had "called attention to the various unsatisfactory conditions in the home" in April 1946.

In February 1949, agent Rosa Mariano had seen Mrs. Flynn after a negative report from the Board of Public Welfare; agent Delia Rosen had visited the Flynns again a few weeks later. It seemed to him that Delia had been a lot kinder. "The house is well cared for with the limitation that it is a poverty stricken home," she'd written. It was almost as if she had met someone else; in her account, Mrs. Flynn "apparently has had a great many dealings with social workers ... [and] realized that there is a feeling that she is mentally deteriorated. She started to say that she recognized me as a social worker because she had insight. She said, 'I'm not stupid at all.' ... It is my impression from this short interview that [she] is very immature, not very intelligent, but quite well-meaning."

O'Neill had been practicing his opening line. He knew clients could be defensive and evasive, but Mrs. Flynn's file suggested that she could be especially difficult. After eight months as an agent for the Massachusetts Society for the Prevention of Cruelty to Children, he was being trusted with his first real cases, and he wanted to get each one right.

He didn't know South Boston very well, but the house was easy enough to find, using the directions he'd written down in his notebook and had examined again on the streetcar on East Broadway. Once up the front steps, he snapped the notebook shut. Reaching for the pen in his top pocket, he discovered that he had put it in upside down, and its clip was now firmly caught on a thread. Try as he might, he couldn't work it loose. He needed to stretch his pocket tight while pulling the pen. That operation required two hands, which meant putting down his notebook. Neither the porch nor the front step looked all that inviting; there were a couple of suspicious stains on the step, and it would take Noah's flood, he thought, to clean off the porch. There wasn't much choice. Putting the notebook between his teeth, he grasped the bottom of his pocket with one hand, the top of the pen with the other, and pulled. With a chilling rip, out came the pen, along with half of the pocket's lining.

He hadn't noticed the door open. "You'd better be coming in. Yes, I am Mrs. Flynn."

A large woman filled the doorway. She was red in the face, and several strands of hair had escaped their clip. She had no expression he could be sure about, but as she glanced at the notebook in his mouth, the beginnings of a smile quivered her top lip.

"But you can call me Mary," she said. "Everyone calls me Mary." Her arms were crossed while she massaged an elbow with careful fingers.

"And what's your name then? You're supposed to tell me your name now. Are you having a little trouble there? It looks like you've ripped your pocket. Pity. It's a nice suit. You'll have to get that mended, won't you?"

She reached out a hand toward his chest. Stepping back, he pulled the notebook from between his teeth and hoped the traces of saliva that now ringed its cardboard base weren't too obvious.

"O'Neill, Mrs. Flynn. I'm Mr. O'Neill. From the Society for the Prevention of Cruelty to Children."

Before he could move into his painstakingly rehearsed summary of the reasons for his visit, the conditions under which the agency was prepared to discuss the possible neglect of the five Flynn children who were still at home and the fact that he would need to do a thorough inspection of the cooking, sleeping, and cleaning arrangements, she interrupted.

"Mr. O'Neill. That's very formal, when we have such a lot to talk about. What's your Christian name, Mr. O'Neill?"

"That's not really routine, Mrs. Flynn."

"Oh, come now, it wouldn't hurt to tell me your name, would it?"

"I guess not. It's Michael, Mrs. Flynn."

"And . . . what about your second name?"

"It's Michael Joseph, Mrs. Flynn."

"Mary, Mr. O'Neill, call me Mary. From around here, then?"

"No, not from here."

"So where? From Dorchester maybe?"

He smiled. "From Malden."

She raised an eyebrow. "How lovely. And what church, what school, way up there in Malden?"

"Malden Catholic High School, but we went to St. Theresa's in Everett."

"I don't know anyone up there." She shifted her stance and folded her arms back across her chest.

"What was your confirmation name? No, no, let me guess." She caught his eye, made sure he was watching, and looked him up and down as if checking for other rips and tears.

"I think you might be a Patrick. Or maybe you're a Xavier, Michael Joseph Xavier."

"It doesn't really matter, Mrs. Flynn. We really must . . ."

"I think your confirmation name matters, Mr. O'Neill. Were you not confirmed, then? Up there at St. Theresa's in Everett? That's terrible, Mr. O'Neill. Not being confirmed. I'm sure I've had all mine confirmed."

"I was confirmed. It's Dominic, Mrs. Flynn."

"Oh, that's lovely. Michael Joseph Dominic. Mr. Michael Joseph Dominic O'Neill. A good Catholic lad."

There was a pause, then a smile that he thought looked almost flirtatious.

"It's nice for the Cruelty Society to send a good Catholic lad to a Catholic family like mine. Not like the Welfare or the Family Society. You don't get anyone nice from there. Oh, you get those vinegar-faced ladies, you know the ones I mean, can't understand our ways. Do you know those kind of ladies, Mr. O'Neill? Anyway, you'd best be coming in, now you've got your notebook out of your mouth and your pen ready to write with. You'll be wanting to write, won't you, Mr. O'Neill?"

She stood aside, pressing her back against one side of the doorframe and beckoning him past her. But she hadn't made enough room, so he was forced to flatten himself against the door as he stepped around her. He was more nervous than he thought he would be, less certain than his training should have made him.

He fidgeted with the pen, rolling it back and forth between his fingers. He stood aside so she could pass him and then followed her as she bustled through the front room and into a darkened kitchen that smelled like sour milk and cabbage. It was bright enough outside, but all the windows in this house looked onto the wall of its neighbor.

"Does your pen still work after all that? Do you want me to cut that lining off for you, Mr. O'Neill? That pocket really is a mess, isn't it? You'll have to explain that to someone, won't you? Is that your suit, or does the Cruelty Society give you that?"

She shooed out a couple of children. He hadn't even noticed them. There was a shy little girl, Margaret, he thought she said, and boy of about ten or eleven. It was hard to forget his name after she'd screeched, "Patrick Joseph Flynn, you get out into that yard and chop some wood, or Mr. O'Neill here will take you away and put you in a home for delinquency."

"Now we can talk," she said. He was still standing near the kitchen door, unsure whether he should move farther in or stay where he was. Mrs. Flynn wasn't helping. She came closer, took a step back as if inspecting him, and then moved close again.

"You'll want to know about my health. It's women's troubles, not something you'd understand." She paused. "Thirty-eight, Mr. O'Neill."

"Pardon?"

"Thirty-eight years old. Would you believe that? Six children, Mr. O'Neill. It's the six children. That's why I look a bit worn, you know. They do wear you out. Do I look a bit worn out to you, Mr. O'Neill? You wouldn't have children yet yourself, college man that you are. Perhaps you've got a nice girl, though. Have you got yourself a nice girl, Mr. O'Neill?"

He stepped back against a rickety dresser, rattling the cracked plates and stained cups.

"Your girl, Mr. O'Neill. What's her name?"

"Let's not talk about that, Mrs. Flynn."

She clucked her tongue and then leaned against the icebox.

"Well, don't you mind, Mr. O'Neill, there will be a girl one day. Good-looking man like yourself. Sure there'll be someone before long. It'll do you the world of good. Someone to look after you a bit."

She moved forward again and pretended to pick a thread out of his cuff.

"Someone who can mend a pocket when you're a bit clumsy." She was smiling again.

"And a lucky girl she'll be too. Professional man, good salary, I'll bet. Is your mother proud, Mr. O'Neill? I'd be proud. Of course, I've got my troubles with my children. No professionals there. I suppose you know that from all your reports. Thomas in the reforming home, and my Benedict didn't finish high school. Mary and Patrick are at St. Brigid's, of course. I'm sure your mother's proud. Is your father a professional man, Mr. O'Neill?"

He opened his mouth. She pressed on, stepping back and walking up and down the space between the icebox and the drop-leaf table.

"Now, Mr. O'Neill, what do you want to talk about? I've had a report, have I? Another report? Oh, dear. I can't remember the last time the Cruelty was around. Is it that crazy neighbor again, that Mr. Docherty? He is a drinker and a danger to all, that one. It wasn't long ago, was it, the last time the Cruelty was here. There was a nice young girl, Miss Roper, was it, or Miss Rosie."

"It was Agent Rosen, Mrs. Flynn."

"And before that, who was that nice young man? Do you know him, Mr. O'Neill? The nice young man, maybe he's left now, though. It was a few years ago now. He was such a friendly one. He didn't mind listening to my troubles, soothing me. He was a lovely young man. I think he was a nice Catholic boy, too. A bit older than you, Mr. O'Neill. Or perhaps he just looked older."

"That was Agent McNulty, Mrs. Flynn."

She stopped pacing and made an exaggerated show of brushing some crumbs from the tablecloth. She wasn't looking at him.

"No, I don't think that was his name, Mr. O'Neill. A small lad, he was, lovely black hair and dark eyes. Nice dark eyes. No, it wasn't McNulty."

He sighed and tried to fix her eyes with his. "It was, Mrs. Flynn. I've read your file. It was Agent McNulty, Thomas McNulty. He is a friend of mine."

"Well, so you say, Mr. O'Neill. I guess you'd know best. And what did agent Thomas McNulty say about me in that file, then? I hope he said nice things. He had such a good manner. Polite. Really listened, Mr. O'Neill. Really listened. He understood my troubles."

Shifting on to one foot, and then the other, she grimaced and pressed her hands together.

"Thirty-eight, Mr. O'Neill. Thirty-eight."

Time to take charge, he thought.

"I'm here to ask some questions, Mrs. Flynn, and then I really must be getting away."

"Yes, Mr. O'Neill, yes, you ask your questions, the questions you have to ask. You go right ahead."

"Does your husband still drink, Mrs. Flynn?"

She turned and looked, that smile near her lips again.

"Do you drink once in a while, Mr. O'Neill?"

"Yes, well, Mrs. Flynn, but . . ."

"So it's not drinking by itself that's the worry then. Is it a question of how much, is that it, Mr. O'Neill? Or is it how often? If you're going to write it down, I need to know exactly what you're asking."

"I mean does he drink too much. That's what I mean."

"Does it say he drinks too much, in the file? Does it say that?"

"I need to ask this about your husband, Mrs. Flynn. He used to drink too much, didn't he? He used to drink his wages and leave you nothing for groceries."

"Well, Mr. O'Neill, you put that down then. In your book. Mr. Flynn used to drink too much and drink his wages."

He found himself biting his lip.

"And the children, Mrs. Flynn?"

"My children don't drink, Mr. O'Neill, what a thing to say. Is that Mr. Docherty saying that my children drink?"

"No, Mrs. Flynn, I mean to say, we think you should keep your children a little cleaner. When they're dirty like they are, when their clothes are dirty, it doesn't reflect well on the home, does it?"

Her eyes flashed. It was unnerving, this sudden ferocity. Her lips had set into a hard, unyielding line.

"Were you never a little dirty yourself, Michael, as a boy, I mean? Did you get a little dirty yourself up there in Malden? Imagine if someone from the Cruelty came along one day without any warning. Would you have been clean and fit for an altar boy yourself? Did your mother scrub you all the time, Michael?"

She smiled again. "And who does your clothes for you now, Michael? Is it still your mother? You're very lucky there, to have a mama still wash your clothes for you."

The smile didn't linger this time. She's angry, he thought. Tom Mc-Nulty wrote about her change of moods.

Perhaps another approach would work better. He complimented her on her clean tablecloth.

"And you'd know about that, Michael, wouldn't you now? About keeping a cloth clean. How you must have helped your mother. Did you do a lot of washing and folding, then, at your home? It's good to meet a nice boy like yourself who appreciates how hard it is to keep things clean."

He looked through the open door, into a bedroom.

"And the sheets look very clean, Mrs. Flynn. That's something we always take careful note of. The clean sheets. On the bed. On that bed, there."

She smiled again and hooked an eyebrow.

"On that bed there? The big bed there? So my sheets go in your file, Michael? My nice big bed with the clean sheets?"

There is little to be found out, he thought, and Agent O'Neill wasn't quite sure on what grounds the latest charge had been made. He knew from his supervisor and his fellow agents that some of the complaints were frivolous or, like this one for Mrs. Flynn, stemmed from a bad reputation. The rooms and the children were untidy, and Mrs. Flynn was not Boston's best housekeeper, but there seemed little evidence of drinking or neglect. There were no liquor bottles he could see, and there must have been bread because the crumbs were scattered right across the table. The interview had taken nearly twenty minutes, and he doubted that much more useful information could be obtained. He might as well leave.

Mrs. Flynn came closer. She was too close, much nearer than before. She touched his shoulder and groaned a little.

"It's my head, Michael," she said. "You feel my head with your hand, you feel it. I'm sure the ache is throbbing right there through my skin."

He murmured something he hoped would sound consoling.

But she takes his hand and brushes it against her forehead. She pulls it downward. Not quickly, but not slowly either. It is a motion made worse by its steadiness, by her calmness. His embarrassment rises. His hand is on her cheek, at her throat, her collar bone, almost to her breast. He pulls it back and tries to grab the doorknob. His face is burning. She takes his hand and compels it down again. She whispers.

"Don't be mean to me. Don't be mean, Michael. Not to me."

· · · · · · · · · · · · RESOLUTION · · · · · · · · · · · ·

How had it ended? In his notes for the file, O'Neill wasn't clear about the details. As he reached the stage of writing about hands and heads and breasts, he recorded simply this: "Agt was unable to decide whether she meant, don't be mean from the standpoint of the agency function or from the standpoint that he refused to be seduced by her." There is much unsaid, much left to ask that the record will not reveal. How had he pulled away? How had Mrs. Flynn reacted?

It is just as important to ask why O'Neill decided to include this clumsy seduction in what he knew was a lasting record. Surely it was included for a reason. He would certainly have been mindful of his training and the society's expectations of veracity, accuracy, and meticulous recording in what it called the client-agent interaction. He was a young agent, recently hired. Perhaps he worried that Mrs. Flynn, a frequent enough client, might tell another worker or paint a false picture. Yet he would have been mindful, too, of the consequences of sharing the story and how he would need to explain his decisions to his case supervisor and even, per-

254 MEN IN SOCIAL WORK

haps, to other agents at a case conference. They might have queried what Mrs. Flynn had meant by "don't be mean." They might have asked if he thought Mrs. Flynn was attracted to him or had perhaps been deliberately undermining him, in which case another agent might have to be assigned the next visit.

There is no reason to consider the story untrue or to disregard O'Neill's honesty in relating it. He probably felt he had to do so. But every story has a point and comes to a conclusion. So there is every reason to ask why O'Neill shaped his story about a difficult client in particular ways and to particular ends and to ponder its details and narrative tactics, perhaps especially its denouement. This was a refused seduction. Mrs. Flynn was pathetic, lonely, and stumbling, but not really malevolent. The agent's authority was preserved and augmented, and the functions of the agency were now possible. He had made the story into one about his own steadfastness and professionalism and his refusal to be diverted from his task.

So it might have ended. But O'Neill retained responsibility for the case and with it the power to conclude Mrs. Flynn's story. I think his subsequent decisions suggest the truer meanings and impact of that strange seduction. He had to visit Mrs. Flynn twice more. So, twice more, he had to tell her story and his story. He had to return to that file and page and write in the space left underneath the record of that first encounter. In April 1950, there is calm authority and a little sympathy. She "showed her resistance to any sort of help" and displayed "a certain amount of hostility toward our agency." But, he wrote, "she is quite pliable and easy to divert . . . [and] she does seem to derive a certain amount of pleasure from talking with me."

But it seems resentments could linger, especially when someone like Mrs. Flynn kept refusing to acknowledge who he was. In September that year came another visit. This time, "she was very upset and disturbed—as usual—and spoke very belligerently to me." "As usual": that's what he chose to write. When one looks at the rest of her file, at all of her encounters with several agents, none of which seems to have involved serious charges or come to anything more than warnings or promises of future surveillance, it seems a strange choice. His conclusions were much harsher: "Problems centered mainly about her extreme limitations, both mentally and emotionally. There was no casework effort possible with her because of her low IQ and personality degeneration. . . . Case is being closed as unimproved and because nothing further can be done either on a protective, authoritative, or case work basis."

In that failed seduction, or in April's benign listening, he had been less sure of what to say. In September, though, she was shouting and angry.

She used things against him, moved toward him, told him to get away, and asked why he was still interested in her situation. She'd done nothing wrong, and still they asked her questions. Now he knew what to say. She was unimprovable. Extreme limitations. Degeneration. Nothing further can be done. It was a fitting end to a story about a troublesome and uncooperative client. It was a fitting and final rebuke to that woman, a rebuke given steel by what she once had tried to accomplish. It is an unforgiving rejection, which seems jarring in the context of other agents' encounters and conclusions. But it is the way he chose to end it. Mrs. Flynn wasn't going to be the measure of his career.

On the basis of his testimony, it is difficult to know whether O'Neill ever pondered what Mrs. Flynn might have been trying to do or why she had attempted what he called his seduction. It is even more difficult to know whether he recognized the play of sexual power that seems to lie at its heart or why he and other male agents might find themselves being maneuvered by female clients. His discomfort with Mrs. Flynn might measure his dismay at her clumsy attentions. But the hard words with which he banished her from the possibility of protection or care might also signify a broader quandary. It was one Mr. O'Neill shared with other male workers, and it concerned the authority that inferiors owed to superiors and that women owed to men. In that sense, it is reasonable to see it as one episode in a larger conflict.

Like most of the other agents, male and female, O'Neill wrote histories in which he tended to have the last word. This one ended with Mrs. Flynn's dismissal and defeat, an outcome no other visitor predicted and no one bar O'Neill seems to have favored. It's the way he chose to end his story, and it is what made me want to rewrite it. I look at the evidence, at the other cases, and at the other encounters in this case. I look at Delia Rosen's account of a woman well used to social workers and increasingly irritated by their assumption that she was stupid and easily diverted. It sets a context and creates a momentum. I wanted to roll his story back to that moment he found himself at Mrs. Flynn's door and began to find himself trapped in a drama he didn't completely understand and made to pay for a resentment he hadn't created by himself.

There are different stories. One is of a thirty-eight-year-old South Boston woman faced with a charge of child neglect who attempted to seduce a male social worker perhaps a dozen or more years her junior. In another, Michael O'Neill was the target, but not of seduction. It mattered that he was a young man, but not because Mrs. Flynn desired him. It mattered because, in that moment, being a young man made him vulnerable to a particular kind of subversion. It wasn't necessarily planned, and perhaps his looks and manner made physical intimacy the more inviting of the dramas she could have explored. Perhaps Mrs. Flynn fancied herself as the knowing woman to Mr. O'Neill's male ingénue. But in this story, Mrs. Flynn sets the stage and writes the opening lines. It is she who seizes the initiative. And in one of the moments that is hidden from us, I think it is she who decided when enough was enough. It took courage, too. If Mrs. Flynn had endured enough insults from social workers, especially young men who thought her slovenly and stupid and pretended they knew better than she did, she must also have known something of what they could do and the damage they could cause her family.

Having written the story from that starting point, I wanted to ask how he had extricated himself, what he thought Mrs. Flynn might have meant, and what he'd said as he left. Most of all, I wanted to ask what she'd done and said. Agent O'Neill is silent on all of these points. He leaves little from which a historian can proceed. But in those later encounters, especially that last angry one in September, might lie some clues. Perhaps his commitment to her defeat stemmed from what he sensed had been her victory. I wonder whether she laughed. I wonder whether he walked away trying not to hear that laughter. Or did he try to believe that the laughter filling his ears came from a different house, from another person's triumph in some other game, or from a joke made at someone else's expense?

CHAPTER 27

In a Women's World

Michael O'Neill's troubles with Mary Flynn began at the very end of the 1940s. By that point, more young men—often from working-class, immigrant, or nonwhite backgrounds, and sometimes taking advantage of the GI Bill—had begun moving into social welfare and especially youth work. Yet even during the 1920s and 1930s, a small number of male agents and visitors worked for the Massachusetts Society for the Prevention of Cruelty to Children and the Family Welfare Association in Minneapolis. Even if attempted seductions were a rare feature of their encounters, tensions between male investigators, female officials, and female clients were not. They have played little part in social work's histories, but the presence of O'Neill and his mostly young peers in the largely female ranks of charity and social workers generates interesting questions about whether they imagined, dramatized, or carried out their social work any differently.

As was true for Agnes Cutler, Elsa Lindstrom, and Laura Wells, we know Michael O'Neill, Thomas McNulty, and the others largely through their depictions of themselves in case files. The records of the agencies provide a few clues: we know their names and sometimes their educations, and with those we can make some reasonable assumptions about their backgrounds. We know they tended to specialize in child protection or what was often called "industrial work," which usually implied dealing with older adolescents adjusting to adulthood. In 1922 men made up seven of the nineteen agents in the Boston office of the MSPCC. By 1927 they made up seven of seventeen. Turnover was relatively rapid for both men and women. Only two men and two women worked at the MSPCC in both 1922 and 1927, though a third female agent—Helen Masters—had been promoted to assistant supervisor. Male agents continued to join and leave the MSPCC during the 1930s; most stayed two or three years, often coming to the society from college or junior positions in other agencies and departing for careers in banking or the law as well as social welfare. One came with a master of laws from Boston University and another with a Harvard master of arts, and others brought professional experience in probation and industrial welfare. During the 1930s, most had college degrees.

By 1930 and probably before, male and female agents were appointed at the same salaries, and the salary cuts of 1932—which were not restored for two years—were also shared equally by men and women.[1] Men's advantages in the broader economy, and their ability to seek a much greater array of jobs outside social work, certainly help explain how the society had a lower proportion of male workers in the late 1930s. Their responsibilities as soldiers help explain their absence in the 1940s.

In Minneapolis the Family Welfare Association's one or two male visitors were a much smaller fraction of the workforce. In 1918 one of the FWA's eleven visitors (and none of the four district secretaries) was a man, and in 1922 another male visitor was hired. Both were gone by 1924, and it seems their absence was something of an issue because the board of directors discussed employing a male worker. By 1926 there was one male visitor, and by 1928 there were three, but the next new male visitor—Earl Pitt—wasn't hired until 1934. He was joined a year later by Vernon Hull, who worked for the FWA until 1937. Earl Pitt stayed until at least 1940, when it appears he may have enlisted in the armed services. The remaining records suggest that in the FWA, as in the MSPCC, male and female visitors were paid the same salaries, which were based on experience and qualifications rather than gender.[2]

As far as names can tell something of people's pasts, the best guess would be that these men differed little from their female coworkers. In 1920s Boston, they were white, Anglo-Saxon, and Protestant, and a few had good Boston names to match their very good Boston educations. By the late 1930s and 1940s, Irish, Italian, and Jewish names began to appear. In Minneapolis there was a strong representation of immigrant backgrounds in the 1920s, especially Germans, Norwegians, and Swedes, which continued into the 1940s. To these sketchy collective biographies can be added the impression—based on what workers chose to tell about themselves or recorded their clients as saying—that these men were all under the age of thirty.

The history of social work's encounters has properly focused on women because women formed the bulk of those who carried casework methods out into the field. Introducing these men into what has been largely a story about women is not a matter of redressing balance but of asking how their manhood mattered. If, as Linda Gordon and others have so persuasively shown, case files open a window into the past performance of class and gender for women, then that is no less true for men. Nor is this a way of simply restoring men to what is in this case an unlikely center stage, something against which early American historian Toby Ditz has so cogently warned.[3] Instead, it is to assume that some particularly important facets of gender are revealed in places where men or women aren't meant to be, places that in some way too closely resemble the supposedly natural realm of the other sex, or places where the anticipated relationships between men and women are somehow different or disordered. In this particular time, one of those places for men was a profession that was not quite a "real" profession (in the way that medicine or the law was), in part because it was so deeply etched by traditions of female benevolence, religiosity, and social activism.

There had always been men in careers of care, but they had usually been wrapped in a mantle of religion that offered some protection—or at least explanation—for the bearers' potential loss of manhood. By 1920, to seek a career in social work, or even a job in a protective or casework agency, was to choose one of the few vocations seen as more naturally suited to women, even if women social workers themselves were more and more likely to reject such characterizations of their calling. These young men were trained in college courses made up largely of women, and their discipline was also one in which intellectual and professional leadership was female. To become a social worker in the 1920s and 1930s meant reading Mary Richmond and Grace Abbott, using the textbook on social case recording by Margaret Cochran Bristol, and understanding Virginia Robinson's and Ada Sheffield's innovations in casework methods. Charity, welfare, and social work agencies were among the first working and professional environments in which older and more experienced women wielded some authority over men, many of whom were junior and just entering the field. Though men began the century in most of the official and overseeing positions, by the 1920s, at least in the American agencies, women were also serving as general secretaries, field officers, and case supervisors. The Minneapolis FWA's district secretaries, who coordinated the caseworkers, were all women during the 1920s and 1930s. In those decades, the FWA was headed by two female general secretaries: Joanna Colcord, who assumed national prominence in social work education and research, and Pearl Salisbury. By 1922 one of the MSPCC's two assistant supervisors was female; by 1927 both were, and by 1930 so was the sole supervisor of casework.

The "problem" of men in feminized places has often been examined in the period around the turn of the twentieth century and in terms of schooling, scouting, and other attempts to "stem the tide of feminization."[4] Although it is important, as James Gilbert has argued, to be wary of a history of masculinity in which men are always and forever wrapped up in one crisis or another, anxieties over the relationship between male authority and women's work certainly continued to shape American public debate.[5] The questions that working women raised about gender, sphere, and skill took on new urgency in the 1920s, especially in terms of "efforts to remasculinize the workplace through [male] bonding," and this increased, if anything, during the Depression decade of the 1930s.[6] In that light, the male welfare workers of the 1920s and 1930s—the boys born around the turn of the century who an earlier campaign about effeminacy had tried to "save"—should raise some interesting questions. How did men in feminized careers define manhood and understand the relationship between manliness and the work of welfare and caring? What characters, dramas, and dilemmas appeared in their case files? What kinds of men was it possible for them to be, and what kinds of manhood did they attempt to describe and implement among others? If we ask how charity shaped the work of men, it is also possible to ask how men shaped the work of charity.

Overall, two kinds of dramas are particularly common in the case notes written by men. Both described and enacted strong anxieties, shaping relationships with their clients in ways that emphasized the fragility of manhood. One focused on effeminacy, which threatened to disrupt the gaining of manhood among boys and teenagers. As they tried to turn those boys and young men back on to the right path, they developed a diagnosis of failure and offered themselves as "true" fathers and authority figures who could ensure the development of manly men. The other was "nagging," which symbolized the troubles men had with overbearing women who threatened the proper relationships of marriage and household. The strength of these young men's reactions to naggers and "foppish" boys is testament, I think, to the anxiety at least some of them felt about how to gain and maintain the kinds of authority men were meant to enjoy. Keeping in mind the emotional states and experiences that language conveys, we can register the intensity of these reactions, and the strength of their words. Manhood mattered to these men, and for most of them, it seemed a fragile privilege.

CHAPTER 28

He Must Be Bent to Our Will and Made into a Man

Just as Boston's child protectors focused on making immigrants into Americans, they also wanted to ensure that the boys among them became manly. This was especially true of the male agents, who in any event tended to be given or to take over cases involving older boys, especially when there was some suspicion of criminal, dangerous, or particularly squalid situations or if there was a charge of delinquency. Of the thirty-five Boston cases in which I could definitely identify the involvement of male workers, two-thirds involved one or both of these characteristics. In Minneapolis, where male workers were definitely involved in seven of the sampled cases, two involved troubled boys, both American and both diagnosed as "unmanly," and two others concerned the criminal activity of bootlegging.

Although the nature and origins of "unmanliness" were sometimes indistinct, its antidotes remained consistent. In the absence of long-term psychiatric treatment or parental support, male charity agents recommended strict control and even harsh punishments. At the same time, they described and enforced a manhood—and fatherhood—in which ideas of eventual independence and self-reliance sat uneasily alongside an unquestioning acceptance of older men's authority. As was true for the Boston male psychiatrists of the 1920s and 1930s studied by Elizabeth Lunbeck, "the man who did not measure up as a man" was very troubling for Boston's younger and more professionally marginal male social workers.[7] Indeed, perhaps the men drawn to child protection and youth work had a particularly keen interest in ensuring a smooth process of masculine transformation. For them, as has been true for other men in other times and places, the fragility of manhood impressed them most, along with the notion that because all men might in some way bear the costs of its failure, strong action was a reasonable response.

Manliness was most often endangered by mothers or by poor genetic inheritance. In one 1937 Minneapolis case, Richard Young, a fifteen-year-old boy, was feared to be approaching delinquency because of his mother's "inability to recognize and cope with [his] problems" and her "selfishness and laxness with him." Although the surface problem, according to both male and female visitors involved in the case, was that "she was incapable of disciplining him," the roots of delinquency, one male worker observed, lay somewhat deeper: "He had been deprived of normal father relationships and she denied him any substitute ones, preferring to keep him close to herself."

The file reveals no attempt to understand why Mildred Young might have kept her only son close. Her own mother had died when she was sixteen. In 1918, at nineteen years of age, she came to Minneapolis from rural Minnesota. She met and married her husband in 1921. His "wanderlust" had seen him take the family to California, where he gambled away his earnings, and then to Chicago, where he finally deserted, taking all of their money. She had arrived back in Minneapolis in 1930 with an eight-year-old son and spent seven years working as a sampler and seamstress. She was involved in a strike in April of 1937 and became even more worried about keeping her job and maintaining payments on her debts. She identified inadequate earnings and indebtedness as her major problems and as the main causes of Richard's "unsettled" nature and anxieties.

Richard became the target of a series of interventions by male workers, teachers, and probation officers. One teacher told FWA visitor Vernon Hull that because Richard was a masturbator he should be put on probation "so they might have some authority to hold over him." A truancy officer agreed with the idea of probation and also suggested removing him from his mother for "intense psychiatric treatment." Richard was on probation in April 1937 for a minor offense; his probation officer's suggestion was for "a little corporal punishment." During a home visit in December 1937, Hull noted only that Richard and another boy were "rather foppishly dressed" and smoking cigarettes. The case was closed in January 1938; "it is futile to attempt to accomplish anything with son because of his mother's attitude and inability to work with those qualified to help her."[8]

In a Boston case from around the same time, teenager Earl Whitfield was seen to suffer from an absence rather than surfeit of maternal affection. The Whitfield family had been seen before. In 1929, just after the parents' separation, Earl's older brother, Robert, then eight years old, had come to the attention of the Family Welfare Service while his mother was in the hospital. He was described as a "sensitive boy" who "cries easily [and] has only recently learned at all to fight." This masculine accomplishment had not escaped Earl, who was a "vigorous, attractive child, gregarious, a good scrapper, full of life and fun, a neighborhood favorite."

But by 1936, fourteen-year-old Earl was on the verge of "serious delinquency." The story developed by the agent, Stanford Johnson, was that Earl had been at first unconsciously and then consciously rejected by his mother because of his similarity to his father. There was also great antagonism between Earl and Robert. In the story told by Johnson, Earl had also become the more effeminate character: he was "very imaginative" and "seemed to live almost entirely in his imagination." He was also an "incessant liar" and "very vain." The Judge Baker Foundation confirmed a "precocious sexual development" (Earl was fifteen at the time of the diagnosis, and his precocity seemed to involve masturbating while he thought about girls). He was also "very evasive, likes movies [and] adventure stories [and] shows considerable resentment in the clinic." In 1936 and 1937, Earl spent time at the Thompsons Island Farm and Trade School. For unclear reasons, he tried to run away to Richmond, Virginia, in 1938, but was found in New York City and brought home. At a meeting in the office, the sixteen-year-old "objected to the stigma" of being a charge of the Children's Aid Society and refused to cooperate any further.

What was wrong with Earl Whitfield? To Stanford Johnson, Earl's problem was his overactive imagination, evasiveness, and vanity, all of which stemmed from a rejecting, vengeful mother and an absent father. To an unnamed female worker who had contact with him in 1938, however, his lying and lack of responsibility were more important. On one occasion, Earl admitted to stealing something and acknowledged his culpability; she wrote a file note and gave it the title "A Real Victory."

Reading Earl's file now, I see him as an achingly sad boy who desperately wanted to be important and to matter to somebody. He was afraid of the consequences of his actions and seemed inordinately frightened about being sent back to Thompsons Island or going to a reform school. Certainly, Johnson had no doubts about the best course of action: "Since he cannot receive the type of psychoanalytical therapy that he needs the attempt to socialize him through the strict discipline in Shirley is the next best procedure."[9] Such was the fate of those who could not afford elite therapies. As best as I can tell, Earl Whitfield remained in reform homes, foster homes, or industrial schools until he was eighteen.

Other male workers attempted to literally replace the absent or ineffective father. There is no evidence that any of them were fathers, but their concern about fatherhood was certainly one shared in most areas of American culture in this period.[10] In the long-running case of Antonio and Marco Pinelli (described in chapter 17), agent Calvin Fletcher clearly understood his role as supplementing and perhaps even replacing the boys' father. Whatever Pinelli Senior's domestic and financial difficulties, his faults were clear in the sins of eldest son Antonio: truancy, begging, masturbation, smoking, coffee drinking, vulgarity, overly adult expressions, sex play with neighborhood girls, and approaches from homosexuals. Marco's adventures were a little less dramatic, but he had "convulsions" as well as "an overly active acquaintance of street life." This was a case of "extremely defective parental control" in which the first remedy was removal from both "a sordid, undesirable environment" and the "world of fantasy which [Antonio] has molded to suit himself."

The boys' problems were rapidly and consistently treated as paternal, not just parental, especially when the first form of treatment—placement in a "normal home"—did nothing to overcome their delinquencies. Strenuous fathering was required, at least for a period. And that had specific objectives: Antonio's world of fantasy had to be "broken," Marco had to "develop inhibitions," and both had to be given "foundations in right living." In other words, the goals of the father were to control the uncontrolled and create obedience. It was to build the foundations for good behavior on submission, and it was to invest much importance in specific rituals through which that submission was enacted. Marco and Antonio were brought to the CAA office for conferences and to be chided for misbehavior. Both boys were more than happy to use dramatic stories, half-truths, and lies in order to secure the outcomes they wanted, so they were occasionally subjected to stern admonishments from agents and foster parents.

The Pinelli brothers also used running away and other, more dramatic forms of noncompliance to engineer ways of leaving unwanted situations and returning either to their own family or to favored foster homes where they could be together. These acts drew out another interpretation of good fathering, and on more than one occasion male agents reminded and encouraged the brothers' father that paternal authority should be enforced through physical punishment.[11]

In their work with delinquent and endangered boys, male workers believed that one of their most important tasks was to combat those deficiencies only real fathers could prevent. In their most involved cases, their descriptions of troubled boys are telling: foppish, languid, evasive, and overimaginative or only interested in movies and fantasy. Some of the hints were even more pointed. For "foppish" Richard in Minneapolis, Vernon Hull darkly warned, "The predictions are he will never adjust to marriage."[12] I don't want to turn these men into ciphers. The male agents and visitors in Boston and Minneapolis were undoubtedly concerned about the future of the boys who came to their attention. In some ways, they showed a capacity to befriend them and offer a kind of guidance that may have been welcomed, especially by those—such as Richard and Earl—whose family situations were complicated, confusing, and very probably traumatic. Behind child rescue and the family welfare approach of the Minneapolis agency lay a genuine commitment to identifying and safeguarding the future prospects of young clients.

But their struggle to care—real as it was—was often stymied by what they took as the responsibilities and inherent nature of manhood. They blamed ineffective (and especially immigrant) fathering, and they blamed deserted mothers for not seeking out sufficiently masculine role models, because in their eyes only real fathers could produce normal, manly boys. In the interests of independence, they demanded obedience. They imagined verbal chastisement and physical punishments as the most convenient means of enforcing compliance with objectives the boys themselves were rarely allowed to discuss or question. Anxious about effeminacy, and convinced that differences between boys measured real levels of masculinity, they found themselves taking control, but rarely taken into confidence.

And they could be strikingly insensitive. Foppish Richard tried to tell Vernon Hull why his mother protected him. As he said, his mother had lost her own mother while still a teenager. His father had deserted them and gambled away their money. In Richard's view, the main cause of his family's distress was his mother's low wages as a seamstress and her constant anxieties about money. It seemed reasonable enough, but no one listened. To a female worker, Dorothy Putnam, who saw Earl Whitfield in 1938, his lying and lack of responsibility were more important than any masculine inadequacy. I wonder, too, about her suggestion of a new issue: "He seems to have a fear that all men will harm him." Neither of the male social workers who dealt with him ever seems to have asked why.

It is possible, too, that this stress on engendering real manhood rested in part on these men's own anxieties and insecurities. They worked in a vocation that had struggled to become a profession and in which questions of authority and control still loomed very large. They questioned and were perhaps questioned by doctors, psychiatrists, judges, and policemen, for whom the privileges of masculinity were more secure. They were a minority of their agencies' staff, and the more experienced workers scrutinizing their notes, reports, and decisions were more and more likely to be women. It was probably, for some, a difficult context. Little wonder, perhaps, that as they molded boys into men, they wrote about manliness as something only men could define and protect. It is sad that the certainties about manliness they perhaps carried into their work as protectors, guides, and defenders had real and sometimes painful consequences for their charges. Most concerned with creating distance and discipline, they were unable to understand why some of the boys for whom they wanted to do so much couldn't or wouldn't accept the manliness they prescribed and could only turn away. By enforcing one kind of manhood, they could sometimes create only misery.

CHAPTER 29

Confronting the Nagger

In their dealings with adult clients, the male workers of the Boston and Minneapolis agencies had to make some important decisions. Although husbands and wives could sometimes present a united front, the arrival of visitors and agents was just as likely to generate real conflict, along with antagonistic revelations. This was especially true in child protection cases, given the nature and possible criminal consequences of the accusations, but it was also common in general welfare, especially when wives or husbands blamed their problems on each other's shortcomings. Compared with their female coworkers, the young men working in these agencies narrated a different kind of encounter, because some female clients, such as Mary Flynn and others with long experience of welfare encounters, failed to recognize their authority over explanations and solutions.

Although Michael O'Neill's seductive Mary Flynn was an extreme case, male workers were more likely than females to find themselves toyed with, as women clients used some weapons the workers had not expected. The MSPCC's Theodore Miller, for instance, endured a variety of moods from a Jewish woman accused at various times of child neglect, public drunkenness, and making and selling liquor. Miller described hysterical garrulousness and a dramatic court performance in which the tearful woman held up her five children and begged for probation; on a subsequent home visit, "she claimed to be delighted to see agent and in nearly every sentence called him 'dear' and danced around quite lively." By describing to him the details of her as yet invisible pregnancy, the woman also gained some temporary respite from further action: "The home was extremely untidy, particularly in the kitchen where pieces of food and clothing were strewn everywhere. However, considering mother's condition, Agt did not believe it would be fair to mother to take neglect action at such a time."[13]

It was the first time for Miller, but not for male workers from his agency; other clients feigned pregnancy, "female troubles," and even nervous collapse. They clearly felt they had the upper hand. Whereas a female agent was likely to check on a bedridden invalid or to step around a strategically placed laundry horse, the young men of the FWA and the MSPCC seem to have been a bit easier to back into a corner. In one almost vaudevillian scene in the 1920s, an Irish housewife in Boston gave Walter Taylor her baby to hold while she continued preparing her children's lunch. Perhaps unused to the practical challenges that a squirming and unchanged infant posed to professional demeanor, Taylor asked only a few questions before deciding that the charge of neglect was "unlikely to be true" and beating a hasty retreat.

The stories that male workers told about clients differed from those of female workers in one very important respect: the men were much more likely to script a drama involving the particular burdens of men's unemployment and low wages. In one way, this gained them a valuable rapport with male clients, with whom most female agents and visitors struggled to develop much beyond a suspicious truce. It could also result in an acceptance that most clients were struggling against very difficult conditions. Agent William Bronson's relationship with the Revere family in 1922 (see chapter 16) was very much helped by his willingness to accept the claims of both husband and wife that their battles were little different from hundreds of others and that the husband's low wages and intermittent employment were the chief culprits.[14] In a similar vein, Thomas Sherman's recognition that an Italian father in South Boston was doing "the best he can" despite casual work, low wages, and bouts of unemployment helped him develop a good relationship with the man. It also helped him initiate a constructive solution to the family's chief problem: a boy of twelve who was very lame and needed an operation.

Both of these cases, however, also show that such a focus on the efforts and insecurities of male breadwinners sometimes led to false conclusions: if men were doing their best, then women were somehow to blame for the family's plight. While women visitors could be dismissive of men's efforts, almost to the point of shaming them for their inability to provide, male visitors could be just as dismissive of women's domestic shortcomings. Their support for men's particular problems could become an endorsement of men's particular prerogatives and a parodying of wives as a husband's worst problem. In his case, William Bronson carefully navigated these potential problems and invested trust in both wife and husband. Thomas Sherman, on the other hand, confronted with a "fresh, smooth cocky sort of woman," whom he later described as "very nagging and abusive" and "very haughty and sarcastic," clearly sided with the husband and, as far as can be told from the file, conceivably created a worse conflict than the one he found. The situation was eventually resolved only through a complaint of neglect, which forced the mother to allow an operation for the child.[15]

Men certainly noticed the dress and adornments of female clients, including one mother "outfitted in brand new fall clothes of the latest cut and of rather expensive quality" and a sixteen-year-old girl with a "satin dress, long red earrings and face rouged."[16] Compared to their female counterparts, men were also more apt to notice and remark on slovenly and dirty home conditions. On a rough count, the MSPCC's male agents were twice as likely as female agents to provide fulsome details of unkempt and unclean houses. Their details were also more likely to resemble the lurid pictures of traditional slum narratives. In one 1922 Boston case, for example, agent Calvin Fletcher described children "alive with vermin" and with an odor "so bad it could not be endured by anyone in the room," and in 1935 Milton Carman visited a house in East Boston that featured flies, rubbish, cheap magazines, "white tablets and a cigarette called a reefer."[17] There is no doubt that they visited some filthy houses; here, as well as in Melbourne and London, were the recognizable sights and smells of poverty's defeat and despair. It is also plausible, on the evidence of the files, that male agents were sometimes called into particularly difficult, dangerous, or suspicious situations. These included a Minneapolis bootlegging case in which Stephen Becker was asked to intervene by a policewoman and had to confront Inge Karlsson, a formidable Swede who was "standing on the porch with her arms akimbo" and "was inclined to carry on the conversation outside."[18] On other occasions, male agents seem to have been used as a means of shocking recalcitrant families; a female MSPCC agent reported with satisfaction that a visit from a male agent had "greatly unnerved" a woman who had seemed "untrustworthy and excitable."[19]

For the male agents, primary responsibilities for solving the problems of poverty lay squarely with wives. In a Boston tenement in 1922, for instance, William Bronson investigated a "miserable dirty" home, "filthy throughout and cluttered up with worn clothing. It was about as dirty a place as the Agt. had ever seen. Agt. warned the mother to start right in to clean up the place from top to bottom and if she did not he would take steps to compel her to do so." The father's responsibilities were also made clear to him: he was directed to visit Bronson at the office "with a view to getting him to move into a better house and neighborhood."[20]

The greatest problem of wives, however, was "nagging." It was a word rarely used by female visitors and agents, but it was often deployed in male workers' accounts. The charge of nagging was particularly common where women were seen to be overstepping the bounds of their legitimate domestic authority. In such cases, male agents endorsed husbands' complaints and even encouraged them in actions against wives. The Bryants, a warring Minneapolis couple, were first visited by Mary Kennan, who suggested that Elizabeth Bryant develop a definite plan and find cheaper housing. John Bryant had already spent time in jail for nonsupport and desertion of their three children, and he was now accused of having an affair. When asked about it, he denied it, but Kennan "told him he might just as well give the information about himself straight from the shoulder so there could be an understanding and an actual accomplishment in the end." The husband spent some time back with the family, but also accused his wife of immorality.

Into this situation stepped young worker Vernon Hull. He visited neighbors who claimed the husband was constantly visiting and also complained of late nights and loud quarreling. Yet it was Elizabeth Bryant to whom Hull directed his attention. "She seemed to be looking around for all of the objections she had ... and yet at the same time seemed to be trying to find things on which to pick on the FWA," he wrote. During the same visit, he described himself intervening decisively on the side of the husband when he "told her she would have to avoid nagging, forget the past, encourage him for the future." He also took a rather charitable approach to John Bryant's various misdemeanors: "[I] told her visitor was not going to tell them whether they should reunite their home or not. That was entirely up to them, but if they did decide to do so, visitor would be glad to settle their little differences and do what he could to make things run smoothly."

"Little differences" might have seemed a little dismissive to Elizabeth Bryant. Still, there was a temporary reunion, but within a year the police referred her again because John had left his wife and now five children (including a new baby) to avoid arrest for forging checks. Found, arrested, and sentenced to twelve months in the workhouse, he was granted probation, and the whole family was referred to the Department of Public Relief. They would reappear at the FWA in 1935, 1936, and 1937, often bouncing back and forth between the Emergency Relief Administration, the Works Progress Administration, and the Department of Public Relief with reports of malnourished children, Elizabeth Bryant's persistent struggles with illness and pregnancies, and John Bryant's drunkenness, which on one occasion almost landed him back in jail because he "threatened bodily injury" to a DPR worker.[21]

Vernon Hull's sympathy for John Bryant rested in part on his identification of Elizabeth Bryant as a "nagger." On the evidence, it was neither reasonable nor helpful to interpret the couple's difficulties in this way. It also represented a form of more or less overt aggression toward women clients, one that most of the male workers included in their case files at some point. In Boston male agents wrote of "speaking sharply" to untruthful, lazy, and nagging mothers about their "responsibilities" and the need to take care of their homes and children. In Minneapolis there were fewer male visitors, but there too Vernon Hull and Earl Pitt were especially prone to an identification of women that emphasized nagging and "demanding," though they rarely went so far as to deny that these women had legitimate claims on husbands' money and support.

Aggression did not lead to refusals of assistance, but it did create misunderstandings. At its worst, it led workers to choose harsh over compassionate interpretations, as in the 1931 case of a young Boston woman who effectively abandoned her baby with a boarding mother. She was arrested on a charge and attempted to explain the situation to agent Thomas Sherman. The child's father had denied paternity and then fled to New York for good measure. She had left the child, she said, because the workers from the Catholic Children's Bureau in Charlestown had frightened her and told her she would be sent to a reform home. Sherman took quite another tack, encouraging the court to find her guilty and to turn the child over to the Child Welfare Department for eventual adoption: "This is a woman of apparent loose character whose finger tips were covered with nicotine. She was dressed very daringly and was what could be called a bleached blond."[22]

In another 1931 incident, agent Theodore Miller was caught up in another family conflict when a police officer reported that a forty-year-old woman and mother of four children "goes out every night and is most often drunk." Ida Martino's going out involved cars and men ("among them negroes"); indeed, "just the other night she went to the bowling alley with a negro and came back dead drunk." Miller visited the home, which was "clean and in good order." Martino denied the accusations and questioned the MSPCC's right to confront her. Even though it was already clear that the accusations stemmed from her estranged husband—who said she was "a very poor manager"—and his sister, who had described Martino as a "heavy drinker," Miller refused to accept her denials: "[She] was advised that at present there were some indications that the complaint was true and that now was her opportunity to make things right. . . . Agt told her that he would come back and that if she continued to carry on as she had been, that she was due for some trouble." No further investigations were undertaken, and no further reports were received. By April 1932, Salvatore Martino had returned to the home. But a new report of neglect sent Miller back in August. This time the complaint had come from Ida Martino's oldest son, who was eighteen years old and had moved out, following conflict with his mother, to live with his paternal grandmother. Despite the strong possibility of another vexatious interfamily dispute, and somewhat unusually for such a vague and potentially unwarranted complaint, Miller took along a policewoman, with a view to removing the younger children (boys aged nine and seven, and a five-year-old girl). There was "no sign of trouble," the house was clean, and the children were "clean and well."[23]

Miller's aggressiveness needs to be explained. It was not evident in some of his other cases, including those with a similarly challenging mix of family conflict, half-truths, and lies. Accusations within families were always difficult, as parents and kin used stories of children's real or alleged suffering as weapons in their disputes. Perhaps Ida Martino's reaction to this second visit provides the best clue: "On leaving mo[ther]. said that agt. and policewoman were welcome to come back any time." In this case, real and reasonable questions about neglect seem to have become subordinated to a larger problem: Ida Martino's belittling sarcasm, her refusal to accept Miller's authority, and her willingness to question his right to exert and enact his professional responsibilities.

As ever, it is interesting to reflect on the kinds of clients particular workers found it easier to dismiss, deny, and denigrate and those who were never extended the constructive and collaborative possibilities of what the agents themselves called "real social work." For the men who worked in this complicated world of difficult judgments, those clients most likely to generate such a response were women who had more or less deliberately refused to defer to the judgments of men, preferring to undermine their authority. They might be morally suspect, but their greater transgression was exemplified in the character of the "nagger," the woman who criticized and belittled men and failed to encourage them in their powers and responsibilities.

. . . .

CHAPTER 30

Mr. O'Neill and Mr. Mattner

Michael O'Neill and the other men of the Boston and Minneapolis agencies certainly faced limited definitions of their possible contributions to care, protection, and policing, definitions that were narrowed further by what were supposedly their natural capacities and incapacities. Conscious yet sometimes unsure of their influence on younger males, they prescribed and enacted a version of paternal care that relied on control and submission and rarely seemed to generate trust or affection. Sometimes meeting women clients who lied and cajoled and flirted, they often seem in their case files to have developed a kind of protective distrust, even of apparently decent wives and mothers, which was not easily overcome. Behind even respectable women lurked the possibility of feminine wiles and shrewd manipulations.

It is particularly important to reflect on what their dramatizations said was wrong with men and with their enemies. Who robbed the effeminate boy of his masculinity? It was normally an overprotective mother. And who was the nagger? She was the bad wife and the inadequate housekeeper. She was a woman who unmanned men. It is particularly interesting that the nagger's most prominent sin was to undermine the confidence of men and their sense of mastery. The nagger in these stories didn't take over from men; instead, she failed to encourage them in the development and deployment of their just and natural powers.

Some of the stories men told in their welfare work during the 1920s and 1930s could have reflected a wider frustration with female power. Perhaps this stemmed from an anxious and rather immature masculinity born of their youth and relative inexperience. But these were also men who confronted dilemmas specific to their own professional lives. Their jobs were unusually unsupportive of the privileges they might have expected their gender to afford them, perhaps especially a straightforward or automatic authority over women. Indeed, those privileges were implicitly and sometimes explicitly challenged. Some female clients, if the risks were justified and the need not too immediate, decided to challenge male workers' right to ask questions and make judgments. Those clients were often being visited in their own homes, streets, and neighborhoods, which could further embolden their efforts to control welfare encounters in their own terms.

Although I don't want to draw too adventurous a conclusion, it is also important to recognize the novelty of the male workers' situation: they were young men being supervised by older and more experienced women. Some of the most crucial changes in modern manhood have reflected men's more or less anxious responses to the changing nature of modern womanhood, especially in relation to paid work and entry into the public sphere. Just as the senior women of these agencies were pioneers in merging professional and managerial authority with femininity, the junior men were pioneers of another kind. The young male agents of the MSPCC and the Minneapolis FWA were among the first men to work in both a broader profession and specific workplaces in which women wielded significant authority as innovators, leaders, managers, employers, and mentors. They

were among the first to confront the problem of meshing female professional authority and expertise, which was based on clear superiorities in
experience and training, with expectations of male privilege and authority. Their gender gained them no advantages in terms of salary or longevity, even if it may have made it easier for them to move into new positions
and careers. Essentially, they were men whose youth or inexperience made
them subject to the control and direction of older women. In the complicated weave of gender relationships, age and generation play a sometimes unacknowledged role in modulating the powers of men and women
alike.

In agencies such as the Melbourne COS, an entirely female inquiry staff
worked with a male secretary and an overseeing committee that included
but was never led by women. Despite the aging Agnes Cutler's occasional
exasperation with "men who seem to think they know everything," the
investigators there left little evidence of any tension between themselves
and Stanley Greig Smith, though they must sometimes have found his penciled questions, exclamation marks, and directions on their case summaries
intrusive and irritating. The same is true of London's COS district offices,
where women inquiry officers worked with committees headed by women
as well as men and with mostly female district secretaries.

In the American agencies, however, some of those workers subordinated to professional authority were men. And some of those doing the
subordinating were women, however reasonably and however much their
authority was absolutely consistent with the structure of experience and
training that they hoped was helping to turn social work into a profession.
If this created tensions in the agencies' offices, there is no record of it. The
greater mobility of male workers might provide some measure of disaffec-
tion, though it is probably more revealing of the fewer opportunities that
women were likely to find outside of welfare work in general and family
casework in particular.

Perhaps, though, some of these men carried something of the contradiction between manliness and subordination out into their investigations
and inquiry work. Perhaps their identification with beleaguered breadwinners, or their aggression toward belittling and disrespectful women, or
their insistence on authoritative fatherhood stemmed in part from the difficulties of reconciling that contradiction. Behind the "nagger," the troublesome wife, and the overly controlling mother there sometimes lurked,
perhaps, the older and more capable women who supervised Michael
O'Neill's placements and queried Vernon Hull's reports. In Melbourne,
London, Boston, and Minneapolis, an occasional sense of identification

between some female workers and clients would come to play a significant role in the changing dynamics of investigation and detection during the 1930s Depression or the Second World War. Before, during, and after that period, however, the occasional sense of brotherhood that male workers felt for men on the other side of the boundary of class reflected a different issue and a different kind of empathy. From their interactions, and from what they chose to preserve as the factual record, we are able to see what kinds of authority these men desired manhood to convey. We also glimpse what they feared manhood might become, not so much in the houses and streets of working-class America as in the professions and public realm of middle-class America.

These decisions also had different practical consequences for male and female clients. Male workers seem to have imagined and sometimes carried out a version of casework and welfare in which punishing inadequate or incorrect gender behavior took precedence over identifying needs and delivering either services or solace. In a number of cases, including, of course, Michael O'Neill's Mrs. Flynn, the men's more aggressive relationships with a client stand in stark contrast to a female worker's more constructive approach to the same person and often the same problem. At some times, though only for some of the male workers, this heightened their focus on restoring masculine authority even when there were doubts that this was the best or even an adequate response to a family's problems. It could also produce approaches to teenage delinquency and juvenile instability that focused less on understanding their fears and dreams and more on convincing them to obey. If the developing profession of social work created difficulties and ambivalence for some of the men who worked in it, their resolutions to those dilemmas could have real costs for the people they were pledged to serve. The making of masculinity is never just about the individual man; it is always about the other men and the women to whom that masculinity is displayed and who sometimes bear the consequences of its anxious wielding.

But there are other possibilities too. There were other men, such as Clark Mattner in Minneapolis and Thomas McNulty in Boston, who rarely used their case files to dramatize gender conflicts. Their professional archive shows little discomfort with women's authority and professional supervision. Although they are not in the center of the stage here, they need to be kept in mind. Although O'Neill and Hull wrote about the harridan, the seductress, and the nagger, other men did not. As mentioned earlier, most men stayed only a few years in these positions before moving back into the more masculine domains of youth work, industrial welfare, administration, law, or business, but others stayed for a decade or more. Some men found working with women and under female authority difficult. But others perhaps enjoyed a shared vocation and drew on the wisdom of a female generation in which the intellectual and professional prominence of women such as Mary Richmond, Frances Marley, Pearl Salisbury, and Joanna Colcord was hard won and well earned. In those other men are perhaps glimpses of a manhood that could come to terms with female competence and seniority and deal more sensitively with the supposed inadequacies of delinquent boys. Perhaps in what they didn't write and record, as well as what they did, they were able to recognize and even endorse different ways of being a man. Perhaps they were more mature and more secure. Perhaps they were homosexual, though this by itself has rarely been a safeguard against misogyny. It's hard to know.

In the history of masculinity, the main characters have been the man in crisis and those who strive to shape, determine, mold, and safeguard his manhood. This is as true of studies in the nineteenth century as in the twentieth. Such has been the case here as well. Yet perhaps it is important to reflect on the diversity of manhood in the past as well as the dramas and difficulties of its mainstream. Although some men attempted to reinscribe authoritative manhood and compliant womanhood in the stories they told and the actions they took, others responded to an environment that challenged those conventions in a way that quietly but effectively disrupted the insistence on male superiority. At any point in the history of masculinity, there are different possibilities and models for manhood, and real men may make choices and decisions that more or less directly challenge what is somehow taken as "natural."

Whatever the reason, I like to imagine Clark Mattner and Thomas McNulty as pioneers too. Less wary of women's power, they might have better understood the bond between a deserted mother and her children or the need for a woman to free herself of the burden of a lazy gambler, a fault-finding grumbler, or a hitter. Perhaps more interested in care than in masculine exertion, or able to link caring and manhood in a way that many men found difficult then and still find difficult now, they might have found a different way to be a man. At the very least, by making their choices, they show how manhood did not have to rest on punishing effeminacy and seeking the proper subordination of women.

I like to imagine, too, the effect they would have had. Like some of the more sensitive and empathetic women workers, they might have listened harder, seen the truth behind evasions and excuses, and trusted people when they tried to explain what was wrong. With them, perhaps, Richard Young might have flicked his foppish hair, swirled by the slow wreath of his cigarette smoke, and not be thought improvable by a thrashing. For them, too, the point of Earl Whitfield's story might not have been what he'd done wrong but what wrong had been done to him and why it had never been redressed. They might have asked why he was so afraid and tried to rescue him, rather than his manhood.

Conclusion

If the case files of social workers were all we had to tell us how they interpreted poverty, we might be impressed by their prejudices or by their self-righteousness and self-satisfaction. We might focus on their dismissals and disdain. But we could and should also be impressed by their courage, by their capacity to listen and to change what they wanted to say. I began this project convinced that these case files could show how the people of the past understood and dramatized poverty's origins and solutions. It was a way of asking them what they wanted to say to each other, and to the wider communities of which they felt a part, about a problem they took seriously enough to make the focus of their professional careers and in many cases their lives. If it is important to unravel and analyze what they said, it is also important to do them justice.

What I have argued here about the dramatization of poverty is advanced with all modesty; as I was inspired by the work of Linda Gordon, Karen Tice, Michael Katz, Beverly Stadum, Eileen Yeo, and others, so I hope that others might go to these files to consider, question, and challenge what I think they tell us about continuity and change, sameness and difference. In emerging work—by Mike Savage and Kathleen Martin in Britain or John Murphy in Australia—there are already significant new perspectives on the links among casework, religious and cultural thought, social analysis, and changing understandings of poverty, entitlement, and welfare.[1] In this work and my work, there is also a response to the call by Stephen Pimpare, among others, for a "new" history of welfare that takes the interactions between poor people and ameliorating institutions as the most significant and compelling drama.[2] I hope that such a "new" history will also and always pay attention to the possibilities of comparative and transnational approaches. I hope that the claims I have ventured about how shifting understandings of poverty could grow out of conversations between the poor and their interpreters can be tested and, if necessary, remade. I also hope that the dramatizations I have attempted suggest something of the possibilities of writing the histories of encounter, understanding, and misunderstanding that will always count among our most powerful ways of looking at the world through different eyes.

Certainly, the hundreds of case files studied here revealed some important variations. Gender mattered. Women and men looked and listened for somewhat different markers of inferiority as they examined the stories and surroundings of the poor; assumptions about the distinctive capacities of women—for benevolence but also for detection—could also generate different possibilities for interaction, collaboration, and conflict with clients. In general, shifts in the dramatization of poverty that emphasized circumstance rather than character came from women listening to women, normally in a context—such as economic crisis or war—that reinforced structural rather than individual explanations. Female workers better understood the struggles of single women, mothers, and girls, even if they tended to underestimate how unreachable their own journeys into independence and self-reliance were for the great majority of their clients. Male workers, on the other hand, were more likely to emphasize the disturbance of men's privileges as both a symptom and a cause of poverty and to insist on the creation of an appropriately resolute manhood as the goal of social work.

By the same token, comparisons across time and place make clear that as charity investigation, child rescue, and "friendly visiting" were molded into casework and social work during the 1920s and 1930s, the dramas that explained poverty's origins and remedies could differ and shift. The certainty that fortune measured character and the enthusiasm for the detective and preventive aspects of "charity organization" were very clear in Melbourne, though the faith in investigation was slightly diminished in London by stronger beliefs in poverty's intractability. In any event, neither certainty provided welfare workers with the tools to cope with the disasters of economic crisis and war, and some began to see themselves as taking part in a larger effort to address the forces that created poverty in the first place. Oregon's dramas continued to focus on the threat of the unfit and the unwanted, and it was here—and only here—that eugenic interventions in poverty's reproduction were embraced by the foot soldiers of social work. In Boston, immigrants had helped shape social work around a transforming, if patronizing, zeal for uplift, though that clearly excluded the city's small "nonwhite" population; in Minneapolis, that zeal was more tempered, but the faith in wise planning and the ability of anyone to rise held strong. These case files dramatized poverty's escape, not its inescapability. Yet even as these American social workers traveled into the 1930s Depression down a somewhat different road, they emerged from it with a greater acceptance of poverty's power, which dimmed their transforming ambitions.

Yet for all of that, this is not a comparative study that reveals sharp gulfs between nations and cultures or rapid and comprehensive change across time. There are shades and shifts, but there is also a strong degree of sameness in how the various investigators, agents, and visitors were building social work's understanding of poverty's causes and cures. In all these places, those who visited, investigated, and asked questions of the needy generally assumed, and generally continued to assume, that the poor were somehow deficient and would have to change. Poverty was persistently understood—and misunderstood—as first and foremost a problem of the poor.

This is perhaps where a "new" history focusing on welfare's interactions and, I would argue, dramatizations might be particularly important and timely. Case files show us how what social workers witnessed and heard was turned into stories that explained problems and solutions. They provide a window into the work that people do to make sense of inequality. In the end, I think these files tell us one thing above all else: that too many well-intentioned people made a tenacious mistake. Whatever the truth of individual circumstances, a good deal of social work then—like the war on welfare fraud now—rests on a larger and more significant conviction: that poor people don't understand poverty. It encouraged and still encourages its practitioners to believe that the poor should be distrusted. And that means you don't need to listen to what they say and the truth they know about security and insecurity, safety and danger. The danger is highlighted, in fact, by what happened when, in the flashes of lightning, that mistake was challenged, as some of the people meant to police charity and welfare began to learn that the poor were telling the truth all along. Those people, who were more likely to be women, had the courage to both care and listen. They managed to put aside their sense of difference from the poor and accept that those who suffered injustice knew something about justice. They began to understand that poverty's imperfections belonged not to the poor but to a society that stood by as they faltered and failed.

There is another and even more consistent view in these files, which came from the poor themselves. Even if it can only be implied from what was included and sometimes twisted in the reports of their questioners, the words of the poor have left their imprint. And what they said then is what those who carefully listen to the poor now and into the future will still hear: that poverty stems from vulnerability, not venality. What outsiders often take as the factors that cause poverty—dependency or inadequacy, for example—are in fact poverty's outcomes. Poverty overwhelms people because they simply don't have the means to make and keep themselves resilient. Poverty is a constant battle against despair and indignity and the anger and helplessness you are never allowed to share. And the poor also said important things about solutions. Poverty's best antidotes are money, jobs, and the measures that improve people's long-term health, security, and opportunity. Poor people want help and intervention, but on terms that make sense and in ways that reflect the hard realities of their lives. Too many of the people who claim to know the solution to poverty—from the right, the left, or the middle—do so because they also think they comprehend poverty better the poor.

As some of the women who appear in this book grew to understand, listening to the poor is difficult, especially if you also trust their answers as a first and fundamental step in an honest and effective solution to poverty. They'll say uncomfortable things that don't fit easily into conservative or progressive mantras. They'll be angry about entrenched inequality and angrier still about the disrespect and indignity that grinds them down. They'll appreciate statements about their needs and their suffering, but not when such statements continue to assume that middle-class interpreters will always have the last word. They'll agree with many observers about the paramount importance of work, especially for men and boys, but they'll suggest—with equal measures of irony and intelligence—that someone will need to create the jobs first.

The most important mistakes of the past stemmed from a conviction played out again and again in these files in different stories and guises: that poverty's remedies lie in changing poor people rather than changing the situations that produce and reproduce their poverty. It seems strange to have to say this again, to have to insist once more that poor people don't cause poverty. As Michael Katz has noted, the "serviceable qualities" of nineteenth-century scientific charity—most especially its focus on the individual rather than structural roots of so-called dependency—were reinforced in the casework of the 1920s (and, I would add, the 1930s) and "reappeared to undergird the 1980s war on welfare."[3] Or, as Alice O'Connor suggests, too many poverty analysts have participated "in what they hitherto had been trying to avoid: they repauperized the poverty problem and heightened the distinction between 'undeserving' and 'deserving' poor."[4]

It has proved surprisingly easy to forget what the poor say. Indeed, current discussions of poverty—in Australia, the United States, and Britain—offer one of the best examples of why history's vigilance is so important. History doesn't repeat itself. But injustice does. Without a sense of history, it has proved very easy to renew the harsh language of blame, denial, and disdain. Those who speak loudly of welfare cheats and the need for welfare reform may not copy the exact terms of seventy or eighty years ago, but they seem to share the sentiments. In Australia, for instance, "necessary gratitude" has become "mutual obligation"; "mendacity" has turned into "welfare dependence"; and the "undeserving" have become the "noncompliant." People are still said to be "truly in need," even by those who should understand that this begs the question of which needs are untrue. Some Americans continue to wage a campaign that targets the supposed "post-industrial pathology" of welfare dependence in terms very similar to those directed against the "pauper."[5] And now in Britain, in the early twenty-first century, people who perhaps don't know any better—and some who most definitely should—are speaking once again of people "deserving" and "earning," forgetting that the hard part of welfare delivery—as opposed to rhetoric—is who gets to be the judge, especially when some of the would-be judges have almost certainly never faced the hard decisions that poor people face every day.

It is likely to get worse. Cost-shifting governments have suspended or seriously weakened long-term and preventive programs, especially in crucial areas such as remedial education and dental care. Universal entitlements are everywhere diminishing, and with them the commitment to anything but a minimum standard for people who can't afford to pay. While the aged have a political presence sufficient to protect them from some of the slurs and suspicions that infect the public welfare system, the same cannot be said for the unemployed, single parents, and invalids. Indeed, the increasing inviolability of the aged—and the unwillingness of some of their advocates to join up with rather than belittle and marginalize other people in need of public support—is making things worse.

Like scientific charity, distrusting and punitive welfare attacks largely invented and insignificant problems. It aims to terrorize the vast honest majority by its assaults on a pathetic and often simply desperate minority. It pretends that a request for assistance—from anybody but "superior types"—usually masks a desire to get something for nothing. It is demonstrably ineffective at deterring the few true villains, who almost always manage to charm their way into charity. It calms the fears and satisfies the prejudices of people who don't know poverty, and it will be just as ineffective in securing the welfare of those who do. Nor will it actually tackle dependencies and weaknesses. It is difficult to think of something less likely to help the despondent and the damaged than the public welfare system being developed, in various forms, in Britain, the United States, and Australia: one that is terrified of taking risks, anxious about trusting its own workers, let alone its clients, and dedicated first and foremost to showing its tabloid audience just how tough it can be. It is not surprising that so many citizens in these countries believe the poor are feckless, deceptive, and dishonest. It's always been one version of what most people are ready to believe. They've been told it so often and so fervently that they have come to accept it as the only true version.

In the end, this is not a history of poverty, or social work, or the poor. It's a narrower study, with a specific target: it is a history of the mistakes that people who are not poor consistently made—and continue to make—about those who are. Among our most urgent political and intellectual tasks is telling true stories about poverty's origins and remedies. Whatever good it does for policy, this does not mean a study of poverty that spends a good deal of money finding out what the poor already know. It means listening first and drawing conclusions later. And in that task, the people who come closest to the poor have a weighty and important role.

Here and now, in the early twenty-first century, amid another debate about poverty, character, dependency, and idleness, it is important to stop this increasingly excited conversation about how much can be saved and make a simple point. Successful responses to poverty are most often distinguished not by the rigor of their inquiry, the strictness of their science, or the wisdom of the experts who design them. They are most often distinguished by their recognition that the poor, by and large, know something about poverty's origins and remedies. They are most often characterized, in other words, by a capacity to trust, rather than distrust, that part of the truth you can only hear from the poor themselves.

In the history of the past lies a different present and future. Those who go among the poor can be our witnesses to capacity and hope. Social workers can be our police and our detectives. Or they can be our ears and our consciences. They can act out our worst and most uncharitable fears. Or they can convey our sense of charity and care. They can insist that everyone must help themselves, or they can assert the wiser position, that because everyone will one day need someone to help them, care for them, and support them, the kindness we are prepared to show strangers is the most important kindness of all.

To do something, really do something, about poverty, more of those talking about the poor need to take the journey that some of these women took, haltingly, uncertainly, driven by a concern to care. Rather than tell the poor what they needed to know, they did something far more important, something glimpsed in some of these hundreds and hundreds of case files, something that stands out across the differences of time and place. They listened to the poor and tried to tell us what we needed to hear. They listened because they had come to know that listening changes what you think about poverty, and then it changes what you are compelled to do about poverty. It helps you understand that poverty is first and foremost an injustice.

Appendix 1

Sources

As for the workers, the names of all clients in this book are fictitious, and I have also changed the details of addresses, jobs, and other characteristics that might identify them. Following the method employed by Linda Gordon in *Heroes of Their Own Lives*, the case file numbers I have used are my own codes, not the actual file numbers. Any researcher who has the permission of the relevant agency to see the case records can obtain the actual file numbers from me.

All files were selected by a random sampling method, except that in London, Boston, Minneapolis, and Oregon, I did not read very short files or inquiries that were not pursued. The number of files analyzed in detail were as follows:

Melbourne	1,271
London	80
Boston	137
Minneapolis	107
Oregon	135
TOTAL	1,730

The high number of Melbourne files is partly a matter of easier access; I was living in Melbourne during the entire period of the research, whereas the American and British files were read during necessarily short international research trips. It also reflects the fact that in Melbourne I included in the sample a larger number of small files that contained very little investigation or information.

MELBOURNE

The case files of the Charity Organisation Society/Citizen's Welfare Service, along with published and unpublished materials, administrative records, and the *Other Half*, are held in the Greig Smith Social Work History Collection, Special Collections, Melbourne University Library. Paul Anderson has written the very valuable *The Greig Smith Social Work Collection: A Bibliography and Guide* (Melbourne: Baillieu Library and Citizens Welfare Assocation, n.d. [1987]). Further published and unpublished material, including case files but mostly relating to the postwar period, is held by the Social Policy Archive, formerly at RMIT University's Department of Youth Studies and now part of RMIT's School of Global Studies, Social Science and Planning. I sampled every tenth case file from 1922–25, 1931–34, and 1945–48.

LONDON

The case files, annual reports, and administrative records of the Charity Organisation Society/Family Welfare Association are held in the London Metropolitan Archives. Almost two hundred files (thirteen boxes) survive from the 1920s and 1930s, all from the Hammersmith and Fulham and what became the Tower Hamlets district (which included the former districts of St. Pancras North, St. Pancras South, Bethnal Green, Islington, and Shoreditch). Another three hundred or so survive from the 1940s, from Hammersmith and Fulham, Tower Hamlets, Greenwich and Lewisham, and Wandsworth. Of the eighty files sampled, forty-nine were from the Hammersmith and Fulham district and thirty-one from Tower Hamlets (mostly St. Pancras, Bethnal Green, and Shoreditch). There are relatively few short files, so those that have been preserved were perhaps regarded as more important or more representative.

BOSTON

I used case files from two organizations—the Massachusetts Society for the Prevention of Cruelty to Children (MSPCC) and the Boston Children's Aid Society/Association (CAA)—held in Archives and Special Collections, Joseph P. Healey Library, University of Massachusetts-Boston. The MSPCC was founded in 1878, and files of cases first opened between 1906 and 1939 are in the collection. Files from 1922, 1928, 1931, and 1935 were randomly sampled. Case files from the Children's Aid Society (1863–1922) and the Children's Aid Association (1923–1960) mostly cover the 1920s. The collection also includes administrative records, papers, correspondence, and publications from both organizations.

MINNEAPOLIS

The case files and administrative records of the Family Welfare Association are held in the Minneapolis Family and Children's Service collection at the Social Welfare History Archives, University of Minnesota. I used a random sample of both hard-copy and microfilmed case files, mostly those first opened in 1922, 1928, 1931, and 1935. I also read all annual reports and a range of records relating to casework, employment, and welfare policy.

OREGON

The files were drawn from the Child Welfare/Family Relief Case Files collection (88A-63) in the Oregon State Archives at Salem. The files were generated between 1909 and 1942, but most were from the 1920s and 1930s. They include files from various public agencies and were randomly sampled, photocopied, and deidentified by the archives before I examined them.

Cast of Characters

Dozens of agents, visitors, inquiry officers, investigators, and social workers from five different locations appear in this book. To ensure their anonymity, as is required by the archives and the depositing bodies who manage their files, I have changed their names and not provided details—addresses, precise educational qualifications, and so on—that would identify them as individuals. Public figures, such as the Melbourne Charity Organisation's Stanley Greig Smith and the Family Welfare Association's Joanna Colcord, retain their actual names, as do workers when their backgrounds or careers but not actual cases are being discussed. However, it is important to ensure that these individuals remain consistent to the case files that they wrote and the encounters in which they participated. To that end, I am listing below the pseudonyms used in each location.

MELBOURNE

Lillian Allen	Ethel Brown	Dorothy Macdonald
Margaret Baker	Elizabeth Cathie	
Celia Bedford	Agnes Cutler	

LONDON

Mildred Harding	Beatrice Tennyson	Marian Wilkinson
Dorothy Hedges		

BOSTON

William Bronson	Eugene Irwin	Sonia Moller
Milton Carman	Stanford Johnson	Evelyn Morris
Elizabeth Carter	Annie Lee	Zillah Nelson
Caroline Cheshire	Dorothy Lynch	Michael O'Neill
Joanna Clapham	Catherine Macdonnell	William Proctor
Foster Derrick	Rosa Mariano	Dorothy Putnam
Joseph Donnell	Evelyn Marks	Bertha Ricketts
Virginia Faulkner	Mary McGuire	Delia Rosen
Calvin Fletcher	Thomas McNulty	Thomas Sherman
Eleanor Graham	Theodore Mercer	Leonora Spencer
Derrick Henderson	Theodore Miller	Jean Stoneham
Benson Swift	Millicent Terry	Clara Weaver
Walter Taylor	Kathleen Walters	Laura Wells

MINNEAPOLIS

Hilda Bakke	Betty Graham	Leontine Kirkham
Stephen Becker	Patricia Griffiths	Elsa Lindstrom
Joan Benson	Rose Grinter	Hilda Lower
Inga Bergson	Vernon Hull	Clark Mattner
Cora Boehm	Vida Johnson	Esther Morwell
Anna Carr	Ilsa Kaufman	Margaret Murray
Ursula Dittmar	Myra Kemmler	Ingrid Neilsen
Cornelia Duchene	Mary Kennan	Catherine Overshaw
Caroline Ewing	Carrie Kennedy	Earl Pitt
Jane Gale	Ella Kirby	Helga Riegel
Lillian Robinson		

OREGON

Helena Atkinson	Alexandra Holton	Jane Lynn
Lisbeth Berry	Thelma Lineker	Edith Perry
Mavis Branston	Hiram Lyell	Ellen Stimson

Case Notes

These are the notes I took from the original files; they allow the reader to gauge the extent to which the six case dramas use a degree of invention. It should also be noted, however, that some of the dialogue is "borrowed" from other cases involving the same worker. All names and identifying information have been removed or changed; changed information appears inside square brackets.

1. Miss Cutler and the Case of the Resurrected Horse
15 January 1931
[Harold Alderman], from England 10 years ago, [residence] (8 years, 15/- week)
34, wife [Ada] (32), 4 daughters (10, 8, 5, 2), son 4 weeks
Painter, odd days' work for past 9 months, owes £3/15 rent, receiving sustenance, needs free treatment at Dental Hospital (ref agency)
Report [Cutler]: impressed favourably, family is buying the house, and also owe £1/12/3 to grocer and 26/- to the baker, Mr. [Alderman] "still suffers a great deal with his chest, due to war service. His wife looks well, but is attending the Women's Hospital for internal trouble, and will probably have to undergo an operation." They are in great need of a horse, as one died a few months ago, and he could make money by taking wood to neighbouring houses. Advised to make enquiries and to contact COS. He greatly needs the artificial teeth, for he has had none for 2 months, which is exacerbating stomach trouble "due to war service." He is given an order for a horse and a pair of boots on 10 February, and COS paid £4 for a horse on 19 March.
22 July 1931
Called asking for advice on placing children with the state and to say he was in rent arrears owing to an accident which prevented him working; "applicant had evidently been drinking. His breath smelt of whiskey, but he was not drunk."
15 October 1931
Called asking for fares for himself and wife, who is to be discharged from hospital, "again smelt strongly of whiskey," told to go through the Hospital, advanced 1/3 to collect her clothing.
23 August 1932
Applicant called with medical certificate: he has TB and will be admitted to Amherst Sanatorium in one week, but needs clothing and shaving equipment,

he is still unemployed and family receiving only 21/6 sustenance per week, he will apply for invalid pension and wife will apply to have children boarded back by Child Welfare Department; given order for new pair of boots, and order for pyjamas and flannels to be sent to Amherst, 14 September.

27 September 1932

Mrs. [Alderman] called: they owe 18 months rent at 15/- a week, and £4 in rates: the mortgagor will allow them to stay on if they can pay the £4 by 5 October. They are receiving 19/- a week sustenance. The horse had to be destroyed 12 months ago following an accident, cart also damaged and unusable.

15 November 1932

Clipping from the *Herald*: Mrs. [Alderman] and 12-year-old daughter knocked down by a motor truck and injured.

19 January 1934

Mrs. [Alderman] calls in: has been ordered special glasses costing £1/1 from Eye and Ear Hospital, is also pregnant, family living on 17/6 week invalid pension and 24/- week from CWD.

Report [Cutler]: visits house, "I noticed that he is not even growing vegetables. He stated that he cannot do this as it has insufficient water.... I noticed that [Alderman] had a horse.... I told [Alderman] that his wife had said on 27.9.32 that the cart was damaged and could not be used. He looked vague. He still impresses me as a decent man, but he and his wife appear to expect a great deal from the Government." She is given order for glasses.

28 February 1939

[Cutler] calls in while visiting another case: house much improved, [Alderman] doing occasional work at Golf Links, two eldest girls earning 35/- a week in Hospital laundry, other children well, though Mrs. [Alderman] again attending Women's Hospital for internal trouble, "all were bright & happy & were very pleased about being visited."

2. Miss Hedges and the Stupid Client

4 May 1933, man 24, wife 27, daughter 3, son 2, son 9 weeks, man is a porter and out of work 4 months; no visit seems to occur until a new application to the Clothing Centre in 1934 and 1935, "a typical hard-working woman, looked rather haggard and worried," rooms "rather grubby," but "the surroundings didn't exactly inspire cleanliness" and the house is "almost falling to pieces."

A new visit is made on 1 November 1935: "dreadful front room. A line of dreadful looking washing was hung across street, in pouring rain"; "a most untidy woman, obviously of very low mentality." Committee advises that the bedclothes in pawn can be redeemed but only if the wife will go to hospital for her confinement and not bring the 4-year old boy home from hospital; "she seems to have an unreasoning fear of hospitals & is really too stupid to invent a logical basis for it." In fact, what the client seems to be resisting is not hospitals per se but the linking of her confinement to the offer of assistance: she is making beds and tidying the house, and a friend of hers is present.

There is another application 25 October 1937 (there is now a son aged 18 months and a son aged 5 months to add to the previous children), referred by Clothing Centre, "seemed a decent sort of woman, but very poor" and "a very nice genuine sort of woman who seems discouraged by her continued misfortune." The husband calls into the office on 20 June 1938, "rather a heavy, dull type of man"; a report is sent to the Friends of the Poor, who are involved: "They have had a great deal of help from charitable sources and are regarded in this whole neighborhood as being quite unhelpable in a constructive sense"; the FOP is advised to leave them to "the statutory authorities."

2 June 1949: reapplication from National Assistance Board for help with a nightgown for wife's hospitalisation, as she is very ill with bronchitis.

3. Miss Wells and the Boy Who Wants to Be an American

3 October 1925: client is boy born 1912 (father born 1882, Poland, Roman Catholic, mother born 1892, Poland, Roman Catholic, 6 other children; child is running away, lives in [Dorchester]. Teacher says he "has none of the peculiarities of a delinquent boy" but truants and sleeps out, when questioned refuses to say anything and "seems to have complete indifference to any method of discipline." Teacher has seen no evidence of anti-social conduct. Father works in a woolen mill. Schoolteacher accompanies visitor to house because she speaks Polish. Fa. "seemed a very slack, irresponsible kind of person." Boy goes to Framingham and Worcester for two weeks in October 1925, examined at JBF 10 November 1925, JBF argue that "something drastic" needs to be done and the boy should be placed in foster home; worker there feels problem "is a combination of dislike for his home on account of his suppression and Americanized aspects and his abundant energy." Children's Aid will meet expenses, and he is placed in a home in [Grafton]. He does not know the "common decencies" of household life, mind is filled with the movies, restless and excited, says his father beats his mother, "has fearful respect for the CAA and JBF."

Returned to his own home in 1927, but runs back to foster home, says his fa is making moonshine, mo encouraging him to steal, has terror of going home, all very dirty; visitor thinks mo is "obviously abnormal," boy starts smoking in 1929, worried that his father will beat him severely for it; clearly sees his own family as "inadequate" and "overly Polish," says his mo is ugly and dirty, calls her a pig, weeps during interviews when confronted with the possibility of returning home, "he wants to grow up to be an American and not a 'Polack.'"

Begins working full-time in a store in 1930, cannot cope with high school. He attends in 1935 for a discharge exam: he is working in a market and living with his foster parents; see as a real success story, and CAA examiner writes "good speaking story." Also, his Polish name is crossed out and his "American" one written above it.

The file makes clear that the parents are paying a weekly board through the entire period, at least from 1927 to 1930, to the foster parents: this is the first time I have seen this in the files, and it seems to be voluntary (no record or mention of any court action).

4. Miss Lindstrom and the Fried Potatoes

1/17/24, woman born 1893 in Minnesota, Norwegian father, Lutheran, husband born 1881 in Norway, Lutheran, in US since 1905, painter. Married 1913 in Iowa, daughter born 1915, son born 1917, son born 1919, daughter born 1922, daughter born 1923, son born 1926, son born 1928, son born 1930. Came to Minneapolis in 1918, [address].

A closing summary of the first stage by agent [Lindstrom]: man not steadily employed during the winter but "when a visit was made he refused assistance. . . . It was impossible to make plans with the family as they were so indefinite and uncooperative"; unemployed again 11/25, employer says due to excessive drinking, wife "protected him in his delinquencies."

Wife applies again for help 12/29, husband unemployed and ill with bronchitis, "rather demanding in her attitude"; referred to Bureau of Public Welfare and given temporary grocery help; case reopened in 1930 when neighbor reports them destitute, referred to Department of Public Relief.

Details: first visit, worker Lindstrom, "wife could not understand visitor's mission and was inclined to cover her confusion by laughing nervously all during the interview. . . . FWA could do nothing unless [husband] was willing to acknowledge his need and accept help." They owe a large grocery bill in 1/25, wife "remarked that the groceryman had plenty of money and did not need to take theirs. Visitor tried to impress her with the fact that it was not how much money the grocer had, but the fact that the money was due him"; she "giggled throughout the interview and continually played with her hair."

November 1925, [wife] in office, "presented a very queer appearance because of the hat she had on. She was very nervous and ill at ease and played with her hands. . . . [Visitor] asked her why she had waited until the very last minute to ask FWA to help with plans and she replied that her husband had not wished her to come"; worker calls in husband and "explained she had sent for him because it was up to him to make the arrangements for taking care of the family. It was not right for him to send his wife on such errands that were embarrassing for him to face and he should not shove them on to her. He admitted that was right." Worker then confronts him with charge that he loses jobs through drinking, which he denies; "all during the interview he tried to evade the issue. He did not want to admit that he was a drinking man [which is actually, on the evidence the worker seems to have, a matter of his word against his employer's] and that he has not shown the right responsibility toward his family."

Another visit 3/26: worker is telling wife to sue husband for non-support when husband comes home; "he said he had heard what visitor said and no one could arrest him for non-support. He was taking care of his family all right. Visitor asked if he thought his family was all right and being actually taken care of when his children had only fried potatoes for lunch."

5. Miss Perry and the Boy Who Knew Numbers

12 December 1921: boy aged 14, Yamhill County, mother deserted in 1919, 2 other boys (12, 9), father reports boy has something like sleeping sickness, fa is a laborer, worker seems to find him a bit "rough." A local doctor committed boy to the FM Institution, "father objects to the confinement and is refusing to allow him to return. Boy was expelled from school for viciousness, a boarding mother says he masturbates continually and has a licentious mind," he is now in St. Mary's under temporary care. Case discussed with father by female CWC visitor; father returns him to FMI but then takes him out again. Father writes in, August 1922, he wants to organize a housekeeper, boy diagnosed as incurable [by whom?] September 1922. Father writes: "I have to do something with the boy and Lord only knows he is such a care.... I wonder if the Doctors would take him to experment on." CWC visitor thinks the county should board the boy pending a final decision and writes to the county board: "We really believe that under present conditions the child is going through an inconceivable amount of trial and suffering and we feel that in this enlightened generation, there is enough heart in any community to prevent that." There is a new diagnosis of lethargic encephalitis, and visitor is directed [by the board, it seems] to organize a commitment to Salem FMI. Father writes in again: "I hear he is to be railroaded to Salem. I had rather he would dy on oppration table can the Dr opprate with any hope tell them to try it." Commitment to FMI takes place in November 1922.

Included in the file are writings and drawings done by the boy while he was at his father's house one day; some are on the back of official letters. There are labeled geometric shapes, complicated multiplications, a poem about driving a car; there is a list of all the children in his town and another list "My Girls." On another page, he has completed a long division of two eight-digit numbers, without any other calculations or notes. He has written "Ha" on one of the sheets: triumph? So many forms of intelligence seem to be indicated. This is incredibly poignant: did the worker see this, look at this stuff? There is little evidence of "feeblemindedness" here.

6. Mr. O'Neill and the Seductive Client

9 October 1945, agents [McNulty-Derrick-Mariano-Rosen-O'Neill]

[Mary Flynn], born 1911, Ireland, husband [Patrick] born 1911 Somerville, son 1932, son 1934, daughter 1936, son 1938, daughter 1943, [South Boston]

Report by maternal grandmother, who says fa drinks and does not support, neighbor says mo is "chasing around" with young boys; previous contacts with BPW [Board of Public Welfare] and Family Society: mo has complained fa is intemperate and abusive; visit by [McNulty], fa is "very small man, ineffectual looking," house "extremely filthy and disorderly. . . . Mother sarcastic, positive of things she does not do, but with a very faulty memory. . . . Was told that this uncooperative spirit she was showing was useless but she replied she did not care. Agt said house must be cleaned up." Visits again, mo more "friendly" and house cleaner, "childlike in her change of moods," another visit is made, "a high-strung woman who seeks to gain an advantage by great show of friendliness."

April 12 1946: mo is "very surprised to have another agt [Derrick] visit case as she had been given to believe that there would not be any further investigation," but "she did not show resentment when agt called attention to the various unsatisfactory conditions in the home."

February 17, 1949: BPW refers, father unemployed, house filthy, new baby (son, born 1947), BPW reports family is "hopeless" and "mo is limited, fa is troublesome," "mo very fearful that chn will be taken away from her," "mo is fond of the chn but is so limited and mentally deficient that she doesn't see their needs. The chn has [sic] nothing to eat because fa uses the money to drink." Agent [Mariano] visits: "The house is well cared for with the limitation that it is a poverty-stricken home. Mo is a very stout woman, who apparently has had a great many dealings with social workers. As I came, looking for the house, she was sitting on the stairs and before I cd approach her, she said 'Yes, I am Mrs. [Flynn].' She immediately invited me in and started telling me her situation, before she asked for my identification. After about ten minutes of discussion, she said, 'Now where are you from?' She realizes that there is a feeling that she is mentally deteriorated. She started to say that she recognized me as a social worker because she had insight. She said, 'I'm not stupid at all.' . . . It is my impression from the short interview that mo is very immature, not very intelligent, but quite well meaning."

Home visit by Agent [O'Neill], 14 September 1949: "a large woman, very untidy and with an apparent very limited mentality. She had one defensive trick or habit of asking agt the same question he had just asked her. Sometimes this was rather embarrassing as many personal points were gone into. Mo talked very quickly and frequently asked agt why he asked certain questions." When [O'Neill] asked if the father drinks, "mo brought up the point about the possibility of agt drinking once in a while, which, of course, he had to admit." "Since agt does not believe she gets much chance to express herself, or to find a sympathetic party, he let her talk about her feelings of ill-health for some time." He then compliments her on having clean sheets. "As we were going to the door, mo touched agt's shoulder and insisted that he feel her head with his hand. Agt obliged and mo grasped his hand and brushed it against her forehead, and then down towards her breast, but agt detached it before it reached that vital point and grasped the door knob with it. Mo kept murmuring 'Don't be mean to me' and agt was unable to decide whether she meant, don't be mean from the standpoint of the agency function or from the standpoint that he refused to be seduced by her."

18 April 1950: another visit, "once again mo showed her resistance to any sort of help.... [Mrs. Flynn] does have a certain amount of hostility displayed toward our agency but she is quite pliable and easy to divert.... She does seem to derive a certain amount of pleasure from talking with me."

26 September 1950 visit: "very upset and disturbed as usual and spoke very belligerently to me. She told me she could not see why we should still be interested in her situation." He writes a closing summary: the problems are "centered mainly about mo's extreme limitations, both mentally and emotionally. There was no casework effort possible with mo because of her low IQ and personality degeneration.... Case is being closed as unimproved and because nothing further can be done either on a protective, authoritative or case work basis."

Notes

INTRODUCTION

1. The phrase is drawn from a very interesting book by Keith Gandal, *The Virtues of the Vicious: Jacob Riis, Stephen Crane, and the Spectacle of the Slum* (New York: Oxford University Press, 1997).
2. The nature and number of the files used in each place are described in appendix 1. Appendix 2 shows the names used for the dozens of women and men who wrote these case files and appear throughout this book.
3. Mary Richmond, *Social Diagnosis* (New York: Russell Sage Foundation, 1917), 106.
4. Mary Birtwell, "Investigation," *Charities Review* 4 (1895): 131.
5. Charity Organisation Society, Money Raising Committee Memorandum, April 1933, in Family Welfare Association/Charity Organisation Society, Records, London Metropolitan Archives, A/FWA/C/A1/18/1.
6. Carolyn Strange, "Stories of Their Lives: The Historian and the Capital Case File," in *On the Case: Explorations in Social History*, ed. Franca Iacovetta and Wendy Mitchinson (Toronto: University of Toronto Press, 1998), 25–48. A similar focus on the agency and interests of those who "consume" welfare characterizes another excellent collection of essays: Anne Borsay and Peter Shapely, eds., *Medicine, Charity and Mutual Aid: The Consumption of Health and Welfare in Britain, c. 1550–1950* (Aldershot, UK: Ashgate, 2007).
7. Eileen Yeo, *The Contest for Social Science: Relations and Representations of Gender and Class* (London: Rivers Oram Press, 1996), 249.
8. Linda Gordon, *Heroes of Their Own Lives: The Politics and History of Family Violence* (London: Virago, 1989), 17.
9. See especially Donileen R. Loseke and Kirsten Fawcett, "Appealing Appeals: Constructing Moral Worthiness, 1912–1917," *Sociological Quarterly* 36 (1995): 61–77.
10. Thomas W. Laqueur, "Bodies, Details, and the Humanitarian Narrative," in *The New Cultural History*, ed. Lynn Hunt (Berkeley: University of California Press, 1989), 204.
11. On this point, see especially Franca Iacovetta, "Parents, Daughters and Family Court Intrusions into Working-Class Life," in Iacovetta and Mitchinson, *On the Case*, 312–37.
12. Karen Dubinsky, "Afterword: Telling Stories about Dead People," in Iacovetta and Mitchinson, *On the Case*, 359–66.
13. Daniel Walkowitz, *Working with Class: Social Workers and the Politics of Middle-Class Identity* (Chapel Hill: University of North Carolina Press, 1999), xi.
14. Angela Woollacott, "From Moral to Professional Authority: Secularism, Social Work and Middle-Class Women's Self-Construction in World War I Britain," *Journal of Women's History* 10 (1998): 108.

15. One of the best examples remains Carolyn Steedman's book *Landscape for a Good Woman* (New Brunswick, NJ: Rutgers University Press, 1987). In an earlier work on Australia, I also emphasize how people living in poverty used apocryphal stories about good and bad welfare workers—almost always portrayed as middle-class women—to convey the broader changes they were experiencing: *The Lowest Rung: Voices of Australian Poverty* (Melbourne: Cambridge University Press, 2003), 38–42.

16. Elizabeth Faue, "Retooling the Class Factory: United States Labour History after Marx, Montgomery, and Postmodernism," *Labour History* 82 (2002): 109–19; Lucy Taksa, "Family, Childhood and Identities: Working Class History from a Personalised Perspective," *Labour History* 82 (2002): 127–33.

17. A similar point is made by Christine Stansell, *City of Women: Sex and Class in New York, 1789–1860* (Urbana: University of Illinois Press, 1987), 66.

18. Woollacott, "From Moral to Professional Authority," 85.

19. Lori D. Ginzberg, *Women and the Work of Benevolence: Morality, Politics and Class in the Nineteenth-Century United States* (New Haven, CT: Yale University Press, 1990), 8, 18.

20. Regina Kunzel, *Fallen Women, Problem Girls: Unmarried Mothers and the Professionalization of Social Work, 1890–1945* (New Haven, CT: Yale University Press, 1993), 48.

21. Walkowitz, *Working with Class*, 110.

22. Karen W. Tice, *Tales of Wayward Girls and Immoral Women: Case Records and the Professionalization of Social Work* (Urbana: University of Illinois Press, 1998), 51.

23. John T. Cumbler, "The Politics of Charity: Gender and Class in Late 19th Century Charity Policy," *Journal of Social History* 14 (1980–81): 99–111; Steven King, *Women, Welfare and Local Politics, 1880–1920: "We Might Be Trusted"* (Brighton, UK: Sussex Academic Press, 2006).

24. Elizabeth Lunbeck, *The Psychiatric Persuasion: Knowledge, Gender and Power in Modern America* (Princeton, NJ: Princeton University Press, 1994), 291.

25. Woollacott, "From Moral to Professional Authority," 109.

26. Ellen Ross, *Slum Travelers: Ladies and London Poverty, 1860–1920* (Berkeley: University of California Press, 2007), 13.

27. Gordon, *Heroes of Their Own Lives*, 298.

28. Roy Lubove, *The Professional Altruist: The Emergence of Social Work as a Career, 1880–1930* (New York: Atheneum, 1972), 48–49; Michael B. Katz, "The History of an Impudent Poor Woman in New York City from 1918 to 1923," in *The Uses of Charity: The Poor on Relief in the Nineteenth-Century Metropolis*, ed. Peter Mandler (Philadelphia: University of Pennsylvania Press, 1990), 227; Gordon, *Heroes of Their Own Lives*, 12–19.

29. Tice, *Tales of Wayward Girls and Immoral Women*, 4.

30. Lunbeck, *Psychiatric Persuasion*, 54.

31. Lynn Hollen Lees, "The Survival of the Unfit: Welfare Policies and Family Maintenance in Nineteenth-Century London," in Mandler, *Uses of Charity* 69; Bruce Bellingham, "Waifs and Strays: Child Abandonment, Foster Care and Families in Mid-Nineteenth-Century New York," in Mandler, *Uses of Charity*, 124.

32. Emily K. Abel, "Valuing Care: Turn-of-the-Century Conflicts between Charity Workers and Women Clients," *Journal of Women's History* 10 (1998): 32–52; Joan

Waugh, "'Give This Man Work!' Josephine Shaw Lowell, the Charity Organization Society of the City of New York, and the Depression of 1893," *Social Science
History* 25 (2001): 217–46; Beverly Stadum, *Poor Women and Their Families: Hard
Working Charity Cases, 1900–1930* (Albany: State University of New York Press,
1992).

33. Ellen Ross, "Hungry Children: Housewives and London Charity, 1870–1918," in
Mandler, *Uses of Charity*, 167.

34. Ross, *Slum Travelers*, 5.

35. Stephen J. Page, "A New Source for the Historian of Urban Poverty: A Note on
the Use of Charity Records in Leicester, 1904–29," *Urban History Yearbook* (1987):
51–60; Pat Starkey, *Families and Social Workers: The Work of Family Service Units,
1940–1985* (Liverpool, UK: Liverpool University Press, 2000), 5. See also John
Welshman, "The Social History of Social Work: The Issue of the 'Problem Family,' 1940–1970," *British Journal of Social Work* 29 (1999): 457–76.

36. Peter Bailey, "'Will the Real Bill Banks Please Stand Up?' Towards a Role Analysis
of Mid-Victorian Working-Class Respectability," *Journal of Social History* 12 (1979):
348.

37. Shurlee Swain, "Destitute and Dependent: Case Studies in Poverty in Melbourne,
1890–1900," *Historical Studies* 19 (1980): 98–107; Tony Birch, "Social Work in Post-
war Fitzroy: A Historical Study of the Citizens Welfare Service," in *Culture and
Control: Boundaries and Identities* (Melbourne: Deakin University, 1996), 26–42;
Nell Musgrove, "Private Homes, Public Scrutiny: Surveillance of 'the Family' in
Post-war Melbourne, 1945–1965," *History Australia* 1 (2003): 8–14; Nell Musgrove,
"'Filthy' Homes and 'Fast' Women: Welfare Agencies' Moral Surveillance in Post-
Second World War Melbourne," *Journal of Australian Studies* 80 (2004): 111–19.

38. Stanley Wenocur and Michael Reisch, *From Charity to Enterprise: The Development
of American Social Work in a Market Economy* (Urbana: University of Illinois Press,
1989).

39. Eric Schneider, *In the Web of Class: Delinquents and Reformers in Boston, 1810s–1930s*
(New York: New York University Press, 1992). My understanding of the history
of social work in Australia and the role of the charity organization movement
also draws on the work of Stephen Garton (especially *Out of Luck: Poor Australians
and Social Welfare* [Sydney: Allen and Unwin, 1985]) and Brian Dickey (*No Charity
There: A Short History of Social Welfare in Australia*, 2nd ed. [Sydney: Allen and Unwin, 1987]).

40. Sarah Deutsch, *Women and the City: Gender, Space, and Power in Boston, 1870–1940*
(New York: Oxford University Press, 2000).

41. Jane Lewis, *The Voluntary Sector, the State and Social Work in Britain* (Aldershot, UK:
Edward Elgar, 1995), 92–94; Kathleen Woodroofe, *From Charity to Social Work in
England and the United States* (London: Routledge and Kegan Paul, 1962).

42. Ian Tyrrell, "What Is Transnational History?" 2007, http://iantyrrell.wordpress
.com/what-is-transnational-history.

43. S. J. Kleinberg, *Widows and Orphans First: The Family Economy and Social Welfare Policy, 1880–1939* (Urbana: University of Illinois Press, 2006).

44. David Goodman, *Gold Seeking: Victoria and California in the 1850s* (Stanford, CA:
Stanford University Press, 1994), xxvi.

45. I draw this phrase from British historian Carolyn Steedman: *Labours Lost: Domestic*

Service and the Making of Modern England (Cambridge: Cambridge University Press, 2009), 215.

46. Franca Iacovetta and Wendy Mitchinson, "Introduction: Social History and Case Files Research," in Iacovetta and Mitchinson, *On the Case*, 6.

47. On this, see especially Nancy L. Green, "To Give and to Receive: Philanthropy and Collective Responsibility among Jews in Paris, 1880–1914," in Mandler, *Uses of Charity*, 197–226.

48 James Scott, *Weapons of the Weak* (New Haven, CT: Yale University Press, 1985).

49. Tim Hitchcock, Peter King, and Pamela Sharpe, eds., *Chronicling Poverty: The Voices and Strategies of the English Poor, 1640–1840* (Basingstoke, UK: Macmillan, 1997), 3–5.

50. Peter Mandler, "Poverty and Charity in the Nineteenth-Century Metropolis: An Introduction," in Mandler, *Uses of Charity*, 1; Katz, "History of an Impudent Poor Woman," 228.

51. Gordon, *Heroes of Their Own Lives*, 83.

52. The debate between Linda Gordon and Joan Scott is a case in point; see *Signs* 15 (1990): 848–60. There is an illuminating discussion of the exchange in Seyla Benhabib, *Situating the Self: Gender, Community and Postmodernism in Contemporary Ethics* (New York: Routledge, 1992), 221–23.

53. Scott, *Weapons of the Weak*, 37.

54. Dominick La Capra, *Writing History, Writing Trauma* (Baltimore: Johns Hopkins University Press, 2001), 40.

55. Antoine De Baecque, *Glory and Terror: Seven Deaths under the French Revolution*, trans. Charlotte Mandel (New York: Routledge, 2003), 10.

56. Scott, *Weapons of the Weak*, 350.

PART ONE

1. Executive Committee minutes, 20 July 1931, in Citizens Welfare Service/Charity Organisation Society, Records, Greig Smith Social Work History Collection, Special Collections, University of Melbourne Libraries (hereafter CWSRM), 1/8.

2. John Murphy, "The Other Welfare State: Non-government Agencies and the Mixed Economy of Welfare in Australia," *History Australia* 3 (2006): 44.1.

3. "Those Nine Women and Their Capable Director, Service, Sympathy and Efficiency," *Truth*, 30 January 1932, in Citizens Welfare Service/Charity Organisation Society, Records, Social Policy Archive, Department of Youth Studies, RMIT University (hereafter CWSRR), 47/726.

4. Executive Committee minutes, 20 February 1928, in CWSRM, 1/8; Executive Committee minutes, 13 April 1925, in CWSRM, 1/7.

5. Stanley Greig Smith, "What We Do with Your Christmas Money," *Herald*, 15 December 1928.

6. "Those Nine Women."

7. *Other Half* 2, no. 1 (March 1929): 4.

8. *Other Half* 2, no. 7 (April 1934): 69, 71.

9. Laurie O'Brien and Cynthia Turner, *Establishing Medical Social Work in Victoria: Discussion and Documents* (Melbourne: University of Melbourne Department of Social Studies, 1979), 23–25.

10. Paul Anderson, *The Greig Smith Social Work History Collection: A Bibliography and Guide* (Melbourne: University of Melbourne, 1987), 8.

11. Richard Kennedy, *Charity Warfare: The Charity Organisation Society in Colonial Melbourne* (Melbourne: Hyland House, 1985), 204.

12. Executive Committee minutes, 26 October 1931, in CWSRM, 1/8.

13. *Other Half*, no. 1 (June 1926).

14. "Distress Relief in Melbourne: Some Comments and Suggestions," February 1932, 2, in CWSRR, 2095.

15. *Thirty-Seventh Annual Report*, 1923–24, 11, in CWSRR.

16. *Other Half* 2, no. 6 (September 1930): 58.

17. *Other Half*, no. 4 (May 1927): 29.

18. *Thirty-Sixth Annual Report*, 1922–23, 5, in CWSRR.

19. "History of the Citizens Welfare Service," n.d., in CWSRR, 975.

20. Smith, "What We Do with Your Christmas Money," 17.

21. *Other Half* 3, no. 5 (August 1933): 51; "Distress Relief in Melbourne," 3; *Other Half*, no. 9 (September 1928): 94.

22. *Other Half* 2, no. 10 (December 1931): 105.

23. O'Brien and Turner, *Establishing Medical Social Work in Victoria*, 20.

24. The first weekly conference was recorded in the Executive Committee minutes on 23 November 1925, CWSRM, 1/7.

25. *Other Half* 3, no. 10 (August 1935): 114. This short account is based largely on O'Brien and Turner, *Establishing Medical Social Work in Victoria*, 1–2 and 19–29; R. J. Lawrence, *Professional Social Work in Australia* (Canberra: Australian National University Publications, 1965), 34–53, and Elaine Martin, "Amy Wheaton and the Education of Social Workers in South Australia, 1935–46," *Historical Studies* 20 (1983): 574–89.

26. *Other Half* 2, no. 1 (March 1929): 3.

27. Shurlee Swain, "Smith, Stanley Greig (1884–1970)," *Australian Dictionary of Biography* (Melbourne: Melbourne University Press, 2002), 16:272–73.

28. Stanley Greig Smith, "Report on Work or Labour Test," June 1924, in CWSRR, 1156.

29. *Other Half*, no. 9 (September 1928): 92.

30. *Other Half* 3, no. 3 (December 1932): 31.

31. Stanley Greig Smith, "The Problem of the Street Mendicant," September 1925, 5, in CWSRR. 1375.

32. *Labor Call*, 7 July 1932, 8.

33. In Melbourne the emergence of Catholic social work was particularly important; see Damian Gleeson, "Catholic Charity during the 1930s Great Depression," *Australasian Catholic Record* 73 (1996): 68–80, and Damian Gleeson, "Professional Social Workers and Welfare Bureaus: The Origins of Australian Catholic Social Work," *Australasian Catholic Record* 77 (2000): 185–202.

34. "An Outline of the Operations of the Charity Organisation Society," in CWSRR, 783.

35. *Other Half* 2, no. 7 (December 1930): 69.

36. *Forty-Fourth Annual Report*, 1930–31, 6, in CWSRR.

37. John Murphy, "Suffering, Vice and Justice: Religious Imaginaries and Welfare Agencies in Postwar Melbourne," *Journal of Religious History* 31 (2007): 287–304, 290.

38. "Notes of Meeting of Social Services Board of Inquiry, held at Parliament House, Melbourne, on Thursday, 1st March, 1932," 242, 248–49, in CWSRR, 2095.

39. Unaddressed letter, 14 June 1911, in CWSRR, 2008.

40. John Murphy, "The Pauper in the New World: On Not Having a Poor Law," unpublished chapter draft, October 2007, 2, gratefully used with permission.

41. These anxieties were first sketched in the pathbreaking book by Karen Halttunen, *Confidence Men and Painted Women: A Study of Middle-Class Culture in America, 1830–1870* (New Haven, CT: Yale University Press, 1982); more recently, it is being brought back into the center of our historical understanding of the nineteenth century by Australian historian Kirsten McKenzie in *A Swindler's Progress: Nobles and Convicts in the Age of Liberty* (Sydney: University of New South Wales Press, 2009) and her broader project on "opportunists and impostors" in the imperial world.

42. Citizens Welfare Service/Charity Organisation Society, Case Files, Greig Smith Social Work History Collection, Special Collections, University of Melbourne Libraries (hereafter CWSCF), ME31145, 27 July 1931.

43. CWSCF, ME32129, 10 November 1932.

44. CWSCF, ME32091, 3 July 1934.

45. CWSCF, ME32100, 11 August 1932.

46. CWSCF, ME33052, 7 June 1933; CWSCF, ME33055, 13 June 1933.

47. CWSCF, ME31029, 10 February 1931.

48. CWSCF, ME31035, 20 June 1933.

49. CWSCF, ME23056, 20 December 1923.

50. CWSCF, ME32120, 30 September 1932.

51. *Other Half* 2, no. 3 (December 1929): 25.

52. "Number of Visits in C.O.S. Case of Mrs Letitia D," n.d. [1932], in CWSRR, 1297.

53. CWSCF, ME31060, 20 March 1931.

54. CWSCF, ME31212, 1 December 1931.

55. CWSCF, ME23027, 29 August 1923.

56. CWSCF, ME31161, 19 August 1931; CWSCF, ME32010, 26 January 1932; CWSCF, ME32127, 2 November 1932; CWSCF, ME320973, 3 June 1932.

57. CWSCF, ME33078, 18 August 1933.

58. *Other Half*, no. 1 (June 1926).

59. CWSCF, ME24055, 13 October 1924.

60. CWSCF, ME31184, 29 September 1931.

61. CWSCF, ME31178, 17 September 1931.

62. CWSCF, ME31013, 22 January 1931.

63. CWSCF, ME31131, 7 July 1931.

64. CWSCF, ME31171, 4 September 1931.

65. CWSCF, ME32011, 2 February 1932.

66. CWSCF, ME32008, 29 January 1932.

67. CWSCF, ME32133, 7 June 1938.

68. CWSCF, ME32127, 2 November 1932.

69. CWSCF, ME33075, 1 August 1933.

70. CWSCF, ME32140, 12 December 1932.

71. CWSCF, ME31156, 12 August 1931.

72. CWSCF, ME31186, 1 October 1931.

73. CWSCF, ME31125, 30 June 1931.
74. CWSCF, ME32054, 29 April 1932.
75. CWSCF, ME33038, 28 April 1933.
76. CWSCF, ME32026, 3 March 1932; CWSCF, ME32065, 24 May 1932.
77. *Thirty-Seventh Annual Report*, 1923–24, 10, in CWSRR.
78. CWSCF, ME31070, 13 April 1931.
79. CWSCF, ME25007, 29 January 1925.
80. CWSCF, ME31160, 12 August 1931.
81. CWSCF, ME33071, 26 July 1933; CWSCF, ME32001, 4 January 1932; CWSCF, ME31217, 9 December 1931.
82. CWSCF, ME33061, 27 June 1933.
83. CWSCF, ME25016, 3 March 1925; CWSCF, ME33069, 15 July 1933.
84. CWSCF, ME32024, 26 February 1932.
85. CWSCF, ME33096, 9 October 1933.
86. Halttunen, *Confidence Men and Painted Women*.
87. Executive Committee minutes, "Note on Main Activities [April 1938]," in CWSRM, 1/10.
88. This is one of the many important points Shurlee Swain derives from her study of Ladies' Benevolent Society cases in nineteenth-century Melbourne; see Shurlee Swain, "Negotiating Poverty: Women and Charity in Nineteenth-Century Melbourne," *Women's History Review* 16 (2007): 99–112.
89. CWSCF, ME50840, 26 July 1932.
90. *Other Half* 2, no. 6 (September 1930): 58.
91. *Other Half*, no. 9 (September 1928): 94.
92. *Other Half* 2, no. 4 (March 1930).
93. *Other Half* 2, no. 8 (March 1931): 86; *Other Half* 3, no. 3 (December 1932): 27.
94. *Other Half* 2, no. 10, (December 1931): 105.
95. Stanley Greig Smith, "A Plea for the Workless," *Argus*, 7 March 1931, 19.
96. *Other Half* 3, no. 7 (April 1934): 79–82.
97. *Other Half* 4, no. 1 (March 1936): 4–5.
98. *Other Half* 3, no. 10 (August 1935): 112.
99. Letter to the Housing and Slum Abolition Board, in Executive Committee minutes, 3 May 1938, in CWSRM, 1/10.
100. Geoff Spenceley, *The Individualist Ethic, the Charity Organisation Society and the Evolution of Unemployment Relief in Melbourne during the Depression of the 1930s* (Melbourne: Monash Papers in Economic History, 1985).
101. CWSCF, ME31039, 24 February 1931.
102. CWSCF, ME22032, 24 June 1922.
103. CWSCF, ME24002, 11 January 1924.
104. CWSCF, ME23011, 30 May 1923.
105. CWSCF, ME32058, 6 May 1932.
106. CWSCF, ME31020, 2 February 1931.
107. CWSCF, ME31120, 5 August 1931.
108. *Other Half* 4, no. 1 (March 1936): 11.
109. CWSCF, ME25009, 31 March 1927.
110. CWSCF, ME31027, 9 February 1931.
111. CWSCF, ME31077, 23 April 1931.

112. CWSCF, ME33088, 18 September 1933.

113. CWSCF, ME31148, 13 February 1934.

114. CWSCF, ME31027, 9 February 1931.

115. CWSCF, ME31190, 7 October 1931.

116. CWSCF, ME32080, 25 June 1932.

117. *Other Half* 3, no. 8 (September 1934): 87.

118. Executive Committee minutes, 17 July 1939, in CWSRM, 1/10

119. *Other Half* 3, no. 7 (April 1934): 82.

120. Executive Committee minutes, 3 August 1945, in CWSRM, 1/11.

121. Executive Committee minutes, 19 October 1953, in CWSRM, 1/13.

122. Executive Committee minutes, 17 January 1944, in CWSRM, 1/11.

123. Executive Committee minutes, 13 January 1947, in CWSRM, 1/12.

124. Ibid.

125. "Report for Executive Committee, 12.1.48," in CWSRR, 783; Executive Committee minutes, 23 May 1949 and 16 October 1950, in CWSRM, 1/12.

PART TWO

1. Cited in Lara V. Marks, *Metropolitan Maternity: Maternal and Infant Welfare Services in Early Twentieth-Century London* (Amsterdam: Rodopi, 1996), 225.

2. Janet McCalman, *Sex and Suffering: Women's Heath and a Women's Hospital* (Melbourne: Melbourne University Press, 1998).

3. Hammersmith and Fulham case files, in Family Welfare Association/Charity Organisation Society, Records, London Metropolitan Archives, A/FWA/HF/B/02–07 (hereafter HFCF), HF042, 1 May 1935.

4. *Fifty-Sixth Annual Report of COS Council*, 1924, 9, in Family Welfare Association/Charity Organisation Society, Records, London Metropolitan Archives, A/FWA (hereafter COSR), C/B1/10.

5. "What Shall We Do to Be Saved?" *Charity Organisation Quarterly* 6, no. 1 (January 1932): 16–26, 18.

6. Kathleen Woodroofe, *From Charity to Social Work in England and the United States* (London: Routledge and Kegan Paul, 1962), 55; Gareth Stedman Jones, *Outcast London: A Study in the Relationship between Classes in Victorian Society* (Harmondsworth, UK: Penguin, 1976), 270.

7. Madeline Rooff, *A Hundred Years of Family Welfare: A Study of the Family Welfare Association (Formerly Charity Organisation Society)* (London: Michael Joseph, 1972), 355–65; Gertrude Himmelfarb, *Poverty and Compassion: The Moral Imagination of the Late Victorians* (New York: Alfred A. Knopf, 1991), 188.

8. Alan J. Kidd, "Charity Organization and the Unemployed in Manchester, c. 1870–1914," *Social History* 9 (1984): 61.

9. A. W. Vincent, "The Poor Law Reports of 1909 and the Social Theory of the Charity Organization Society," *Victorian Studies* 27 (1984): 362.

10. Eileen Yeo, *The Contest for Social Science: Relations and Representations of Gender and Class* (London: Rivers Oram Press, 1996), 257, 272; on the development of casework, I also draw on José Harris, "The Webbs, the Charity Organisation Society and the Ratan Tata Foundation: Social Policy from the Perspective of 1912," in

The Goals of Social Policy, ed. Martin Bulmer, Jane Lewis, and David Piachaud, 27–63 (London: Unwin Hyman, 1989), and the earliest account, A. F. Young and E. T. Ashton, *British Social Work in the Nineteenth Century* (London: Routledge and Kegan Paul, 1956).

11. Jane Lewis, *The Voluntary Sector, the State and Social Work in Britain* (Aldershot, UK: Edward Elgar, 1995), 82, 88.

12. Robert Humphreys, *Poor Relief and Charity, 1869–1945: The London Charity Organization Society* (Basingstoke, UK: Palgrave, 2001), 161.

13. Ibid., 189.

14. "Memorandum of Interview with the Representatives of the Senior Secretaries Group, July 30th 1942," in COSR, C/A21/1, 31, 5.

15. "Report of Discussion on the 'Aims and Policy' Pamphlet and on Case Selection and Case Finance at the Meeting of Council on 24th January 1949," COSR, C/A1/18/1.

16. *Sixty-Fifth Annual Report of COS Council*, 1934, quoted in Humphreys, *Poor Relief and Charity*, 183.

17. "COS at the Crossroads: Summary of the Points Made by Speakers at the Council Meeting on the 24th February [1936] and the Adjourned Meeting on March 9th," in COSR, C/A1/18/1. My understanding of this period also draws on Rooff, *Hundred Years of Family Welfare*, 135–65.

18. Bernard Harris, *The Origins of the British Welfare State: Social Welfare in England and Wales, 1800–1945* (Basingstoke, UK: Palgrave Macmillan, 2004), 197–242; Humphreys, *Poor Relief and Charity*, 96–110.

19. Rooff, *Hundred Years of Family Welfare*, 139.

20. Minutes of Fulham District Committee, in COSR, HF/A4/7/1.

21. Hammersmith and Fulham case files, in HFCF, HF007, 7 December 1932.

22. My understanding of women in the COS, as well as other social work organizations, draws on Ronald G. Walton, *Women in Social Work* (London: Routledge and Kegan Paul, 1975), 102–56.

23. Council Minute Book, 40, in COSR, C/A1/17.

24. *Fifty-Second Annual Report*, 1920, 7, in COSR, C/B1/9.

25. Pat Thane, "Girton Graduates: Earning and Learning, 1920s–1980s," *Women's History Review* 13 (2004): 347–61. See also Anne Logan, "Professionalism and the Impact of England's First Women Justices, 1920–1950," *Historical Journal* 49 (2006): 833–50.

26. Committee to Consider the Question of the Training of Social Workers, 1929–31, 5, in COSR, C/A69/1.

27. Quoted in George K. Behlmer, "Character Building and the English Family: Continuities in Social Casework, ca. 1870–1930," in *Singular Discontinuities: Tradition, Nostalgia and Identity in British Culture*, ed. George K. Behlmer and Fred M. Leventhal, 58–74 (Stanford, CA: Stanford University Press, 2000), 72.

28. Vera Brittain, *Women's Work in Modern Britain* (London: Noel Douglas, 1928), 59; Ray Strachey, *Careers and Openings for Women* (London: Faber and Faber, 1935), 158.

29. F. D. Meredith, "The Impressions of a Student," *Charity Organisation Quarterly*, n.s., 6, no. 4 (October 1932): 167.

30. Prudence Montagu-Pollock, "Change in Methods of Case Treatment since 1900," *Charity Organisation Quarterly*, n.s., 11, no. 3 (August 1937): 202–3.

31. T. E. Lloyd, "Social Service and the Volunteer," *Charity Organisation Quarterly*, n.s., 5, no. 3 (August 1931): 110.

32. Minutes of Council Meeting, 15 April 1918, 6, in COSR, C/A1/17.

33. N. M. O'Connor, "The Charity Organization Society," Occasional Paper No. 20, August 1917, in COSR, C/H/06.

34. *Fifty-Third Annual Report of COS Council*, 1921, 3, in COSR, C/B1/10.

35. "Report of Committee Appointed to Consider the Best Way of Making the Council and Its Work More Effective," Council Minute Book, 29 April 1918, in COSR, C/A1/17.

36. "Report of the Lambeth Council of the Charity Organization Society on 'Standardization,'" n.d. [1918], 16–17, in ibid.

37. "Charity, True and False," *Charity Organisation Quarterly*, 1st ser., 1, no. 1 (1921): 5.

38. Council Minute Book, 17 January 1923, 172, and 13 January 1925, 214, in COSR, C/A1/17.

39. Secretaries Meeting, 2 May 1928, in COSR, C/A61/2/1.

40. Lewis, *Voluntary Sector*, 97.

41. *Sixty-Fifth Annual Report*, 1930, 15, in COSR, C/B1/11.

42. Money Raising Committee Memorandum, April 1933, Council Minute Book, COSR, C/A1/18/1.

43. "COS at the Crossroads," in COSR, C/A1/18/1.

44. Both cited in Humphreys, *Poor Relief and Charity*, 127.

45. *Seventy-Third Annual Report*, 1938, 7, in COSR, C/B1/12.

46. *Sixty-Seventh Annual Report*, 1932, 20, in COSR, C/B1/11.

47. Memorandum on Interview with Representatives of 1941 Secretaries Group, 9 July 1942, in Minutes of the Sub-Committee to Consider the Memoranda of the Junior and Senior Secretaries Group, in COSR, C/A21/1.

48. Minutes of the Training Sub-Committee, 37, in COSR, C/A57/2.

49. Ibid.

50. Committee to Consider the Question of the Training of Social Workers, 1929–31, 31–32, in COSR, C/A69/1.

51. Minutes of Secretaries Meetings (1921–1935), COSR, C/A61/2/1. On the limits of casework training at this time, see Behlmer, "Character Building and the English Family," 70–73.

52. *Sixty-First Annual Report*, 1930, 2 in COSR, C/B1/11.

53. *Fifty-Seventh Annual Report*, 1925, 1, in COSR, C/B1/10.

54. O'Connor, "Charity Organization Society," 4.

55. "Charity, True and False," 6, 7.

56. *Sixty-Fifth Annual Report*, 1934, 14, in COSR, C/B1/11.

57. HFCF, HF017, 21 July 1938.

58. HFCF, HF019, 17 March 1938.

59. HFCF, HF007, 25 October 1928.

60. HFCF, HF029, 19 March 1940.

61. HFCF, HF001, 14 May 1926.

62. HFCF, HF002, 2 February 1925.

63. HFCF, HF023, 26 November 1937.
64. HFCF, HF032, 14 January 1942.
65. HFCF, HF024, 24 May 1938.
66. Tower Hamlets case files, in Family Welfare Association/Charity Organisation Society, Records, London Metropolitan Archives, A/FWA/TH/B/02–07 (hereafter THCF), TH016, n.d. [1943].
67. THCF, TH015, 20 July 1937.
68. HFCF, HF049, 30 June 1924.
69. HFCF, HF047, 17 November 1920.
70. HFCF, HF048, 7 February 1922.
71. THCF, TH006, 27 January 1939.
72. HFCF, HF003, 18 November 1925; HFCF, HF025, 5 December 1938; HFCF, HF011, 7 March 1928; HFCF, HF018, 15 November 1934; THCF, TH003, 27 April 1938; THCF, TH008, 3 January 1927; THCF, TH009, 28 August 1934; HFCF, HF038, 30 January 1942.
73. HFCF, HF003, 18 November 1925.
74. *Sixty-Third Annual Report*, 1932, 20, in COSR, C/B1/11.
75. Ian Gazeley, *Poverty in Britain, 1900–1965* (Basingstoke, UK: Palgrave Macmillan, 2003), 103–10.
76. THCF, TH020, 31 May 1940; HFCF, HF013, 26 May 1930.
77. HFCF, HF019, 19 November 1936.
78. HFCF, HF007, 25 October 1928.
79. HFCF, HF044, 9 March 1945.
80. HFCF, HF009, 19 October 1936.
81. HFCF, HF018, 15 November 1934.
82. THCF, TH013, 10 July 1925.
83. HFCF, HF035, 22 March 1944.
84. THCF, TH011, 8 July 1929.
85. HFCF, HF038, 30 January 1942.
86. HFCF, HF005, 20 November 1928.
87. HFCF, HF015, 30 December 1932.
88. HFCF, HF012, 20 July 1922.
89. THCF, TH004, 14 July 1936.
90. HFCF, HF006, 26 October 1928.
91. HFCF, HF021, 30 August 1935.
92. HFCF, HF026, 13 February 1939.
93. HFCF, HF020, 2 March 1936.
94. *Fifty-Fifth Annual Report*, 1923, 3, in COSR, C/B1/10.
95. *Sixtieth Annual Report*, 1928, 9, in COSR, C/B1/11.
96. A COS Secretary, "Failure," *Charity Organisation Quarterly*, 1st ser., 1, no. 16 (January 1926): 288–89.
97. *Charity Organisation Quarterly*, n.s., 1, no. 1 (1927): 154, 156.
98. "Unemployment Insurance and Public Assistance," *Charity Organisation Quarterly*, n.s., 4, no. 4 (October 1930): 167.
99. *Fifty-Ninth Annual Report*, 1925, 4, in COSR, C/B1/10.
100. HFCF, HF013, 26 May 1930.

101. THCF, TH002, 17 December 1924.
102. HFCF, HF005, 20 November 1928.
103. HFCF, HF011, 7 March 1928.
104. HFCF, HF007, 25 October 1928.
105. HFCF, HF002, 2 February 1925.
106. THCF, TH001, 26 April 1921.
107. HFCF, HF012, 11 December 1939.
108. HFCF, HF025, 5 December 1938.
109. HFCF, HF018, 15 November 1934.
110. THCF, TH010, 1 December 1930.
111. HFCF, HF016, 4 May 1933.
112. *Sixty-Third Annual Report*, 1931, 15, in COSR, C/B1/11.
113. Report of the Lambeth Council of the Charity Organization Society on "Standardization," n.d. [1918], 3, Council Minute Book, in COSR, C/A1/17.
114. *Sixty-Fourth Annual Report*, 1932, 20, in COSR, C/B1/11.
115. *Seventieth Annual Report*, 1938, 7, 9, in COSR, C/B1/12.
116. "COS at the Crossroads," in COSR, C/A1/18/1.
117. "Memorandum of Interview with the Representatives of the Senior Secretaries Group, July 30th 1942," in COSR, C/A1/1, 31.
118. Memorandum of Interview with Miss Eileen Younghusband (September 14, 1942), in Minutes of Special Committees, 57, 60, in COSR, C/A21/1.
119. Ibid., 63.
120. *Seventy-Fifth Annual Report*, 1943–44, 12, in COSR, C/B1/12.
121. Lewis, *Voluntary Sector*, 18–19.
122. Ibid., 105. I also draw here on Rooff, *Hundred Years of Family Welfare*, 169–85.
123. "Memorandum on the Function of the Family Welfare Association," 18 November 1949, in Minutes of Aims and Policy Committee, in COSR, C/A1/18/1.
124. Central Committee on Aims and Policy, Minutes, 21 April 1952, 260, in COSR, C/A19/1.
125. "COS at the Crossroads," in COSR, C/A1/18/1.
126. HFCF, HF042, 19 August 1942.
127. HFCF, HF021, 30 August 1935; THCF, TH007, 15 May 1941.
128. THCF, TH018, 30 June 1944; THCF, TH001, 25 July 1944.
129. THCF, TH027, 28 August 1940.
130. Ross McKibbin, *The Ideologies of Class: Social Relations in Britain, 1880–1950* (Oxford: Oxford University Press, 1990), 300.
131. Seth Koven, *Slumming: Sexual and Social Politics in Victorian London* (Princeton, NJ: Princeton University Press, 2004), 288.
132. Ibid., 222–27.

PART THREE

1. MSPCC, 47th Report, 1927, 23, in Massachusetts Society for the Prevention of Cruelty to Children, Records, 1878–1970, Archives and Special Collections, Joseph P. Healey Library, University of Massachusetts, Boston (hereafter MSPCC Records), Box 257.
2. MSPCC, 43rd Report, 1923, 21, in ibid.

3. MA099, 23 May 1928, in ibid, Box 18.

4. MA042, 1925, in Boston Children's Aid Association, Records, 1915–1960, Archives and Special Collections, Joseph P. Healey Library, University of Massachusetts, Boston (hereafter CAA Records), Box 10.

5. John H. Ehrenreich, *The Altruistic Imagination: A History of Social Work and Social Policy in the United States* (Ithaca, NY: Cornell University Press, 1985); Don S. Kirschner, *The Paradox of Professionalism: Reform and Public Service in Urban America, 1900–1940* (New York: Greenwood Press, 1986); Walter I. Trattner, *From Poor Law to Welfare State: A History of Social Welfare in America*, 6th ed. (New York: Free Press, 1998); Jacob Fisher, *The Response of Social Work to the Depression* (Boston: G. K. Hall, 1980).

6. Daniel Walkowitz, *Working with Class: Social Workers and the Politics of Middle-Class Identity* (Chapel Hill: University of North Carolina Press, 1999), 57–85.

7. Regina Kunzel, *Fallen Women, Problem Girls: Unmarried Mothers and the Professionalization of Social Work, 1890–1945* (New Haven, CT: Yale University Press, 1993), 115; Karen W. Tice, *Tales of Wayward Girls and Immoral Women: Case Records and the Professionalization of Social Work* (Urbana: University of Illinois Press, 1998), 98–99.

8. Charles H. Trout, *Boston, the Great Depression, and the New Deal* (New York: Oxford University Press, 1977), 20.

9. Susan Traverso, *Welfare Politics in Boston, 1910–1940* (Amherst: University of Massachusetts Press, 2003), 2.

10. Trout, *Boston, the Great Depression, and the New Deal*, 16.

11. Linda Gordon, *Heroes of Their Own Lives: The Politics and History of Family Violence* (London: Virago, 1989), 35.

12. Trout, *Boston, the Great Depression, and the New Deal*, 33.

13. Ibid., 307–8.

14. Relationships between middle- and working-class women in Boston are particularly well described in Sarah Deutsch, *Women and the City: Gender, Space, and Power in Boston, 1870–1940* (New York: Oxford University Press, 2000), 161–218.

15. MSPCC, 42nd Report, 1922, 20, in MSPCC Records, Box 257. Caseloads are taken from all of the reports (1922–29) in ibid.

16. Gordon, *Heroes of Their Own Lives*, 63.

17. Ibid., 61–68. See also Joyce Antler and Stephen Antler, "From Child Rescue to Family Protection: The Evolution of the Child Protective Movement in the United States," *Children and Youth Services Review* 1 (1979): 177–204. On children, delinquency, and law in Boston during this period, I rely especially on Eric C. Schneider, *In the Web of Class: Delinquents and Reformers in Boston, 1810s–1930s* (New York: New York University Press, 1992), 148–87.

18. MSPCC, 43rd Report, 1923, 21, in MSPCC Records, Box 257.

19. MSPCC, 47th Report, 1927, 22, in ibid.

20. These descriptions are derived from MSPCC bulletins between January 1928 and March 1936, in "Early Papers of the MSPCC," MSPCC Records.

21. Gordon, *Heroes of Their Own Lives*, 21.

22. Tice, *Tales of Wayward Girls*, 143.

23. MA008, 6 February 1922, in MSPCC Records, Box 126; MA126, 16 September 1931 in ibid., Box 206; MA033, 20 January 1922, in ibid., Box 127.

24. MA034, 25 January 1922, in ibid.

25. MA123, 29 August 1931, in ibid., Box 206.

26. MA018, 16 March 1922, in ibid., Box 126.

27. MA030, 16 May 1922, in ibid., Box 127.

28. MA015, 2 March 1922, in ibid., Box 126.

29. MA016, 11 April 1922, in ibid.

30. MA020, 17 March 1922, in ibid.

31. MA088, 24 May 1928, in ibid., Box 174.

32. MA102, 4 June 1928, in ibid.

33. MA132, 6 October 1931, in ibid., Box 207.

34. MA017, 6 April 1922, in ibid., Box 126.

35. MA075, 27 July 1935, in ibid., Box 249.

36. MA026, 14 July 1922, in ibid., Box 127.

37. MA098, 6 February 1930, in ibid., Box 174.

38. MA035, 18 January 1922, in ibid., Box 127.

39. MA069, 9 September 1935, in ibid., Box 249.

40. MA009, 25 January 1922, in ibid., Box 126.

41. MA004, 16 January 1922, in ibid.

42. MA012, 20 February 1922, in ibid.

43. MA021, 26 April 1922, in ibid., Box 127.

44. MA039, 20 February 1922, in ibid.

45. MA023, 9 June 1922, in ibid.

46. Gordon, *Heroes of Their Own Lives*, 68.

47. MSPCC, 42nd Report, 1922, 6, in MSPCC Records, Box 257.

48. MSPCC, 47th Report, 1927, 23, in ibid.

49. MA051, 18 June 1925, in CAA Records, Box 10.

50. MA050, 29 September 1925, in ibid.

51. Tice, *Tales of Wayward Girls*, 176.

52. MA052, 4 December 1925, in CAA Records, Box 10.

53. Yoosun Park and Susan P. Kemp, "'Little Alien Colonies': Representations of Immigrants and Their Neighborhoods in Social Work Discourse, 1875–1924," *Social Service Review* 80 (2006): 728.

54. MA125, 4 February 1932, in MSPCC Records, Box 206.

55. MA061, 15 August 1935, in ibid., Box 249.

56. Gordon, *Heroes of Their Own Lives*, 187.

57. MA058, 12 July 1935, in MSPCC Records, Box 249.

58. MA045, 13 October 1925, in CAA Records, Box 10.

59. S. J. Kleinberg, *Widows and Orphans First: The Family Economy and Social Welfare Policy, 1880–1939* (Urbana: University of Illinois Press, 2006), 84–90, 93–95.

60. MA044, 19 October 1925, in CAA Records, Box 10.

61. MA001, 17 March 1922, in MSPCC Records, Box 126.

62. MA041, 24 September 1925, in CAA Records, Box 10.

63. MA093, 24 May 1928, in MSPCC Records, Box 174.

64. MA029, 8 May 1922, in ibid., Box 127.

65. *Annual Report*, 1932, in MSPCC Records, Box 257. On this period, see also Traverso, *Welfare Politics in Boston*, 90–115.

66. *Annual Report*, 1933, in MSPCC Records, Box 257.

67. Beverly Stadum, "The Uneasy Marriage of Professional Social Work and Public Relief, 1870–1940," in *The Professionalization of Poverty: Social Work and the Poor in the Twentieth Century*, ed. Gary R. Lowe and P. Nelson Reid (New York: Aldine de Gruyter, 1999), 37.

68. Gary R. Lowe and P. Nelson Reid, "Poverty, Public Welfare and Professionalism: Opportunity Lost," in *Professionalization of Poverty*, ed. Lowe and Reid, 90.

69. Walkowitz, *Working with Class*, 121.

70. Gordon, *Heroes of Their Own Lives*, 149.

71. Ibid., 152.

72. These are the real names of agents first employed during the 1930s.

73. MA047, 30 November 1925, in CAA Records, Box 10.

74. MA100, 30 May 1928, in MSPCC Records, Box 174.

75. MA112, 19 August 1931, in ibid.

76. MA105, 18 November 1936, in ibid.

77. MA107, 15 July 1939, in ibid.

78. MA052, 4 December 1925, in CAA Records, Box 10.

79. MA136, 29 September 1931, in MSPCC Records, Box 207.

80. MA108, 31 October 1941, in ibid., Box 206.

81. Alice O'Connor, *Poverty Knowledge: Social Science, Social Policy and the Poor in Twentieth-Century U.S. History* (Princeton, NJ: Princeton University Press, 2001), 61.

PART FOUR

1. Beverly Stadum, *Poor Women and Their Families: Hard Working Charity Cases, 1900–1930* (Albany: State University of New York Press, 1992).

2. "The Associated Charities" (1922), in Minneapolis Family and Children's Service, Records, ca. 1889–1960, SW75, Social Welfare History Archives, University of Minnesota Libraries (hereafter FWA Records), Box 1, Folder 4. My account of the charity and welfare agencies in Minneapolis also relies on David J. Klaassen, "'The Deserving Poor': Beginnings of Organized Charity in Minneapolis," *Hennepin County History* 47 (1988): 15–25; Robert G. Neal, "Welfare in the Early Years of Hennepin County (1857–1934)," *Hennepin History* 59 (2000): 23–34; Robert G. Neal, "Welfare in Hennepin County: Depression, War, and Civil Rights (1934–65)," *Hennepin History* 60 (2001): 5–19; and Beverly Stadum, "Family Casework with the Minneapolis Poor, 1900–1930," *Minnesota History* 51 (1988): 43–47.

3. Aims of the Associated Charities, n.d. [1915], in FWA Records, Box 1, Folder 4.

4. "Department of Relief and Service," draft report, 1915, 9, in ibid. My understanding and account of the history of the FWA is also much influenced by Stadum, *Poor Women and Their Families*, 12–18.

5. Draft report of an Associated Charities study of family casework in Minneapolis, n.d. [1921], in FWA Records, Box 8, Folder 12.

6. Board of Directors, Minutes, 18 January 1922, in FWA Records, Box 5, Folder 8.

7. Board of Directors, Minutes, 13 June 1922 and 26 April 1922, in ibid.

8. Board of Directors, Minutes, 18 October 1922 and 4 September 24, in FWA

Records, Box 5, Folder 9. See also a chronology of the agency between 1926 and 1935 in FWA Records, Box 1, Folder 5.

9. Board of Directors, Minutes, 5 October 1927, in FWA Records, Box 5, Folder 12, and 20 January 1926, in FWA Records, Box 5, Folder 11.

10. Board of Directors, Minutes, 20 February 1924, in FWA Records, Box 5, Folder 9.

11. Family Welfare Association, untitled document showing caseloads from 1915–1935, in FWA Records, Box 8, Folder 2. In these same years, the total caseload was 2,189 (1918), 2,753 (1920), 3,814 (1922), and 5,447 (1925).

12. Board of Directors, Minutes, 16 January 1930, in FWA Records, Box 5, Folder 14.

13. Minneapolis Council of Social Agencies, Community Survey of Social and Health Work in Minneapolis, Agency Report: Family Welfare Association, July 1938, 32, in FWA Records, Box 8, Folder 2.

14. William Millikan, *Union against Unions: The Minneapolis Citizen's Alliance and Its Fight against Organized Labor, 1903–1947* (Minneapolis: Minnesota Historical Society Press, 2001). My understanding of Minneapolis in this period also draws on Elizabeth Faue, *Community of Suffering and Struggle: Women, Men and the Labor Movement in Minneapolis, 1915–1945* (Chapel Hill: University of North Carolina Press, 1991).

15. M090, Minneapolis FWA, 22 September 1922, in Minneapolis Family and Children's Service, Case Records, ca. 1895–1945, Social Welfare History Archives, University of Minnesota Libraries, SW Film 19 (hereafter FWACR), Reel 178.

16. M082, 29 January 1924, in ibid.

17. M007, 16 September 1935, in FWA Records, Box 20.

18. M045, 11 November 1932, in FWA Records, Box 19.

19. M039, 5 February 1924, in FWACR, Reel 225.

20. M010, 26 December 1935, in FWA Records, Box 20.

21. M094, 20 April 1931, in FWA Records, Box 18.

22. M066, 4 January 1934, in FWA Records, Box 19.

23. M101, 10 June 1929, in FWA Records, Box 18.

24. M033, 15 January 1924, in FWACR, Reel 225.

25. M035, 22 January 1924, in ibid.

26. M038, 31 January 1924, in ibid.

27. M036, 26 March 1934, in ibid.

28. M048, 29 November 1932, in FWA Records, Box 19; M091, 16 October 1922, in FWACR, Reel 178.

29. M097, 24 October 1925, in FWA Records, Box 18.

30. M052, 15 December 1933, in FWA Records, Box 19; M055, 23 December 1933, in ibid.

31. M065, 6 August 1935, in ibid.

32. Stadum, *Poor Women and Their Families*, 124.

33. M088, 14 September 1922, in FWACR, Reel 178.

34. On these conflicts and relationships, I draw also on Stadum, *Poor Women and Their Families*, 133–55.

35. M047, 22 November 1932, in FWA Records, Box 19.

36. M025, 13 April 1936, in FWA Records, Box 20.

37. M055, 6 December 1933, in FWA Records, Box 19.
38. M068, 22 January 1934, in ibid.
39. M080, 11 December 1923, in FWACR, Reel 224.
40. M096, 5 May 1927, in FWA Records, Box 18.
41. M035, 22 January 1924, in FWACR, Reel 225.
42. M004, 21 February 1935, in FWA Records, Box 20.
43. M103, 28 March 1934, in FWA Records, Box 18.
44. M100, 5 July 1934, in ibid.
45. M020, 9 November 1936, in FWA Records, Box 20.
46. M056, 28 December 1933, in FWA Records, Box 19.
47. M063, 22 October 1934, in ibid.
48. M070, 15 March 1934, in ibid.
49. M049, 5 December 1932, in ibid.
50. M063, 22 October 1934, in FWA Records, Box 19.
51. Board of Directors, Minutes, 20 January 1932, FWA Records, Box 6, Folder 1.
52. "A Five Year Analysis of Social Data regarding Clients Given Full Care by the Minneapolis FWA from 1928 to 1932," in FWA Records, Box 8, Folder 3.
53. Neal, "Welfare in Hennepin County."
54. M019, 16 October 1936, in FWA Records, Box 20.
55. "Statement of Function" [n.d., 1942?], in FWA Records, Box 1, Folder 5.
56. Minneapolis Council of Social Agencies, "Community Survey of Social and Health Work in Minneapolis Agency Report: Family Welfare Association," July 1938, in FWA Records, Box 8, Folder 2.
57. FWA Records, Box 7, Folder 11. A study of a Chicago agency shows a similar timing for this transition; see Martha Heineman Field, "Social Casework Practice during the 'Psychiatric Deluge,'" *Social Science Review* 54 (1980): 482–507.
58. M001, 7 June 1935, in FWA Records, Box 20.
59. M024, 3 March 1937, in ibid.; M026, 29 May 1937, in ibid.
60. M050, 24 August 1932, in FWA Records, Box 19.
61. M068, 22 January 1934, in ibid.

PART FIVE

1. OR53 [Associated Charities], 11 December 1914, in Oregon Public Welfare Commission, Child Welfare/Family Relief Case Files, Oregon State Archives, 88A-63 (hereafter OPWC Records), Folder 71/8.
2. OR131 [Public Welfare Bureau], 24 May 1924, in OPWC Records, Folder 74/12.
3. OR13 [Public Welfare Bureau], 11 April 1933, in OPWC Records, Folder 70/16.
4. W. H. Slingerland, *Child Welfare in Oregon* (Salem: Oregon Child Welfare Commission, 1919); Mrs. Frederic Schoff, "The National Congress of Mothers and Parent-Teacher Associations," *Annals of the American Academy of Political and Social Science* 67 (1916): 139–47.
5. ORM6 [Child Welfare Commission], 19 November 1924, in OPWC Records, Folder 70/1.
6. ORM20 [Child Welfare Commission], 7 February 1922, in ibid.
7. OR24 [Child Welfare Commission], n.d. [1924?], in OPWC Records, Folder 70/20.

8. ORM15 [Child Welfare Commission], 11 June 1923, in OPWC Records, Folder 70/1.

9. OR111 [Child Welfare Commission], 19 August 1927, in OPWC Records, Folder 73/8.

10. ORM16 [Child Welfare Commission], 19 November 1922, in OPWC Records, Folder 70/1.

11. OR3 [Child Welfare Commission], 15 September 1920, in OPWC Records, Folder 70/8.

12. OR66 [Child Welfare Commission], 13 April 1925, in OPWC Records, Folder 71/20.

13. ORM14 [Child Welfare Commission], n.d., in OPWC Records, Folder 70/1.

14. OR23, 28 January 1932, in OPWC Records, Folder 70/20.

15. OR63 [Child Welfare Commission], 19 January 1933, in OPWC Records, Folder 71/20.

16. OR133 [Public Welfare Bureau], 9 February 1931, in OPWC Records, Folder 74/12.

17. OR120 [Public Welfare Bureau], 25 February 1932, in OPWC Records, Folder 73/16; OR118 [Public Welfare Bureau], 28 February 1933, in ibid.

18. OR110 [Public Welfare Bureau], 18 May 1934, in OPWC Records, Folder 73/8; OR10 [Public Welfare Bureau], 12 May 1941, in OPWC Records, Folder 70/12; OR95 [Public Welfare Bureau], 6 October 1931, in OPWC Records, Folder 72/20.

19. OR92 [State Relief Commission], 21 December 1932, in OPWC Records, Folder 72/16.

20. ORM15 [Child Welfare Commission], 11 June 1923, in OPWC Records, Folder 70/1; OR16 [Public Welfare Bureau], 1 December 1933, in OPWC Records, Folder 70/16.

21. OR45 [State Relief Committee], 13 June 1934, in OPWC Records, Folder 71/1.

22. OR27 [Public Welfare Bureau], 8 February 1933, in OPWC Records, Folder 70/20.

23. OR124 [Public Welfare Bureau], 21 December 1925, in OPWC Records, Folder 74/1.

24. OR41 [Child Welfare Commission], 22 March 1923, in OPWC Records, Folder 71/1.

25. OR121 [Child Welfare Commission], 16 January 1924, in OPWC Records, Folder 74/1.

26. OR49 [State Relief Committee], 7 February 1931, in OPWC Records, Folder 71/4.

27. OR92 [State Relief Committee], 21 December 1932, in OPWC Records, Folder 72/16.

28. OR95 [Public Welfare Bureau], 6 October 1931, in OPWC Records, Folder 72/20.

29. OR108, 1 April 1913, in OPWC Records, Folder 73/8.

30. OR67 [Child Welfare Commission], 3 January 1923, in OPWC Records, Folder 71/20.

31. OR91 [Public Welfare Bureau], 26 January 1928, in OPWC Records, Folder 72/16.

32. Some recent and excellent local studies include Robert D. Johnston, *The Radical Middle Class: Populist Democracy and the Question of Capitalism in Progressive Era Portland* (Princeton, NJ: Princeton University Press, 2003), Dmitri Palmateer, "Charity and the 'Tramp': Itinerancy, Unemployment and Municipal Government from Coxey to the Unemployed League," *Oregon Historical Quarterly* 107 (2006): 228–53, and Janice Dilg, "'For Working Women in Oregon': Caroline Gleason/Sister Miriam Theresa and Oregon's Minimum Wage Law," *Oregon Historical Quarterly* 110 (2009): 96–130. Earlier works—such as Carl Abbott's *Portland: Planning, Politics, and Growth in a Twentieth-Century City* (Lincoln: University of Nebraska Press, 1983) and E. Kimbark MacColl, *The Growth of a City: Power and Politics in Portland, Oregon, 1915–1950* (Portland: Georgian Press, 1979)—remain crucial.

33. ORM10 [Public Welfare Bureau], 24 January 1922, in OPWC Records, Folder 70/1.

34. ORM12 [Child Welfare Commission], 13 March 1924, in ibid.

35. ORM21 [Child Welfare Commission], 22 January 1923, in ibid.

36. ORM2 [Child Welfare Commission], 11 March 1922, in ibid.; ORM3 [Child Welfare Commission], 26 October 1927, in ibid.

37. ORM18 [Child Welfare Commission], 28 December 1923, in ibid.

38. OR94 [Child Welfare Commission], 2 December 1921, in OPWC Records, Folder 72/20.

39. Nicole Hahn Rafter, ed., *White Trash: The Eugenic Family Studies, 1877–1919* (Boston: Northeastern University Press, 1988).

40. Johnston, *Radical Middle Class*, 53. For ideas about understandings of marginality and threat in the American West, I also draw on David Peterson del Mar, *What Trouble I Have Seen: A History of Violence against Wives* (Cambridge, MA: Harvard University Press, 1996), 97–134, and *Beaten Down: A History of Interpersonal Violence in the West* (Seattle: University of Washington Press, 2002), 92–135.

41. ORM19 [Child Welfare Commission], 20 February 1923, in OPWC Records, Folder 70/1. It is important to note del Mar's argument that sexual and family violence seems to have increased in the first two decades of the twentieth century in part because of increased assertiveness and independence by wives and children and, as he argues, "flourished in the shrinking parts of the north Pacific slope that were least modern" and in "highly isolated pockets" (*Beaten Down*, 130).

42. OR21 [Child Welfare Commission], August 1924, in OPWC Records, Folder 70/16.

43. OR28 [Child Welfare Commission], 30 July 1927, in OPWC Records, Folder 70/20.

44. OR45 [Public Welfare Bureau], 9 March 1929, in OPWC Records, Folder 71/4; OR31 [Child Welfare Commission], 5 May 1922, in OPWC Records, Folder 70/24; OR88 [Child Welfare Commission], 28 August 1921, in OPWC Records, Folder 72/12; OR72 [Child Welfare Commission], 22 September 1923, in OPWC Records, Folder 72/1.

45. OR62 [Child Welfare Commission], 23 February 1922, in OPWC Records, Folder 71/16.

46. OR71 [Child Welfare Commission], 3 August 1925, in OPWC Records, Folder 72/1.

47. OR 17 [Child Welfare Commission], 14 March 1923, in OPWC Records, Folder 70/16.
48. OR 40 [Child Welfare Commission], 17 October 1923, in OPWC Records, Folder 71/1.
49. OR 42 [Child Welfare Commission], 12 June 1924, in ibid.
50. OR 19 [Child Welfare Commission], 11 January 1924, in OPWC Records, Folder 70/16.
51. OR 36 [Child Welfare Commission], 24 January 1923, in OPWC Records, Folder 71/1.
52. OR 26 [Child Welfare Commission], 30 April 1928, in OPWC Records, Folder 70/20; OR 22 [Child Welfare Commission], 3 May 1926, in ibid.; OR 15 [Public Welfare Bureau], 11 May 1921, in OPWC Records, Folder 70/16.
53. OR 59 [Child Welfare Commission], 23 July 1926, in OPWC Records, Folder 71/16.
54. OR 116 [Child Welfare Commission], 26 April 1926, in OPWC Records, Folder 73/12; OR 114 [Child Welfare Commission], 24 April 1934, in ibid.
55. OR 83 [Child Welfare Commission], 15 June 1921, in OPWC Records, Folder 72/4.
56. OR 106 [Child Welfare Commission], 26 April 1923, in OPWC Records, Folder 73/1.
57. OR 98 [Child Welfare Commission], 8 November 1922, in OPWC Records, Folder 72/20.
58. OR 32 [Child Welfare Commission], 19 July 1921, in OPWC Records, Folder 70/24.
59. OR 65 [Child Welfare Commission], 7 August 1938, in OPWC Records, Folder 71/20.
60. OR 93 [Child Welfare Commission], 31 July 1928, in OPWC Records, Folder 72/16.
61. OR 126 [Child Welfare Commission], 14 May 1929, in OPWC Records, Folder 74/4.
62. OR M4 [Public Welfare Bureau], 5 October 1923, in OPWC Records, Folder 70/1.
63. OR 117 [Child Welfare Commission], 18 October 1924, in OPWC Records, Folder 73/12.

PART FIVE

1. Based on MSPCC Annual Reports, 1922–36, in Massachusetts Society for the Prevention of Cruelty to Children, Records, 1878–1970, Archives and Special Collections, Joseph P. Healey Library, University of Massachusetts Boston (hereafter MSPCC Records), Box 257, and MSPCC Executive Committee minutes, in MSPCC Records, Box 258.
2. Figures taken from General Historical file, in Minneapolis Family and Children's Service, Records, ca. 1889–1960, SW75, Social Welfare History Archives, University of Minnesota Libraries (hereafter FWA Records), Box 1, Folder 4, and Board of Directors, Minutes, various meetings, in FWA Records, Box 5, Folders 8–14, and Box 6, Folders 1–3.

3. Toby Ditz, "The New Men's History and the Peculiar Absence of Gendered Power: Some Remedies from Early American Gender History," *Gender and History* 16 (2004): 1–35.

4. Michael Kimmel, *Manhood in America: A Cultural History*, 2nd ed. (New York: Oxford University Press, 2006), 124.

5. James Gilbert, *Men in the Middle: Searching for Masculinity in the 1950s* (Chicago: University of Chicago Press, 2005).

6. Kimmel, *Manhood in America*, 131; Lois Scharf, *To Work and to Wed: Female Employment, Feminism and the Great Depression* (Westport, CT: Greenwood Press, 1980); Alice Kessler-Harris, "Gender Ideology in Historical Reconstruction: A Case Study from the 1930s," *Gender and History* 1 (1989): 31–49.

7. Elizabeth Lunbeck, *The Psychiatric Persuasion: Knowledge, Gender and Power in Modern America* (Princeton, NJ: Princeton University Press, 1994), 244.

8. M024, 3 March 1937, in FWA Records, Box 20.

9. MA047, 30 November 1925, in Boston Children's Aid Association, Records, 1915–1960, Archives and Special Collections, Joseph P. Healey Library, University of Massachusetts, Boston (hereafter CAA Records), Box 10.

10. Robert L. Griswold, *Fatherhood in America: A History* (New York: Basic Books, 1993); Ralph LaRossa, *The Modernization of Fatherhood: A Social and Political History* (Chicago: University of Chicago Press, 1997).

11. MA044, 19 October 1925, in CAA Records, Box 10.

12. M024, 3 March 1937, in FWA Records, Box 20.

13. MA012, 20 February 1922, in MSPCC Records, Box 126.

14. MA018, 16 March 1922, in ibid.

15. MA125, 4 February 1932, in MSPCC Records, Box 206.

16. MA072, 25 June 1935, in MSPCC Records, Box 249; MA094, 8 June 1928, in MSPCC Records, Box 174.

17. MA033, 20 January 1922, in MSPCC Records, Box 127; MA066, 23 August 1935, in MSPCC Records, Box 249.

18. M037, 28 January 1924, in Minneapolis Family and Children's Service, Case Records, ca. 1895–1945, Social Welfare History Archives, University of Minnesota Libraries, SW Film 19, Reel 125.

19. MA099, 23 May 1928, in MSPCC Records, Box 174.

20. MA025, 20 April 1922, in MSPCC Records, Box 127.

21. M099, 26 November 1927, in FWA Records, Box 18.

22. MA134, 19 October 1931, in MSPCC Records, Box 207.

23. MA137, 15 October 1931, in ibid.

CONCLUSION

1. Kathleen Callanan Martin, *Hard and Unreal Advice: Mothers, Social Science and the Victorian Poverty Experts* (Basingstoke, UK: Palgrave Macmillan, 2008). I am grateful to both Mike Savage and John Murphy for sharing with me chapters from unpublished manuscripts.

2. Stephen Pimpare, "Toward a New Welfare History," *Journal of Policy History* 19 (2007): 234–52.

3. Michael B. Katz, "The History of an Impudent Poor Woman in New York City from 1918 to 1923," in *The Uses of Charity: The Poor on Relief in the Nineteenth-Century Metropolis*, ed. Peter Mandler (Philadelphia: University of Pennsylvania Press, 1990), 241.

4. Alice O'Connor, *Poverty Knowledge: Social Science, Social Policy, and the Poor in Twentieth-Century U.S. History* (Princeton, NJ: Princeton University Press, 2001), 244.

5. Nancy Fraser and Linda Gordon, "A Genealogy of *Dependency*: Tracing a Keyword of the U.S. Welfare State," *Signs* 19 (1994): 309–36.

Index

Abbott, Grace, 259
Abel, Emily, 10
African Americans, 13, 162–65, 172, 188
Alderman family (COS clients; pseud.),
  23–32, 289–90
Allen, Lillian (COS worker; pseud.), 37,
  52, 63, 65, 69, 75, 77, 102
Anderson, Paul, 283
Anna (CAA client; pseud.), 157–58
Arnesen, Anna and Ole (FWA clients;
  pseud.), 177–83, 292–93
Atkinson, Helena (AC worker; pseud.),
  221

Bailey, Peter, 10
Baker, Margaret (COS worker; pseud.),
  68, 74
Bakke, Hilda (FWA worker; pseud.), 201,
  202, 205
Becker, Stephen (FWA worker; pseud.),
  268
Bedford, Celia (COS worker; pseud.), 37,
  52, 63
Bellingham, Bruce, 10
Benson, Joan (FWA worker; pseud.), 201
Bergson, Inge (FWA worker; pseud.), 197
Bergson family (FWA clients; pseud.),
  199–200
Berry, Lisbeth (CWC worker; pseud.), 232
Birch, Tony, 11
Birtwell, Mary, 4
Boehm, Cora (FWA worker; pseud.), 207
Bosanquet, Helen, 47
Boston, 4, 10, 11, 13, 69, 70, 83, 95, 108,
  123, 188, 227, 234, 235, 242, 261, 273,
  278; Associated Jewish Philanthropies,
  141; Boston State Hospital, 169; Catho-
  lic Children's Bureau, 270; Chardon
  Street Home, 169; Child Welfare De-
  partment, 270; Children's Hospital, 146;
  156; Denison House ,148; Eye and Ear
  Infirmary, 148; Homeopathic Hospital,
  154; Judge Baker Foundation, 154, 157,
  158, 160, 161, 263; Judge Baker Guidance
  Center, 134, 143; Massachusetts General
  Hospital, 146; Overseers of the Public
  Welfare, 142, 247; poverty and welfare
  in, 141–42; Society of St. Vincent de
  Paul, 141; Thompsons Island Farm and
  Trade School, 263
Boston Children's Aid Society/Associa-
  tion, 3, 133, 139, 141, 143, 145, 153–54,
  263, 264; and African American clients,
  163–64; and Americanization, 136–38,
  159–61; case files, 284
Boulton, Jeremy, 18
Branston, Mavis (CWC worker; pseud.),
  231
Bristol, Margaret Cochran, 259
Brittain, Vera, 101–2
Bronson, William (MSPCC worker;
  pseud.), 146–47, 148, 267, 268
Brown, Ethel (COS worker; pseud.), 37,
  55, 57, 58, 63, 64, 69, 78
Bruno, Frank, 185
Bryant, Elizabeth and John (FWA clients;
  pseud.), 268–69
Buckley, Alma (MSPCC client; pseud.),
  170

Cage, R. A., 11
Carman, Milton (MSPCC worker;
  pseud.), 268
Carr, Anna (FWA worker; pseud.), 207
Carrie (CAA client; pseud.), 154–55
Carstens, Carl C., 143, 144
Carter, Elizabeth (MSPCC worker;
  pseud.), 147–48
case files: as historical sources, 2–3, 4–6,
  10–11, 14–20, 277–80

casework: Boston 144, 149–53, 155, 168; and child rescue, 149–52, 156; and degeneration, 234–43; history of, 9–11, 277; investigation of bodies, 52–53, 229; London, 96, 100–101, 108–10, 111–16, 118; Melbourne, 39–45, 47–61; Minneapolis, 186–89; Oregon, 222–24, 234, 239; and "respectable" clients, 61–66

Cathie, Elizabeth (COS worker; pseud.), 63

Cavin, Edward H., 144

Charity Organisation Society (London), 3, 91, 92, 221, 228, 273; case files, 98, 284; Central Committee for Aims and Policy, 125; *Charity Organisation Quarterly*, 96, 99, 104, 105, 117; Council, 72; during the Second World War, 125–30; history of, 96–98, 103–7; internal dissent and debate, 97, 99–100, 103–5, 117, 124; methods and assumptions, 95–96, 98, 107–11; Senior Secretaries Group, 97; and social policy, 99–100; social work training, 106; views of the poor, 111–17, 118–23; women in, 100–103, 126, 129–30

Charity Organisation Society (Melbourne), 3, 11, 33, 35–36, 187, 221, 228, 273; case files, 283–84; 'detective' work and, 47–49, 52–61; during the Depression, 71–80, 83–84; during the Second World War, 81–82; Executive Committee, 33, 36, 45, 51, 67, 79, 81, 82; history of, 38–45; 'imposture' and fraud, 39–40, 44, 58–59, 64–67, 68–69; methods and assumptions, 46–61, 67–71; *Other Half*, 36, 45, 50, 69, 71, 76, 79, 80, 284; social work training, 42–43; transformation in the 1940s, 82–83; women in, 35–38

Cheshire, Caroline (MSPCC worker; pseud.), 148

Child Welfare Commission (Oregon), 3; case files 222; casework methods, 223–28, 242–43; and feeblemindedness, 238–42; focus on policing entitlement, 228–33; and race, 238; and rural degeneracy, 235–43

Child Welfare Committee (Oregon), 223

Chivers, June (COS client; pseud.), 55

Citizen's Welfare Service (Melbourne), 11, 41, 72, 82, 283

Clapham, Joanna (MSPCC worker; pseud.), 147

Colcord, Joanna, 47, 100, 185, 186, 259, 275, 287

Coles family (CWC clients; pseud.), 240–41

Collins, Walter (COS client; pseud.), 122

comparative and transnational history, 11–14, 277–79

Concord Reformatory (Massachusetts), 168

Cook, Arthur (COS client; pseud.), 119–21

Crichton family (PWB clients; pseud.), 230–32

Cross, Angela (FWA client; pseud.), 207

Cumberland, Doris, 33

Cumbler, John, 8

Cushing, Grafton D., 152

Cutler, Agnes (COS worker; pseud.), 23–32, 33, 36, 37, 38, 48, 49, 50, 52, 54–58, 61, 62, 63, 64, 65–66, 69, 73, 75, 77, 78–79, 102, 108, 109, 140, 191, 257, 273, 289–90

Davis, Charlie (COS client; pseud.), 122

Davis, Isabella and Gerald (COS clients; pseud.), 75–76

Dawson, Millie (CWC client; pseud.), 232–33

De Baecque, Antoine, 18

Derrick, Foster (MSPCC worker; pseud.), 247

Deutsch, Sarah, 11

Dickinson, Mrs. (COS client; pseud.), 115

Ditchburn, Mary (COS client; pseud.), 115

Dittmar, Ursula (FWA worker; pseud.), 198

Ditz, Toby, 258

Dodge family (PWB clients; pseud.), 235

Donaldson, Letitia (COS client; pseud.), 51

Donnell, Joseph (MSPCC worker; pseud.), 169

Dorroh, Thelma, 208

dramatization of poverty and inequality, 4–6, 9, 15, 43–45, 63, 67–71, 72–80, 83,

95–96, 108–10, 111–17, 123–24, 139–40, 146–49, 167–72, 189–90, 192, 205–6, 242, 277–80; comparative aspects, 12–14, 47–48, 69–70, 83, 95–96, 98–99, 108, 117, 123, 139–40, 142–43, 146, 152, 163, 165, 167, 172, 187–88, 206, 234–35, 242, 277–79

Duchene, Cornelia (FWA worker; pseud.), 192

Dyson family (CWC clients; pseud.), 241

Edison family (MSPCC clients; pseud.), 171

Elfman, Hanna (FWA client; pseud.), 203–4

Elliott, Gilbert, 117

eugenics, 70, 145, 239–40, 242, 278

Ewing, Caroline (FWA worker; pseud.), 193

Family Welfare Association (Minneapolis), 3, 163, 242, 266; and African American clients, 188; case files, 284; "colored workers," 186, 188; during the Depression, 183–84, 206–9; during the 1940s and 1950s, 207–8; focus on independence, 197–206, 208–9; Gateway Bureau, 184, 186, 204; history of, 185–87; and immigrant clients, 188; male social workers, 186, 257–59, 272–73; planning and "pauperization," 189–97; and women clients, 195–97; workers and caseloads, 186–87, 206–7

Farmer, Beryl (MSPCC client; pseud.), 172

Faulkner, Virginia (pseud.), 144, 148, 150

Firth, Patrick and Ellen (PWB clients; pseud.), 229

Fletcher, Calvin (CAA worker; pseud.), 159–61, 263, 268

Flynn, Mary (MSPCC client; pseud.), 247–56, 266, 274, 294–95

Foley, Kathleen, 82

Gale, Jane (FWA worker; pseud.), 192

gender: in histories of poverty and social work, 6–9, 258–60, 272–76, 278. *See also* men in social work; women in social work

Gilbert, James, 259

Ginzberg, Lori, 7

Glen Lake Sanatorium (Minnesota), 199

Glenn, Myra and Steven (FWA clients; pseud.), 202–3

Godfrey family (COS clients; pseud.), 122

Golding, Lillian (COS client; pseud.), 87–93, 95, 290–91

Goodman, David, 12, 13

Gordon, Linda, 5, 9, 10, 16, 18, 142, 145, 151, 157, 167, 171, 173, 258, 277, 283

Goss, Ellen (COS client; pseud.), 55

Graham, Betty (FWA worker; pseud.), 205

Graham, Eleanor (MSPCC worker; pseud.), 139, 157

Griffiths, Patricia (FWA worker; pseud.), 207

Grinter, Rose (FWA worker; pseud.), 192, 196

Groener family (CWC clients; pseud.), 233–34

Halttunen, Karen, 63, 67

Hamilton, Freda (COS client; pseud.), 56

Hardeman family (COS clients; pseud.), 119

Harding, Mildred (COS worker; pseud.), 95, 108, 120

Harrison family (COS clients; pseud.), 77

Hedges, Dorothy (COS worker; pseud.), 87, 91–92, 290–91

Hellstrom family (FWA clients; pseud.), 198

Henderson, Derrick (MSPCC worker; pseud.), 162

Hilton, Alma and William (FWA clients; pseud.), 193–94

Himmelfarb, Gertrude, 96

historical writing: fiction and imagination, 16–20

Hitchcock, Tim, 16, 18

Hoagland, Madeleine, 168

Hoban, Ruth, 82

Holmes, Dorothy (COS client; pseud.), 65–66

Holton, Alexandra (CWC worker; pseud.), 239

Houston, Dora (COS client; pseud.), 121

Hull, Vernon (FWA worker; pseud.), 202, 258, 262, 264, 265, 269, 273, 274

Humphreys, Robert, 11, 97, 116

Iacovetta, Franca, 10, 14

Irwin, Eugene (MSPCC worker; pseud.), 144

Jackson, Belle (FWA client; pseud.), 188–89

Jackson, Rosa (CAA client; pseud.), 163–64

Johnson, Stanford (MSPCC worker; pseud.), 149, 165, 262, 263

Johnson, Vida (FWA worker; pseud.), 199

Johnston, Robert, 235

Jones, Gareth Stedman, 96, 116

Karlsson, Inge (FWA client; pseud.), 268

Katz, Michael, 9, 16, 18, 277, 280

Kaufman, Ilsa (FWA worker; pseud.), 191

Kemmler, Myra (FWA worker; pseud.), 204, 207

Kennan, Mary (FWA worker; pseud.), 196, 268

Kennedy, Carrie (FWA worker; pseud.), 199

Kennedy, Richard, 11, 39

Kidd, Alan J., 97

King, Frank and Thea (MSPCC clients; pseud.), 171

King, Peter, 16

King, Steven, 8

Kirby, Ella (FWA worker; pseud.), 188

Kirkham, Leontine (FWA worker; pseud.), 191

Kleinberg, Susan, 13, 158

Knight, Arthur (COS client; pseud.), 115–16

Koven, Seth, 10, 129

Koziorek, Jerzy/George (CAA client; pseud.), 133–38, 143, 156, 291–92

Kunzel, Regina, 7, 141

La Capra, Dominick, 17–18

Lamb, Geraldine, 208

Laqueur, Thomas, 5

Larue, Calvin and Mary (FWA clients; pseud.), 192–93

Lee, Annie (CAA worker; pseud.), 153–55

Lees, Lynn Hollen, 10

Lewis, Jane, 11, 12, 97, 104, 116, 125

Lindner, Hanna (FWA client; pseud.), 195–97

Lindstrom, Elsa (FWA worker; pseud.), 177–84, 257, 292–93

Lineker, Thelma (CWC worker; pseud.), 227

Liverpool, 10

Lloyd, T. E., 102, 105

London, 7, 8, 11, 12, 13, 14, 69, 70, 82, 83, 106, 139, 140, 142, 145, 147, 163, 165, 168, 188, 206, 230, 268, 273, 278; Battersea Polytechnic, 106; Bedford College, 106; bombing of, 125, 126–28; Catholic Council for International Relations, 113; Friends of the Poor, 93, 100; General Council for the Assistance of the British Repatriated from Russia, 111; London Metropolitan Archives, 98; London School of Economics, 106, 124; Professional Classes Aid Council, 100; Relief Fund for British Refugees from Russia, 111; welfare and poverty in, 96–98, 99, 106, 113, 123; West London Hospital, 112

Lothrop, Theodore A., 143

Lowe, Gary, 166

Lower, Hilda (FWA worker; pseud.), 200

Lubove, Roy, 9

Lunbeck, Elizabeth, 8, 10, 261

Lyell, Hiram (PWB worker; pseud.), 222

Lyman School for Boys (Massachusetts), 159, 160

Lynch, Dorothy (MSPCC worker; pseud.), 169

Lynn, Jane (CWC worker; pseud.), 233

Macadam, Elizabeth, 101

Macdonald, Dorothy (COS worker; pseud.), 50, 68

Macdonnell, Catherine (MSPCC worker; pseud.), 169

Macintyre, Agnes, 42

Manchester, 97

Mandler, Peter, 16

Marchetti family (MSPCC clients; pseud.), 148

Mariano, Rosa (MSPCC worker; pseud.), 247

Markert, Julius, 168

Markham, Thomas and Carrie (AC clients; pseud.), 221–22

Marks, Evelyn (MSPCC worker; pseud.), 150

Marks, Lara, 91, 92

Marley, Frances, 144, 275

Martin, Kathleen, 277

Martino, Ida and Salvatore (MSPCC clients; pseud.), 270–71

Mary (CAA client; pseud.), 153–54

Massachusetts Reformatory for Women, 169

Massachusetts Society for the Prevention of Cruelty to Children, 4, 139, 266; and African American clients, 162–65, 172; case files, 141–43, 284; caseloads and agents, 144–45, 166; characterizations of clients, 145–50; during the Depression and New Deal, 165–73; focus on transformation, 152–62, 165, 173; history of, 143–45; and immigrant clients, 147–50, 152–53, 156–57, 161–62, 164–65; male social workers in, 257–59, 272–73

Masters, Helen, 257

Mattner, Clark (FWA worker; pseud.), 274, 275

McCalman, Janet, 63, 92

McGuire, Mary (MSPCC worker; pseud.), 164

McKibbin, Ross, 129

McLeod, Mary (FWA client; pseud.), 199

McNulty, Thomas (MSPCC worker; pseud.), 144, 247, 251, 252, 257, 274, 275

McRae, Dorothy (FWA client; pseud.), 203

Melbourne, 7, 11, 12, 13, 14, 95, 101, 108, 109, 123, 139, 140, 142, 145, 147, 163, 165, 168, 194, 203, 206, 230, 268, 273, 278; Brotherhood of St. Laurence, 83; Catholic charities in, 35, 75; Dental Hospital, 34, 55; Depression in, 34, 71–80, 83; Eye and Ear Hospital, 34; hospital almoners, 42; Jewish charities in, 35; ladies' benevolent societies, 35, 40, 46–47, 52, 56, 60; Legacy Club, 45; Melbourne Hospital,

45, 54, 61; poverty and welfare in, 33–35, 81–82; Wesley Central Mission, 35

men in social work, 6, 257–60, 278; and fathering, 263–65; and ideas about manhood, 260, 261–65, 271–76; and men clients, 267–68, 271–72, 274; and women clients, 260, 266–71, 272

Mercer, Theodore (MSPCC worker; pseud.), 148

Meredith, F. D., 102

Miller, Theodore (MSPCC worker; pseud.), 266, 270–71

Minneapolis, 9, 10, 11, 13, 69, 70, 83, 95, 108, 123, 139, 140, 147, 163, 165, 227, 234, 235, 242, 261, 273, 278; Board of Public Welfare, 183, 186; Council of Social Agencies, 207; Department of Public Relief, 192, 198, 199, 200, 203, 206, 269; Depression and New Deal in, 197–98, 204, 206–7; Division of Public Relief, 183, 207; poverty and welfare in, 187; Union City Mission, 186

Mitchell, Earl and June (FWA clients; pseud.), 200–202, 203

Mitchinson, Wendy, 10, 15

Moller, Sonia (MSPCC worker; pseud.), 172

Morris, Evelyn (MSPCC worker; pseud.), 144

Morwell, Esther (FWA worker; pseud.), 189

Mullowney, Catherine, 144

Multnomah County Public Welfare Bureau, 221, 222–23, 225, 226, 234, 235, 236; methods and assumptions, 228–33, 242–43

Murphy, John, 34, 46, 47, 277

Murray, Margaret (FWA worker; pseud.), 191, 199

Musgrove, Nell, 11

National Assistance Board (Britain), 93

Neilsen, Ingrid (FWA worker; pseud.), 201

Nelson, Zillah (CAA worker; pseud.), 153–54

New York City, 10

Oates, May (COS client; pseud.), 57

O'Brien family (MSPCC clients; pseud.), 169–70

O'Brien, Laurie, 37
O'Connor, Alice, 172, 280
O'Connor, N. M., 107
O'Neill, Michael (MSPCC worker; pseud.), 247–56, 257, 266, 271, 273, 274, 294–95
Oregon, 11, 13, 70, 108, 123, 139, 278; Boys and Girls Aid Society, 239, 241; Boys and Girls Association, 237; Children's Farm Home, 239; Pacific Coast Rescue and Protective Society, 239, 240; Public Assistance Bureau, 3; Red Cross, 224, 226, 233, 238; State Archives, 218; State Hospital, 241; State Institution for the Feeble-Minded, 213–16, 218, 225–26, 236, 240; State Relief Committee, 229; welfare in, 222–24, 227, 234–35, 242
Overshaw, Catherine (FWA worker; pseud.), 182

Page, Stephen, 10
Patrick (CAA client; pseud.), 153–54
Pearce, Mary (COS client; pseud.), 57
Penney, Dolores (FWA client; pseud.), 205
Perry, Edith (CWC worker; pseud.), 213–19, 293
Pimpare, Stephen, 277
Pinelli, Antonio and Marco (CAA clients; pseud.), 159–61, 263–64
Pitt, Earl (FWA worker; pseud.), 258, 269
Portland, Oregon: Associated Charities, 3, 221, 222, 230; Court of Domestic Relations, 235; Catholic Charities, 240; Louise Home for Girls, 240; poverty and welfare in, 234–35; Salvation Army Home, 237
poverty: contemporary debates, 280–82; perspectives of the poor, 14, 15, 59–60, 73–76, 128–30, 170–71, 204, 279–82. *See also* dramatization of poverty and inequality
Powell family (MSPCC clients; pseud.), 168–69
Pringle, J. C., 104
Proctor, William (MSPCC worker; pseud.), 146–47
Putnam, Dorothy (MSPCC worker; pseud.), 149, 158, 265

Rafter, Nicole, 235
Reid, Nelson, 166
Reisch, Michael, 11
Richards, Doris (COS client; pseud.), 48
Ricketts, Bertha (CAA worker; pseud.), 164
Richmond, Mary, 4, 47, 259, 275
Riegel, Helga (FWA worker; pseud.), 191
Roberts, Gloria (COS client; pseud.), 55
Robinson, Lillian (FWA worker; pseud.), 189
Robinson, Victoria (COS client; pseud.), 57–58
Robinson, Virginia, 259
Robson, Ellen (COS client; pseud.), 52
Rochester State Hospital (Minnesota), 193
Rooff, Madeline, 96, 99
Rosen, Delia (MSPCC worker; pseud.), 247, 251, 255
Ross, Ellen, 8, 10
Rowthorn, William (COS client; pseud.), 95, 99
Roxburgh, Margaret, 124

Salisbury, Pearl, 259, 275
Salvation Army: Boston, 141; Melbourne, 35, 40, 75; Minneapolis, 182, 186, 194
Sambell, Joyce, 82
Savage, Mike, 277
Schneider, Eric, 11
Scott, James, 16, 17, 19
Sharpe, Pamela, 16
Sheffield, Ada, 259
Sherman, Thomas (MSPCC worker; pseud.), 156, 267, 270
Shirley Reformatory (Massachusetts; pseud.), 159, 168
Simms, Gloria (COS client; pseud.), 78
Smith, Stanley Greig, 33, 36, 37, 38–45, 46, 48, 52, 64, 65, 69, 71, 72, 78, 79, 80, 81, 82, 83, 100, 273, 287
social work: during the Depression and New Deal, 166–67; history of, 9–11, 140–41. *See also* casework
Spenceley, Geoff, 11
Spencer, Leonora (CAA worker; pseud.), 157, 158
Spiller, Franklin and Earl (CWC clients; pseud.), 213–19, 243, 293

Stadum, Beverly, 9, 10, 166, 183, 187, 195, 277
St. Agnes Home (Oregon City, OR), 217, 238
Starkey, Pat, 10
State War Council (Victoria), 50
Steedman, Carolyn, 18
Stimson, Ellen (PWB worker; pseud.), 223
St. Mary's Home for Boys (Beaverton, OR), 214, 227
Stoneham, Jean (MSPCC worker; pseud.), 151, 158
Strachey, Ray, 101–2
Stratton, Celia (COS client; pseud.), 78–79
Sustenance Branch (Victoria), 42, 55, 66, 78
Sutton, William and Dora (COS clients; pseud.), 110–11
Swain, Shurlee, 11
Swift, Benson (MSPCC worker; pseud.), 169–70

Taylor, Walter (MSPCC worker; pseud.), 144, 266–67
Tennyson, Beatrice (COS worker; pseud.), 119–20
Terry, Millicent (CAA worker; pseud.), 163
Thane, Pat, 101
Thompson, Roy and Gloria (COS clients; pseud.), 64–65
Tice, Karen, 7, 10, 18, 141, 145, 155, 277
Tierney, Leonard, 82
Towle, Charlotte, 47
Traverso, Susan, 11, 141
Trout, Charles, 141, 142
Turner, Cynthia, 37
Tyrrell, Ian, 12

United Unemployment Relief Committee (Victoria), 43

Victorian Association of Ladies' Benevolent Societies, 46
Victorian Association of Social Workers, 43

Victorian Council for Social Training, 37, 42
Victorian Institute for Almoners, 42
Victorian Society for the Prevention of Cruelty to Children, 43, 56
Vincent, A. W., 97

Walker, Ellen (COS client; pseud.), 115
Walkowitz, Daniel, 6, 7, 10, 141, 166, 167
Walters, Kathleen (MSPCC worker; pseud.), 172
Watson family (CWC clients; pseud.), 239–40
Waugh, Joan, 10
Weaver, Clara (MSPCC worker; pseud.), 148
Wells, Laura (CAA worker; pseud.), 133–38, 257, 291–92
Wencour, Stanley, 11
Whitfield, Earl and Robert (CAA clients; pseud.), 262–63, 264, 265, 276
Wild, Harriet (CWC client; pseud.), 241–43
Wilkinson, Marian (COS worker; pseud.), 93
Williams, Mavis (COS client; pseud.), 75
Wilson, Beatrice (COS client; pseud.), 122
Wilson, Edward (COS client; pseud.), 56
Wiseman, Meryl, 37
women in social work, 6–9, 35–38, 100–103, 144–45, 148, 258–59; and changes in ideas about poverty, 72–80, 126, 129–30, 278, 280; as "detectives," 53–54; as leaders, 272–75; and women clients, 57–58, 73–75, 78–79, 126, 129–30, 142, 151–52, 158–59, 204–5, 273–74
Woodroofe, Kathleen, 12, 96
Woollacott, Angela, 7, 8

Yeo, Eileen, 5, 97, 277
Young, Richard and Mildred (FWA clients; pseud.), 261–62, 264, 265, 275–76
Younghusband, Eileen, 72, 102, 124

Ziskind, Frances, 168

HISTORICAL STUDIES OF URBAN AMERICA

Edited by Timothy J. Gilfoyle, James R. Grossman, and Becky M. Nicolaides

SERIES TITLES, CONTINUED FROM FRONTMATTER

Colored Property: State Policy and White
Racial Politics in Suburban America
by David M. P. Freund

Selling the Race: Culture, Community, and
Black Chicago, 1940–1955
by Adam Green

The New Suburban History
edited by Kevin M. Kruse and
Thomas J. Sugrue

Millennium Park: Creating a Chicago
Landmark
by Timothy J. Gilfoyle

City of American Dreams: A History of Home
Ownership and Housing Reform in Chicago,
1871–1919
by Margaret Garb

Chicagoland: City and Suburbs in the
Railroad Age
by Ann Durkin Keating

The Elusive Ideal: Equal Educational
Opportunity and the Federal Role in Boston's
Public Schools, 1950–1985
by Adam R. Nelson

Block by Block: Neighborhoods and Public
Policy on Chicago's West Side
by Amanda I. Seligman

Downtown America: A History of the Place
and the People Who Made It
by Alison Isenberg

Places of Their Own: African American
Suburbanization in the Twentieth Century
by Andrew Wiese

Building the South Side: Urban Space
and Civic Culture in Chicago, 1890–1919
by Robin F. Bachin

In the Shadow of Slavery: African Americans
in New York City, 1626–1863
by Leslie M. Harris

My Blue Heaven: Life and Politics in the
Working-Class Suburbs of Los Angeles,
1920–1965
by Becky M. Nicolaides

Brownsville, Brooklyn: Blacks, Jews, and the
Changing Face of the Ghetto
by Wendell Pritchett

The Creative Destruction of Manhattan,
1900–1940
by Max Page

Streets, Railroads, and the Great Strike
of 1877
by David O. Stowell

Faces along the Bar: Lore and Order in the Workingman's Saloon, 1870–1920
by Madelon Powers

Making the Second Ghetto: Race and Housing in Chicago, 1940–1960
by Arnold R. Hirsch

Smoldering City: Chicagoans and the Great Fire, 1871–1874
by Karen Sawislak

Modern Housing for America: Policy Struggles in the New Deal Era
by Gail Radford

Parish Boundaries: The Catholic Encounter with Race in the Twentieth-Century Urban North
by John T. McGreevy